50 Years a Keynesian and Other Essays

Also by G.C. Harcourt

A 'SECOND EDITION' OF *THE GENERAL THEORY* (*two volumes, edited with P.A. Riach*)

CAPITAL AND GROWTH: Selected Readings (*edited with N.F. Laing*)

CAPITALISM, SOCIALISM AND POST-KEYNESIANISM: Selected Essays of G.C. Harcourt

CONTROVERSIES IN POLITICAL ECONOMY: Selected Essays of G.C. Harcourt

ECONOMIC ACTIVITY (*with P.H. Karmel and R.H. Wallace*)

KEYNES AND HIS CONTEMPORARIES: The Sixth and Centennial Keynes Seminar held in the University of Kent at Canterbury (*editor*)

INCOME AND EMPLOYMENT IN THEORY AND PRACTICE: Essays in Memory of Athanasios Asimakopulos (*edited with Alessandro Roncaglia and Robin Rowley*)

INTERNATIONAL MONETARY PROBLEMS AND SUPPLY-SIDE ECONOMICS: Essays in Honour of Lorie Tarshis (*edited with Jon Cohen*)

ON POLITICAL ECONOMISTS AND MODERN POLITICAL ECONOMY: Selected Essays of G.C. Harcourt (*edited by Claudio Sardoni*)

POST-KEYNESIAN ESSAYS IN BIOGRAPHY: Portraits of Twentieth-Century Political Economists

READINGS IN THE CONCEPT AND MEASUREMENT OF INCOME (*edited with R.H. Parker*)

READINGS IN THE CONCEPT AND MEASUREMENT OF INCOME: Second Edition (*edited with R.H. Parker and G. Whittington*)

SOME CAMBRIDGE CONTROVERSIES IN THE THEORY OF CAPITAL

THE DYNAMICS OF THE WEALTH OF NATIONS: Growth, Distribution and Structural Change – Essays in Honour of Luigi Pasinetti (*edited with Mauro Baranzini*)

THE MICROECONOMIC FOUNDATIONS OF MACROECONOMICS (*editor*)

THEORETICAL CONTROVERSY AND SOCIAL SIGNIFICANCE: An Evaluation of the Cambridge Controversies

SELECTED ESSAYS ON ECONOMIC POLICY

THE SOCIAL SCIENCE IMPERIALISTS: Selected Essays of G.C. Harcourt (*edited by Prue Kerr*)

50 Years a Keynesian and Other Essays

G.C. Harcourt
Emeritus Reader in the History of Economic Theory
Emeritus Fellow
Jesus College, Cambridge, and
Professor Emeritus
University of Adelaide

First published 2001 by
PALGRAVE
Houndmills, Basingstoke, Hampshire RG21 6XS and
175 Fifth Avenue, New York, N. Y. 10010
Companies and representatives throughout the world

PALGRAVE is the new global academic imprint of
St. Martin's Press LLC Scholarly and Reference Division and
Palgrave Publishers Ltd (formerly Macmillan Press Ltd).

ISBN 0–333–94633–2

This book is printed on paper suitable for recycling and
made from fully managed and sustained forest sources.

A catalogue record for this book is available
from the British Library.

Library of Congress Cataloging-in-Publication Data
Harcourt, Geoffrey Colin.
    50 years a Keynesian and other essays / G.C. Harcourt.
        p. cm.
    Includes index.
    ISBN 0–333–94633–2 (cloth)
    1. Keynesian economics. 2. Economists. 3. Economics—History—20th
century. I. Title: Fifty years a Keynesian and other essays. II. Title.
    HB99.7 .H317 2000
    330.15'6—dc21
                                                                00–040462

10   9   8   7   6   5   4   3   2   1
10 09 08 07 06 05 04 03 02 01

Printed and bound in Great Britain by
Antony Rowe Ltd, Chippenham, Wiltshire

Contents

Preface   vii

Acknowledgements   x

1   50 Years a Keynesian (1999)   1

Part I   Keynes Now

2   Is Keynes Dead? (1992)   33

3   A 'Second Edition' of Keynes's *General Theory* (1997)   46

4   *The General Theory of Employment, Interest and Money*: Three
    Views (1996) (with Claudio Sardoni)   57

5   A Note on 'Mr Meade's Relation' and International Capital
    Movements (with Paul Dalziel) (1997)   72

Part II   Intellectual Biographies

6   Joan Robinson, 1903–1983 (1995)   91

7   Lorie Tarshis, 1911–1993: In Appreciation (1995)   114

8   Edward Austin Gossage Robinson, 1897–1993 (1997)   131

9   Karl Marx, 1818–83 (with Prue Kerr) (1996)   157
10 Keynes, John Maynard (1997)   169

Part III   Tributes

11 George Shackle: A Tribute (1993)   175

12. What Josef Steindl Means to My Generation (1994)   177

13 A Left Keynesian View of the Phillips Curve Trade-Off
    (2000)   183

14 The Results of the Capital Theory Controversies and
    General Equilibrium Theory: Some Reflections on
    Concepts and History (1998)   188

v

15 Investment Expenditure, Unrealised Expectations and
    Offsetting Monetary Policies (1998)   197

Part IV   Review Articles

16 Joan Robinson and the Economics Profession (1991)   209

17 Fifty Years of Measurement: A Cambridge View (1993)
    (with Michael Kitson)   219

18 The Kaldor Legacy (1997)   238

Part V   Survey

19 Post-Keynesian Thought (1999)   263

Part VI   General Essays

20 Critiques and Alternatives: Reflections on Some Recent
    (and Not So Recent) Controversies (1996–97)   289

21 Mrs Robinson and the Classics (1998) (with Prue Kerr)   300

22 Two Views on Development: Austin and Joan Robinson
    (1998)   306

23 How I Do Economics (1996)   323

24 The Cambridge Contribution to Economics (1998)   334

Index   354

Preface

I include in this selection, essays which have been written and/or published in the 1990s, most since 1995 when *Capitalism, Socialism and Post-Keynesianism* (Harcourt, 1995a) was published. Occasional minor amendments only have been made to provide consistency of book style. The title essay covers the period from my intellectual birth as an economist until the present day – hence '50 years a Keynesian'. In it I describe the evolving structure of my ideas and their *rationale* ultimately, hopefully, in sensible and humane policy proposals.

It is followed by six categories of essays. The first comes under the rubric of 'Keynes Now'. The section starts with the rhetorical question 'Is Keynes Dead?', a lecture I gave at UNSW in 1992, and ends with a joint note with fellow Antipodean, Paul Dalziel. We built on 'Mr Meade's Relation' to tackle the modern heresy that, again, saving determines investment in individual economies and the world economy. In between I discuss the principal findings of the research project which Peter Riach and I organised with over 40 Keynes scholars during the 1990s with the title, *A 'Second Edition' of The General Theory* (two volumes, Harcourt and Riach, 1997). The findings confirm that there is much life left in JMK as we enter a new century. The third essay, written with Claudio Sardoni, measures Paul Davidson's deep view of the significance of *The General Theory* against the demanding *numeraire* of the assessments in the Moggridge and Skidelsky biographies of Keynes.

Part II contains intellectual biographies written in the second half of the 1990s. The first two, on Joan Robinson and Lorie Tarshis, are reprinted from the *Economic Journal* where, from 1990 on, I was honorary obituary editor until the recent revamping of the journal, when I was made redundant two years before my second term was up. The Council of the RES ignored the drawbacks of the Kaldor–Scitovsky criteria and kindly compensated me with life membership of the RES. The third essay is the memoir of Austin Robinson in the *Proceedings* of the British Academy. The last two in the section concern the seamless web of Marx and Keynes: In

Warner (1996), Prue Kerr and I provided business people and managers with all they need to know about Marx. The essay on Keynes comes from Tom Cate's fine *Encyclopedia of Keynesian Economics* (1997). The *Encyclopedia* has had a bad press in some quarters, but I think it (and its subject) will last much longer than much that is fashionable now in the teaching of macroeconomics.

In Part III are tributes large and small to former economists, all of whom I knew and much admired: George Shackle, Josef Steindl, Bill Phillips, Piero Sraffa and Hy Minsky. The first two essays are personal tributes; the other three were written on the occasion of conferences and/or volumes honouring their lives and contributions. I hope they serve the purpose of reminding readers what remarkable and fine people we have had in our trade!

Modern technology is threatening to banish the old art of reviewing, at least in journals. I think this a great pity for reviews and review articles, if done seriously, serve to enlighten as well as inform. I hope I have come within cooee of doing so in the three reprinted in Part IV: a *HOPE* piece on Marjorie Turner's and George Feiwel's volumes on Joan Robinson; a review article, written with Mike Kitson, which celebrates 50 years of the NBER for the *Review of Income and Wealth*; and an account of the themes in Nicky Kaldor's Mattioli Lectures (published 10 years after his death in 1986).

Part V contains a survey of Post-Keynesian thought. It is based on the entry written with Luke Spajic for the Italian *Encyclopedia*, but it has not been published before in this particular form. As we move further and further away from the lives and deaths of the original founders, it is more important than ever that survivors such as myself report what we learnt first hand from the pioneers. It worries me how false interpretations and nuances (inevitably, of course), get into the history of the issues and their resolutions or lack of resolution.

Part VI contains general essays. The first is one which was written in 1980 but not published until 1996–97 in the *Journal of Post Keynesian Economics*, for reasons which I have explained in a number of places, for example, Harcourt (1995b). I think its moral and messages are still relevant today. In the second essay, written with Prue Kerr, we discuss Joan Robinson's relationship to our classical forebears. In the other essays in this section, the 1996 Kingsley Martin Memorial Lecture gave me the opportunity to compare and contrast the views of Austin and Joan Robinson on development issues; Steven Medema's and Warren Samuels's project, *How do Economists do Economics* (1996), allowed me to write on 'How I do Economics'; and, lastly, Sarah Ormrod's splendid series of Summer School Lectures in Cambridge let me reflect on the Cambridge contribution to Economics. This is an opportune theme on which to finish, as all the essays in the volume reflect my Australian and Cambridge upbringing.

Personal acknowledgements

I am especially indebted to Tim Farmiloe for asking me to put together this selection of essays, 'one of the first fruits of my retirement'; to Susan Cross for her expert help in preparing the volume and preface; and, as ever, to Joan for her love and support.

November 1999   G. C. HARCOURT

References

Cate, T. (ed.) (1997) *An Encyclopedia of Keynesian Economics* (Cheltenham, Glos: Edward Elgar).
Harcourt, G. C. (1995a) *Capitalism, Socialism and Post-Keynesianism. Selected Essays of G. C. Harcourt* (Cheltenham, Glos: Edward Elgar).
— (1995b) 'Recollections and Reflections of an Australian Patriot and a Cambridge Economist', *Banca Nazionale del Lavoro Quarterly Review*, XLVIII, 225–54.
— and P. A. Riach (eds) (1997) *A 'Second Edition' of The General Theory*, 2 vols (London: Routledge).
Medema, S. and W. J. Samuels (eds) (1996) *Foundations of Research in Economics. How do Economists do Economics* (Cheltenham, Glos: Edward Elgar).
Warner, M. (ed.) (1996) *International Encyclopedia of Business and Management* (London: Routledge).

Acknowledgements

The author and publishers wish to acknowledge with thanks the following for permission to reproduce copyright material:

The editor of *History of Economics Review* for permission to reprint 'Is Keynes Dead?', *History of Economics Review*, no. 18, Summer 1992, 1–9.

The editor of *The Cambridge Review* for permission to reprint 'A "Second Edition" of Keynes's *General Theory*', *Cambridge Review*, vol. 118, May 1997, 21–5.

Edward Elgar Publishing Ltd, Cheltenham, Glos. and Claudio Sardoni for permission to reprint '*The General Theory of Employment, Interest and Money*: Three Views', Chapter 1 of P. Arestis (ed.), *Keynes, Money and the Open Economy. Essays in honour of Paul Davidson*, vol. 1 (Cheltenham, Glos.: Edward Elgar, 1996), 1–13.

Oxford University Press and Paul Dalziel for permission to reprint 'A Note on "Mr Meade's Relation" and International Capital Movements', *Cambridge Journal of Economics*, vol. 21, September 1997, 621–31.

The editors of *The Economic Journal* for permission to reprint 'Joan Robinson, 1903–1983', *Economic Journal*, vol. 105, September 1995, 1228–43 and 'Lorie Tarshis, 1911–1993: In Appreciation', *Economic Journal*, vol. 105, September 1995, 1244–55.

The British Academy for permission to reprint 'Edward Austin Gossage Robinson, 1897–1993', *Proceedings of the British Academy*, vol. 94, *1996 Lectures and Memoirs*, 1997, 707–31.

Routledge and Prue Kerr for permission to reprint 'Marx, Karl Heinrich (1818–83)' in M. Warner (ed.), *International Encyclopedia of Business and Management* (London: Routledge, 1996), 3388–95.

Edward Elgar Publishing Ltd, Cheltenham, Glos, and Thomas Cate for permission to reprint 'Keynes, John Maynard' in T. Cate (ed.), *An Encyclopedia of Keynesian Economics* (Cheltenham, Glos.: Edward Elgar), 278–81.

The editors of *Review of Political Economy* for permission to reprint 'George Shackle: A Tribute', *Review of Political Economy*, vol. 5, no. 2, 1993, 272–3 and 'What Josef Steindl Means to My Generation',

Review of Political Economy, Josef Steindl Memorial Issue, vol. 6, no. 4, 1994, 459–63.

Cambridge University Press for permission to reprint 'A Left Keynesian View of the Phillips Curve Trade-Off', Chapter 32 of R. Leeson (ed.), *A. W. H. Phillips: Collected Works in Contemporary Perspective* (Cambridge: Cambridge University Press, 2000), 304–7.

Edward Elgar Publishing Ltd, Cheltenham, Glos, for permission to reprint 'Investment Expenditure, Unrealised Expectations and Offsetting Monetary Policies', in R. Bellofiore and P. Ferri (eds), *Financial Fragility and Investment in the Capitalist Economy: The Economic Legacy of Hyman Minsky* (Cheltenham, Glos: Edward Elgar, 2000), pp. 69–75.

The editors of *History of Political Economy* for permission to reprint 'Review of Turner, *Joan Robinson and the Americans*; Feiwel (ed.) *Joan Robinson and Modern Economic Theory* (Vol. 1) and *The Economics of Imperfect Competition and Employment: Joan Robinson and Beyond* (Vol. 2)', *History of Political Economy*, 23, Spring 1991, 158–64.

The review editor of *Review of Income and Wealth* and Michael Kitson for permission to reprint 'Fifty Years of Measurement: A Cambridge View', *Review of Income and Wealth*, series 39, no. 4, December 1993, 435–47.

The editors of *Journal of International and Comparative Economics* for permission to reprint 'The Kaldor Legacy: Reviewing Nicholas Kaldor, *Causes of Growth and Stagnation in the World Economy*, Cambridge: Cambridge University Press, 1996', *Journal of International and Comparative Economics*, vol. 5, 1997, 341–57.

The editor of *Journal of Post Keynesian Economics* for permission to reprint 'Critiques and Alternatives: Reflections on Some Recent (and Not So Recent) Controversies', *Journal of Post Keynesian Economics*, vol. 19, Winter 1996–97, 171–80.

Edward Elgar Publishing Ltd, Cheltenham, Glos, and Prue Kerr for permission to reprint 'Robinson, Joan, as an Interpreter of the Classical Economists: Mrs Robinson and the Classics', in H. D. Kurz and N. Salvadori (eds), *The Elgar Companion to Classical Economics L–Z* (Cheltenham, Glos: Edward Elgar, 1998), 324–8.

Oxford University Press for permission to reprint 'Two Views on Development: Austin and Joan Robinson', *Cambridge Journal of Economics*, vol. 22, May 1998, 367–77.

Edward Elgar Publishing Ltd, Cheltenham, Glos, for permission to reprint 'How I do Economics', in S. G. Medema and W. J. Samuels (eds), *Foundations of Research in Economics. How do Economists do Economics* (Cheltenham, Glos: Edward Elgar, 1996), 93–102.

Cambridge University Press for permission to reprint 'The Cambridge Contribution to Economics' in S. J. Ormrod (ed.), *Cambridge Contributions* (Cambridge: Cambridge University Press, 1998), 65–87.

1
50 Years a Keynesian*

Introduction

I expect that like most people I shall never cease to be surprised by the perceptions which other people have of who you are, what you have done and why. When I retired in September 1998 and that most courageous and supportive of editors, Tim Farmiloe, offered to publish two volumes of my selected essays,[1] I re-read some essays about my life and work by John Hatch and Colin Rogers (1997), John Hatch and Ray Petrides (1997), Philip Arestis, Gabriel Palma and Malcolm Sawyer (1997a, 1997b) and Sheila Dow (1997). These authors all have differing time periods and views[2] from which to observe me. These are naturally reflected in their observations. Nevertheless, there is a dominant theme in all their accounts, that, as Hatch and Rogers put it (1997: 97), I have 'always been a Keynesian economist in the very broadest sense [, that I have always] identified with the elegance of Keynes's economics [and] also with its social purposes'. In this essay I try to explain the how and why of their evaluation.

* I thank but in no way implicate Stephanie Blackenburg, Giuseppe Fontana, Tim Harcourt, John Hatch, Prue Kerr, Bob Rowthorn, Trevor Stegman and Tom Wilson for their comments on a draft of this essay. Most of the policy papers referred to in the essay are gathered together in a companion volume, Harcourt (2000).

1

First introductions to economics and to Keynes

I was not consciously aware of Keynes and his economics until 1950 when I started a four-year honours course in economics at the University of Melbourne. Yet I had already done four years of economics as a schoolboy. The two texts that dominated those schoolboy years were *Supply and Demand* (1922) by H. D. Henderson and *The Social Framework* (1942) by J. R. Hicks. With hindsight, they may be seen as excellent starting points from which to come to Keynes's writings. The first is a very clear exposition of the essentials of the supply and demand approach of Marshall's *Principles* (1890) without Marshall's own ifs and buts and smokescreens. (It is instead shot through with Henderson's sceptical view of life in general and economics in particular.) Hicks's book provided an illuminating way to learn the essentials of the Keynesian national accounting framework, Keynesian in the sense that the theoretical system of *The General Theory* (1936) was the principal impetus for the systematic development of the national accounting framework in the war and postwar years. When I wrote my first book (*Economic Activity* (1967), written jointly with Peter Karmel and Bob Wallace), I found that being forced to think through the logic of the national accounts (the topic of chapters 2 and 3 of *Economic Activity*) was extremely enlightening, not least because at the time I wrote the first draft (1963) I was also struggling to understand the logic of the system of production interdependence that is the core of Piero Sraffa's (1960) *Production of Commodities*, and of the interrelations between these two systems.[3]

My first explicit introduction to J. M. Keynes was not through *The General Theory* (or even the *Treatise on Money*, 1930) but through the *Tract* (1923) in the first-year lectures by Alf ('Sammy') Weller to those students electing to do the honours questions in their exams. Though it was 1950, 27 years on from its publication, I think in retrospect that it was still a stroke of good fortune to start from there. For in the *Tract*, while Keynes was still a resolute quantity theory of money person *à la* Marshall, he was already kicking against the constraints of his teacher's system, especially the long-period character of its propositions and their irrelevance as a guide to monetary policy. Moreover, though he still accepted the real/money dichotomy, he had already singled out deflation as a worse short-term situation of economies than inflation (even hyperinflation) and, within this, the social evils of unemployment as opposed to the economic effects of falling price levels. So we took on board the appropriate passages and we were given the basis with which eventually to understand the full significance of the context within which is placed Keynes's best-known remark, '*In the long run* we are all dead' Keynes (1923: 65, emphasis in original).[4] Furthermore, our fledgling intellectual muscles were flexed by the detailed analysis of the forward exchanges in chapter 3. It is one of Keynes's most incisive contributions to economic theory; understanding it is a must for understanding his analysis in later years of the implications of an inescapable environment of uncertainty for decisions and decision-makers in an economy.

I did not read *The General Theory* until our second year when it was one of the set texts for the lectures given by Don Cochrane (of Cochrane and Orcutt fame) and Joe Isaac (my first mentor and the first economist to be made a 'judge' of the Australian Arbitration Commission, as it was called then). I tried to read *The General Theory* over the long vacation. Though it excited me tremendously, I cannot pretend that I got very far with it, as my tutors gently pointed out when I came to write my first faltering essays on its concepts. Cochrane did not help by sending me prematurely to Duesenberry's 1949 book when I told him I had read *The General Theory*. By the end of the lectures I think I was becoming clear on the outlines of the theory, helped – I thought at the time – by Paul Samuelson's Keynesian cross diagram.[5] We did not meet 'Mr. Keynes and the "Classics"', Hicks (1937), until our third year (the first year of the two-year honours programme known as Final Division). By then we were also reading *Value and Capital* (1939) and even the *Foundations* (1948). We were introduced to Michal Kalecki's writings on distribution and, in microeconomics, to Robert Triffin's (1942) *Monopolistic Competition and General Equilibrium Theory* following on from the 1933 classics by Joan Robinson and Edward Chamberlin and the reviews and articles they spawned.

The most significant of these articles for me was Kurt Rothschild's 1947 classic, 'Price Theory and Oligopoly'. The central theme of his article was that oligopolists were as interested in secure profits as in maximum profits and therefore that Clausewitz's (1943) *Principles of War*, rather than the theories of Joan Robinson or Chamberlin or the then emerging game theory, was the appropriate framework within which to analyse their behaviour.

When I came to choose a topic for the 30 000-word honours dissertation we were required to do, my two loves came together in an ambitious (one of the examiners thought it over-ambitious!) attempt to work out the implications for systemic behaviour in a Keynesian framework of microeconomic foundations containing Rothschild's Clausewitzian oligopolists. The particular issue I homed in on was Keynes's remarks in the chapters on the consumption function (see Keynes, 1936: 98–104) on the implications of 'financial prudence' – writing off the book values of fixed assets well ahead of their actual wearing out and replacement – for the impact of current investment expenditure on activity. I used Lou Goldberg's wonderful collection of company accounts (Lou was then Professor of Accounting at the University of Melbourne); I tried to test the implications of my attempted marriage against the reserve policy of Australian companies during the Great Depression. I used a case-studies approach, taking the accounts of individual companies and constructing flow-of-funds statements. The results of my labours could most favourably (charitably) be summed up by the Scottish verdict 'not proven'. I suspect that the essence of what I was getting at is to be found in a pithy paragraph in Joan Robinson's writings (see *Collected Economic Papers*, Vol III, 1965: 177) and the analysis of this on pp. 210–14 of Harcourt (1972). Oligopolists have some discretionary power over the setting of prices *and* also wish, as far as is possible, to finance their investment expenditures internally from retained profits. If we now consider a world of oligopolists, it follows that the expansionary effects of a rise in overall planned investment may be offset, always to some extent and sometimes more than offset, by the contractionary effects of the accompanying rise in planned savings. The latter results from the redistribution of income implied by the rise in profit margins and prices designed to bring about the required rise in internal finance.[6]

Partly simultaneously with and partly preceding these developments in my thoughts about economic theory were radical changes, first in my political beliefs, and subsequently in my religious ones. The direct stimulus for the changes was not J.M.K. but the first-year lectures on economic geography (eat your heart out, Paul Krugman) which constituted, in essence, a course on comparative economic systems. It was a shock to my system for while they revealed great variations in the nature of the organisation of different social systems, they also revealed two common characteristics in all – that injustice and poverty thrived and that the rationality of the different forms of organisation was conspicuous by its absence. The result was my conversion from being a doctrinaire free marketeer – my parents' views absorbed uncritically (for details see Harcourt, 1998: 3–7) – to, I suppose, an equally doctrinaire socialist (soon and later, respectively, to be coupled with the adjectives, 'democratic' and 'Christian'). These philosophical changes were given practical content when I joined the Australian Labor Party (ALP) in early 1954.

Other influences

I have stressed the influence of Keynes and the writers on price formation in different market structures. But I want also to mention the discussion of Joseph Schumpeter's work on business cycles in my second year in a course on economic history, and of the great economists in my third year when I took HET (*History of Economic Thought*) as the first of my honours options. (In my fourth year I took mathematical economics.) The small group taking HET read Smith, Ricardo, Malthus, J. S. Mill, Marx, Jevons, Marshall and others in the originals. I confess that Marx's *Capital* defeated me and I had to depend on Maurice Dobb and, later, Paul Sweezy to give me what few clues I acquired. That had not stopped me from calling myself a Marxist in my second year, nor from writing an economic history essay on an industrial revolution in the sixteenth century within a Marxist framework. In the essay I foolishly used terms such as exploitation, surplus labour and value, proletariat and capitalist – much to the annoyance of one of my teachers, a Latvian who was opposed to anything Marxist. Unfortunately he also marked the essay.

I graduated at the beginning of 1954 and spent the next 19 months or so working for a Master's degree by dissertation as the research assistant to R. I. Downing, who had just taken up the prestigious Ritchie Chair at Melbourne University, one of the very few pure research chairs in Australia. Downing, an Australian and a graduate of Melbourne University, was also a Cambridge buff, an enthusiastic Keynesian (he had been at King's just before the Second World War) who also knew and admired Kalecki. The project I worked on was financed by the Reserve Bank of Australia (the Central Bank). I had to design and carry out a pilot survey of income and saving in Melbourne, to see whether an annual Australia-wide survey along the lines of Harold Lydall's work in Oxford and George Katona's at Ann Arbor was a practical possibility. This was Keynesian economics in a down-to-earth mode, examining the feasibility of acquiring information at the level of the household on three fundamental variables in the Keynesian system – income, saving, wealth – in order to estimate their aggregate values from the bottom up, as it were.

The project was successfully completed in 1955 (though not without many trials and extreme tribulations, of which I shall say nothing, in print anyway). I subsequently received the degree in 1956. My first article, 'Pilot Survey of Personal Savings', written jointly with Duncan Ironmonger (who had been the excellent expert advisor from the Australian Bureau of Statistics (ABS) on the stratified sampling procedures used to gather the information) was published in the *Economic Record* in 1956. By then I was married to Joan (30 July 1955) and we were in Cambridge. I was doing a PhD at King's, supervised first by Nicky Kaldor and then, when he went on leave for the academic year 1956–57, by Ronald Henderson.[7]

At Cambridge in the 1950s

My PhD topic was initially on the implications for the theory of the firm and the trade cycle of the assumption that secure profits are as important as maximum profits in oligopolistic market structures. When I told Robin Marris[8] this at the first meeting of the new/old research students in Michaelmas Term 1955 to set up the seminar series, he pounced – 'You're first!'. So two weeks or so into Full Term, I gave a preliminary paper on my topic to the seminar. Joan Robinson was there, chain-smoking and startling us all in the subsequent discussion by saying (of business people's behaviour) 'I think the buggers do...'. Despite surviving this rather traumatic beginning, I quickly lost my way in the first term, partly because Nicky and I did not hit it off at all.[9] So being assigned to Henderson at the start of 1956 literally saved my academic life. Henderson had a look at my honours dissertation and sent me to the NIESR (National Institute for Economic and Social Research) to work on a then emerging data-set, the preparation of aggregate profit and loss, balance sheet and funds statements for all the quoted public companies in the UK for 1949–53. Bryan Hopkin, the then Director, wanted some reports written on a sample of the data – the chemical industry and the woollen and worsted industry – and its uses. That was my task for the first eight months of 1956. It was hard work – the nearest thing to mechanisation was a Marchand calculator – but invaluable. In addition I came to know the research officers at the NIESR, especially Max Corden, a fellow Australian, Sig Prais and Christopher Dow. Dow took me for a beer on the evening he finished the first draft of his celebrated imported-cost inflation model (Dow, 1956), an approach I subsequently was to take in my own research though I cannot pretend that I had then other than the merest inkling of what he had done, due in equal measure to his euphoric account and my response to English pints.

After many ups and downs my topic became the implications of using historical cost-accounting procedures for setting prices and measuring incomes for dividend and taxation purposes in an inflationary period. I put the historical-cost pricing models of Trevor Swan, Eric Russell and Russell Mathews and John Grant into the Marxian–Kaleckian framework of Joan Robinson's (1956) *Accumulation of Capital* to derive my inferences, which were tested against the NIESR data referred to above. My first policy proposals were that the measurement of profits for taxation and dividend purposes should be on a replacement-cost rather than an historical-cost basis, as should the setting of prices by firms. I also started a long-to-continue investigation of the impact of investment-incentive schemes on investment decisions and outcomes.

In 1955 I had gone, usually with Tom Asimakopulos and Keith Frearson, to Joan Robinson's lectures on what was to become *The Accumulation of Capital* (1956). I found them as stimulating as they were frustrating, not least because Joan dropped her voice whenever she came to a critical proposition. So when the book was published in 1956 I took off a term from 'research' (much to Ronald Henderson's displeasure, he had no love for either Joan or her influence), locked myself away with the book and then emerged to

read a paper on what I thought it was all about to the research students seminar over two successive meetings. Marris chaired the ses-
sions and Joan came to a third session to answer questions. She was
not impressed by us, she thought we could not see the wood for the
trees (even those she planted) because we asked nit-picking questions about, for example, price and real Wicksell effects rather than
about broad conceptual issues. Probably she was right, but she was
not without blame as she was to admit when in 1962 she published
her own tell-it-to-the-children version (just as she had done in 1937
for *The General Theory*).

This detour was an invaluable experience because it gave me a
framework and focus for my subsequent work, a framework which
obviously I think I understand much better now than when I was
first developing it. That is to say, I was starting to work on mainly
classical problems done in the modern post-Keynesian, Kaleckian
and Marxian manner. The first fruits were, as I said, to be found in
my PhD dissertation. It allowed me to analyse the relationships
between pricing practices (in this case, whether historical or replacement costs were marked-up), the level of activity and the aggregate
distribution of income in periods of inflation. It also allowed me to
link these outcomes back to the temporal structure of the liabilities
side of balance sheets through the impact on the need for firms to
borrow short-term and long-term because of what was happening to
their cash flows.

In retrospect, I see that I put too much emphasis on the allocation-
of-resources aspect of what was going on. I argued that by using
replacement costs the price mechanism would be able the better to
do its grand (neo-classical) job, signal where resources should move
to and from because of the 'true' costs of production involved –
clearly a naive inference in a world of oligopolists. Moreover, it
distracts attention from the need explicitly to consider what
determines the sizes of the mark-ups used (regardless of the cost-
base to which they are applied) and so to look at the relationships
between accumulation plans, financial needs and price-setting.
Because of Keynes's realisation in 1937 that he had neglected the
finance motive in his discussion of the determination of the rate of
interest, proceeding from *The General Theory* alone meant that
readers sometimes missed the significance of the vital distinction
between finance on the one hand, and saving on the other, and the

role that finance, *not* saving, played as the ultimate constraint on the achievement or not of planned accumulation.[10] This emphasis was to be found in the later (and earlier) Keynes and in the writings of Kalecki and Hy Minsky. It is part of the modern agendas of both the post-Keynesian and mainstream literature; see, for example, the many papers which Asimakopulos (1983) spawned and the huge literature created by Feldstein and Horioka (1980), to which Paul Dalziel and I made a modest critical contribution in the *Cambridge Journal* in 1997. We defended Keynes's fundamental insight that, as James Meade put it, nationally and internationally, the investment dog wags the saving tail and not the other way around.[11]

Cambridge themes in first Adelaide years

In March 1958 I started a lectureship at the University of Adelaide. In 1960 I gave some lectures on Kaldor's postwar writings which resulted in me asking why such an eminent Keynesian as Kaldor *insisted* that full employment was the natural long-period position of a growing capitalist economy (see Harcourt, 1963a). There was a convenient analytical dichotomy which provided a rationale for his view. For if it were true that prices and money-wages were sticky in the short period but flexible in the long period, with prices being the 'more' flexible of the two, the Kahn–Keynes multiplier would serve to determine output and employment in the short period and (providing $s_\pi > s_w$) the distribution of income in the long period. A crucial proviso was that full employment was 'given' by the requirement that accumulation proceeded at a pace which allowed Harrod's g_n to be realised; for then Kaldor's long-period mechanism ensured the equality of g_w with g_n. This was a neat logical solution but why should anyone believe that it described the world, especially when we had the prior contributions of Kalecki in which both employment and the distribution of income were determined simultaneously and in the short period, without there being any constraint to be at full employment.

Because of my earlier work, it was natural for me to ask: what pricing policies must be followed in the consumption and investment goods sectors in order that the Kaldor mechanism works in the short period (by 1957, Kaldor was arguing that his mechanism applied to the short period as well as the long period)? Note that I was old-fashioned enough to believe it necessary to distinguish explicitly between the roles of the two sectors and also to have investment leading and saving following. Moreover, it was also made explicit that the chief decision-makers were business people, that it was their accumulation, profit-making and employment and output decisions which drove the economy along (sometimes well, sometimes poorly), not those of lifetime utility maximisers whose consumption/saving patterns led and all other institutions were but neo-classical agents devoted to helping them fulfil their plans, as if a Ramsey optimiser ruled the world. I stress these points because if we examine the helpful, if misguided, article by Chari (1998), a Lucas admirer, on Robert Lucas's influence on macroeconomics in the last quarter of a century, we see that the whole Marx–Kalecki–Keynes view has been completely suppressed in most macroeconomic analysis, in Chari's view, a good thing too.[12] If I have not persuaded you, do have a read of an insightful article by John Lodewijks (1999) in which he sets out the core characteristics of the macroeconomic sections of three leading modern texts, Mankiw (1998), Parkin (1996) and Taylor (1995). His account supports my generalisation. God alone knows what harm it has done to the now too many cohorts of undergraduates brought up on this fare. I was relieved to see that Bob Solow takes a broadly similar view on these general matters: see the many wise remarks in his recently published Frederico Caffé Lectures, *Monopolistic Competition and Macroeconomic Theory* (Solow, 1998).

Not surprisingly, the answers to my question of what pricing polices must be followed in order that planned investment becomes actual investment and full employment is maintained produced some very peculiar behaviour both within and between the consumption goods sector and the investment goods sector. For example, in one scenario we find that the entrepreneurs in the investment goods sector are active, bidding for or sacking labour and raising or lowering production in response to changes in planned demands. In contrast, their counterparts in the consumption goods sector are passive, accepting the loss or return of labour and the consequent changes in production. Their only active role is to set the prices of consumption goods appropriate to each situation. There is a glaring weakness in my analysis. I implicitly treated each sector as one giant firm (the modern representative agent heresy) and so derived sector results. I needed to delve one layer deeper in order to find out the behaviour of individual firms which would give those sector results. Solow (1998) takes on such considerations head on (but it is over 30 years later). Robin Marris also worked on similar themes for many decades; his mature views are to be found in Marris (1991, 1997).

At much the same time I reviewed Wilfred Salter's 1960 classic (see Harcourt, 1962; 1982). I found it one of the most illuminating books I have ever encountered in economics. Salter built on the insight as to why old machines could operate side by side with new and better ones (old machines only have to cover their *variable* costs, new machines have to expect to cover their *total* costs), to make serious and profound policy recommendations concerning the rate of change of nominal incomes in a fully employed economy. In order to have high levels and rates of growth of overall productivity in a fully employed economy, the ground rule for adjusting money incomes should be that they increase at the rate of *overall* productivity plus prices.

At the time I read Salter's book there was a heated debate occurring in Adelaide (indeed, in Australia) on an appropriate wages policy for Australia. Eric Russell, my mentor at Adelaide, was virtually the odd (but ultimately correct) man out in the debate. With James Meade he had written the definitive account of how the Australian economy works (see Meade and Russell, 1957). (I always preferred Russell's Kaleckian means of establishing the paper's main results; see Harcourt, 1977a; Sardoni, 1992.) With Salter, alas, to die at the ridiculously early age of 34 in 1963, he had given crucial evidence combining his theoretical analysis with Salter's empirical work to the Australian Arbitration Commission on behalf of the wage-earners in the 1959 Basic Wage Case. Eric's arguments were opposed by those economists who gave tremendous weight to the 'evils' of inflation and who were not prepared to allow changes in prices to influence the setting of the rate of increase of money incomes. It seemed to me at the time, albeit through the proverbial glass darkly, that Eric was correct. I am comforted by the fact that my other Australian mentor, Joe Isaac, also agreed with Eric in the debates.

I recently returned to these themes, together with the implications of Kalecki's remarkable 1943 article on the political aspects of full employment, especially his vital distinction between the political economy of *getting* to full employment, on the one hand, and *sustaining* it, on the other (see Harcourt, 1997). I argued that if economies followed the Russell/Salter rule of adjusting *money* incomes for effective productivity *plus* prices, they would greatly improve their chances of entering virtuous regimes of Salter processes in which *overall* productivity would grow at agreeable rates because low productivity industries would be knocked out and investment in high productivity industries would be encouraged. This would enhance the chances of restraining increases in nominal incomes, so allowing full employment to be maintained because *real* incomes would be growing at relatively satisfactory rates. These ideas were put by the Australian Council of Trade Unions (ACTU) advocate to the Industrial Relations Commission in the 1996–97 Living Wage case (partly through the good offices of our son, Tim, who was then a research officer at the ACTU). Alas, they did not carry the day with the Commission that year but received a more sympathetic hearing the next year. The current emphasis on the need to create flexible labour markets and to introduce enterprise bargaining threatens to produce a pattern of wage levels and changes in wages which will throttle the benefits of Salter processes by allowing old machines longer lives in declining or low productivity industries and frustrating the rate of introduction of new machines in high productivity or expanding industries, so perpetuating sluggish growth in overall productivity.

While I supported Eric in the discussions at Adelaide and in letters to him when he was on leave in Oxford in 1960, I did not write directly about the issues, except to list Salter's policy conclusions in my 1962 review article. My own writings at the time were on much more basically microeconomic policy proposals – investment allowances for primary producers (Barton and Harcourt, 1959), a rather silly article with Jim Bennett (Bennett and Harcourt, 1960) on reforming the company taxation system (silly because it mixed up a neoclassical with a post-Keynesian approach) – and on theoretical issues – the critique of Kaldor's theories, a note on Joan Robinson's 1956 volume and Harry Johnson's critique of it, Harcourt (1963b) and the first draft of 'The Accountant in a Golden Age' (Harcourt,

1965a; Sardoni, 1992), my second most cited paper after the survey of capital theory in the *Journal of Economic Literature* (Harcourt, 1969).

Cambridge in the 1960s: an insider's view

In the autumn of 1963 I returned to Cambridge on study leave and almost immediately (the day after President Kennedy was killed) was offered a University Lectureship in the Faculty, soon to be followed by a Fellowship at Trinity Hall. I took leave without pay from Adelaide and stayed until near the end of December 1966. This was possibly the most productive, certainly the most exciting period of my working life. Themes and issues which I had been looking at separately now came together. A major catalyst was hearing Bob Solow's 1963 Marshall Lectures on the Cambridge theories of distribution and growth associated especially with Kaldor and Joan Robinson. These spurred me on to write my own favourite theoretical paper on employment and distribution in a two-sector model in the short period – Harcourt (1965b); Sardoni (1992). It combined a macroeconomic theory of distribution, a Kaleckian/Keynesian theory of employment, a Salterian discussion of the choice of technique, a Kaleckian/Robinsonian approach to price-setting and Sraffa's emphasis on production interdependence.[13] The macroeconomic theory of distribution and the Kaleckian/Keynesian theory of employment led to an expression for the multiplier which reflected the distribution process through its effect on the size of the leakage into saving. The approach to price-setting emphasised retained profits as a source of finance for investment expenditure and as a determinant, together with the level of aggregate demand, of the sizes of the mark-ups in the two sectors.

The paper made explicit the structure of my approach to understanding the processes at work in modern economies from then on. A major item missing was an explicit role for Keynes's monetary insights and the determination of the rate of interest, always something of a mystery to me. That is one reason why in 1974 when my old teacher, Jim Cairns, who was then Deputy Prime Minister and Federal Treasurer, asked me whether I would consider being Governor of the Reserve Bank of Australia, I said 'no', adding 'You know me, Jim, I'm a real man, not a money man'.

My interest in inflationary situations and Salter's contributions came together when I examined the choice of technique in inflationary conditions, comparing and contrasting the outcomes of different investment-decision rules and, in a subsequent paper, Harcourt (1968), the impact of different investment-incentive schemes on the choice of technique. I also used the analysis of 'The Accountant in a Golden Age' to analyse what effects the Russian system of bonus payments for managers, then all the rage, had on the choice of technique in planned economies (see Harcourt, 1966). I queried whether the results had an economic rationale or were even what the proponents of the bonus scheme intended. As I have said elsewhere, I see with hindsight that I was using the post-Keynesian method of starting from real world observations, what people actually do, what economic societies they operate in, rather than an axiomatic one of, say, an assumption of profit-maximisation. The object was to work out the results of businesspeople's behaviour and policy-makers' declared aims and to compare the results with those arising from the application of standard economic theory.[14] For example, I showed that with the orders of magnitude likely to be met in the real world, the pay-off period criterion resulted in a more investment-intensive, less labour-intensive technique being chosen than would have occurred if a DCF (Discounted Cash Flow) procedure had been used.

In 1966 I wrote the first draft of 'Pricing and the Investment Decision' (Harcourt and Kenyon, 1976; Sardoni, 1992). In it I tried to develop an endogenous theory of the size of the mark-up, relating it to investment plans and the desire for internal finance and trying to make sure that the model was set in historical time as Joan Robinson called it (to contrast it with logical time), and which we now include under the rubric of path-dependence.

The paper had a long gestation period (see Harcourt, 1995a: 233), and by the time it was published Al Eichner's and Adrian Wood's writings on similar themes had captured centre-stage. Both, of course, made splendid contributions but Eichner's model has a weakness associated with the use of Keynes's MEC (Marginal Efficiency of Capital) schedule and Wood's analysis is explicitly in the logical time of a Golden Age model. (Jim Ball (1964) preceded us all.) An implication of our analysis was that in the oligopolistic industries with which we were concerned, margins would be greater, the greater was the investment planned, *ceteris paribus.* But investment would be less, the higher were the margins and therefore prices set. In microeconomic terms at least, this is a drawback on accumulation, productivity growth and attaining and sustaining full employment. Furthermore, the higher price levels may make the control of inflation more difficult. These arguments may not go though at the level of the system as a whole but, at the least, they need to be explored. Salter processes are at their most effective when competitive market structures are present. (Oligopolists *may* behave like competitors but they cannot be forced to do so.) The increase in international competitiveness of the last two decades may have brought the world economy closer to the competitive model than when the writings referred to above were first developed. If so, our minds may be put more at ease on this particular score.

Capital theory controversies and policy proposals

Soon after I returned home I was asked by Mark Perlman to write a survey article on capital theory for the newly formed *Journal of Economic Literature* (see Harcourt, 1999a, for the full story). This made me read intensively the literature, much of which had been created around me in the 1950s and 1960s by people mainly from the two Cambridges. Especially did it force me to try to make sense of the heated discussions I had witnessed in Cambridge between Joan Robinson, Kaldor and Pasinetti on the one hand, and Solow, Hahn, Meade, Christopher Bliss and others on the other. Ken Arrow also participated and was respected by both sides, both, for example, claiming learning by doing (Arrow, 1962), for themselves. Sraffa mostly stood aside from the day-to-day skirmishes, though he did ask me to show why Levhari's claim (1965) that reswitching and capital-reversing could not occur in the economy as a whole was wrong when I drew his attention to the article (see Harcourt, 1999a). Writing the survey while simultaneously taking an active, time-consuming role in the anti-war movement radically changed my approach to economics, teaching and politics, changes which were to affect the policy debates and proposals with which I was associated in the 1970s.

Once my 1972 book on capital theory was published, I turned to its policy implications and to policy issues in general. The 'long boom' or 'Golden Age of capitalism'[15] was coming to its end, Australia as with the rest of the advanced world was experiencing rising inflation and, soon, rising unemployment. Two papers from the first half of the 1970s set out the theoretical background and the social and political philosophies involved. Fittingly, the first paper, Harcourt (1974), arose from a lecture to the South Australian accounting profession, for it has always been my belief that the Australian training of economists, whereby some knowledge of the rationale and procedures of double-entry book-keeping is required, is a *sine qua non* for understanding how capitalism originated, developed and works.

In the lecture, I outlined the ingredients of the package deal of policies that came to be called the Adelaide Plan: so-called, because it was the outcome of discussions between Eric Russell, Barry Hughes, Philip Bentley and myself in Adelaide. In Harcourt (1999b) I summarised its essentials. Sufficient, therefore, to say here that it was an attempt to provide a sensible, effective and more just and humane alternative to what we saw to be the misguided attempts to tackle accelerating inflation by short sharp shock procedures; their professed aim was to quickly push unemployment above the then fashionable concept of its natural rate. This was designed to force decision-makers and wage-earners to revise their inflationary expectations and then move slowly back to the natural rate with a lower rate of inflation in mind.

In Harcourt (1977b; 1982) (the paper arose from a seminar I gave in Melbourne in 1975), I compared and contrasted the three rival theories then on offer (and the policies that flowed from them) from policy-makers and academics alike in Australia – Monetarist, Bastard Keynesian and Post-Keynesian. (Mervyn Lewis identified a fourth group, the structuralists, who came at macroeconomic policy from an essentially orthodox microeconomic base, forerunners of Gordon Brown's supply-siders.) When discussing policies I tried explicitly to identify the political constraints on the possibility of acceptance and implementation. I did this also later in the decade in a paper given at a symposium on unemployment at the Winter School of the Economic Society of Australia and New Zealand (Harcourt, 1978). There, I wrote:

When putting forward these suggestions, I shall try to operate within the constraints imposed by the present Federal government and *its* advisors, to try to devise a package that is acceptable to *their* philosophy, and to *their* political and economic outlook. I do this, not because I agree with them – they are in the main repugnant to me – but because I find the present level of unemployment so *unnecessarily* wickedly high as to make unthinkable *either* an emasculated Pontius Pilate act *or* the attitude of let them – the pollies, their advisors *and* the unemployed – stew in their own juice, it can only hurry on the time when the whole system may be overturned (p. 61).

Like much of the rest of the industrialised world, Australia was caught in what the late Arthur Okun (1978) called 'The great stagflation swamp'. In those years, prices and money-wages were relatively sticky and so any contractionary fiscal and monetary policies designed to drive inflation out of the system had a seemingly irreducible floor, in the USA of about 6 per cent per annum 'despite massive excess supplies of idle people, machines and plant' (Okun, 1978: 7), a situation which was prolonged for over three years in the USA.

The Federal government and its advisors seemed not to have learnt from the American experience. Nevertheless, I tried to persuade them to attempt a cautious increase in government expenditure, concentrating on expenditure with a low import content and directed to social purposes. I mentioned the balance of payments constraint but said that if the value of the multiplier was less than two we could probably take it in our stride. If there were to be an accelerator effect, that would be a problem – but with the then level of excess capacity and finance puzzles any lift to investment would be a while coming – by which time I hoped the other measures I outlined would have given Australia a more competitive cost structure.

At that time virtually all governments in Australia were against a rise in government spending and so the second-best policy was a cut in taxes (accompanied by a rise in interest rates). I actually advocated a cut in sales taxes, not only because of the effect on spending but also because of its favourable impact on the rate of inflation. (By the early 1990s I had changed my mind to argue that government spending should be designed according to the longer term needs of the community – subject to the political philosophy of the party in power – and counter-cyclical policy should be through changes in taxes and interest rates, see Harcourt, 1993b; 1995b.)

I coupled the macroeconomic proposals with a plea for the return of indexation through the Arbitration Commission. I argued that the relationship between real wages and unemployment in Australia (as a dyed-in-the-wool Keynesian, I should have written unemployment and real wages) was complicated, certainly not obviously negative, as was then argued in official circles, and therefore *real* wage cuts were not needed, if they ever were. I also coupled this with an earlier suggestion of a relativities wages fund, whereby the groups who thought they had fallen behind in past years in the wage–wage spiral could argue before the Arbitration Commission for a share in a predetermined amount granted overall, over and above the indexation procedures, in order to restore relativities. The full restoration might well be spread over a number of periods, but the justice of the claim would have been established from the beginning. Such procedures would require further coordination and cooperation – agreement as to what *was* a fair structure of relativities, the target to be aimed at and eventually reached.[16] I concluded by saying that my suggestions for Australia were in accord with the suggestions made overseas by the best Keynesians, Bastards and otherwise – I cited Jim Tobin and Sid Weintraub. I closed by saying that:

> If we were not operating within the political constraints imposed by the present government, I would repeat again the need for what Joan Robinson calls 'a real social contract which would satisfy the reasonable demands of the workers for more control over their own work, more security against redundancy, better social services and so forth; but that [I feared], must await our return to another [better] world'. (p. 69)[17]

In the late 1970s the ALP set up a National Committee of Inquiry into why the party had done so badly in the 1975 and 1977 elections and I was appointed as the economist on the committee. This allowed me to feed these and other ideas into the discussion paper on economic policy and the future of Australia which we produced, Discussion Paper no. 6 (1979). I drew on a paper I wrote with Prue Kerr (Harcourt and Kerr, 1979), and a review of Hy Minsky's 1975 book on Keynes (Harcourt, 1977c).

I would like to think that the combination of explicit theory and policies within a judgement of what was politically feasible in a given situation and specific period of time would have had Keynes's blessing for it was his own practice that, at least implicitly, I had in mind. Certainly, the most important ingredient of the package deal of policies of the Hawke–Keating governments in the 1980s and early 1990s – the Accord – may find its rationale in these arguments. Of course, I do not claim any originality for them – Ralph Willis, a lone voice crying in the ALP wilderness for many years, was making the same arguments and I was merely making explicit what I had learnt from Russell, Salter, my Cambridge mentors and Kalecki, together with my maturing understanding of Marx's analysis of capitalism.

At the same time as Tommy Balogh and Nicky Kaldor in the United Kingdom were identifying Monetarism as the incomes policy of Karl Marx, I was scandalising the increasingly technocratic and value-free economics profession in Australia by talking explicitly about these attempts to recreate the reserve army of labour. The objectives were to make the sack effective again, to produce a cowed and acquiescent workforce for international and domestic capital to exploit, and to reverse the swing of economic, social and political power to labour which had occurred over the Golden Age back to capital, disguised as a laudable attempt to control inflation. I publicly attacked as hired prize-fighters those economists who were supporting the monetarist/Bastard Keynesian measures designed to bring all this about. In retrospect, I bitterly regret not 'spilling the beans' on a secret meeting I attended at the University of Melbourne sometime in the 1970s at which Heinz Arndt argued that the economics profession had a duty to wean the public off the acceptance of full employment, as it was then understood anyway, as an indispensable object of policy. Of the ten or so Australian Professors of Economics there, only one other was as scandalised by the argument as I was (see Harcourt, 1995b: 31).

Return to Cambridge in the 1980s

In 1975 I chaired a small IEA (International Economic Association) conference at S'Agaro on the microeconomic foundations of macroeconomics. Its theme was, of course, the principal theoretical theme with which I had been grappling since the early 1950s. The volume of the conference, Harcourt (1977d), was not well-received either by its reviewers or the true initiator of the conference, John Hicks, who was distressed by our inability to come up with definitive or at least suggestive solutions to the issues we raised. Nevertheless, I think we acknowledged the difficulties I documented in the introduction to the volume and made some progress towards understanding their source.

In February 1977 Eric Russell died after playing squash. While I had felt torn up by the roots when I left Cambridge at the end of 1966, I nevertheless wanted to stay in Adelaide while Eric was there. Moreover, in 1972 my mother had had a severe stroke and we did not feel justified in leaving Australia while she was alive. But when she died in 1981 and openings occurred in the Faculty and at Jesus, I decided with the selfless support of my family to take them up. The major task I set myself was to write the intellectual history of Joan Robinson and her circle – Austin Robinson, Richard Kahn, Piero Sraffa, Nicky Kaldor, Michal Kalecki, Dick Goodwin, Luigi Pasinetti. I wanted to see whether there was a coherence to the tradition this group of economists both inherited from the classical political economists, Marx and Keynes and passed on, adding, of course, their own very considerable contributions. Virtually all of the group are now dead and since I nearly joined them four times between September 1992 and September 1994 I am rather lagging in getting it all down in book form. But there are now well over 30 separate essays which provide an essential background to the project and now I am retired I hope to get into King's Archives more often to examine the papers of these economists, most of which are housed there. Prue Kerr and I have just started collecting the critical articles on Joan Robinson's contributions for a series of readings which Routledge publishes. Reading these and writing the introduction to the volumes should be a great help in focusing my mind on the other project. I believe it to be a vital project, necessary in order to help to salvage the wisdom contained in the writings of Keynes, his immediate colleagues and their followers, and Kalecki and his, together with the other strands that fall under the rubric of post-Keynesianism.

I have supplemented this principal project in two ways: first, with Peter Riach who suggested to me that we organise the writing of A *'Second Edition' of The General Theory* by Keynes scholars from all over the world (Harcourt and Riach, 1997, 2 vols). Of course, the title may be jokey and pretentious, but the intent was serious. We wanted, first, to document as well as could be done what Keynes himself might have written in, say, 1938 or 1939 on certain aspects of *The General Theory*, had he not been so ill from 1937 on. Secondly, we asked the scholars concerned to explain what and why they had done on certain aspects of *The General Theory* (and extensions under the Keynesian umbrella) in the postwar period. Together, this would serve to provide up-to-date reports within an historical perspective at, I believe, a peculiarly significant and appropriate juncture in the development of economics itself and, more importantly, the particular economic problems of much of the world. These were (are) sensible aims, explicitly stated, but, I have to say, wilfully overlooked in two savage reviews of the volumes. If Freudian ideas were still in vogue I would hazard an explanation of the rationale for the reviews. But as they are not, I won't. Moreover, other reviews have been positive and favourable, indeed generous. For example, Tony Thirlwall (1999) has written a veritable *tour de force*, writing most convincingly as John Maynard Keynes reflecting on and reacting to the various themes in the volumes.[18]

Secondly, following the request to give the Second Donald Horne Address in February 1992 I have written a series of policy papers (Harcourt, 1992, 1993a, 1993b, 1994, 1997) which have pulled together the strands of my previous incursions into policy and added new ones in a way which, I hope, is up-to-date, properly relevant and infused with the spirit of the economics of Keynes – and his contemporaries and followers.

The idea of the Horne Addresses is to ask an Australian living abroad to come home to give a wide-ranging address on issues of vital importance for Australian citizens. The conjunction of events to which mine was addressed was the launching of the Republican movement in Australia and the U-turn on economic policy of the Federal ALP government that was then occurring. The background was the emerging reaction against the 'let the market rip' policies of the 1980s which characterised part of economic policy in Australia, and the crowing over, and then second thoughts about, the implications of the collapse of Communism. I never held any brief for the awful regimes of the USSR and the Eastern European economies but I did point out that the achievements of those Western industrialised capitalist economies that had gone overboard on Hayekian/Friedmanite policies from the 1970s on were not that much to write home about either. There was therefore a case to be made for middle ways – the Kaleckian approach to democratic socialism, for example, for Eastern Europe, the Keynes/Kaleckian (with modern additions) post-Keynesian blueprints for Australia and other similar countries.

I preceded my outlines of middle ways with an account of what modern (and not so modern) theory had to say about the conditions which need to be satisfied for markets to be safely left to do their thing, pointing out that these conditions are spectacularly *not* satisfied in the markets for labour, foreign exchange, financial assets and housing. I recognised that it was a *non sequitur* to jump to the proposition that some form of intervention and regulation would necessarily do better – the case for this had always to be made.

The common theme connecting these papers was the argument that many markets and indeed economic systems themselves are characterised by cumulative causation processes. This viewpoint implies that very different policy proposals and institutions are needed than those associated with the more orthodox view that there are strong equilibrating forces present. Radically different attitudes would be taken towards, for example, speculators and speculation because their systemic effects would not be the benign ones identified by, for example, Milton Friedman (1953) in his well-known article on the case for flexible exchange rates.

The essays on macroeconomic policy in the collection relate principally to the problems of small open economies. It allowed me to ride some hobby-horses, for example, as mentioned above (see pp. 17–18), that government expenditure should not principally be used for pump-priming but rather should fit in with the longer-term needs of economies, taking into account the social and political philosophy of the government in power. I also drew attention to the danger of forgetting those old-fashioned but profound lessons from the writings of Russell and Salter concerning the macroeconomic effects of incomes policies on rates of accumulation, and from Kalecki concerning the vital differences between getting to, and then sustaining, full employment. Because at the economy-level capital and labour are complements, changing money incomes according to changes in the cost of living *and* overall productivity is not only equitable, it is also efficient. It allows income-receivers to benefit from the growing overall real output of the economy and it encourages investment in profitable, productivity-enhancing industries and hastens the decline of industries whose time has not only come but gone.

In Harcourt (1994), which was entitled 'A "Modest Proposal" for Taming the Speculators and Putting the World on Course to Prosperity,' I tried to set out the problems of the various broad regions of the world, show how they are interrelated and what particular combination of policies and institutions might serve to tackle their problems effectively and simultaneously. I included various 'carrot and stick' measures to induce speculators to behave in ways which were less systemically harmful. My proposal for inducing less speculation on foreign exchange markets was in a sense a generalisation of the Tobin tax (without, I must confess, me having read Tobin's proposal). I suggested that the taxation authorities identify what proportions of foreign exchange transactions of both buyers and sellers could be regarded as speculation and that these proportions carry with them penal rates of taxation on the incomes of the transactors concerned. I resurrected Keynes's suggestion (1936: 160) that there be an inverse relationship between the levels of tax rates and the lengths of time for which shares were held. I argued that unless housing purchases and sales could be shown to be for legitimate social purposes, penal rates of taxation should go with them. There is a Utopian tinge to such an exercise (though I did try to take into account the constraints imposed by present political and ideological climates). Nevertheless, unless such interrelationships and schemes are explicitly set out, it is difficult to get people of good will to think about the causes and cures of the world's ills.

Conclusion

So: here it is, nearly 50 years a Keynesian, still pottering on and thinking about the themes which excited me so much when I started economics at the University of Melbourne in 1950. I am glad that I have been able to write accounts of many of the leading actors in the drama I have witnessed and documented in places of lasting public record (see for example Harcourt, 1993c, 1995b; Baranzini and Harcourt, 1993; Pesaran and Harcourt, 2000). But, ultimately, it has been the policy aspects of what I have tried to do that I care most about. I am not sure that I really want to be an economic dentist – one actual dentist in the family is enough, I would have thought – but I would like to do my damnedest to make sure that those least able to protect themselves from the malfunctioning, natural and also, now, more often man-made, of modern societies are in fact protected. That, for me, as I believe it was for Keynes and his followers, is the proper rationale for our 'miserable subject'.

October 1999

Notes

1. The present volume of recent essays and the volume of my essays on policy from the 1950s on.
2. John Hatch and I go back to the 1960s when he was a research student and I was a young don at Cambridge. Subsequently we were to be colleagues for many years in Adelaide. I first met Colin Rogers in the 1980s. When he decided to leave his native South Africa and settle in Australia, he came to Adelaide to the post that became vacant when, having left for Cambridge in 1982, I resigned in 1985. I had known Ray Petrides from the 1970s, both in Australia and on his frequent visits to Cambridge. Philip Arestis, Gabriel Palma and Malcolm Sawyer came to know me well personally when I returned to Cambridge in 1982. I first met Sheila Dow in 1980 but we had corresponded before that.
3. A précis of the insights so gained is in paras 12 and 13 of Harcourt and Massaro (1964a; 1982: 178–9).
4. 'But this *long run* is a misleading guide to current affairs ... Economists set themselves too easy, too useless a task if in tempestuous seasons they can only tell us that when the storm is long past the ocean is flat again' (Keynes, 1923: 65, emphasis in original).
5. We were also referred to Lorie Tarshis's (1947) marvellous textbook, but I was too dumb to see that it was the better basis for a proper

understanding of the economics of Keynes. I also read Harrod's (1951) *Life* which is often more his than Keynes's.

6. Tom Wilson (20 August 1999) writes that in the 1950s he 'rejected the generally accepted claim that oligopolists didn't try to maximise profits. The empirical evidence did not support the assumption [it was an error to suppose] that profit margins and ... prices were ... arbitrary ... price competition was present in price setting.'

7. Henderson subsequently went to Australia to set up an Australian equivalent of the DAE/NIESR at Melbourne University. I first met him in 1957 when he was a 'small l' liberal aligned with the isolated minority around Dennis Robertson in the Cambridge Faculty (and the much respected Treasurer and Fellow of Corpus). He was on leave from Cambridge at Melbourne and we shared a room. Downing suggested that I try out my questionnaire for the pilot survey on Henderson as he had a most complicated income and wealth situation. He agreed, the questionnaire 'worked' – but he told me that had I or one of the other interviewers knocked on his door because he had been chosen in our sample, he would have refused to answer on grounds of invasion of privacy. I tell this anecdote because Ronald was to become famous for his pioneering enquiry into poverty in Australia which required much more intrusive questions than those of my questionnaire. He also became an early proponent of an incomes policy, including the indexation of money-wages, to complement monetary and fiscal policies in Australia – a very changed (for the better) set of principles.

8. Marris helped Piero Sraffa run the research students' seminar and generally offer pastoral and other advice.

9. This was to be a temporary, not a permanent state; see Harcourt (1988) for my appreciative evaluation of Nicky.

10. Trevor Stegman (2 June 1999) writes that I should add 'in an economy operating below full employment'. There are vital differences between the two situations, in that more saving – not spending – would be required in the full employment situation, but planned additional investment would still need to be financed before it could become actual investment. I hope this goes someway towards answering Tom Wilson's criticism (20 August 1999) of the same passages.

11. Of course, inflation proved disobliging by 'going away' for several years after I submitted my dissertation. In the 1970s I appeared before Russell Mathew's committee on taxation reforms in Australia and replacement cost accounting (Russell and John Grant were the Australian pioneers on these issues). In response to questions from Russell, I said: 'The trouble with you and me being so far ahead of our time is that when our time comes, I at any rate have forgotten what I said.'

12. In my view Lucas should get credit for independently rediscovering the essence of Keynes's critique of Tinbergen's 1930s empirical work on the investment function, renaming it the Lucas critique – otherwise, I think his influence has been disastrous.

13. At this time Vincent Massaro and I were reading Sraffa's 1960 book and discussing his sub-systems with him prior to writing our two papers (1964a, 1964b) on it.

14. Many of these ideas went into my lectures at Cambridge as well as the chapters of *Economic Activity* which was then nearing completion. I also used the latter for the course on macroeconomics I gave to British civil servants at the Civil Service training centre near London Zoo. Roger Opie gave the microeconomics lectures, so there are several cohorts of British civil servants who were first introduced to economics by two dinky-di Australian Keynesian economists. I understand there was a file in the UK Treasury on my investment-incentive writings; I hope it was more benign than the one which was soon to be started by the Australian spooks when, having returned home in early 1967, I became one of the leaders of the anti-Vietnam war movement in South Australia.

15. Tom Wilson (20 August 1999) suggests that we are now in the Second Golden Age in the USA and the UK – low unemployment, low inflation, decent growth with a lousy (my word) distribution of income and wealth. I would prefer to call it, following Joan Robinson, a Bastard Golden Age because I do not think that by the standards of the first Golden Age, unemployment may be regarded as 'low'.

16. Tim Harcourt e-mails (30 June 1999) that something similar to this was actually brought in by Bill Kelty (the General Secretary of the ACTU) during the Accord years, showing that 'the Australian system provided the institutional flexibility to deliver such measures.'

17. I had started the paper by saying I was going to be 'very old-fashioned' in it. I look now as if I had just come out of the Ark.

18. Tony also gave me an earlier opportunity to help keep the Keynesian tradition alive by asking me to chair the sixth and centennial Keynes seminar at the University of Kent in 1983, on Keynes and his contemporaries (see Harcourt, 1985).

References

Arestis, P., G. Palma and M. Sawyer (eds) (1997a) *Capital Controversy, Post-Keynesian Economics and the History of Economics. Essays in Honour of Geoff Harcourt*, vol. 1 (London: Routledge).

Arestis, P., G. Palma and M. Sawyer (eds) (1997b) *Markets, Unemployment and Economic Policy. Essays in Honour of Geoff Harcourt*, vol. 2 (London: Routledge).

Arrow, K. J. (1962) 'The Economic Implications of Learning by Doing', *Review of Economic Studies*, vol. 28, 155–73.

Asimakopulos, A. (1983) 'Kalecki and Keynes on Finance, Saving and Investment', *Cambridge Journal of Economics*, vol. 7, 221–33.

Ball, R. J. (1964) *Inflation and the Theory of Money* (London: Allen & Unwin).

Baranzini, M. and G. C. Harcourt (eds) (1993) *The Dynamics of the Wealth of Nations. Growth, Distribution and Structural Change. Essays in Honour of Luigi Pasinetti* (London: Macmillan).

Barton, A. D. and G. C. Harcourt (1959) 'Investment Allowances for Primary Producers', *Australian Journal of Agricultural Economics*, vol. 3, 12–18.

Bennett, J. W. and G. C. Harcourt (1960) 'Taxation and Business Surplus', *Economic Record*, vol. 36, 425–8.

Cate, T. (ed.) (1997) *An Encyclopedia of Keynesian Economics* (Cheltenham: Edward Elgar).

Chamberlin, E. H. (1933) *The Theory of Monopolistic Competition. A Re-orientation of the Theory of Value* (Cambridge: Harvard University Press).

Chari, V. V. (1998) 'Nobel Laureate Robert E. Lucas, Jr: Architect of Modern Macroeconomics' *Journal of Economic Perspectives*, vol. 12, 171–86.

Clausewitz, C. Von (1943) *Principles of War*, translated and edited by Hans W. Gratzke (London: John Lane (The Bodley Head)).

Dalziel, P. C. and G. C. Harcourt (1997) 'A Note on "Mr. Meade's Relation" and International Capital Movements' *Cambridge Journal of Economics*, vol. 21, 621–31.

Discussion Paper no. 6 (1979) 'Economic Issues and the Future of Australia', in Australian Political Studies Association, Australian Labor Party National Committee of Inquiry, *Discussion Papers*, APSA Monograph no. 28, 1979, Flinders University of South Australia.

Dow, J. C. R. (1956) 'Analysis of the Generation of Price Inflation, a Study of Cost and Price Changes in the United Kingdom, 1946–54, *Oxford Economic Papers* (N.S.), vol. 8, 252–301.

Dow, S. C. (1997) 'Endogenous Money', in Harcourt and Riach (1997), vol. 2, 61–78.

Duesenberry, J. S. (1949) *Income, Saving and the Theory of Consumer Behaviour* (Cambridge, Mass.: Harvard University Press).

Feldstein, M. and C. Horioka (1980) 'Domestic Saving and International Capital Flows', *Economic Journal*, vol. 90, 314–29.

Friedman, M. (1953) 'The Case for Flexible Exchange Rates' in *Essays in Positive Economics* (Chicago: The University of Chicago Press), 157–203.

Harcourt, G. C. (1962) 'Review Article of W. E. G. Salter, *Productivity and Technical Change*', *Economic Record*, vol. 38, 388–94.

— (1963a) 'A Critique of Mr Kaldor's Model of Income Distribution and Economic Growth', *Australian Economic Papers*, vol. 1, 20–36.

— (1963b) 'A Simple Joan Robinson Model of Accumulation with One Technique: A Comment', *Osaka Economic Papers*, January, 24–8.

— (1965a) 'The Accountant in a Golden Age', *Oxford Economic Papers*, vol. 17, 66–80.

— (1965b) 'A Two-Sector Model of the Distribution of Income and the Level of Employment in the Short Run', *Economic Record*, vol. 41, 103–17.

— (1966) 'The Measurement of the Rate of Profit and the Bonus Scheme for Managers in the Soviet Union, *Oxford Economic Papers*, vol. 18, 58–63.

— (1968) 'Investment-Decision Criteria, Investment Incentives and the Choice of Technique', *Economic Journal*, vol. 78, 77–95.

— (1969) 'Some Cambridge Controversies in the Theory of Capital', *Journal of Economic Literature*, vol. 7, 369–405.

— (1972) *Some Cambridge Controversies in the Theory of Capital* (Cambridge: Cambridge University Press).

— (1974) 'The Social Consequences of Inflation', *Australian Accountant*, October, 520–8.

— (1977a) 'Eric Russell, 1921–77: A Great Australian Political Economist', The 1977 Newcastle Lecture in Political Economy Research, Report no 36, pp. iii–26, reprinted in Sardoni (1992), 344–56.

— (1977b) 'On Theories and Policies', chapter 4 of J. P. Nieuwenhuysen and P. J. Drake (eds), *Australian Economic Policy* (Melbourne: Melbourne University Press), 40–52.

— (1977c) 'Review of Hyman P. Minsky (1975) *John Maynard Keynes*, New York: Columbia University Press; London: Macmillan, 1976', *Economica*, vol. 44, 306–7.

— (ed.) (1977d) *The Microeconomic Foundations of Macroeconomics* (London: Macmillan).

— (1978) 'Policy and Responses for Australia', *Economic Papers*, no. 60, December, 61–9.

— (1982) *The Social Science Imperialists, Selected Essays. G. C. Harcourt*, edited by Prue Kerr (London: Routledge & Kegan Paul).

— (ed.) (1985) *Keynes and his Contemporaries. The Sixth and Centennial Keynes Seminar held in the University of Kent at Canterbury 1983* (London: Macmillan).

— (1988) 'Nicholas Kaldor, 12 May 1908–30 September 1986', *Economica*, vol. 55, 159–70.

— (1992) 'Markets, Madness and a Middle Way', *The Second Annual Donald Horne Address*, Melbourne, 1992, published in *Australian Quarterly*, vol. 64, 1–17.

— (1993a) 'The Harcourt Plan to "Save" the World', *At the Margin*, issue 1, Lent, 2–5.

— (1993b) 'Macroeconomic Policy for Australia in the 1990s', *Economic and Labour Relations Review*, vol. 4, 167–75.

— (1993c) *Post-Keynesian Essays in Biography: Portraits of Twentieth Century Political Economists* (London: Macmillan).

— (1994) 'Taming Speculators and Putting the World on Course to Prosperity: A "Modest Proposal"', *Economic and Political Weekly*, vol. xxix, 2490–2.

— (1995a) 'Recollections and Reflections of an Australian Patriot and a Cambridge Economist', *Banco Nazionale del Lavoro Quarterly Review*, vol. xlviii, 225–54.

— (1995b) *Capitalism, Socialism and Post-Keynesianism. Selected Essays of G. C. Harcourt* (Cheltenham: Edward Elgar).

— (1997) 'Pay Policy, Accumulation and Productivity' *Economic and Labour Relations Review*, vol. 8, 78–89.

— (1998) 'Political Economy, Politics and Religion: Intertwined and Indissoluble Passions', *The American Economist*, vol. xxxii, 3–18.

— (1999a) '"Horses for Courses": The Making of a Post-Keynesian Economist', in Arnold Heertje (ed.), *The Makers of Modern Economics*, vol. 4 (Cheltenham: Edward Elgar), 32–69.

— (1999b) '"The End of a Perfect Day". "Horses for Courses" and Policy Proposals', *Economic Issues*, vol. 4, 7–20.

— (2000) *Selected Essays on Policy* (Basingstoke: Palgrave).

— and D. Ironmonger (1956) 'Pilot Survey of Personal Savings', *Economic Record*, vol. 32, 106–18.

— , P. H. Karmel and R. H. Wallace (1967) *Economic Activity* (Cambridge: Cambridge University Press).

— and P. Kenyon (1976) 'Pricing and the Investment Decision', *Kyklos*, vol. 29, 449–77.

— and P. M. Kerr (1979) 'The Mixed Economy', chapter 14 in J. North and P. Weller (eds), *Labor* (Sydney: Ian Novak), 184–95.

— and V. G. Massaro (1964a) 'A Note on Mr Sraffa's Sub-Systems', *Economic Journal*, vol. 74, 715–22.

— and V. G. Massaro (1964b) 'Mr Sraffa's *Production of Commodities*', *Economic Record*, vol. 40, 442–54.

— and P. A. Riach (eds) (1997) *A 'Second Edition' of The General Theory*, 2 vols (London: Routledge).

Harrod, R. F. (1951) *The Life of John Maynard Keynes* (London: Macmillan).

Hatch, J. and R. Petridis (1997) 'A Cambridge Economist *but* an Australian Patriot', in Arestis *et al.* (1997a), vol. 1, 1–10.

— and C. Rogers (1997) 'Distinguished Fellow of the Economic Society of Australia, 1996: Professor Emeritus Geoff Harcourt', *Economic Record*, vol. 73, 97–100.

Henderson, H. D. (1922) *Supply and Demand* (London: Nisbet).

Hicks, J. R. (1937), 'Mr. Keynes and the "Classics": A Suggested Interpretation', *Econometrica*, vol. 5, 147–59.

— (1939) *Value and Capital* (Oxford: Clarendon Press).

— (1942) *The Social Framework: An Introduction to Economics* (Oxford: Clarendon Press).

Kalecki, M. (1943) 'Political Aspects of Full Employment', *Political Quarterly*, reprinted in Kalecki (1971), 138–45.

— (1971) *Selected Essays on the Dynamics of the Capitalist Economy 1993–1970* (Cambridge: Cambridge University Press).

Keynes, J. M. (1923) *A Tract on Monetary Reform* (London: Macmillan), *Collected Writings*, vol. IV, 1971.

— (1930) *A Treatise on Money*, 2 vols (London: Macmillan), *Collected Writings*, vol. V, VI, 1971.

— (1936) *The General Theory of Employment, Interest and Money* (London: Macmillan), *Collected Writings*, vol. VII, 1973.

— (1937) 'Alternative Theories of the Rate of Interest', *Economic Journal*, vol. 47, 241–52, *Collected Writings*, vol. XIV, 1973, 201–15.

Levhari, D. (1965) 'A Nonsubstitution Theorem and Switching of Techniques', *Quarterly Journal of Economics*, vol. 79, 98–105.

Lodewijks, J. (1999) 'Hicks and the Crisis in Keynesian Economics', *Indian Journal of Applied Economics*, vol. 8, 141–6.

Mankiw, N. G. (1998) *Principles of Macroeconomics* (Sydney: Dryden).

Marris, R. L. (1991) *Reconstructing Keynesian Economics with Imperfect Competition* (Aldershot: Edward Elgar).

— (1997) 'Yes, Mrs. Robinson! *The General Theory* and Imperfect Competition', in Harcourt and Riach (1997), vol. 1, 52–82.

Marshall, A. (1890) *Principles of Economics* (London: Macmillan), ninth (variorum) edition 1961.

Meade, J. E. and E. A. Russell (1957) 'Wage Rates, the Cost of Living and the Balance of Payments', *Economic Record*, vol. 33, 23–8.

Okun, A. (1978) 'The Great Stagflation Swamp', *Challenge*, vol. 20, 6–13.

Parkin, M. (1996) *Economics* (Sydney: Addison-Wesley).

Pesaran, M. H. and G. C. Harcourt (2000) 'Life and Work of John Richard Nicholas Stone 1913–1991', *Economic Journal*, vol. 110, F146–65.

Robinson, J. (1993) *The Economics of Imperfect Competition* (London: Macmillan), 2nd edition 1969.

— (1937) *Introduction to the Theory of Employment* (London: Macmillan), 2nd edition 1969.

— (1956) *The Accumulation of Capital* (London: Macmillan).

— (1965) *Collected Economic Papers*, vol. 3 (Oxford: Blackwell).

Rothschild, K. W. (1947) 'Price Theory and Oligopoly', *Economic Journal*, vol. 57, 299–320.

Salter, W. E. G. (1960) *Productivity and Technical Change* (Cambridge: Cambridge University Press), 2nd edition 1966.

Sardoni, C. (ed.) (1992) *On Political Economists and Modern Political Economy. Selected Essays of G. C. Harcourt* (London: Routledge).

Samuelson, P. A. (1948) *Foundations of Economic Analysis* (Cambridge, Mass.: Harvard University Press).

Solow, R. M. (1998) *Monopolistic Competition and Macroeconomic Theory* (The Frederico Caffé Lectures) (Cambridge: Cambridge University Press).

Sraffa, P. (1960) *Production of Commodities by Means of Commodities. Prelude to a Critique of Economic Theory* (Cambridge: Cambridge University Press).

Tarshis, L. (1947) *The Elements of Economics. An Introduction to the Theory of Price and Employment* (Boston: Houghton Mifflin), 2nd edition 1966.

Taylor, J. B. (1995) *Economics* (Sydney: Houghton Mifflin).

Thirlwall, A. P. (writing as J. M. Keynes) (1999) 'A "Second Edition" of Keynes' *General Theory*', *Journal of Post Keynesian Economics*, vol. 21, 367–86.

Triffin, R. (1942) *Monopolistic Competition and General Equilibrium Theory* (Cambridge, Mass.: Harvard University Press).

Part I
Keynes Now

2
Is Keynes Dead?*

I want to argue today that Keynes is not dead. The impetus for giving this talk arises from a number of events. The first one was the death of Keynes' favourite pupil Richard Kahn in 1989. (A special issue of the *Cambridge Journal of Economics* is being prepared as a memorial to Richard and for that I have written a paper called 'Kahn and Keynes and the Making of *The General Theory*' (*Cambridge Journal of Economics*, vol. 17, 1994, 11–23.))

Secondly, a very fine book by a Brazilian economist came out in the late 1980s: Edward Amadeo's *Keynes's Principle of Effective Demand* (1989, Aldershot, Edward Elgar). I think it is the best analytical account of the transition in Keynes's thought from the *Treatise on Money* to *The General Theory*. I think the best historical account is Peter Clarke's marvellous book on *The Keynesian Revolution in the Making, 1924–1936* (1988, Oxford, Oxford University Press). There, he uses the skills of the historian, goes to the archives and shows what an extraordinary quick thinker Keynes was because he would appear before the Macmillan Committee during the day and then rush back and revise the proofs of the *Treatise on Money* to take into account the latest arguments raised before the Committee or ideas he had during the day. Keynes did his first draft always in galleys. He had an agreement with Macmillan that he could do everything in galleys, and then he would rewrite the second draft as corrections

* Originally published in *History of Economics Review*, no. 18, Summer 1992, 1–9, as an edited transcript of a lecture delivered at the University of New South Wales, 21 February 1992.

33

to the galleys and send the galleys back again. I don't think anyone would do that now because you don't have galleys with modern printing.

The third event was the publication for the first time in English of Kahn's *The Economics of the Short Period* (1989, London: Macmillan) which he wrote in eighteen months in 1928–29 as his Fellowship dissertation for King's College, Cambridge, after he had spent *one year* learning economics. We can see that virtually all the major innovations we need for imperfect competition theory were worked out here. The work was then hidden away till the early 1980s when it was published in Italian and then, in the late 1980s, in English just after he died, although he had corrected the proofs.

Kahn had an extraordinary fertile and innovative mind. This is relevant for thinking about Keynes then and Keynes now because the object of Kahn's work was, first of all, to put the short period at centre stage rather than just a station on the way to the long-period cross which is how Marshall saw the short period. Marshall regarded, as Kahn argued, Book V on the long-period theory of normal prices and quantities as the core of the *Principles*. Kahn's first major change of emphasis was to make the short period a subject of study in its own right. This was tremendously important, not because Keynes had not been coming independently to a similar opinion, but because he could now work with someone who had that point of view.

It is very interesting if you look through, say, Gerald Shove's Principles Lectures in 1928–29 – of which we have copies in Cambridge – to find that you are three-quarters of the way through before he even mentions the short period. If you look at Dennis Robertson's Principles Lectures, the long period dominates, in terms of a Say's Law position, even though Robertson's major innovative contributions, as opposed to expositions, were on the theory of the trade cycle and of monetary-real sector interaction.

Secondly, Kahn departed from perfect or even pure competition. The difference between perfection and purity is that to be perfect you have to know the future as well as have no power, to be pure, you just have no power. So Kahn developed a very realistic theory of imperfectly competitive markets and firms, including the kinked demand curve and the reverse L-shaped cost curve and all the paraphernalia of modern monopolistic competition or imperfectly competitive theory.

Now, the mystery is why did Keynes take over the first change of emphasis and concentrate on the short period when he came to write *The General Theory*, but resolutely refuse to use microeconomic foundations which were imperfectly competitive when Kahn had them all there?

Then there is the multiplier article, which takes the apparatus of the *Treatise on Money* and works out in quantitative terms what Keynes and Hubert Henderson did not do in their pamphlet *Can Lloyd George Do It?* They could not answer even the crude Treasury view because they could not address two issues: (a) what would be the total rise in employment and (b) they had not developed the idea that investment created the saving, if you started from a situation of some unemployment.

Kahn answered both those questions in a very rigourous and careful way. Nevertheless, he had Marshallian competitive supply and demand structures as the microfoundations. And they went into *The General Theory*. It was not until 1939, when Keynes responded to Tarshis's and Dunlop's findings (also Kalecki's) about real wages and money wages, that he had a rather reluctant flirtation with what we now call normal cost pricing theory. When he wrote to Ohlin, who had noted that it almost seemed that Keynes had never talked to Mrs Robinson, or read her theory of imperfect competition, Keynes said that he was very puzzled about his comments on this because he had showed his proofs to Mrs Robinson and she had never suggested imperfect competition, and he did not see how it was relevant. He continued that as to the criticism of diminishing marginal productivity in the short period, he thought that that was 'one of the very few incontrovertable propositions of our miserable subject'.

The other thing I want to say about Keynes himself is although Keynes read mathematics as an undergraduate, he really spent as much if not more time on philosophy and he was a philosopher, a innovative and outstanding philosopher, before he became an economist. (The definitive work on Keynes's philosophy and economics was written by Rod O'Donnell who is here today.)

This is so important for understanding (a) Keynes himself, and (b) some facets of modern economics, because he brought at least three things from his philosophy, which are very important for understanding economics. People like Rod, Anna Carabelli, John Coates and Athol Fitzgibbons have brought this to our attention.

First of all, the whole is not necessarily the sum of the parts, and that paved the way for Keynes to do macroeconomics in a way which was very innovative. And secondly, his use of philosophy, particularly in the *Treatise on Probability*, to explain how sensible people behave in uncertain circumstances, doing the best they can. That dovetails very well with Marshall's account of business-people's behaviour. Marshall had a very realistic account of this and the things they have to cope with, the uncertainty of the future, whenever they are making their production and investment decisions. Keynes could take his philosophical views on that and adapt them to his understanding of what would happen in systems where uncertainty was an inescapable fact of life. Then you try to explain the behaviour, both of the people in the system and of the system itself.

Those were two very important things which I think he took from his philosophical training and because we didn't know, or we had not thought how important that was, it was not until people like O'Donnell mentioned it to us that we could reread *The General Theory* and the contributions there in a new light. The third thing that came over, which I think is the most important lesson we can take both about understanding Keynes but also about doing economics, is that Keynes thought that in a discipline like economics there was a whole spectrum or continuum of languages which range all the way from intuition and poetry to lawyer-type arguments to formal logic and mathematics. All had a part to play according to the issues that you were looking at and the aspects of the issues that you were dealing with; so that as you go through *The General Theory*, the language continually changes.

The most striking example is where Keynes struggles with being formal about investment theory in chapter 11 and makes one heck of a mess of it. I think he was eleventh wrangler, that means he got the eleventh best first-class honours in maths, but I think he probably had forgotten all his maths by the time he was in his late forties, so there are a lot of errors running through the maths of *The General Theory*. His incoherent conception of specified rigorous models in chapter 11 cannot be straightened out. As Tom Asimakopulos, Joan Robinson and Kalecki have shown, the ingredients are there, but you need a new recipe to make it sensible.

But then having written the chapter on the MEC, he went off into probably the best chapter of *The General Theory*, chapter 12, which is about the state of long-term expectations, where he uses beautiful English language to try and capture how people behave under uncertainty, how stock exchanges work, how valuations of stock exchanges feed through into real investment expenditures, the conditions under which speculation is beneficial, the conditions under which it's harmful and so on … all beautifully written. And it is interesting that when Shove wrote to him about *The General Theory* to say how much he enjoyed it and what a revolutionary book it was and so on, he wrote that in his own work on the firm and industry, he had not been able to analyse the effects of expectations precisely. Keynes wrote back to say that when dealing with the influence of expectations, one is, in the nature of things, outside the realism of the formally exact (*C. W.*, XIV, 1973, 1–2). If we look at the change in language that occurs between chapter 11 and chapter 12, Shove would presumably be better able to understand what was going on. So that's the third of many things that you can take from Keynes' philosophy as far as his economics is concerned.

I suppose to economists these days *The General Theory* is a relatively easy book, which can be put down into one or two diagrams, so we wonder why he spent three or four hundred pages writing it. We have to think back to what he was facing when he was doing it, not only because it is interesting historically but because as Keynesianism is now rising again like a phoenix from the ashes, it is confronting exactly the same system conceptually, I mean much more squiggly sophisticated than Keynes was facing, but it is exactly the same system of thought as Keynes himself was liberating himself from. So it's interesting to see what were the steps of his liberation.

The first thing that he was brought up on by Marshall was that if you are going to write the *Principles of Economics* in three books (which is what Marshall set himself to do, though he never did get round satisfactorily to doing it) then in the first book, you talked analytically about real things, real quantities, relative prices; money and money prices had no analytical role to play. Marshall used partial equilibrium analysis, so he just showed how there was a tendency for individual markets to clear. But then the question arose of whether it would be analytically interesting to ask what determined total employment and total output. The answer was no, because although he had only used partial equilibrium to show this tendency for markets to clear with supply and demand being equal, there was an appendix where you had a general equilibrium model and the same argument went through. So while it was an important practical problem, because Marshall knew about the trade cycle and all that, as an analytical or long-period problem it was not an interesting one; so it was all done in real terms and Say's Law was really a deduction from Volume I.

Secondly, when you came into the saving-investment market, there was the concept of a real rate or a natural rate of interest which was the clearing price. Where on the saving side this reflected time preferences while on the investment side it reflected some sort of Fisherian rate of return over cost curve transforming present consumption into future consumption. That explained how the composition of Say's Law output was divided up between consumption and investment.

When you arrived in Volume II, you carried over for the version of the quantity theory of money that you used, the Say's Law long-period equilibrium output level to fit into the equation so that output and employment were in fact given, you had V and M and therefore you had a theory for the general price level. That is where money and absolute prices came in and then you discussed why the economy could fluctuate round that position and how one might design monetary institutions which allowed the economy to recover from shocks and get back to that position as quickly as possible. If the fundamental determinants of that position changed, the tastes or the endowments or the techniques of production, the role of Volume II was to tell you how to go with as little pain as possible from the old to the new equilibrium position.

That was the sort of constraint on Keynes when he wrote the *Treatise on Money*, even though he was getting more and more interested in the cycle and lapses from full employment. He notes that he felt constrained from following out too far the intricate theory of short-period production because that was not the acceptable way to proceed when you are writing a treatise on money. You are not supposed to be talking about those things, by and large. He still thought that what he was doing in *A Treatise on Money* was providing a more usable version of the quantity theory of money and that his fundamental equations, which explain the price levels for available and unavailable goods, were just other ways of writing down the quantity theory of money. Indeed, as Amadeo shows, they were in fact that, particularly in the long-period position so that you could either express the general price level in the fundamental equations or you could express it in quantity theory terms, you got the same answer.

In the *Treatise on Money* it is still true that real things rule and monetary things all had to adjust to them. For example, if you had malfunctioning in the economy, that meant that the banking system had set a money rate of interest which was inconsistent with the underlying natural rate or real rate and you would get malfunctioning until the banking system came to its senses.

He did try to talk about short-period production and employment problems in the famous banana plantation parable. In this parable, there is no endogenous process which stops a cumulative process once it has started. Keynes has a thrift gospeller to come in to help the people in this economy, where investment is making plantations and consumption is making bananas, and the gospeller tells them to save more. Then on the *Treatise on Money* equations, there is a cumulative downturn in prices, employment and production until they either all starve to death or they decide to change their saving function.

What Kahn did in the multiplier article was really to provide the endogenous process which would bring the process to an end. If you start off with investment rising then output and employment rise till saving is equal to investment again, even on the *Treatise on Money* definitions. That was a tremendously liberating move to allow Keynes to go from *A Treatise on Money* to *The General Theory*.

Especially is this so because Kahn's work was accompanied by what is called Mr Meade's relation. James Meade was sent to Cambridge for a year to learn economics before he could teach it in Oxford, and while he was there he was working in the Cambridge 'Circus' discussing the *Treatise on Money*. Mr Meade's relation was doing the multiplier by the saving leakage rather than leakage through the *mpc* and of course that was very important because it showed where the saving, which matched the investment, came from.

I am very careful to say 'matched'. Keynes, I think, was always very careful to say that investment led and saving responded and therefore, as he showed in 1937, because he had forgotten it in *The General Theory*, investment in turn is constrained by finance. You have to have the finance that allows the investment to occur, then the saving is created. But you still read in the textbooks about there being a need for the saving to finance the deficit and the investment: as though the saving had to come first in an unemployed situation, and then the investment followed.

But what Keynes argued when he brought in the finance motive in his article in 1937 was that the investment market can become congested through a lack of finance or cash; it can never become congested through a lack of saving. And he was explicitly assuming unemployment when he said that. Everybody would accept, I think, that at full employment saving has to come first to release the resources. As long as you have unemployment there is such a thing as a free lunch. You can have saving, investment and consumption, all at the same time, without one being the alternative to the other. But you still need finance as well, even at full employment.

Anyway, the point about Mr Meade's relation was that he made explicit where the saving came from and that was the explicit answer to the Treasury View, that there is only a certain amount of saving around so if you use so much in the public sector, there is that much less left to the private sector to invest. Of course, Keynes rather blew it as a debator in doing this because he revealed prematurely his answer to the Treasury View and they said 'that's not our view at all. What we're really saying is that the public sector is so inefficient you should not let them do investment anyway because private people would do it so much more efficiently'. That has a certain modern ring to it, in light of what Donald Horne calls 'the economic fundamentalists' and others call the 'economic rationalists'.

Keynes then realised that Say's Law did not hold and therefore the quantity theory of money was not an explanation of the general level of prices. This had occurred in the *Treatise on Money*, although he could not see at that time that it was inconsistent with his system. But by the time Kahn wrote the multiplier article, he began to see it clearly. So he started to build up his system again, with money there right from the start rather than having it as a veil, as it were, in Volume II. He argued that Marshall's dichotomy, between the real and then the money, was quite wrong. You have to have a theory of a monetary production economy where money had a role to play as a medium of exchange, unit of account and store of value right from the start of the story.

What other changes occurred, because Keynes liked to make things always very stark so that you could see in very simple outlines what the fundamental changes were before he put the modifications in? In the *Treatise on Money* it was the natural rate of interest which equilibrated real saving and investment, and then the monetary rate of interest had to be consistent with it. By the time Keynes got to *The General Theory*, he turned this round 180 degrees and he argued the money rate of interest, determined by the demand for money including liquidity preference and the supply of money, ruled the roost because of the peculiar nature of liquidity preference. His version of the natural or real rate of interest, which had become the expected rate of profit or the marginal efficiency of investment, had to measure up to the money rate of interest. That is the subject principally of Chapter 17 of *The General Theory*.

It is fashionable to be particular types of Keynesians, chapter 3, ch. 12, ch.11, and the most sophisticated and really trendy thing to be in recent years is a chapter 17 Keynesian. If you can understand own rates of interest, and that the money rate of interest rules the roost, and the peculiar nature of the liquidity variable, then you are a chapter 17 Keynesian. Barry Hughes pointed out to me that there are a number of hard-nosed financial American journalists who suddenly became chapter 17 Keynesians because they have recently discovered the liquidity trap level of the money rate of interest on American financial markets and they've given Keynes great credit for this theoretical idea. They have suddenly rediscovered liquidity preference, including a real life liquidity trap, which Keynes just conjectured as a theoretical possibility.

The other major change was to build up the theory of the consumption function with the leakages and saving, and the theory of investment. Finally, there was chapter 21 on the general theory of prices where he said we will bring back to the fore those homely but intelligible concepts of short-period elasticities of supply and marginal costs. Again, he was quite Marshallian, but he just adjusted it or adapted it to get an aggregate short-period Marshallian supply curve which was the basis of the aggregate supply function.

Incidentally, much of this was clearly presented in Lorie Tarshis's PhD dissertation. Tarshis used Gardner Means's theory of administered prices and built up a macro theory of distribution which is very like Kalecki's and then put in Kahn's, Joan Robinson's and Means's microfoundations in *The General Theory*. But that's never seen the light of day because when Tarshis submitted it to a publisher, a jealous and envious contemporary was the reviewer and, seeing his chance, rejected the manuscript for publication. Lorie went off to liberate Italy from the Germans in the American army and to meet his second wife in the process. So his PhD thesis was never published which was a great tragedy, but he did put Keynes's model in the 250 pages of his textbook published after the war. This was written in terms of aggregate demand and aggregate supply, which was always his framework of thought, and which he derived from Keynes's lectures, having been brought up on the *Treatise on Money* before he did *The General Theory*.

Tarshis fell victim to the US Right Wing. His book was being prescribed by virtually every economics department in America when suddenly the Right got to hear about it, and fearing for the subversion of American youth, got Rose Wilder Lane to write a pamphlet condemning it and sent the pamphlet to every university in America. As a result a lot of the universities decided not to adopt the book. Lorie's book had only modest sales and the next year Samuelson's book, which was to teach generations of American economists, came out. Now I am not saying that Paul escaped the Right because he didn't. He got the remnants of its backlash; but he survived and his book took off. I think that it was a tragedy that it was Samuelson's book with the Keynesian cross which took over. Many people who have read Tarshis's text still say that his was the best account of Keynesian economics at a textbook level.

It is unfortunate in many respects that we have all been brought up on Samuelson instead of Tarshis. Let me explain why it is a tragedy (this relates very much to why Keynes is still very much alive). The monetarists and the rational expectations people thought that they had a cast-iron empirical case in the 70s and 80s with which to reject Keynesianism. They believed that the stagflation episode conclusively disapproved the claims of Keynesianism.

Partly that was because the Americans Keynesians in the 1960s were grossly overconfident. It was Samuelson and Solow who said society could dine *à la carte* on any combination of inflation and unemployment they wished to choose. That was a very naive application of the Phillips Curve, and it meant that the Phillips Curve became identified as an important part of Keynesianism. Now you cannot find the Phillips Curve in *The General Theory*. It is completely foreign to Keynes's philosophy and understanding of the world to expect to find a sustainable empirical relationship of the nature of the Phillips Curve. Bill Phillips never claimed that it was other than an interesting empirical relationship, it was what people made of it and grafted it onto their view of Keynesianism that did the damage.

If we had used Lorie Tarshis's version of *The General Theory* we would have had no trouble at all in having the start – not the end but the start – of an understanding of the stagflation episode. If you had built an imported cost inflation or an autonomous money-wage rise into Lorie's version of *The General Theory*, the aggregate supply function would have moved in such a way that it would have given you a lower level of employment and a higher general price level, which could have precipitated a stagflationary process. That is how Lorie saw it but given that we were not brought up on that, and instead on *IS–LM* or the Keynesian cross, we just did not think in that way and so no one, with the exception of Lorie and the people who were influenced by Lorie, ever challenged the monetarists and rational expectationists on this.

Such a framework, however, would have led you to reply that stagflation is perfectly predictable from the analysis that comes out of *The General Theory*. I think that's a very important message to remember, especially since Lorie developed the aggregate supply function in an imperfectly competitive setting and not a purely competitive setting. He had made the step forward to put in the sort of micro foundations which Kalecki and later Sidney Weintraub also used.

The reason why I think that Keynes is alive and is also relevant, is that his framework of thought, which arose out of his struggle against the ideas that preceeded him, created an approach which, suitably adapted, is still relevent for understanding the world today and for mounting a critique of the present day alternative framework of thought which in its essence is the very framework from which Keynes liberated himself.

Of course, there are a number of adaptations that have to be made. I mentioned the change in the microfoundation. Secondly, it is very interesting that Keynes who spent most of his life writing and thinking about open economies, on the whole wrote *The General Theory* in terms of a closed economy. In the modern world, that is just impossible because we are so interrelated and so have to bring back the open economy aspects of Keynes's macroeconomics.

Thirdly, Keynes for the most of his life was an endogenous money person, rather than an exogenous one. In *The General Theory*, for quite wrong tactical reasons, he had money as exogenous. The quantity theory of money as an explanation of prices properly understood is a long-period proposition, not a short-period proposition. Most of *The General Theory* model, however, is short-period and yet he is saying if you start from unemployment and you change the quantity of money, you may get patches of time where there is very little change in prices at all, because the marginal cost curves are rather flat. Most of the impact is on output and employment. So the quantity theory stands refuted, but that is a cheap debating point because you have changed the rules by which you are playing.

Now Kahn was always sceptical about the quantity theory of money. He could not understand why Dennis Robertson and Keynes thought of it as a causal relationship. Kahn kept pounding on at Keynes not to use quantity theory in a causal way. I think this had one bad result; Keynes then became an exogenous money person and that let Friedman in the door, which was a very serious error, not only for economic theory but much more so for the people who have been made unemployed as a result of contractionary monetarist policies.

Another change that has to be brought into Keynes's theory before we can say that Keynes has been suitably resurrected is that there is an implicit assumption in *The General Theory* that the long-term movement in prices is neither up or down, that there are cyclical ups and downs but there is no secular upward trend. That runs through the model and as Vicky Chick has pointed out you have to redo the model in the light of an expectation of rising prices before the model is suitable for understanding modern problems.

If Keynes is resurrected in the hands of Stiglitz, Blinder and Akerlof, and Solow and Hahn redo *The General Theory* in modern terms, then post-Keynesian growth theory is going to make a come-back. Not only in the form of Kaldor's contribution but also Joan Robinson's contributions, suitably adapted to take in the cyclical growth theories of Kalecki and Richard Goodwin. Richard Goodwin is already becoming flavour of the month with many of the discerning young Turks in Italy and America.

Kaldor has come back even though he has not been acknowledged on the whole in the new growth theory – Lucas, Romer, Helpman and Grossman. Sometimes they remember to say that these ideas actually came from Kaldor, Myrdal and Allyn Young, but since the way they now train youngsters in America is that economics began ten years ago, these writers are unknown to them. What is worthwhile in the new growth theory is the taking up of the ideas of Kaldor, Myrdal and Young. I am sorry it is done in the way in which it's done. On the other hand, there is a very bright young fellow from Harvard, a Korean now at Notre Dame, and he has been doing the new growth theory but in a sort of post-Keynesian – post-Marxian cum Marglin framework. He has an article coming out on endogenous technical progress which I think will be the classic counter-blast, it certainly will be the seminal answer to the new growth theorists.

If what Stiglitz and company have been doing does take on and attracts the bright young minds into Keynesian economics again then they will start reading about Keynes: and this, despite Mankiw saying that the best way to become a Keynesian is never to read *The General Theory*, which is a prejudice of his mentor, Bob Solow. Bob says that he is very glad that he learnt Keynes through Oscar Lange and Hicks' *IS* and *LM* rather than from *The General Theory* itself. I think that this is an aberration by Solow, and I hope that when people come back they will actually read *The General Theory* and the literature that is growing up around it on its philosophical basis. But I also think that growth theory, in the form of cyclical growth, will come back into its own.

So for those reasons I would like to put to you the proposition that Keynes will come back, because Keynes is not dead, Keynes is very much alive and kicking.

3
A 'Second Edition' of Keynes's *General Theory**

The year 1996 marked sixty years on from the publication of *The General Theory of Employment, Interest and Money* by J. M. Keynes. There are definite signs that the profession is becoming interested again in the approaches, theories and policies which flow from his *magnum opus*, following the abortive attempts of the last twenty years or so to destroy Keynes and all his ways by conservative elements in the profession and body politic. In the advanced capitalist countries, mass unemployment has again emerged as a sustained and disgraceful problem, not least because so much of it was deliberately created by government actions in the first place. The need for a combination of policies and the creation of appropriate institutions with which to tackle this blight is at least being recognised, even if the political will to act is still largely conspicuous by its absence. All this is the background to the present essay.

Some years ago Professor Peter Riach of De Montfort University suggested to me that, following the example of unfinished musical compositions sometimes being completed by others after the deaths of the composers concerned, we ought to consider making a 'second edition' of *The General Theory*. We were also inspired by Keynes's letter to Ralph Hawtrey in August 1936 (*Collected Writings*, Vol. XIV (1973): 47) in which he mentioned that he was thinking of writing some 'footnotes' to *The General Theory* once he had absorbed his own new ideas and the critics' reactions to them. His heart attack in

---

* Originally published in *The Cambridge Review*, May 1997, 21–5.

1937, the Second World War and his untimely death soon after the end of the war, on Easter morning 1946, meant that he never did get to write those 'footnotes'.

Peter and I therefore decided to approach a group of Keynes scholars, ranging from the Golden Oldies to the up-and-coming, to ask them to write chapters setting out what they thought Keynes might have written in, say, 1939 on particular aspects of *The General Theory*, and then why have they done what they have on those aspects in the postwar period. *A 'Second Edition' of The General Theory* (2 vols, hereafter GT^2) was published by Routledge in January 1997. The chapters in the first volume of GT^2 broadly track the chapters of *The General Theory* itself; those in the second volume contain overviews, extensions and new developments under the rubric of the economics of Keynes and comparisons of Keynes's contributions with those who have followed similar paths.

Sixty years on there inevitably need to be major changes to the foundations of the system set out in the original *General Theory*. The first is the necessity to have more explicitly imperfectly competitive microeconomic foundations. This is still a controversial issue. Both Paul Davidson and Jan Kregel are sceptical, to say the least, of the necessity for them in a theory of effective demand, not least because Keynes himself took as 'given' the degree of competition (*The General Theory*, p. 245). Robin Marris (1991; 1997) is an outstanding pioneer here. He argues that only when we allow imperfectly competitive market structures to rule (he takes as an example what he calls 'imperfect polipoly') is it possible to set up simple yet believable models which produce Keynes-type results: in particular, sustained involuntary unemployment of labour due to a lack of overall – effective – demand in the product market. In GT^2 his chapter is followed by a thoughtful one by Nina Shapiro (1997) who argues against this viewpoint. Her principal point is that the failure of the economic system *when left to itself* to be able to signal appropriately to decision-makers operating in necessarily uncertain environments means that investment expenditure (even on average) by businesspeople may not be sufficient to absorb the saving that would be made voluntarily from full employment incomes. This implies that market structures are in principle irrelevant for this central proposition. She argues, I think correctly, that matters would be worse – there would be higher average levels of unemployment and greater fluctuations in prices, output and employment – in a competitive economy than in an imperfectly competitive one.

Secondly, endogenous money processes rather than a given money supply (the quantity of money is more determined by demand from its users than by the monetary authorities as its supplier) are seen to be more appropriate in the present environment. Sheila Dow (1997) is a notable innovator on this issue. She reminds us that while Keynes was essentially an endogenous money person for all of his life, in *The General Theory* he had, for expositional and possibly for tactical purposes, taken the quantity of money as *given*, not exogenous in any absolute sense. Keynes usually concentrated his arguments on one set of issues at a time; he therefore took, as provisionally given, values of variables which ultimately would have to be explained when all the arguments concerning all the issues were brought together. Dow shows that Keynes's theory of liquidity preference may be used in an endogenous money world because demand as well as supply factors play key roles in determining the patterns of rates of interest.

Thirdly, the assumption of a constant *long-term* price level has to be replaced by the assumption of 'rising prices for ever' as a reasonable (if not a rational) expectation. Arthur Brown (1997) and Brian Reddaway (1997) have written eminently sensible evaluations of the consequences of this assumption. Interestingly enough Brown, like Keynes, is more wedded to the goal of attaining a constant general price level than is Reddaway. Reddaway feels that there is enough flexibility and innovation in society's institutions and practices to allow adjustments for rising prices to be made, rather than to have a single overriding goal of a constant price level which almost certainly would unnecessarily damage both employment and growth. Keynes and Brown gave more weight to the role of money as a unit of account and, I suggest, to having the operations of the economy consistent with the conventions of historical-cost, double-entry book keeping, an innovation which was essential for the rise of capitalism in the first place.

Finally, the open economy aspects of the functioning of economies needed to be emphasised more explicitly and systematically than in the first edition and the design of international institutions and policies had to be rethought accordingly. Paul Davidson (1997) has made a notable start on this. Having observed that with both fixed and floating exchange rates there are inbuilt contractionary and deflationary biases in the operation of the world economy, Keynes set about designing institutions to offset them. The key objective was to gain time for economies which tended to run into deficits on their current accounts (in a fixed exchange rate regime) and continuing devaluations (in a floating exchange rate regime) to make the structural and cost adjustments needed to correct these faults: otherwise they were forced to impose measures which led to contracting output and employment, declining investment expenditure, and so a cumulative downward spiral in their external competitive position. Those countries which were blessed in the other direction, so that surpluses accumulated or exchange rates appreciated, were not subject to powerful forces which made them take corrective actions and so behave in a socially beneficial way. Hence, the contractionary biases in the working of the system as a whole were reinforced. At Bretton Woods Keynes tried to overcome this, but his suggestions were not accepted; the seeds of the ultimate destruction of the system were planted at its inception.

Davidson has the same aims as Keynes, but advocates different measures in order to fit in with the changed climate of the 1990s. Sensing that the political time is not yet ripe for the world economy to have either an international mechanism whereby to finance international trade and capital movements or a World Central Bank, Davidson designs a half-way house instead. The main features are institutional pressures which would serve to make creditor nations behave in a socially responsible manner at a world level, a 'currency' between central banks to provide liquidity and the creation of an environment wherein all countries can aim for full employment without running into external constraints. The overall aim is to reduce the contractionary bias in the world's operations without running into inflationary pressures which spread world-wide. This will allow the economies of the world to advance steadily, with each allowing the others 'free lunches'. It is a scheme fittingly in the spirit of Keynes and only the dark forces of ignorance and self-interested greed stand in the way of discussion of its principles and details – and its implementation.

In recent years the link between Keynes's philosophical contributions and his economics has been the subject of some outstanding research work. It relates to both the nature and the method of theorising in a subject such as economics. A number of contributors to GT^2 have written about this issue. In the second volume we have a chapter by Rod O'Donnell who wrote the seminal work (1982; 1989) on this aspect of Keynes's contributions. In his chapter, O'Donnell (1997) puts to rest for ever (I hope) the canard that Keynes was a techniques luddite as far as the use of mathematics in economic theory and of econometric techniques in applied work were concerned. Another chapter is by John Coates (1997), who draws on his profound researches into the relationship between Keynes and the Cambridge philosophers, especially Wittgenstein, and what he has dubbed 'ordinary language economics'. He discerns in Keynes's philosophy at the time of the writing of *The General Theory* an anticipation of the modern work on fuzzy logic and fuzzy sets. Coates conjectures that these recent developments may allow a bridge to be erected between the complex, multi-dimensional yet often vague concepts of economics and the powerful analytical procedures of mathematics. Fuzzy sets evidently allow us to handle in a precise analytical manner vague concepts such as 'baldness' – a contribution appreciated by the editors of GT^2, to whom the notion of membership or non-membership of a category which is gradual rather than abrupt gives comfort.

Keynes sensed the conflict between precision and relevance due to the omission of crucial factors which was often associated with the former. Keynes also sensed what the recent developments allow. Furthermore, he understood the rich and widely ranging fund of common knowledge on which economists, by using ordinary language as much as possible, could draw.

One consequence of the findings on method has been a rethinking of the nature and implications of uncertainty in the Keynesian system. This had led to a reappraisal of the possibility of ever fitting Keynes's ideas satisfactorily (or even at all) into the dominant neo-Walrasian framework of modern economics, because it cannot handle either historical (calendar) time or money itself. Peter Howitt (1997) has contributed a courageous account of this and of his own change of mind, writing of Keynes's intuitive and innovative mind and of his refusal ever to be constrained by past intellectual capital, and certainly not by his own.

Finally, Keynes's intuitions still have to be related back to his predecessors – especially Marx, but also to other 'heretics' under the rubric of underconsumption. John King (1997) has summarised this admirably. In 1987 Claudio Sardoni published a fine book on Marx's and Keynes's theories of effective demand and crisis. It was based on thorough research into what the two authors actually wrote. Reading his account, it could quickly be realised that after allowing for differences in terminology and attitudes to the survival of the capitalist system and its accompanying institutions as such, whenever these two great analysts of capitalism tackled the same questions, they came up with broadly the same answers. Yet it is known that Keynes had a very low opinion of Marx. We think that this tells us more about Keynes than Marx and Sardoni's chapter in the second volume of GT^2 (1997) confirms our view.

Sardoni does not think that Keynes would have changed his opinion of Marx despite Joan Robinson's attempts to make him see that coming at Keynes's puzzles through Marx's approach was a more rewarding way to tackle them. Sardoni shows how, initially, as Keynes moved towards *The General Theory*, he found Marx's emphasis on the circuits of capital and the fact that entrepreneurs want to make money profits rather than produce commodities as such were clues both to understanding how capitalism works (well and poorly) and to the critique of 'classical' economics, especially of Say's Law. These arguments were contained in the sections on the cooperative, neutral and entrepreneur economies which did not make it to the published version of *The General Theory*.

Keynes's contributions also must be related to his contemporaries, most of all to Michal Kalecki; Peter Kriesler (1997) has done this. Kriesler is the author of the definitive book on Kalecki's microeconomics: Kriesler (1987). He has prepared himself admirably for the task of comparing and contrasting the *'General Theories'* of Kalecki and Keynes and of comparing them in turn with the system of their classical/neoclassical rivals. Kriesler is more partial to Kalecki's solution of the realisation problem than to that of Keynes. The only aspect of their respective analyses in which he argues that Keynes is superior concerns the role of expectations, financial matters and especially the determination of the rate of interest. Of course Kriesler admires Keynes, but he thinks that Kalecki's approach, which derives from Marx and the classical economists (in the non-Keynes sense), so that Kalecki's version of *The General Theory* emphasises accumulation and cyclical growth, and the role that distribution between classes plays in these processes, is a more natural way to analyse modern capitalism.

We ended GT^2 with a consideration of the relationship of Keynes's contributions to those of his successors. We took Axel Leijonhufvud as a foremost example. Bruce Littleboy (1997) looks back on the Keynes–Leijonhufvud saga nearly thirty years on from Leijonhufvud's great book, *Keynesian Economics and the Economics of Keynes* (1968). Since that date a huge literature has emerged, and Leijonhufvud himself has backed off from some of his major suggestions, especially on the reversal of quantity versus price movements in Marshall (and Keynes) and Walras. Littleboy is one of the most insightful surveyors of these developments. His PhD thesis on the topic was the basis of a well-regarded book published in 1990. In his chapter in the second volume of GT^2 he compares and contrasts Leijonhufvud's views on Keynes then and now with those of some leading post-Keynesians, especially Shackle, whose views are discerned to be at odds with those of Leijonhufvud. Littleboy argues persuasively that in many instances this is *not* the case, and that when it appears to be so, it is largely because the post-Keynesians or Leijonhufvud or, most of all, Keynes, have themselves been misunderstood.

It is also fitting that Leijonhufvud's own mentor, Robert Clower (1997) should have written a deeply thought-out evaluation of the nature of the chapters 2 and 3 of *The General Theory* and that James Tobin (1997) has set out his own thoughts nearly sixty years on from his first encounter with *The General Theory* as a freshman at Harvard in the year it was published. Clower rewrites chapter 3, 'The Principle of Effective Demand', as he thinks Keynes would have (up to 1946) so as to make crystal clear the outlines of the new system as Keynes saw them – in Keynes's own words actually. (A feature of several of the chapters is that parts at least are written by 'the authors as J.M.K'.) Clower next sets the scene by suggesting that Keynes was more preoccupied with existence problems than with stability ones, in particular, the existence of a rest state with unemployment. He then examines the Marshallian base of Keynes's system. He argues that it grew straight out of Marshall's partial equilibrium demand and supply analysis with quantity leading to price rather than price leading to quantity, as in Walras. (Clower nevertheless identifies Walras as belonging, when Keynes was learning his trade, to the same tradition as Marshall.) Clower next works through the various ways Keynes has been interpreted, usually in terms of the Keynesian cross, relating these analyses back to Marshall's models. Clower 'does a Marshall on Keynes', that is, not so much taking literally what exactly Keynes wrote but instead interpreting him so as to mean what Clower argues he needed to say and mean. Finally, Clower quotes from chapter 18 the passage which other commentators have taken to be evidence for a long-period interpretation of *The General Theory*:

> In particular, it is an outstanding characteristic of the economic system in which we live that, whilst it is subject to severe fluctuations in respect of output and employment, it is not violently unstable. Indeed it seems capable of remaining in a chronic condition of sub-normal activity for a considerable period without any marked tendency either towards recovery or towards complete collapse.
>
> (*Collected Writings*, Vol. VII (1973): 249)

Clower, though, argues that Keynes's vision – as set out now by Clower – is the basis for a research programme which, if successful, will constitute a second Keynesian revolution that actually does for economics what Keynes intended to do by publishing the 'first edition' in February 1936.

In the opening chapter of the second volume of GT^2 Tobin sums up a lifetime of reflecting on the messages of *The General Theory* and presents his considered judgements, many of them based on his own outstanding contributions to the development of Keynesian economics.

First, in the guise of John Maynard Keynes, he amends the original definition in chapter 2 of involuntary unemployment in order to make it more simple, operational – and convincing: if people want to work at existing conditions of employment and cannot get jobs, they are involuntarily unemployed. Otherwise, as both Keynes *and* himself, he remains unrepentant. Demand deficiencies rather than supply constraints bite most of the time in capitalist economies. Policy can do something about this without having radically to change either institutions or political systems. Money is integrated in the workings of the system as a whole; it is *not* a veil. Price and wage flexibility are beside the point theoretically as far as determining the levels of activity and unemployment are concerned, though there is much to be said for relative money-wage stability if we want a stable economy overall. Wage-earners do not and do not have to 'suffer' from money illusion to make Keynes's system 'work', their behaviour is perfectly consistent with sensible behaviour, with the balancing of pros and cons, so that it is sensible for wage-earners to resist cuts in money-wages in order to protect relative positions, but not to go in for industrial unrest every time the prices of wage goods go up a little.

When we come to the mid-1990s and Tobin writes as Tobin, he argues that we have to come to grips with what we mean by equilibrium when there is unemployment. He tells us that he prefers to use the phrase 'rest state' because, clearly, the labour market is *not* clearing at the given price if, as is usually the case, there is involuntary unemployment present. He then tackles head-on the disequilibrium interpretation of Keynes. Keynesian rest states are centres of gravitation for short-period flow equilibria, given inherited stocks of capital goods, labour supplies and technical knowledge. But clearly all these change over time, some from the very attainment of short-period flow equilibrium. So we must consider the characteristics of the next period's centre of gravitation, taking into account what has happened in the previous period(s) and the implications for stocks, short *and* long-term expectations and so on, for this period. It is an open question whether, either in fact or in theory, the disequilibrium dynamics so released will produce a succession of short-period equilibria which, left to themselves, will converge on a long-period, full stock and flow equilibrium. Tobin, like Keynes, is not sure that this is a very interesting or relevant question anyway.

These are some of the themes and chapters to be found in our GT^2 volumes. Space and time prevent me from discussing John Cornwall's and Robert Skidelsky's very different evaluations of the social philosophy and policy measures which, originating in *The General Theory*, have now been updated by our two scholars; or referring to the intricate analysis by Jan Kregel, Ingo Barens and Volker Caspari, and Colin Rogers and Tom Rymes of that most difficult of all chapters in *The General Theory*, chapter 17; and much else besides. I must, though, mention the two chapters on investment by Robert Eisner (1997) and Luigi Pasinetti (1997). In essence, these two scholars accept Keynes's original formulation, Eisner by stressing recent empirical findings, Pasinetti by making a subtle argument which both defends Keynes and holds off a critique of Keynes's formulation. The critique is based on the results of the capital theory debates of the 1950s to 1970s: see Harcourt (1972). In any event I hope I have written enough to tempt my readers to browse through the volumes themselves.

References

Brown, A. J. (1997) 'The Inflationary Dimension', in Harcourt and Riach, Vol. II.

Clower, R. W. (1997) 'Effective Demand Revisited', in Harcourt and Riach, Vol. I.

Coates, J. (1997) 'Keynes, Vague Concepts and Fuzzy Logic', in Harcourt and Riach, Vol. II.

Davidson, P. (1997) '*The General Theory* in an Open Economy Context', in Harcourt and Riach, Vol. II.

Dow, S. C. (1997) 'Endogenous Money', in Harcourt and Riach, Vol. II.

Eisner, R. (1997) 'The Marginal Efficiency of Capital and Investment', in Harcourt and Riach, Vol. I.

Harcourt, G. C. (1972) *Some Cambridge Controversies in the Theory of Capital* (Cambridge: Cambridge University Press).

— and P. A. Riach (eds) (1997) A *'Second Edition' of The General Theory*, 2 vols (London: Routledge).

Howitt, P. (1997) 'Expectations and Uncertainty in Contemporary Keynesian Models', in Harcourt and Riach, Vol. I.

Keynes, J. M. (1936) *The General Theory of Employment, Interest and Money*, in *Collected Writings*, Vol. VII. (1973) (London: Macmillan).

— (1973) *The General Theory and After, Part II: Defence and Development*, in *Collected Writings*, Vol. XIV (London: Macmillan).

King, J. E. (1997), 'Underconsumption', in Harcourt and Riach, Vol. I.

Kriesler, P. (1987) *Kalecki's Microanalysis: The Development of Kalecki's Analysis of Pricing and Distribution* (Cambridge: Cambridge University Press).

— (1997) 'Kalecki, Keynes and *The General Theory*', in Harcourt and Riach, Vol. II.

Leijonhufvud, A. (1968) *On Keynesian Economics and the Economics of Keynes: A Study in Monetary Theory* (London: Oxford University Press).

Littleboy, B. (1990) *On Interpreting Keynes: A Study in Reconcitiation* (London: Routledge).

— (1997) 'On Leijonhufvud's Economics of Keynes', in Harcourt and Riach, Vol. II.

Marris, R. (1991) *Reconstructing Keynesian Economics with Imperfect Competition* (Aldershot: Edward Elgar).

— (1997) 'Yes, Mrs Robinson! *The General Theory* and Imperfect Competition', in Harcourt and Riach, Vol. I.

O'Donnell, R. (1982) 'Keynes: Philosophy and Economics, An Approach to Rationality and Uncertainty', PhD dissertation, University of Cambridge.

— (1989) *Keynes: Philosophy, Economics and Politics, The Philosophical Foundations of Keynes's Thought and Their Influence on his Economics and Politics* (London: Macmillan).

— (1997) 'Keynes and Formalism', in Harcourt and Riach, Vol. II.

Pasinetti, L. (1977) 'The Marginal Efficiency of Investment', in Harcourt and Riach, Vol. I.

Reddaway, B. (1997) 'The Changing Significance of Inflation', in Harcourt and Riach, Vol. II.

Sardoni, C. (1987) *Marx and Keynes on Economic Recession* (Brighton: Wheatsheaf Books).

— (1997) 'Keynes and Marx', in Harcourt and Riach, Vol. II.

Shapiro, N. (1997) 'Imperfect Competition and Keynes', in Harcourt and Riach, Vol. I.

Tobin, J. (1997) 'An Overview of *The General Theory*', in Harcourt and Riach, Vol. II.

4

The General Theory of Employment, Interest and Money: Three views*

with Claudio Sardoni

In responding to Philip Arestis's request for a contribution to the volume of essays in honour of Paul Davidson, a good friend of G.C.H. of well over 30 years' standing, and of C.S. for 15 years or more, we thought that a 'compare and contrast' essay on interpretations of *The General Theory* would be a peculiarly suitable and appropriate subject. For it would enable us both to outline Paul's own deep and astute interpretation and to compare it with the interpretations in two recent biographies of Keynes – Donald Moggridge's magisterial economist's life (1992) and Volume II of Robert Skidelsky's superb biography (1992), which is centred on the creation, content and criticism of *The General Theory*. Moreover, his original and compelling interpretation has earned the reproach of Don Patinkin because of its post Keynesian characteristics (see Skidelsky, 1992: xi), so it seemed a good idea also to compare his arguments and approaches with those of one of America's leading post Keynesian economists.[1]

Davidson's Keynesian antecedents

Ever since G.C.H. has known Paul Davidson – they first met in Bristol in the early 1960s when Davidson gave him Hell all the way through his paper to John Whitaker's seminar – he has always

---

* Originally published in Philip Arestis (ed.) (1996) *Keynes, Money and the Open Economy. Essays in Honour of Paul Davidson*, Vol. 1 (Cheltenham: Edward Elgar) 1–13.

referred G.C.H. (and everyone else) back to the Old Testament (*A Treatise on Money*) and the New Testament (*The General Theory*) for the evidence and authority for his propositions. (The *Tract on Monetary Reform* (1923) also receives honourable mention at times – perhaps it is the central core of the economists' Dead Sea Scrolls?) We doubt if there is anyone else in the profession so adept and thorough at backing up their analytical arguments with telling and clinching quotes from Keynes. Davidson himself was introduced to these great texts by his mentor, the late Sidney Weintraub, who was himself a latter-day St Paul. They both also regarded Marshall as a modern Moses, one who was not only the channel through which the Law was received but also *the* guide to theoretical analysis.[2] In the essay we want to show how this background has shaped Davidson's views of *The General Theory* and of the Keynesian approach to economic theory in general.

Davidson's interpretation of Keynes – and after

Davidson developed his ideas over many years in articles and in his *magnum opus, Money and the Real World* (1972, 1978). We have already mentioned how strong an influence Marshall was on Sidney Weintraub and Davidson. It is no accident then that the analytical structure of Davidson's work is usually in terms of supply and demand functions and curves, sometimes Marshall's, sometimes, of course, the aggregate versions of *The General Theory*. So partial is Davidson to supply and demand curves that when he came to analyse the determination of investment in *Money and the Real World* (and in articles leading up to it), he departed from Keynes's emphasis on a comparison between the marginal efficiency of capital and the money rate of interest. He argued instead in terms of stock and flow supply and demand curves, using present value calculations containing the external rate of interest as the discount factor. Furthermore, the analysis takes in Keynes's own (in the *Tract on Monetary Reform*) of spot and future markets (applied there to the analysis of the forward exchanges) in order to determine the short-period flow of expenditure on new capital goods in the economy as a whole. In this way Davidson was able to combine the demand for capital goods in the present situation with the determination of the planned addition to capacity relative to the existing stock of capital goods, taking in both their current costs of production and the cost and availability of finance. This is an integral part of the real world which both Keynes and Davidson analyse so well.

When it comes to considering the money part of the equation, as it were, Davidson is equally illuminating. He has many wise things to say about the inescapable fact of uncertainty giving rise to the need for a liquidity variable with the peculiar and essential properties of money. He has also written on many occasions in scathing tones about the impossibility of finding a place for money in any significant sense other than as a ticket in an Arrow–Debreu general equilibrium system where everything has been coordinated before the 'action' starts. (This is about the only proposition that Paul and Frank Hahn agree on.) Formally, he associates 'a non-neutrality of money analytical system' with Keynes's need to reject the

> three basic axioms of orthodox neoclassical theory: (1) the axiom of gross substitution ... everything ultimately a substitute for everything else (2) the axiom of reals ... the objectives of agents [ugh!] that determine their actions and plans do not depend on ... nominal magnitudes ... and (3) the axiom of an ergodic economic world ... whereby the future [is] predictable in [a] probability sense.
>
> (Davidson, 1990: 333–4)[3]

Because money is there right from the start and because its creation does not create employment, output or income directly, when important decision makers shift their demand for goods to a demand for money, there is a failure in effective demand which the system is *not* equipped automatically to make good either in the short or in the long term.

Even more so, both Davidson and Sidney Weintraub stressed, as Keynes did, the essential role of the wage unit in securing stability in both the general price level *and* the level of activity of the system. This theme runs through their analysis of both unemployment and inflation. Moreover, because the emphasis is on money's role as a store of value, they are both probably, again as Keynes was all his life, in favour of the long-term stability of the general price level (see Brown, 1997). This not only ensures the pre-eminence of money as a store of value, but also helps to minimise the dangers of crisis in a system which is run basically by decision makers trying to make $M' > M$ by the end of the period of production, as Marx stressed in a proposition of which Keynes approved (we are not sure that either Sidney or Paul knew about it!). The point is that the ultimate driving force is a desire to make as large money profits as possible, so that the commodities produced, the labour employed and the accumulation planned are but the means to this end. Not having to worry about a declining long-term value of money is therefore a boon, *ceteris paribus*, though Keynes, from at least the *Tract on Monetary Reform* on, argued passionately that deflation and depression caused greater evils than inflation.

Of course, Davidson does not argue that money-wages are necessarily sticky, nor that an assumption of stickiness is essential for Keynes-type results to occur – perish the thought! Nor does he argue that a sticky money-wage by itself would ensure an optimum as opposed to, often, a stable systemic outcome. It is rather that he sees very clearly the intricate relationships between the wage unit, on the one hand, and the price level and activity, on the other – and so makes it an essential *policy* variable to be influenced if not controlled. (Both Weintraub and Davidson are rather right-wing when it comes to policy, always preferring a Marshallian–Pigovian carrot and stick approach to directives or controls or administered incomes policies.)

In so far as the wage unit is relevant for the determination of the general price level, Davidson has a soft spot for the fundamental equations of the *Treatise on Money*. With them Keynes advanced one of the earliest analyses of the possibility of cost-push (as well as demand-pull) inflation, an emphasis which Richard Kahn stressed for most of his own working life after the publication of *The General Theory*. But Davidson also clearly expounded the link between the general price level and the demand for money and hence the determination of the rate of interest and its role in turn in determining the level of investment.

Davidson is most subtle in his analysis of the demand for money. Not only is his interpretation of the speculative aspects of the liquidity preference function much in keeping with the original spirit of Keynes's analysis, but also he should receive considerable credit for putting the finance motive, originally introduced by Keynes in 1937, centrally back on the agenda in a series of articles in the 1960s (see Davidson, 1990, Part II). Davidson recognised very clearly that in modern capitalist economies availability of finance (*not* saving) is the ultimate constraint on the rate of accumulation. (This is even true of a situation of full employment, though there, adequate finance has also to be coupled with a release of real resources associated with, say, a rise in the saving ratio.) Not, of course, that the financial constraint will always bite – limp animal spirits may bring investment to an end (or, at least, make it too low a level) before the limits of, for example, bank finance have been reached, especially in a system which includes unused overdraft limits as a feature. But if we may put animal spirits to one side for the moment, the investment market may become congested before investment itself has reached the level which matches full employment saving.

As Bibow (1995) has shown, Davidson overlooked the subtle point that the finance motive only operates in a disequilibrium situation, that it is essentially a disequilibrium phenomenon. But that does not detract from his conceptual insight about the role of finance as the ultimate constraint – an insight which Kalecki also had, so that it is strange that Paul has always been hostile to the latter's contributions. Perhaps there is an ideological and political rather than a purely technical economic reason for this? In any event the factors associated with the finance motive are even more relevant today than when Keynes and then Davidson wrote about them. With the deregulation of so many capital markets, coupled with the great rate of technical advance in the same markets, the resulting imbalance between finance capital and industrial capital has been one of the principal sources of crisis and instability in the world economy. To the analysis of this, Paul Davidson, with his sound grounding in Keynes's writings and his own insights, has made thoughtful and essential contributions (see, for example, Davidson, 1997).

Finally, Davidson has never been especially interested in (perhaps we should say dogmatic about) the exact nature of the microeconomic foundations of the Keynesian system. He has been happy to use markets with Marshallian competitive structures in his models. This reflects Keynes's claim that he took as one of his givens 'the degree of competition' (*The General Theory*, p. 245) and that he did not expect the particular market structures of various industries to make any significant difference to his new and fundamental propositions.[4] In following his lead Davidson is probably reflecting the methodological view that we should try to get by with as simple assumptions as possible in our models in order to make them both tractable and understandable. Nevertheless, a more thorough treatment by Davidson of the nature of the markets in which firms operate would certainly be welcome. An analysis of the actual working of capitalist markets would give Davidson's economics for the real world greater power and conviction. Furthermore, his contribution on this topic would be especially appropriate at a time when most of the so-called New Keynesians argue that 'Keynesian results' can be obtained at the analytical level only by introducing some *ad hoc* hypotheses of imperfect competition.

Skidelsky's post-Keynesian Keynes

As we mentioned above, Robert Skidelsky was criticised by Don Patinkin for 'having adopted a "post-Keynesian" interpretation of Keynes's economics' (Skidelsky, 1992: xi).[5] He was also criticised by Rod O'Donnell for challenging the notion of evolutionary continuity in Keynes's thought from the earliest times to *The General Theory* and beyond. We think Skidelsky is right on both counts. Most of all, Patinkin never properly took on board how very Marshallian in method Keynes was. Skidelsky points out that it was not natural for Keynes to think in a Walrasian general equilibrium manner of everything depending on everything else simultaneously. He was much more accustomed to going around the economy, brilliantly spotlighting each (relevant) part of it in turn. He ignored the rest for the moment – they were at best kept at 'the back of our heads' – while he identified causal relationships – or, if there was mutual determination, he judged whether the two-way influences were of equal importance in both directions, or of overwhelming importance in one. He was, moreover, acutely conscious of the different periods of time associated with nevertheless intertwined processes. Not only was it his own way of seeing processes, it also contrasts starkly with how those he was criticising saw them. There are obvious examples: investment determining saving as opposed to saving determining investment; the marginal efficiency of capital having to square up against the money rate of interest as opposed to the money rate of interest needing to be consistent with the natural rate of interest; aggregate demand determining output, income and employment as opposed to employment determining output and income; and so on.

No doubt Keynes exaggerated, and Skidelsky highlights this, in order to bring out the contrasts and to try to change *our* ways of looking at things, to get a better feel on processes and to understand better Keynes's 'vision'. But if, as Skidelsky argues (and so does Davidson), Walras's way of doing economics was alien to Keynes, a convinced Marshallian on method, then the method of *The General Theory* does fit correctly under the post Keynesian rubric.

As for Rod O'Donnell's masterly account of Keynes's philosophy and economics (O'Donnell, 1989), if it has one limitation as an account of Keynes's thought processes, it is *too* systematic, explicit and formally logical. It thus leaves too little room for Keynes's leaps of intuition so well documented by Austin Robinson, Skidelsky, Davidson and Moggridge. Moggridge quotes Keynes's letter to O. T. Falk, 19 February 1936: 'The extent to which one sees one's destination before one discovers the route is the most obscure problem of all in the psychology of original work ... it is the destination which one sees first [though] a good many of the destinations so seen turn out to be mirages' (Moggridge, 1992: 552). Moggridge comments that

> For all his books ... *in every case* Keynes drew up a draft table of contents. He ... thought of the structure of his argument as a whole even before he put pen to paper on any details ... his table of contents [were] sketch maps of how he intuitively thought of the route through the larger problems in book form... [For] the complex major works ... the multiplicity of 'maps' illustrates his struggles to find the route and to keep the whole and the parts together.
>
> (*Ibid.*: 551–2, emphasis in original)

Rod O'Donnell is so systematic a thinker himself – to the benefit of us all – that he may not have fully perceived or appreciated how Keynes could have done what he did without following the same systematic path. Skidelsky, though, is more akin to Keynes in his psychological make-up and approach and so has more naturally, and intuitively, appreciated the mode of thought of the complex person whose life and works he has analysed.

Skidelsky puts much emphasis on the psychological nature of Keynes's economics: the central role which Keynes gave to an inescapable uncertain environment within which decisions have to be made, the roles of expectation formation and conventions, the psychologies of the main actors in Keynes's economic dramas – the speculators, investors, rentiers, consumers, money-holders, wage-earners. He draws subtle portraits of them all; some of the most memorable passages occur, for example, in *The Economic Consequences of the Peace* (1919) as much as in chapter 12 of *The General Theory*. All this no doubt reflects Keynes's fascination with the Freudian ideas of his day, brought to the UK by some of Keynes's friends, his Moorean philosophical background and his own artistic leanings and understandings. For example, Skidelsky points out how many ideas and arguments of *The General Theory* were expressed in ordinary language, as much in the drafts as when writing to Lydia. John Coates (1990, 1997) especially has documented this in his studies of Keynes and ordinary language economics.

Skidelsky also brings out Keynes's strong anti-thrift prejudices which he argues were linked to Keynes's many-sided rebellion against Victorian values and morality. This shows itself in his passages on the motives behind the consumption function and in his stress on the residual nature of saving as contrasted with the explicit positive aspects so beloved of the Victorians including Marshall – and Skidelsky's modern Victorian heroine, Margaret Thatcher. All these ideas and attitudes are hard to fit into the formal aspects of neo-Walrasian systems such as Patinkin was accustomed to use, though not, of course, into the all-round thoughts of that passionate socialist, Leon Walras, which are to be found in his later volumes and which are associated with his single-minded commitment to carrying on his father's political and philosophical aims. Certainly Davidson and Skidelsky join company with their emphasis on the overriding influence of uncertainty in the investment and money markets, in the determination of investment and the rate of interest in a monetary production economy. Those themes are reiterated in Davidson's writings, often on his own, but also in significant joint papers with Sidney Weintraub.

We, however, wish to close this section on a note of caution. To lay too much emphasis on psychology could be dangerous, for it could lead to an interpretation of Keynes which relies excessively on methodological individualism. Although, undoubtedly, Keynes speaks of 'psychological laws', it should be emphasised that he almost never refers just to isolated individuals. In general, Keynes speaks of the psychology of specific social groups (speculators, entre-preneurs, wage-earners, for example). When we consider issues of social psychology, we must remember that history, institutions and conventions play a crucial role in the determination of attitudes. Similar observations may be made about an explanation of Keynes's anti-thrift attitude which is based only on his rebellion against the attitudes of Victorian England. Although Keynes's position on saving and consumption can be partly explained by his personal rebellion, it is also true that his views essentially derive from his awareness that capitalist economies, with the end of the First World War, entered a new historical phase, in which saving and parsimony no longer played the same central role as before. In particular, for Keynes, it is the almost 'natural' link between saving and invest-ment which disappeared (see, for example, the first pages of *The Economic Consequences of Peace* (1919)). Keynes's theory is well-grounded on knowledge not only of the actual working of the economy but also of its historical developments.

Moggridge's historical Keynes

Donald Moggridge's account of *The General Theory* is indispensable for the authoritative dating of the development of the system which became *The General Theory*. It is also fascinating for its revelation of Hawtrey's discovery of the multiplier in his comments on the proofs of the *Treatise on Money*, only to reject it out of hand ever after (Moggridge, 1992: 535). This throws into relief Keynes's relatively slow appreciation of its meaning – that it was the endogenous process which brought either falls or rises of income to an end – for which he had been searching ever since the banana plantation parable of the *Treatise on Money* and the lack of a clinching argu-ment in *Can Lloyd George Do It?* (1929). He needed to put a precise figure on the change in employment (and output) which could be expected, under precisely defined conditions, from a primary change in employment associated with, say, public works expendi-ture or an induced rise in private investment expenditure.

Associated with this precision would be an account of where the saving came from to match the increased investment. Kahn had provided both in 1931 but Keynes does not appear to have seen the full significance of it all until early 1933 (Moggridge, 1992: 563).

Moggridge accepts Keynes's own account (for example, in his letter to Harrod, *C.W.*, Vol. XIV, 1973: 85–6) of the chronology of discovery and of what the key ingredients of the new system were: the consumption function, the liquidity preference function and the marginal efficiency of capital schedule. He does not put much emphasis on the central importance of uncertainty and expectations though he accepts that the 1937 *Quarterly Journal of Economics* reply to the critics (which does) is a true index of Keynes's assessment of the significance of his new system.

Moggridge also wrote one of the best accounts of the strengths and weaknesses of *IS/LM* as a means of getting a first grip on the new system. It is to be found in the appendix to his book on Keynes (1976) in the *Modern Masters* series. In it he agrees with Davidson that though formally the *IS* and *LM* curves are set out as independent of one another, once actual movements are analysed this assumption is no longer tenable. Hence their limited role is to give us an actual feel for the interrelationships, for existence *including* its fragility, if you like, a 'first glimpse', as Keynes put it, but no more than that, at our own peril. Keynes himself was explicitly aware of this:

> We have now introduced money into our causal nexus for the first time, and we are able to catch a first glimpse of the way in which changes in the quantity of money work their way into the economic system. If, however, we are tempted to assert that money is the drink which stimulates the system to activity, we must remind ourselves that there may be several slips between the cup and the lip. For whilst an increase in the quantity of money may be expected, *cet. par.*, to reduce the rate of interest, this will not happen if the liquidity-preferences of the public are increasing more than the quantity of money; and whilst a decline in the rate of interest may be expected, *cet. par.*, to increase the volume of investment, this will not happen if the schedule of the marginal efficiency of capital is falling more rapidly than the rate of interest; and whilst an increase in the

volume of investment may be expected, *cet. par.*, to increase employment, this may not happen if the propensity to consume is falling off. Finally, if employment increases, prices will rise in a degree partly governed by the shapes of the physical supply functions, and partly by the liability of the wage-unit to rise in terms of money. And when output has increased and prices have risen, the effect of this on liquidity-preference will be to increase the quantity of money necessary to maintain a given rate of interest.

(*The General Theory*, p. 173)[6]

And, as with Moggridge, so with another famous Fellow of Clare, Brian Reddaway, who, fresh from his supervisions as an undergraduate with Keynes while *The General Theory* was being written, wrote in his splendid review of the book in the *Economic Record* (1936, reprinted in Lekachman, 1964):

Are we then reasoning in a circle? ... no, we are merely faced with the inevitable difficulty of trying to describe a system where the four variables [*I, S, Y* and *r*] *mutually* determine one another ... our four propositions are represented approximately by

(1) $S = f(Y)$
(2) $I = g(r)$
(3) $I = S$
(4) $M = L_1 (Y) + L_2 (r)$

... Keynes ... deprecates the spurious air of exactness introduced by too much mathematics ... in his endeavour to describe the system without this sort of shorthand he has tended to obscure the fact that the determination is mutual.

(pp. 106–7)

One point where Moggridge is out of step with received opinion is that he does not regret that Keynes scrapped the distinction between the cooperative (and neutral) economy models, on the one hand, and the entrepreneur economy model, on the other, as being the best way of showing the essential difference between the classical system and his own. As we know, these passages, which Moggridge (1992) judges to constitute 'an analytically unsatisfactory distinction' (p. 566), ended up in the laundry basket at Tilton. Keynes's account of Say's Law and his emphasis on the classical postulates in the labour market took their place in the published volume, as did Pigou's *Theory of Unemployment* (1933) as the archetypal representative of the position and propositions of the classical economists.

We have pointed out Davidson's relative lack of interest in the issues raised by different market forms. A similar attitude may be detected in both biographies of Keynes. The issue of the relationship between Keynes and the 'imperfect competition revolution' receives little attention from Moggridge and Skidelsky. 'Imperfect competition' is conspicuous by its absence from the indexes of both their books. Moggridge ignores the issue altogether. Skidelsky does not get beyond stating 'it remains a puzzle that the two escape routes from Marshallian orthodoxy – the one associated with Sraffa and imperfect competition, the other with Keynes and effective demand – never converged in Keynes's lifetime though leading disciples like Kahn and Joan Robinson were heavily involved in both "revolutions"' (Skidelsky, 1992: 290). The explanation of Davidson's position, as we have seen, is essentially analytical (his Marshallian – Keynesian view of competition); an explanation, or a justification, of why both the biographers have virtually ignored the problem is harder to find.

From a historical point of view, which of course is central in a biography, the issue of the relationship, or the absence of relationships, between the Keynesian 'revolution' and the other revolution which took place in Cambridge more or less at the same time, whose leaders were all very close friends and colleagues of Keynes, is a fascinating topic. Many questions arise: why did Keynes ignore the contributions on imperfect competition from Kahn, Joan Robinson, and Sraffa? Was this a 'tactical' decision (not to open too many fronts in the struggle against old ideas)?; was Keynes skeptical about the possible macroeconomic implications of the assumption of imperfect competition?; did Kahn or Joan Robinson ever try to involve Keynes in the debate on imperfect competition?; and many more. Given the very high quality of the two biographies, we would have liked to have seen their answers to some of the questions which are raised by the 'puzzle', not least because other scholars in recent days have tackled these themes; see, for example, Darity

(1985), Harcourt (1987), Kregel (1985), Marcuzzo (1994), Marris (1991, 1992, 1997), and it would be enlightening to have Moggridge's and Skidelsky's views on and reactions to the issues as well.[7]

Summary and conclusions

To sum up: with one or two exceptions the three views examined are complementary and reinforcing. Most importantly, all are agreed that Keynes's great book does constitute a revolution in 'vision', analysis and method, so that the attempt to derive Keynes-type results *within* the dominant neo-Walrasian framework of modern economic theory (or even the New Keynesian one) is doomed to failure. This has been recognised explicitly and coura-geously by, for example, Peter Howitt (1997) and, at least implicitly, by Frank Hahn who admits that he has been forced to rely at times on 'plausible' rather than 'clinching' arguments when tackling Lucas and company; see Hahn (1982: xi). All this is reassuring for the three authors concerned – Davidson, Moggridge and Skidelsky – have very different backgrounds and temperaments; yet, after so much of their lifetimes studying the evidence, they *in the main* agree on 'what Keynes really meant'.

Notes

1. We would like to record here our great sadness that Don Patinkin has died. Though we seldom agreed on economic matters, he was a most admirable and likeable person and a scholar to whom the entire profes-sion is in debt.
2. In the 1950s, and the following decades, Weintraub made important contributions concerning the microeconomic foundations of Keynes's *General Theory*. In particular, Weintraub based Keynes's aggregate demand and supply functions on Marshallian microeconomic foundations, see, for example, Weintraub (1957).
3. Davidson has devoted much effort to his criticism of the axiom of an ergodic world; see, for example, Davidson (1991).
4. See Shapiro (1997) for a deeply illuminating analysis of this point.
5. Robert's disarming reply – 'If I am guilty of this fallacy, I can say only that this is how Keynes's economics appeared to me, being the person I am' – makes good sense to us and, we imagine, to Paul too. Mark Blaug (1994: 1211n) comments on Patinkin's complaint: 'But all that this seems to mean is that Skidelsky treats Keynes as having been obsessed through-out his life by the problem of economic behavior under uncertainty; if this is a post-Keynesian interpretation, we are all post-Keynesians now'.

6. G.C.H. has always been grateful to his teacher and friend Keith Fearson for pointing out the significance of this passage to him.
7. In his judicial and highly readable review article of the two biographies, Mark Blaug (1994: 1211–12) also regrets the omission.

References

References to Keynes's works are from the following edition: *The Collected Writings of John Maynard Keynes*, 29 vols, 1971–79 edited by A. Robinson and D. Moggridge, London: Macmillan for the Royal Economic Society. The listing gives *C.W.*, followed by volume number and date.

Bibow, J. (1995) 'Some Reflections on Keynes's Finance Motive for the Demand for Money', *Cambridge Journal of Economics*, vol. 19, 647–66.

Blaug, M. (1994) 'Recent Biographies of Keynes', *Journal of Economic Literature*, vol. 32, 1204–15.

Brown, A. J. (1997) 'The Inflationary Dimension', in Harcourt and Riach, Vol. 2, (1997).

Coates, J. (1990) 'Ordinary Languages Economics. Keynes and the Cambridge Philosophers', unpublished PhD dissertation, Cambridge.

— (1997) 'Keynes, Vague Concepts and Fuzzy Logic', in Harcourt and Riach Vol. 2 (1997).

Darity Jr, W. (1985) 'On Involuntary Unemployment and Increasing Returns', *Journal of Post Keynesian Economics*, vol. 7, 363–72.

Davidson, P. (1972) *Money and the Real World* (London: Macmillan), 2nd edn 1978.

— (1990) *Money and Employment. The Collected Writings of Paul Davidson*, I, edited by L. Davidson (London: Macmillan).

— (1991) 'Is Probability Theory Relevant for Uncertainty?', *Journal of Economic Perspectives*, vol. 5, 129–43.

— (1997) '*The General Theory* in an Open Economy', in Harcourt and Riach Vol. 2, (1997).

Hahn, F. H. (1982) *Money and Inflation* (Oxford: Basil Blackwell).

Harcourt, G. C. (ed.) (1985) *Keynes and his Contemporaries, The Sixth and Centennial Keynes Seminar held at the University of Kent at Canterbury, 1983* (London: Macmillan).

— (1987) 'Theoretical Methods and Unfinished Business', in Reese (1987), 1–22; reprinted in Sardoni (1992).

— and P. A. Riach (eds) (1997), *A 'Second Edition' of The General Theory*, 2 vols. (London: Routledge).

Howitt, P. (1997) 'Expectations and Uncertainty in Contemporary Keynesian Models', in Harcourt and Riach, Vol. 1, (1997).

Kahn, R. F. (1931) 'The Relation of Home Investment to Unemployment', *Economic Journal*, vol. 41, 173–98; reprinted in Kahn (1972).

— (1972) *Selected Essays on Employment and Growth* (Cambridge: Cambridge University Press).

Keynes, J. M. (1919) *The Economic Consequences of the Peace*, *C.W.*, II (1971).

— (1923) *A Tract on Monetary Reform*, *C.W.*, IV (1971).

— (1930) *A Treatise on Money*, 2 vols, C.W., V, VI (1971).
— (1936) *The General Theory of Employment, Interest and Money* (London: Macmillan), C.W., VII (1973).
— (1937) 'The General Theory of Employment', *Quarterly Journal of Economics*, vol. LI, 209–23; C.W., XIV (1973), 109–23.
— (1937) *The General Theory and After: Part II, Defence and Development*, C.W., XIV (1973).
— and H. D. Henderson (1929) *Can Lloyd George Do It?*, C.W., IX (1972), 86–125.
Kregel, J. A. (1985) 'Harrod and Keynes: Increasing Returns, The Theory of Employment and Dynamic Economics', in Harcourt (1985), pp. 66–88.
Lekachman, R. (1964) *Keynes' General Theory. Reports of Three Decades* (London: Macmillan; New York: St Martin's Press).
Marcuzzo, M. C. (1994) 'At the Origin of Imperfect Competition: Different Views', in Vaughn (1994), pp. 75–84.
Marris, R. L. (1991) *Reconstructing Keynesian Economics with Imperfect Competition* (Aldershot: Edward Elgar).
— (1992) 'R. F. Kahn's Fellowship Dissertation: A Missing Link in the History of Economic Thought', *Economic Journal,* vol. 102, 1235–43.
— (1997) 'Yes, Mrs Robinson! *The General Theory* and Imperfect Competition', in Harcourt and Riach, Vol I (1997).
Moggridge, D. E. (1976) *Keynes* (London: Macmillan).
— (1992) *Maynard Keynes. An Economist's Biography* (London: Routledge).
O'Donnell, R. M. (1989) *Keynes: Philosophy, Economics and Politics* (London: Macmillan).
Pigou, A. C. (1933) *The Theory of Unemployment* (London: Macmillan).
Reddaway, W. B. (1936) 'The General Theory of Employment, Interest and Money', *Economic Record*, vol. 12, 28–36; reprinted in Lekachman (1964), pp. 99–108.
Reese, D. A. (ed.) (1987) *The Legacy of Keynes*, Nobel Conference, XXII, San Francisco: Harper & Row.
Sardoni, C. (ed.) (1992) *On Political Economists and Modern Political Economy. Selected Essays of G. C. Harcourt* (London: Routledge).
Shapiro, N. (1997) 'Imperfect Competition and Keynes', in Harcourt and Riach, Vol. 1 (1997).
Skidelsky, R. (1992) *John Maynard Keynes. Volume Two. The Economist as Saviour* (London: Macmillan).
Vaughn, K. (ed.) (1994) *Perspectives in the History of Economic Thought, Vol. X; Method, Competition, Conflict and Measurement in the Twentieth Century* (Aldershot: Edward Elgar).
Weintraub, S. (1957) 'The Micro-foundations of Aggregate Demand and Supply', *Economic Journal*, vol. 67, 455–70.

5
A Note on 'Mr Meade's Relation' and International Capital Movements*

with Paul C. Dalziel

Recognition that a change in investment expenditure always leads to an equal increase in voluntary saving has been highlighted by several commentators as one of the key innovations in Keynes's *General Theory*; see especially Hicks (1936: 239), Robinson (1937, ch. 2), Meade (1975: 82), Patinkin (1976: 65; 1993: 647), and Skidelsky (1992: 554). Following a reference in Kahn's (1931: 189) seminal presentation of the multiplier, this identity relationship between investment and voluntary saving has been called 'Mr Meade's Relation', and in a brief note Meade (1993) has described how he first discovered and presented it to the Cambridge 'Circus' in the first half of 1931.[1] First, Meade set out the 'causal relationships' among increases in investment, income and saving in the form of arrowed lines within a sequential diagram. This method of 'process' or 'period' analysis, often using Robertson's (1936, 1940) equivalent tabular presentation, remains an important part of post-Keynesian textbooks (see Harcourt *et al.*, 1967, ch. 10; Chick, 1983, ch. 14; and Davidson, 1994, ch. 3), but has virtually disappeared from modern-

* Originally published in the *Cambridge Journal of Economics*, vol. 21, 1997, 621–31. We are very grateful to Amit Bhaduri, the late James Meade, Dominic Prtak, Bob Rowthorn, Claudio Sardoni, Sunanda Sen and three anonymous referees of this journal for their insightful comments on an earlier draft. We are also grateful to Robert Pollin for providing us with a chapter outline of his forthcoming book, *The Macroeconomics of Finance, Saving, and Investment*, Pollin (1997), and to Robert Blecker for providing us with a copy of his chapter for that volume, Blecker (1997).

day research. As far as we are aware, Chick (1985), Cottrell (1986), Earl (1990) and Dalziel (1996a,b) are the only recent authors to advocate its wider use. Second, Meade assumed a constant marginal propensity to save in every round of his process analysis. This allowed him to apply the formula for the summation of a geometric series when the common ratio is less than one, which provided a neat closure for his problem and became the standard approach in the various developments of the Keynesian model that occurred after *The General Theory*; for example, the dynamic supply-side analysis of Harrod (1939), the disaggregated analysis of Goodwin (1949) and the income distribution analysis of Kaldor (1955–56).

In this note we comment on two aspects of Mr Meade's Relation, particularly as it is presented in Meade (1993). First, we confirm in a process analysis supplemented with some simple algebra that the identity between changes in investment and voluntary saving does not require a fixed propensity to save. Indeed, nothing more is required than the structure of identities which make up the multiplier process; something that Meade himself recognised 60 years earlier in a pamphlet on Public Works published at the beginning of 1933 (see Patinkin, 1994: 1144).[2] Based on this recognition, we argue in the first section that a 'conservation of saving' principle is a better way of understanding how Mr Meade's Relation is produced than the more common explanation that it is national income which acts as an equilibrating mechanism between investment and saving (comparable to the rate of interest mechanism in the classical model).

Our second comment relates to Meade's (1993) assumption of a closed economy. This is a perfectly reasonable heuristic device, of course, but some authors have claimed that the modern-day importance of international capital flows for open economies invalidates Mr Meade's Relation (beginning with Feldstein and Horioka, 1980: 319; see Baxter and Crucini, 1993; Blecker, 1995; and Coakley *et al.*, 1996, for recent surveys of this literature). The next section of this paper extends the model of section 1 to include international trade and capital movements, and demonstrates that investment expenditure continues to create an equal amount of voluntary saving. This turns out to be a simple consequence of our conservation of saving principle, and the role of capital account movements is not to allow domestic investment in excess of domestic saving, but rather is the result of saving (or, equivalently, of ownership in the new capital stock) being redistributed between domestic and foreign residents.

Our purpose in making these comments is in part methodological and in part due to a belief that more attention should be paid to Mr Meade's Relation in its open economy context. With respect to methodology, a well-established strand in post-Keynesian thought has argued in favour of analysis based on historical processes, rather than analysis based on equilibrium conditions (see, especially, Robinson, 1974; Kaldor, 1985). The process analysis used by Meade (1993), and extended in this note, is a tool well suited to this method, and is able to produce important and robust insights (the conservation of saving principle, for example) that we hope will encourage its wider use. With respect to open economy analysis, reliance on pre-Keynesian understandings of the relationship between investment and saving has led to a widespread interpretation of balance of payments deficits as being caused by a level of domestic saving that is inadequate to finance domestic investment (see, for example, Boskin, 1990: 161; and the criticism by Harcourt and Kitson, 1993: 440). This, in turn, has led many policy advisers to advocate reductions in private and public consumption as a way of addressing persistent external deficits, without recognising the effect such policies can be expected to have on aggregate incomes. The note concludes in the final section with a brief discussion of these methodological and open economy issues.

A process analysis of investment and saving

The process analysis in Mr Meade's 1993 version of his Relation is made up of three rows showing the causal relationships among, and the respective values of, increases in the levels of investment, income and saving in successive rounds of Kahn's (1931) multiplier expenditure – income process, after a one-off increase in investment expenditure. It includes a number of implicit assumptions that will be repeated in the analysis of this note. First, and perhaps most important, it is assumed that there are unemployed resources in the economy that can be used to increase the levels of capital and consumption good production. Second, the monetary counterparts of the real transactions are ignored (see Dalziel, 1996a, for a relaxation of this restriction in a similar process analysis). Third, it is assumed that income receivers immediately determine how much of their income they will consume, so that the very difficult empirical problem of lag structures is excluded (see, for example, Harcourt *et al.*, 1967, ch. 10). Similarly, no account is made of the impact of the structure of intermediate goods in the economy (Harcourt and Massaro, 1964) or of the distribution of income between wages and profits (Kalecki, 1937). Fourth, the analysis examines a single process only, following Kahn's (1931: 197) original example in holding constant other possible influences such as induced changes in the state of business confidence. Finally, contrary to Kahn's approach, an analysis of the public sector is not included. The issues arising out of international trade and capital movements are postponed until the next section below.

Three small adjustments are made in Figure 5.1 below to Meade's (1993) analysis. First, the middle row of Meade's diagram has been expanded to include induced consumption expenditure. This allows the process's underlying mechanism to be explicitly recorded, namely that the increased income of each round is caused by the round's induced consumption expenditure. Second, there is no requirement that the level of saving in any round of the process must be a fixed proportion of the previous round's induced income; that is, there is no marginal propensity to save in the diagram. Finally, Meade's first and second rows have been merged to conserve space.

$$\Delta I \ \rightarrow \ \Delta Y_0 \ \rightarrow \ \Delta C_1 \ \rightarrow \ \Delta Y_1 \ \rightarrow \ \Delta C_2 \ \rightarrow \ \Delta Y_2 \ \rightarrow \ \Delta C_3 \ \rightarrow \ \Delta Y_3 \rightarrow \text{etc.}$$
$$\qquad\qquad \downarrow \qquad\qquad\qquad \downarrow \qquad\qquad\qquad \downarrow$$
$$\qquad\qquad \Delta S_1 \qquad\qquad\quad \Delta S_2 \qquad\qquad\quad \Delta S_3$$

Figure 5.1   *Process analysis of investment and saving*

The analysis begins with an increase in investment expenditure, ΔI. When the expenditure takes place, the workers and owners involved in the capital goods sector receive new income equal to ΔY_0, as shown in the first causal arrow of Figure 1. Subsequently, these agents spend a proportion of their income on consumption goods, ΔC_1, and the remainder is added to voluntary savings, ΔS_1 (including the retained profits of the capital goods producers). The consumption expenditure passes as increased income, ΔY_1, to workers and owners in the consumption goods sector. In round 2 of the process, the receivers of that income spend a portion as ΔC_2, generating further income, ΔY_2, and the remainder is saved, ΔS_2. The multiplier process continues in this way until a round occurs in which all income from the previous round's induced consumption expenditure is saved (which may occur only asymptotically: for example, if Meade's assumption is made that the marginal propensity to save is constant). At this point, no further expenditure takes place, and so no further income is generated and the expenditure – income circular flow stops.

The process analysis in Figure 5.1 can be expressed algebraically.[3] Consider the following equations, which are true for all rounds of the process, $r \geq 1$:

$$\Delta I = \Delta Y_0 \tag{1}$$
$$\Delta S_r = \Delta Y_{r-1} - \Delta C_r \tag{2}$$
$$\Delta C_r = \Delta Y_r \tag{3}$$

The second step in Meade's analysis, applying the formula for the sum of a geometric series, is not available to us in our analysis, since we have not assumed a constant marginal propensity to save in every round. Nevertheless, note that equations (1) to (3) yield at the end of any round $r \geq 1$:

$$\Delta I = \sum_{i=1}^{r} \Delta S_i + \Delta Y_r \tag{4}$$

Thus, at the end of the first round, some of the new investment expenditure is held as voluntary saving, ΔS_1, while the remainder is held as induced income, ΔY_1, in advance of the second round. At the end of that second round, the previous round's induced income has become further saving, ΔS_2, and further induced income, ΔY_2, so that $\Delta I = \Delta S_1 + \Delta S_2 + \Delta Y_2$. This pattern continues throughout the process, until eventually (or perhaps asymptotically) a round occurs in which all of the additional income is voluntarily held as saving. In this terminal round (denoted R), $\Delta Y_r = 0$ in equation (4), which becomes:

$$\Delta I = \sum_{i=1}^{R} \Delta S_i = \Delta S \qquad\qquad (5)$$

Both equations (4) and (5) warrant further comment. Equation (5) is Mr Meade's Relation, and records that the multiplier process concludes with exactly sufficient voluntary saving to match the initial increase in investment expenditure. Thus Mr Meade's Relation, and the subsequent Keynesian emphasis on changes in investment as the explanatory cause of economic fluctuations, do not rely on the special assumption of a fixed marginal propensity to save, but simply on the identities in equations (1) to (3).

More importantly, equation (4) explains how this result is achieved. In every round of the multiplier process, there is a 'conservation of saving' principle in operation. That is, at the end of every round, the value of the initial increase in investment expenditure always equals increased saving, made up by the accumulated increases in voluntary saving in each round so far, plus the income generated by the current round's induced consumption expenditure (which is involuntarily held until there is the opportunity to spend or voluntarily to save it in the following round). Thus any act of consumption during the multiplier process does not reduce aggregate savings, but simply redistributes savings in the form of new income to the supplier of the purchased consumption goods.

Readers will notice that our approach, with its emphasis on the underlying processes of Mr Meade's Relation and the conservation of saving principle, is in accord with the strand of post-Keynesian methodology that argues in favor of analysis based on historical processes (see, especially, Robinson, 1974; Kaldor, 1985). Nevertheless, we should acknowledge that Mr Meade's Relation is frequently expressed in equilibrium terms – a practice which Patinkin (1993: 647) reminded us is derived from Keynes himself:

> The novelty in my treatment of saving and investment consists, not in my maintaining their necessary aggregate equality, but in the proposition that it is, not the rate of interest, but the level of incomes which (in conjunction with certain other factors) ensures this equality.
>
> (Keynes, 1937b: 211)

Our analysis confirms that aggregate income changes in response to an increase in investment expenditure until voluntary saving increases by the same amount, but it does not support treating this change in aggregate income as an equilibrating mechanism – certainly not in the same sense that the rate of interest equilibrates investment and saving in the classical model. A rise in the rate of interest in the classical model, for example, is presumed to *cause* an increase in saving. In our analysis, the level of saving is fixed once the investment expenditure takes place, and any further increases in aggregate income are the *result* of saving being redistributed, through consumption expenditure, until all of the investment-created saving comes to be held voluntarily.[4]

This insight may be expressed another way if it is recognised that saving is not only 'the excess of income over expenditure on consumption' (Keynes, 1936: 61), but is also the mechanism by which ownership in the new capital goods produced by investment is allocated among income earners. Once the investment expenditure takes place, the level of new ownership (new saving) is fixed, and the multiplier process simply determines how that ownership is distributed (producing further income by way of consumption expenditure as it does so). Within this framework, modern-day policy disputes that appear to be about private and public saving rates can be seen to be in fact about the distribution of ownership in society's rising level of capital stock – a conflict that is as old as capitalism itself.

Throughout this section, it has been assumed that there are no supply-side constraints to interrupt the multiplier process in Figure 5.1. A referee suggested that we should indicate the relevance of our analytical framework as the economy approaches full employment. If the economy is at full employment, of course, then the increase in investment expenditure which initiates the process in Figure 5.1 is not possible without the release of some resources from the industries producing consumption goods. In this sense, properly understood, saving is a prerequisite to investment at full employment, although note that the saving which releases resources does not guarantee their reemployment. Hence the Keynesian focus on investment decisions rather than on saving decisions remains valid, even at full employment. A more interesting case, perhaps, occurs when there is sufficient unemployment to permit the initial increase in investment, ΔI, but there is insufficient excess capacity to absorb all of the induced increase in consumption demand during the multiplier process. This does not affect our conservation of saving principle. Rather, it is a simple matter to add nominal values to the model so that the rising price of consumption goods produced by the excess demand eventually causes the real quantity of saving produced by the investment to be willingly held, as long as the conditions discussed by Keynes (1936: 64) are satisfied.

International capital movements

The previous section has demonstrated the general validity of Mr Meade's Relation between investment and saving for a closed economy. An influential paper by Feldstein and Horioka (1980), however, has argued that this validity does not remain in an open economy with international capital flows:

> [T]he assumption of perfect capital mobility is inconsistent with the traditional Keynesian interpretation that exogenous changes in the level of investment cause income to vary until the resulting saving equals investment; whatever the validity of this argument for a closed economy, it is inappropriate if domestic saving is added to the worldwide pool of capital.
>
> (Feldstein and Horioka, 1980: 319)

A recent paper by Blecker (1997) points out that the Feldstein and Horioka study found that changes in investment and saving for countries are very highly correlated, so that their empirical work did not support their disregard of 'the traditional Keynesian interpretation'. Blecker's paper investigates the role of retained profits (corporate savings) in financing investment in order to explain the close empirical relationship between domestic investment and saving, but our approach here is to extend Meade's theoretical analysis to include international trade and capital flows. Let foreign purchases of domestic consumption goods (exports) be denoted as X, and imported consumption goods as Z. Without loss of generality, it is assumed that the domestic economy does not export any capital goods, but allowance is made for the possibility that part of the original rise in domestic investment is produced in the rest of the world, and a proportion of the saving held in domestic equity is under-taken by foreigners. Let imported capital goods (including imported intermediate goods contributing to circulating capital) be denoted as K^f, and saving as S^f or S^d depending on whether the saving is undertaken by foreign or domestic residents.

$$
\begin{array}{cccc}
\Delta S_0^f & \Delta S_1^f & \Delta S_2^f & \Delta S_3^f \\
\uparrow & \uparrow & \uparrow & \uparrow \\
\Delta K^f \to \Delta X_0 & \Delta Z_1 \to \Delta X_1 & \Delta Z_2 \to \Delta X_2 & \Delta Z_3 \to \Delta X_3 \\
\uparrow \qquad \downarrow & \uparrow \qquad \downarrow & \uparrow \qquad \downarrow & \uparrow \qquad \downarrow \\
\Delta I \to \Delta Y_0 \to \Delta C_1 \to \Delta Y_1 \to \Delta C_2 \to \Delta Y_2 \to \Delta C_3 \to \Delta Y_3 \to \text{etc.} \\
\downarrow \qquad\qquad \downarrow \qquad\qquad \downarrow \\
\Delta S_1^d \qquad\qquad \Delta S_2^d \qquad\qquad \Delta S_3^d
\end{array}
$$

Figure 5.2   *Process analysis incorporating international capital movements*

Consider Figure 5.2. The analysis begins as before with an increase in domestic investment expenditure, ΔI. Part of this investment is imported, ΔK^f, and this component increases foreign rather than domestic incomes. The increase in foreign incomes will initiate an expenditure – income multiplier process in the rest of the world, but the details of that process need not be considered here, because the balance of payments accounting identity requires that the imported goods be matched by the value of exported goods plus increased saving by foreigners held in domestic equity (which might be nega-tive). This is simply the external counterpart to the internal deci-sions made about consumption and saving; that is, the income received by foreigners from domestic expenditure, ΔK^f, must be divided between consumption of the home country's goods and ser-vices, ΔX_0, and saving in domestic equity, ΔS_0^f. The expenditure on exports, together with the share of investment expenditure going to domestic producers, increases domestic income by ΔY_0, as shown in the process diagram.

   In the following round, some of this new income is spent on con-sumption goods, ΔC_1, and the remainder is saved, ΔS_1^d. Of the con-sumption expenditure, some is spent on imports, ΔZ_1, and the rest contributes to increased domestic income, ΔY_1. Once again, the increased expenditure on imports must be matched by increased exports, ΔX_1, and by increased foreign saving, ΔS_1^f. Induced income in round one is therefore given by $\Delta C_1 + \Delta X_1 - \Delta Z_1$, initiating the next round of the process. This process continues until there is no further expenditure (domestic or foreign) on domestic consumption goods.

As in the previous section, the logic of the process analysis allows us to draw a robust conclusion about the relation between invest-ment and voluntary saving. The processes in Figure 5.2 can be sum-marised in the following set of equations for all $r \geq 1$:

$$\Delta I = \Delta K^f - \Delta X_0 + \Delta Y_0 \tag{6}$$
$$\Delta S_0^f = \Delta K^f - \Delta X_0 \tag{7}$$
$$\Delta S_r^d = \Delta Y_{r-1} - \Delta C_r \tag{8}$$
$$\Delta C_r + \Delta X_r - \Delta Z_r = \Delta Y_r \tag{9}$$
$$\Delta S_r^f = \Delta Z_r - \Delta X_r \tag{10}$$

Equations (6) and (7) imply that at the end of the initial round, ΔI equals the extra voluntary saving of foreigners, ΔS_0^f, plus the induced domestic income, ΔY_0. In subsequent rounds, the five equa-tions imply that at the end of any round $r \geq 1$:

$$\Delta I = \sum_{i=1}^{r} \Delta S_i^d + \sum_{i=0}^{r} \Delta S_i^f + \Delta Y_r \tag{11}$$

That is, the initial value of increased investment expenditure always equals the accumulated increases in domestic and foreign saving held in domestic equity, plus the round's induced rise in domestic income, which is the open economy equivalent of the conservation of saving principle described in the previous section. At the end of the process (when induced income equals zero in the terminal round, R), it follows that:

$$\Delta I = \sum_{i=1}^{R} \Delta S_i^d + \sum_{i=0}^{R} \Delta S_i^f \tag{12}$$

Equation (12) confirms for an open economy the proposition that it is changes in the level of investment expenditure which determine changes in the aggregate value of saving, and confirms Mr Meade's Relation that the multiplier process operates until all the new saving is voluntarily held. Meade, as ever, brought out the central point with crystal clarity, when he wrote to us in a letter dated 7 August 1994:

> In a national closed economy, an increase in investment which takes place in one county (e.g. Somerset) may cause a regional movement of capital funds, and a regional movement of goods, from another county (e.g. Dorset), the net movement of capital funds of one kind or another being necessarily equal to the net movement of goods and services. The world economy is a closed economy, and this same net movement of capital funds and goods and services takes place from one country to another, the total multiplier being simply what happens in a world closed economy.

What then of the approach that treats balance of payments deficits as the result of deficient domestic saving? If we substitute equations (7) and (10) into equation (12), and use non-subscripted variables to represent the aggregate values of the respective variables in Figure 5.2 summed over all the rounds of the process, then the above analysis produces the change in the balance of payments deficit given in equation (13):

$$(\Delta K^f + \Delta Z - \Delta X) = \Delta I - \Delta S^d \qquad (13)$$

Equation (13) records that any excess of new domestic investment expenditure over new domestic saving must be matched by an equal increase in the country's balance of payments current account deficit. Note carefully, however, how equation (13) has been derived. There is no 'worldwide pool of capital' to which excess domestic saving can be added or from which deficient domestic saving can be supplemented, as is assumed in the analysis of Feldstein and Horioka (1980). Rather, the investment expenditure must take place first, which creates a particular item of capital in a particular location.[5] The operation of the multiplier process then determines how ownership of that new capital (voluntary saving) comes to be distributed. The change in the balance of payments deficit measures how much of the ownership is retained by (in the case of imported capital), or transferred to (in the case of domestically produced capital), overseas residents. Of course, whereas a country's policy-makers may be indifferent about the distribution of ownership of capital between residents in Somerset and Dorset, there may well be disquiet if the distribution of ownership becomes weighted towards non-domestic residents, and this may justify a policy response. The important point to observe is that such a balance of payments problem is not an issue about whether low domestic saving is acting as a constraint on domestic investment, but is an issue about whether low domestic saving is causing an undesired distribution of wealth ownership.

Conclusion

Over twenty years ago, Meade argued that 'Keynes's intellectual revolution was to shift economists from thinking normally in terms of a model of reality in which a dog called *savings* wagged his tail labelled *investment* to thinking in terms of a model in which a dog called *investment* wagged his tail labelled *savings*' (1975: 82, emphasis in original). This note has demonstrated the basic simplicity and strength of this intellectual revolution by using Meade's original method of process analysis to reveal how a conservation of saving principle produces the identity between investment and subsequent voluntary saving for both closed and open economies. In both cases, investment determines the aggregate value of saving and the multiplier operates until all saving is voluntarily held.

From our analysis, we endorse Chick's (1985) call for wider use of the method of process analysis in macroeconomic research. While recognising the almost intractable empirical problem of determining an appropriate unit of time for each period – the problem that caused Keynes (1937a: 184) to doubt the usefulness of the method – its major strength is that it allows the researcher to explore the underlying mechanisms and structures of a modern economy in a way that equilibrium analysis cannot. In this note, for example, the analyses in Figures 5.1 and 5.2 are very rudimentary in character, and yet are able to reveal general insights into the underlying relationship between investment and saving that are important for effective policy design. Thus, process analysis is an analytical tool that should be of particular interest to economists working within a critical realist framework (Bhaskar, 1987; Lawson, 1994, 1997). More importantly, the analysis in this note highlights the dangers of economic policies designed to encourage higher saving rates as a means of addressing low economic growth and persistent balance of payments deficits in many Western countries. For any individual country, an increase in saving rates will reduce aggregate expenditure, by reducing induced income in each round of the multiplier process. Indeed, in theory the multiplier process could be choked off immediately if all of the income generated from increased investment expenditure was saved by its first recipients in the initial round – a particularly striking example of Keynes's famous 'paradox of thrift'. While it is true that the resulting reduction in consumption goods production would release resources for increased investment goods production, the former is not a sufficient condition to guarantee increased investment expenditure, and nor should it be a necessary condition in a period of high and sustained unemployment throughout the world. Further, while it is true that a reduction in domestic economic activity is likely to reduce imports (particularly imported intermediate goods), this will not necessarily reduce a balance of payments problem if other countries adopt a similar strategy, but may only increase the international economy's susceptibility to widespread recession. Instead, our analysis suggests that economic recovery towards full employment will require policies coordinated at the international level, aimed at increasing investment directly and designed to control balance of payments deficits through surplus country expansion rather than deficit country contraction (as argued in Harcourt, 1995, for example).

Notes

1. This interpretation is disputed by Dimand (1994), but see Patinkin's (1994) rejoinder. Mr Meade's Relation, of course, should not be confused with Robertson's 'composite Aunt Sally of uncertain age' who appeared in a subsequent exchange on the former's validity (Robertson, 1937: 436; Keynes, 1937c: 215).
2. We are grateful to Daniele Besomi for bringing to our notice the importance of this pamphlet by allowing us to see a preliminary transcript of correspondence between Meade and Roy Harrod that he has prepared as part of his work editing Harrod's papers and correspondence in the interwar years. In this correspondence Meade adopted the assumption of fixed propensities to import to derive an open economy version of his Relation.

3. We are grateful to Ken Courts for this point.
4. 'The amounts of aggregate income and of aggregate saving are the *results* of the free choices of individuals whether or not to consume and whether or not to invest' (Keynes, 1936, p. 65, emphasis in original).
5. It will perhaps come as no surprise that our analysis brings us to an argument about the meaning of 'capital' – an issue that absorbed considerable efforts by 'the Cambridge School' in the 1950s to the 1970s (Joan Robinson, 1975: vi–vii; Harcourt, 1976: 29; see Dalziel, 1997, for a lengthier discussion in this context).

References

Baxter, M. and M. J. Crucini (1993) 'Explaining Saving–Investment Correlations', *American Economic Review*, vol. 83, 416–36.

Bhaskar, R. (1987) *Scientific Realism and Human Emancipation* (London: Verso).

Blecker, R. A. (1997) 'Policy Implications of the International Saving-Investment Correlation', final draft of a chapter in Pollin (1997), 173–229.

Boskin, M. J. (1990) 'Issues in the Measurement and Interpretation of Saving and Wealth', ch. 5 in E. R. Berndt and J. E. Triplett (eds), *Fifty Years of Economic Measurement: The Jubilee of the Conference on Research in Income and Wealth* (Chicago: University of Chicago Press).

Chick, V. (1983) *Macroeconomics After Keynes: A Reconsideration of The General Theory* (Oxford: Philip Allan).

— (1985) 'Keynesians, Monetarists and Keynes: The End of the Debate – Or a Beginning?' chapter 4 in P. Arestis and T. Skouras (eds), *Post Keynesian Economic Theory: A Challenge to Neo-Classical Economics* (Sussex: Wheatsheaf).

Coakley, J., F. Kulasi and R. Smith (1996) 'Current Account Solvency and the Feldstein–Horioka Puzzle', *Economic Journal*, vol. 106, 620–27.

Cottrell, A. (1986) 'The Endogeneity of Money and Money–Income Causality', *Scottish Journal of Political Economy*, vol. 33, 2–27.

Dalziel, P. (1996a) 'The Keynesian Multiplier, Liquidity Preference and Endogenous Money', *Journal of Post Keynesian Economics*, vol. 18, 311–31.

— (1996b) 'The Relevance of the Keynesian Multiplier Process after Sixty Years', paper presented to the 24th Conference of Economists, University of Adelaide, *History of Economics Review*, vol. 25, 221–31.

— (1997) 'The Savings Debate in Australia and the Meaning of Capital', ch. 3 in P. Arestis, G. Palma and M. Sawyer (eds), *Capital Controversy and the History of Economic Thought: Essays in Honour of Geoff Harcourt* (London: Routledge).

Davidson, P. (1994) *Post Keynesian Macroeconomic Theory* (Aldershot: Edward Elgar).

Dimand, R. (1994) 'Mr Meade's Relation, Kahn's Multiplier and the Chronology of the *General Theory*', *Economic Journal*, vol. 104, 1139–1142.

Earl, P. (1990) *Monetary Scenarios: A Modern Approach to Financial Systems* (Aldershot: Edward Elgar).

Feldstein, M. and C. Horioka (1980) 'Domestic Saving and International Capital Flows', *Economic Journal*, vol. 90, 314–29.

Goodwin, R. M. (1949) 'The Multiplier as Matrix'. *Economic Journal*, vol. 59. Reprinted (1983) as ch. 1 in *Essays in Linear Economic Structures* (London: Macmillan).

Harcourt, G. C. (1976) 'The Cambridge Controversies: Old Ways and New Horizons – Or Dead End?' *Oxford Economic Papers*, vol. 28. Reprinted in C. Sardoni (ed.) (1992), *On Political Economists and Modern Political Economy: Selected Essays of G. C. Harcourt* (London: Routledge).

— (1995) 'A "Modest Proposal" for Taming Speculators and Putting the World on Course to Prosperity', *Economic and Political Weekly*, vol. 29. Reprinted as ch. 3 in *Capitalism, Socialism and Post Keynesianism: Selected Essays of G. C. Harcourt* (Aldershot: Edward Elgar).

— P. H. Karmel and R. H. Wallace (1967) *Economic Activity* (Cambridge: Cambridge University Press).

— and M. Kitson (1993) 'Fifty Years of Measurement: A Cambridge View', *Review of Income and Wealth*, vol. 39, Essay 17.

— and V. G. Massaro (1964) 'A Note on Mr Sraffa's Subsystems', *Economic Journal*, vol. 74. Reprinted as ch. 12 in P. Kerr (ed.) (1982), *The Social Science Imperialists* (London: Routledge).

Harrod, R. F. (1939) 'An Essay in Dynamic Theory', *Economic Journal*, vol. 49, 14–33.

Hicks, J. R. (1936) 'Mr Keynes' Theory of Employment', *Economic Journal*, vol. 46, 238–53.

Kahn, R. F. (1931) 'The Relation of Home Investment to Unemployment', *Economic Journal*, vol. 41, 173–98.

Kaldor, N. (1955–56) 'Alternative Theories of Distribution', *Review of Economic Studies*, vol. 23, 83–100.

— (1985) *Economics Without Equilibrium* (New York: M. E. Sharpe).

Kalecki, M. (1937) 'A Theory of the Business Cycle', *Review of Economic Studies*, vol. 4, 77–97.

Keynes, J. M. (1936) *The General Theory of Employment, Interest and Money* (London: Macmillan).

— (1937a) 'Letter to B. Ohlin, 27 January 1937', reprinted in *The Collected Writings of John Maynard Keynes*, vol. XIV (London: Macmillan for the Royal Economic Society, 1973).

— (1937b) 'Alternative Theories of the Rate of Interest', *Economic Journal*, vol. 47. Reprinted in *The Collected Writings of John Maynard Keynes*, vol. XIV (London: Macmillan for the Royal Economic Society, 1973).

— (1937c) 'The "Ex Ante" Theory of the Rate of Interest', *Economic Journal*, vol. 47. Reprinted in *The Collected Writings of John Maynard Keynes*, Vol. XIV (London: Macmillan for the Royal Economic Society, 1973).

Lawson, T. (1994) 'A Realist Theory for Economics', ch. 13 in R. E. Backhouse (ed.), *New Directions in Economic Methodology* (London: Routledge).

— (1997) *Economics and Reality* (London: Routledge).

Meade, J. E. (1933) *Public Works in their International Aspect*, pamphlet published by the New Fabian Research Bureau. Reprinted as ch. 2 in S. Howson (ed.) (1988), *The Collected Papers of James Meade: Volume 1, Employment and Inflation* (London: Unwin Hyman).

— (1975) 'The Keynesian Revolution', ch. 10 in M. Keynes (ed.), *Essays on John Maynard Keynes* (Cambridge: Cambridge University Press).

— (1993) 'The Relation of Mr Meade's Relation to Kahn's Multiplier', *Economic Journal*, vol. 103, 664–5.

Patinkin, D. (1976) *Keynes' Monetary Thought: A Study of its Development* (Durham: Duke University Press).

— (1993) 'On the Chronology of the General Theory', *Economic Journal*, vol. 103, 647–63.

— (1994) 'Mr Meade's Relation, Kahn's Multiplier and the Chronology of the *General Theory*: Reply', *Economic Journal*, vol. 104, 1143–46.

Pollin, R. (ed.) (1997) *The Macroeconomics of Finance, Saving, and Investment* (Michigan: University of Michigan Press).

Robertson, D. H. (1936) 'Some Notes on Mr Keynes' General Theory of Employment', *Quarterly Journal of Economics*, vol. 51, 168–91.

— (1937) 'Alternative Theories of the Rate of Interest', *Economic Journal*, vol. 47, 428–36.

— (1940) 'Effective Demand and the Multiplier', ch. 9 in *Essays in Monetary Theory* (London: P. S. King).

Robinson, J. (1937) *Introduction to the Theory of Employment* (London: Macmillan).

— (1974) 'History Versus Equilibrium', *Thames Papers in Political Economy*. Reprinted (1979) in *Collected Economic Papers*, Vol. V (Oxford, Blackwell).

— (1975) *Collected Economic Papers*, Vol. II, 2nd edn (Oxford: Blackwell).

Skidelsky, R. (1992) *John Maynard Keynes*: Volume two: *The Economist as Saviour, 1920–1937* (London: Macmillan).

Part II
Intellectual Biographies

6
Joan Robinson, 1903–1983*

1

It is now over a decade since Joan Robinson died in Cambridge on 3 August 1983. Though there have been volumes of essays, articles, including issues of journals, and at least one book devoted to an evaluation of her contributions, no obituary article of Joan Robinson has been published in this *Journal*.[1] In one sense this is shameful, but it does offer an opportunity for a longer-term perspective to be taken on her influence and achievements. Just before she died Harvey Gram and Vivian Walsh (1983) published in the *Journal of Economic Literature* a judicious evaluation of Joan Robinson's impact on the profession, based on her six volumes of collected papers (Robinson, 1951–79, *Collected Economic Papers* (*C.E.P.*) (one of which was the index compiled by Prue Kerr and Murray Milgate in language and with wit which must have delighted the author). Gram and Walsh's conclusions have stood the test of time but developments in the subject since then allow us now to reinforce their view that she *had* made lasting contributions, despite her own distress and near nihilism in the last years of her life.

* Originally published in *The Economic Journal*, vol. 105, September 1995, 1228–43. I am most grateful to Ann Bailey, John Bailey, Willy Brown, Ha-Joon Chang, Phyllis Deane, Peter Groenewegen, Alan Hughes, Barbara Jeffrey, Robin Jeffrey, Jan Kregel, Bruce McFarlane, Cristina Marcuzzo, Peter Nolan, Mića Panić, Luigi Pasinetti, Hans Singer and Ajit Singh for their comments on a draft of this essay.

The essay is in eight sections. In section II I give a brief outline of her life and career. The rest of the essay is concerned with the development of her thought; it includes an account of the sharp changes of view and direction over her working life and possible reasons for them. Her favourite saying of Keynes was: 'If someone persuades me that I'm wrong, I change my mind. What do *you* do?' Her own life was a splendid example of this attitude.

II

Joan Robinson was born in 1903 into an upper-middle-class family with a tradition of dissent. Her great-grandfather was Frederick Maurice, the Christian Socialist, her father was Major-General Sir Frederick Maurice, of the infamous Maurice debate in 1918. Joan was one of five children. She read history at St Paul's Girls' School and came up to Girton in 1922 to read economics because she wanted answers to questions about unemployment and poverty. (She felt she did not get them from the Economics Tripos and certainly not from her supervisor Marjorie Tappan-Hollond – they did not get on at all.) She 'graduated' with a second in 1925 – 'a great disappointment'. Joan and Austin Robinson, who was then at Corpus Christi, married in 1926 and went to India for two years. This started Joan's life-long love affair with the sub-continent, together with her abiding interest in the problems of developing countries. Though Cambridge was the base to which she always returned, Joan Robinson loved travelling: she visited China several times in the postwar years and, in her later years, spent part of each year in Kerala State in India. Her first visit to the United States of America in 1961 is still remembered with awe and – sometimes – affection by those who were at MIT and elsewhere at the time, see Turner (1989, ch. 14). Joan Robinson became a University Assistant Lecturer in 1934, a University Lecturer in 1937, a Reader in 1949, and a Professor in 1965. She 'retired' in 1971, remaining active into the last year of her life, despite poor health in the last few years, a fact which her indomitable spirit always refused to accept.

III

The critical Marshallian

> The more I learn about economics the more I admire Marshall's intellect and the less I like his character.
> Joan Robinson (1953; *C.E.P.*, vol. IV: 125)

It is no accident, therefore, that Marshall had a profound influence on the development of her thought, both directly from the *Principles* and indirectly through the teachings of Pigou, Keynes, Gerald Shove, Dennis Robertson and Austin Robinson. Her delightful 'spoof', 'Beauty and the Beast' (*C.E.P.*, vol. I, 1951), written with her friend Dorothea Morison when Joan was still an undergraduate, shows that she understood well his theoretical method and that she already despised his pious moralising and what she took to be fudges designed to hide unpleasant truths emerging. All his characteristic tools are displayed – an awareness of time, elasticities, consumers' and producers' surpluses, balance at the margin, maximising utility not only as mankind in the ordinary business of life but in social relationships too.

Her first major publication was *Economics is a Serious Subject* (1932). Here Pigou's tool-making imagery is much to the fore. She was wary of direct application to explanation and, especially, to policy, of the box of tools which, she argued, then made up economic theory. She discerned a conflict in the models between realism and tractability, warning that inevitably there must be a trade-off between the two. (Ronald Coase (1937: 386) responded to her challenge by providing a definition of the firm which was both.)

Yet it was a real problem which led her to develop what became in 1933 *The Economics of Imperfect Competition* (1933*a*) – why had not the depressed conditions of the 1920s and early 1930s caused many more firms actually to close down, at least temporarily, an inescapable inference of the Marshallian/Pigovian theory of the firm?[2] The answer was to be found, she argued, in Piero Sraffa's 'pregnant suggestion' in 1926 that it was demand rather than rising marginal costs which determined levels of production in firms. The firms concerned should be analysed as mini-monopolies operating in competitive environments, setting rather than adapting to prices set by the impersonal forces of the market. The concept of the marginal revenue curve, which arose, as far as Joan Robinson and Richard Kahn were concerned, in an essay by Austin Robinson's pupil, Charles Gifford, provided the immediate impetus and appropriate tool, allowing Joan Robinson to make a unified survey of the issues classified under the rubric of the economics of imperfect competition. She may well have seen Kahn's Fellowship Dissertation, 'The Economics of the Short Period' (1929, 1989), before her first draft was written and she had his help, advice and criticism during much of the book's creation: '... I have had the constant assistance of Mr R. F. Kahn. The whole technical apparatus was built up with his aid and many of the major problems ... were solved as much by him as by me' (1933*a*: v).[3]

Many years later, she argued that the principal result of the book was to throw doubt on the marginal productivity theory of distribution, destroying the equality of the real wage with the marginal product. But this is hindsight history – certainly, the claim does not 'hit you in the eye' when you read the relevant sections of the 1933 book (Books VIII and IX). It is true, of course, as Cristina Marcuzzo (29 December 1994) reminded me, that Joan Robinson's discussion implies that '*when* monopoly is introduced the equality does not hold, and [that] this is a blow to the theory of distribution based on perfect competition'. Nevertheless, as just one example, in Joan Robinson's 1937 paper on disguised unemployment she discussed the nature of disguised unemployment explicitly in terms of wages and marginal products: 'The wage received by a man who remains in employment in a particular industry measures the marginal physical productivity of a similar man who has been dismissed from it' (1937*a*, 1947: 61). (The quote is from the second edition, published in 1947.)

That the unfit were not necessarily eliminated by a slump was, though, a damaging indictment of the workings of competitive capitalism and, thus, of its justifications, second in importance only to the Kalecki/Keynes demonstration in the early to mid 1930s that a lack of effective demand was characteristic of the uncontrolled workings of the system. Joan Robinson herself was subsequently to repudiate the book, essentially for its confinement within the Marshallian method which entailed the 'shameless fudge' that demand curves stayed still while businesspeople found their equilibrium prices by trial and error. Here is a succinct statement, dating from 1953, from her article in the *Economic Journal*, '"Imperfect competition" revisited.'

'In my opinion, the greatest weakness of the *Economics of Imperfect Competition* is one which it shares with the class of economic theory to which it belongs – the failure to deal with time. It is only in a metaphorical sense that price, rate of output, wage rate or what not can move in the plane depicted in a price–quantity diagram. Any movement must take place through time, and the position at any moment of time depends upon what it has been in the past. The point is not merely that any adjustment takes a certain time to complete and that (as has always been admitted) events may occur meanwhile which alter the position, so that the equilibrium towards which the system is said to be tending itself moves before it can be reached. The point is that the very process of moving has an effect upon the destination of the movement, so that there is no such thing as a position of long-run equilibrium which exists independently of the course which the economy is following at a particular date' (*C.E.P.*, vol. II, 1960: 235). In later years she was to sum up this critique in the phrase 'History versus Equilibrium', see Joan Robinson (1974*a*).

She continued to believe that the analysis in Book V on 'Price Discrimination' retained its essential validity. It had long been standard fare in textbooks, the sort of received wisdom that is so deeply entrenched that the originator no longer gets any credit for it.

IV

The pioneering Keynesian

As we noted, Joan Robinson read economics at Cambridge because she wanted to know why poverty and unemployment existed. Her time in India in the 1920s deepened her hatred of poverty and injustice. Keynes's *Treatise on Money* was published in 1930. Joan Robinson saw Keynes as trying guiltily to break out of the confines of the Marshallian dichotomy in order to analyse the causes and cures of prolonged unemployment as well as deflations and inflations of the general price level. The discussions of the 'Circus' about the *Treatise on Money* and Keynes's lectures in the 1930s as the embryonic *General Theory* emerged were an obvious outlet for Joan Robinson's passionate search for truth.

She wrote two perceptive interim progress reports in the early 1930s on the emerging ideas, Robinson (1933*b*, *c*). It is interesting to see that in one of them, while she perceived what Keynes was doing (possibly even more clearly than he did himself), she was still, like him, enough under Marshall's influence to call his hints and outlines those of a *long-period* theory of underemployment equilibrium. Keynes 'had failed to notice [when he wrote the *Treatise on Money*] that he had incidentally evolved a new theory of the long-period analysis of output' (1933*c*, *C.E.P.*, vol. I, 1951: 56). The methodology of the *Treatise on Money* is explicitly in evidence: the full stock-flow equilibrium is a long-period one, with only normal profits being made and saving equal to investment (on the *Treatise on Money*'s definitions).

By the time *The General Theory* was written and published the emphasis had changed firmly to the short period, as is witnessed to, first and foremost, by Keynes's list of what is locked up in the *ceteris paribus* pound, see Keynes (1936: 245), and, secondly, by Joan Robinson's own excursion into long-period analysis. She did this mainly in order to see whether the results of *The General Theory*, e.g. the paradox of thrift, see Joan Robinson (1937*a*), were robust, even though she regarded the exercise by then as very much economics for the economists and certainly not the principal province of *The General Theory* itself, see her letter to Keynes about her long-period analysis, in his *Collected Writings* (*C.W.*, vol. 13, 1973: 647–8). Nevertheless, in her 'told to the children' exposition of the new propositions, Joan Robinson remained distinctly old-fashioned when considering long-period propositions: 'For the discussion of problems involving broad changes over the course of generations, in population, the rate of technical progress or the general social forces influencing thriftness, it is possible to regard fluctuations in employment as a secondary consideration, and to conduct the discussion in terms of a self-regulating system' (1937*b*: 84).

Joan Robinson's important set of essays (1937*a*) also contained her discussion of the concept of disguised unemployment, so (ultimately) bringing together her observations while in India with her understanding of and contributions to the new theory emerging in Cambridge. They also contain an exposition of what was to become known in the literature as the Harris–Todaro model of migration (1970). Pervez Tahir (1990) has documented this in telling detail.

V

Marx, money, distribution and growth

Now a sea change starts to occur in her approach and views. Probably the single most important stimulus was meeting Michal Kalecki for the first time in 1936, a meeting which marked the beginning of their long, close friendship and vigorous intellectual exchanges. Joan Robinson was the greatest champion of the clear-cut case for the independent discovery by Kalecki of the principal propositions of *The General Theory*. Most important for her own subsequent development was her introduction to a framework of analysis which originated via Tugan-Baranovsky in Marx's writings and which Kalecki used for his solution of the realisation problem. Increasingly, Joan Robinson came to feel that this framework was more appropriate for understanding the workings of capitalism (and, indeed, at a very basic level, of economic systems generally).

Before she met Kalecki, Joan Robinson had become interested in Marxist thought. She reviewed John Strachey's 1935 book in this *Journal* in 1936 but she had not then fully mastered the structure of Marx's ideas. That she eventually did, for Keynesian/Kaleckian issues, is shown most convincingly in her superb account of 'Kalecki on capitalism' in the memorial issue for Kalecki in the Oxford Institute *Bulletin* in 1977. There, she shows how the pricing policies of firms, the different saving behaviour of the wage-earners and the capitalists (the latter sub-divided into entrepreneurial and managerial decision-makers, on the one hand, and a passive rentier class, on the other), and the dominant importance of profit-making and accumulation, may be combined in a simple short-period model of the determination of employment and distribution to illustrate the possibility of an under employment rest state. The same structure underlay the analysis of her *magnum opus* of 1956 and its follow-up in 1962 but it was not as clearly set out as in 1977.

We shall never know whether in their first discussions Kalecki employed the apparatus of his 1936 review in Polish of *The General Theory*, see Kalecki, *Collected Works* (*C.W.*, vol. I, 1990: 223–32); but certainly his use there of a micro foundation in which imperfect competition was the general, and pure competition the special, case from which to build upwards to the central result of *The General Theory* would have been congenial to her later thoughts and expositions. And his critique in his review of the details of Keynes's theory of investment was mirrored in her own subsequent critique, that it was an unholy mass of *ex ante* and *ex post* factors which needed to be separated by taking account of the two-sided relationship between profits and investments. Actual investment helped to create actual profits, expected profits (themselves related to actual profits) helped to determine planned investment. The relationship originally suggested by Kalecki became the substance of her famous banana diagram in Essay 2 of the 1962 *Essays in the Theory of Economic Growth* (1962*a*: 48). She now presented the arguments in a more digestible form than in the 1956 book.

But this is running ahead to her postwar contributions. We must mention, first, her *Essay on Marxian Economics* (1942), written during the early days of the war. Gerald Shove (1944) was more sympathetic to her interpretation of Marx than to her exposition of what the 'academic economists' (read, principally Marshall) had to say on overlapping issues. A throw-away remark in the book – to the effect that as there had been growth since the Industrial Revolution began and as the equilibrium rate of profits was associated with zero investment, '[A]bnormal profits [must have been] the normal rule' (1942: 60–1) – precipitated an extraordinary exchange of letters between Joan Robinson, Maurice Dobb and Shove. The subsequent story is discussed in Araujo and Harcourt (1993; 1995). Keynes's response to her *Essay* (in a letter to Mrs Austin Robinson [*sic*] 20 August 1942) – that it was 'as well written as anything you have done ... despite the fact that there is something intrinsically boring in an attempt to make sense of what in fact is not sense [and that he was] left with the feeling ... that [Marx] had a penetrating and original flair but was a very poor thinker indeed' – reveals more about Keynes than Marx.

Joan Robinson developed Keynesian ideas in at least two directions in the postwar years. First, she had a deep understanding of money and its roles in economic systems, something which is often forgotten – but not by Frank Hahn (1972: 205), who quotes with approval her remark that 'Money ... gets the blame for the fact that the future is uncertain', adding that he 'for one, [is] ready to forgive and forget'. She was active in Labour Party circles in making the case for permanently cheap money, using uncompromising Keynesian arguments, see Howson (1988). She also played a prominent part in the liquidity preference, loanable funds debates which so split members of the Faculty of Economics and Politics at Cambridge at the time. (Harry Johnson tried to build a bridge – 'Some Cambridge Controversies in Monetary Theory' (1951–2) – only to be criticised by both sides of the debate for his efforts.) Joan Robinson's main concern was with the determination of the rate of interest which gave the title to an influential set of essays (1952*b*). She emphasised Keynes's insight that in macro analysis we must always be on our guard against the fallacy of composition. The use of *one*–representative–agent models to analyse systemic behaviour will never do, certainly not in an analysis of the determination of prices in the market for financial assets. There, as Keynes and then Kahn and Joan Robinson argued, the equilibrium rate of interet is the level which brings about at least a momentary if uneasy truce between the bulls and the bears (and bullishness and bearishness). If there were *not* differences of opinion between the two groups no balance or state of rest, not even momentarily, would be possible.

Her essay is a particularly good example – Kahn's 1931 article on the multiplier is another – of the Marshallian/Keynesian method of looking at parts of the economy in sequence, holding constant or abstracting from what is going on, or least the *effects* of what is going on elsewhere, for the moment.[4] In this way Marshall hoped we would get definite, if partial, results and that, if we went right round the economy, we would eventually be able to bring all our results together to give a full, overall picture. That the procedure was inconsistent with his deeper vision that economic processes were akin to systemic interrelated biological processes he – as well as Joan Robinson and Kahn – seem to have forgotten. This may be one of the reasons why in the end both Marshall and Joan Robinson (but not Keynes nor Kahn?) thought that they had ultimately failed – not, I suppose, from realising that by following the procedure, they were attempting the impossible, but because it was the procedure itself which was at fault.[5]

The other development was what Joan Robinson called 'generalising *The General Theory* to the long period' – the distinctively Cambridge contributions by Kahn, Kaldor, Joan Robinson, Piero Sraffa and, later, Luigi Pasinetti – to the postwar theory of growth, itself sparked off by Harrod's article (1939) just before the war and given fresh impetus by the publication of his book (1948) just after it. Kahn dates the birth of these developments in Cambridge as the early summer of 1948. Kahn, Joan Robinson and Sraffa were staying in the Dolomites. They read together the proofs of Harrod's book because there was too much snow to allow much rock-climbing. Nevertheless, long before this there were signs of prior conception, as far as Joan Robinson was concerned, e.g. in her work on Marx and her pioneering work on the long-period aspects of *The General Theory* in 1935, utilising the then fashionable concept of the elasticity of substitution and Marshall's definition of the long period, both of which she subsequently abandoned as incoherent and/or inappropriate, see Kregel (1983). Subsequently she wrote an introduction to the English translation of Rosa Luxemburg's *Accumulation of Capital* (1951), and exploratory articles in this *Journal* (1949, 1952). These insights came to fruition in 1956 as *The Accumulation of Capital*, the same year in which two illustrious *Keynesians*, Trevor Swan (remember him?) and Bob Solow, independently published their explicitly styled neoclassical growth models as partial answers to Harrod's conundrums. (Both explicitly assumed background Keynesian policies to prevail in order to allow 'the dynamical principle of "substitution" ... seen ever at work' (Marshall, 1961: p. xv) to do its thing unhampered. Swan took the further precaution (in an appendix) of putting up 'a scare crow ... to keep off the index number birds and Joan Robinson herself' (pp. 343–4)).

In an (unpublished) preface to later editions, Joan Robinson identified the four major issues the book was intended to address. She developed a model of an unregulated free enterprise economy in which firms 'within limits set by their command of finance' determine the rate of capital accumulation, while members of the public, constrained 'by their command of purchasing power, are free to make the rate of expenditure what they please ... [a] model ... not unrealistic in essential respects'.

The model was to be used 'to analyse the chances and changes of the development of an economy as time goes by [by considering] four distinct groups of question':

(1) We make comparisons of situations, each with its own past, developing into its own future, which are different in some respects (for instance the rate of accumulation going on in each) in order to see what the postulated difference entails.

(2) We trace the path which a single economy follows when the technical conditions (including their rate of change) and the propensities to consume and to invest are constant through time.
(3) We trace the consequences of a change in any of these conditions for the future development of the economy.
(4) We examine the short-period reaction of the economy to unexpected events.

In the original preface she explained the rationale of the analysis and of the scenarios examined, together with the thrusts of the approach: a return to classical analysis of growth, distribution and technical progress over time while abstracting, for the most part, from the details of the theory of value and other aspects of the neoclassical interlude between the Classicals and Marx, on the one hand, and Keynes, on the other, but taking in the new ideas associated with the Keynesian revolution. (The latter were to be set, though, in a Marxian framework due primarily, I believe, to Kalecki's influence.)

But, of course, the positive enterprise – Golden Age relationships and so on, all of which were to be preparatory to the examination of motion and processes – was bedevilled by the simultaneous and parallel fights over distribution theory and the meaning (which was sidetracked into questions of the measurement) of capital in the neoclassical supply and demand approach as compared to its meaning and role in a Marxian/Keynesian view of the world. Thus, the Wicksellian analysis of the choice of technique in the economy as a whole (which started in Joan Robinson's famous 1953–4 *Review of Economic Studies* paper on the production function and the theory of capital) found a place in the arguments of *The Accumulation of Capital* only after the main propositions of the comparative dynamic analysis had been established within a model containing only one technique at any moment of time. Though Joan Robinson clearly stated her positive methods and contributions in the 1956 book and again, more succinctly, in *Essays in the Theory of Economic Growth* (1962a), especially Essay 2, the capital theory debates tended to overshadow them all, especially when they hotted up in the mid 1960s with the *Quarterly Journal of Economics* (*QJE*) symposium on reswitching and capital-reversing. The symposium was the response to the attempt by

David Levhari (1965) to rid the system of the implications of the Ruth Cohen Curiosum and so preserve the robustness of the crucial neoclassical conceptual stance that price was an index of scarcity in both the market for onions and the market for 'capital'.

Certainly Joan Robinson contributed to this aspect of the debate – the Ruth Cohen Curiosum was named by her, called 'a perverse relationship' and explicitly set out in the 1953–4 article and 1956 book (pp. 109–10) under the subheading, 'A Curiosum'. She joined in the *QJE* exchanges in 1967, in the company of K. A. Naqvi. Increasingly, however, she thought it was all beside the point. For example, there is her cryptic injunction to Gallaway and Shukla (1974) – 'Do not bother. Neoclassical theory is no better off even when there is no reswitching (p. 348n*)' – and her last *Quarterly Journal of Economics* article, 'The Unimportance of Reswitching' (1975). Rather, she pursued relentlessly her methodological critique, the illegitimacy of using comparisons (differences) to analyse processes (changes), History versus Equilibrium, the need to be clear about the limitations and applicability of models in logical time *vis à vis* those in historical time. The former are able to answer questions framed as 'what would be different if...?' The latter are concerned with those which may be posed as 'what would follow if...?'[6] It is shameful that despite the great emphasis that has been put on path dependency in recent years (by Franklin Fisher and Frank Hahn amongst many others) rarely is Joan Robinson (or Nicky Kaldor) ever given credit for identifying the issues and setting out the conceptual framework for the subsequent analysis. But it is arguable that she was too dismissive of the doctrinal critique for it was a critique in an appropriate setting for the task in hand, of the conceptual foundations and intuitions of the supply and demand approach.

VI

Planning, the price mechanism and China

There was, moreover, a practical aspect to her work on the choice of technique. In the 1950s, on a visit to China, she gave a series of lectures, one of which was devoted to the question. It was set within the context of the Galenson and Leibenstein (1955), and Dobb (1954) and Sen (1960) analysis of the appropriate techniques to embody in accumulation in a developing country. Dobb and Sen had the Stalinist model at the back of their heads, whereas Joan Robinson insisted on a middle way, giving weight to employment creation as well as to rapidly increasing the surplus to be reinvested.[7] The analysis she sketched at the time was developed in much greater detail in the student's 'do-it-yourself' book, *Exercises in Economic Analysis* (1960). Though she always said she went to China to learn, not to teach, evidently she could not resist temptation at this particular juncture.

In the same set of lectures she discussed the role of the price mechanism in developing countries. Her published views on this may be found in her difficult but profound essay, 'The Philosophy of Prices' (*C.E.P.*, vol. II, 1960: 27–48) (which was too much for the Russians to take).[8] Joan Robinson always argued that to understand an economy we must start from its history, institutions and 'rules of the game', especially when we are trying to influence the form which the latter two should take. Here, however, she grappled with the inescapable facts of life of any society in which commodities are exchanged, having been produced by labour and commodities, and a price mechanism rules: that there is a two-way interchange between incomes and prices and that the appropriate price structure for the desired development of the economy may not throw up for significant sections of the population incomes which are consistent with society's perception of what is a decent, acceptable and humane standard of life. This problem is made even more complicated by the fact that in one form of (pure) price system incomes arise from prices which are related to commodities produced by specific factors while in the other form of pure price system which she identifies, factors are not specific, can operate in any sector.

In outline and intent, the lectures, together with her views on population control, are very close to the pragmatic, gradualist, trial and error, mix of the market, openness, and central control which now characterises the Chinese economy. This is possibly an interesting thought about lectures which were first written in the 1950s.[9]

VII

The last years

Joan Robinson was ill for much of the last decade of her life and deeply distressed about the arms race, see her Tanner Lectures on this theme, Joan Robinson (1981). She became more and more pessimistic, even nihilistic, in her last years. Two late papers reflect these attitudes. Both were either written or published in 1980. The more optimistic of the two is a joint paper with Amit Bhaduri in the *Cambridge Journal of Economics*. The more pessimistic one is 'Spring Cleaning' which was published after her death as 'The Theory of Normal Prices and the Reconstruction of Economic Theory' in Feiwel (1985).

In the first article, Bhaduri and Joan Robinson define the role and application of Sraffa's critique and analysis.[10] His contribution is interpreted not only as a fundamental critique of the neoclassical concept of prices as indexes of scarcity within the supply and demand framework, but also as the starting point for thinking in terms of thought experiments about production, distribution and technical change – 'the influence of changes in technology on demand for labour, on accumulation and on effective demand' (p. 111). The results were then to be grafted onto the Keynesian approach, as Joan Robinson saw it, whereby in a Marxian/Kaleckian framework, the laws of motion could be analysed in historical time rather than in the logical time of neoclassical analysis and the Sraffian critique. 'Spring Cleaning' was much more radical – a plea to clear out the whole house, not only the attic – and start again.[11]

VIII

Conclusion

Joan Robinson died in August 1983. She had had a rewarding period in Autumn/Winter 1982 teaching at Williams College in the United States, see Juliet Schor's account in Marjorie Turner's *Joan Robinson and the Americans* (1989: pp. 204–7). On her return to Cambridge in late December she became depressed and disoriented for the month or so before she had a massive stroke from which she never recovered.

In her late years Joan Robinson used to say of her critics: 'I wish they would stop paying me compliments and answer my questions instead'. For one critic in particular this is a harsh judgment. Paul Samuelson did try to answer them when she was alive and he paid Joan Robinson a fine tribute after her death. He described in Samuelson (1989) how she altered his prior perceptions of a major long-term process:

What I learned from Joan Robinson was more than she taught. I learned not that the general differentiable neoclassical model was special and wrong but that a general neoclassical technology does not necessarily involve a high steady-state output when the interest rate is lower. I had thought that such a property generalised from the simplest one sector Ramsey-Solow parable to the most general Fisher case.

(p. 137)

In probably their last ever public exchange (Joan Robinson (1975), Solow (1975)), Bob Solow (who liked, admired and was irritated by Joan in equal measure), agreed with Samuelson that: 'More generally, and more important, it is not true, even with all the standard assumptions, that steady states with lower interest rates have higher consumption per worker. [He did] not find the result hard to live with [because it occurred] within the framework of the neoclassical assumptions [so that at worst he had] to kiss a neat generalization good-by[e]' (pp. 51–2).

Frank Hahn (1989, p. 909) remained unrepentant, saying that he did not think she, or rather her writings, would be much remembered though he conceded that she had asked some important questions and that she had deep insight in monetary theory. Lawrence Klein (1989) appreciated her all-round abilities, arguing that the first 100 pages or so of *The Accumulation of Capital* were among the best for introducing anyone to our 'miserable subject' (Keynes, *C.W.*, vol. 14, 1973: 190), by 'laying bare [its] fundamental aspects' (p. 258). As ever, Ken Arrow (1989) is perceptive and generous and Dick Goodwin, a long-time fan, who always acknowledged the major influence she had been on his thought, described her remarkable economic intuition (unaided, in her case, by trained mathematical facility): 'Once I was giving a paper on a two-sector dynamical model ... of which I said that both sectors would exhibit both motions. She interrupted me to say that I was wrong: ... only one. I denied this ... But I was bothered and later ... discovered she was right' Goodwin (1989: 916).

Luigi Pasinetti's *New Palgrave* entry on Joan (1987) is a brilliant account of the person and of the nature of her contributions. Pasinetti particularly emphasises the aspect of team work in her contributions, while stressing as well her originality. These characteristics are obvious in both the making of *The Economics of Imperfect Competition* and of *The General Theory*, to which vols. XIII, XIV and XXIX of the *Collected Writings* bear eloquent witness, even though much of the discussion was oral. Pasinetti illustrates the theme in his discussion of the capital theory controversies and the ultimate downplaying of them by Joan. He writes: 'at this point the works of Joan Robinson merge into those of that remarkable group of Cambridge economists [he singles out Sraffa, Kaldor and Kahn as well as Joan] ... who took up, continued and expanded the challenge that Keynes had launched on orthodox economic theory. [They] started a stream of thought which is obviously far from complete. Its basic features ... are clear enough ... [–] a determined effort to shift the whole focus of economic theorizing away from the problems of optimum allocation of given resources ... and move it towards the fundamental factors responsible for the dynamics of industrial societies' (p. 216).

In his authoritative appreciation of Joan, the late Sukhamoy Chakravarty (1983) stressed her seriousness, that 'economics was not a "game" played for its own sake. She was profoundly concerned with [its] social relevance [and] attached much greater importance to the seriousness and integrity of an economist than to her/his ability to solve intellectual puzzles' (p. 1716). Profound as her own answers have been, she has also 'left us with a very rich set of questions to which we can devote ourselves profitably for years to come' (p. 1716).

Finally, in the obituary of her for the King's College *Annual Report* in October 1984 – it was drafted by her colleague, close friend and rival, Nicky Kaldor – we read:

It would be no exaggeration to say that, after Keynes, Joan Robinson would be widely regarded as the most prominent name associated with the Cambridge School of Economics. As a teacher she was brilliant ... As a writer she was prolific ... As a controversialist she was sometimes alarming ... She held her views with great conviction yet at the same time she was eager to look at every economic 'fact' and was ready to modify her views if these contradicted some of the assumptions on which she had been working. But behind her somewhat forbidding presence she possessed great warmth and sympathy.

(p. 34)

What did I learn from Joan and what do I think are the most valuable lessons she has for future generations in the trade? First, she taught us always to look at the conceptual basis of our theories. The theories themselves should start off from actual situations, from actual societies with explicit 'rules of the game', institutions, past histories and defined sociological characteristics. In analysing them we should ask what are the levels of abstraction at which we wish to argue and what exactly are the sorts of questions we are trying to answer. (In her later years, for example, she left us two, sometimes overlapping, agendas, her Ely Lecture, 'The Second Crisis in Economic Theory' (1972)[12] and 'What are the Questions?' (1977*b*).) Our aim should be to produce theories which contain the essential elements of the reality from which they start as the basic ingredients, in a sufficiently simplified form to allow us to see clearly the relationships at work and how exactly they intertwine. Moreover, we should always be careful to specify explicitly what sort of analysis is appropriate for the question asked. Perhaps, most of all, we should always keep at the back of our heads the injunction that: 'The purpose of studying economics is not to acquire a set of ready-made answers to economic questions, but to learn how to avoid being deceived by economists', Joan Robinson (1955; *C.E.P.*, vol. II, 1960: 17).

Let me close by saying that while Joan Robinson could often be harsh and unfair to others, she was quite as hard on herself; she was, most of all, as Dick Goodwin (1989) says, 'a passionate seeker after truth'. Ruth Cohen (1983) told us at the Memorial Service in October 1983: 'She was unrelenting in her arguments on matters she was working on ... and often frightening'. As she grew older, her writings became more 'tip of an iceberg' in character. Like many another great economist who aged, she assumed that readers knew as much as she did about the submerged portion. Future generations ought to follow up the tantalising hints revealed and reread her works for their wisdom, vigour, insight and sheer intelligence, and for the honesty and courage which they reveal.

She was basically a shy person, though not in the conventional sense – it was, rather, that she had very few words to say outside 'shop' (which nevertheless included a huge number of issues, many of which were outside even her broad boundaries of economics). Moreover, she responded to friendship and she was a warm person who was passionately and often quixotically loyal.[13] She could be very perceptive and kind and she had been known to apologise, albeit succinctly and gruffly. She is on record as saying that she was a bad mother but a good grandmother. As ever she was too harsh in her judgement – the first part is not a judgement her daughters agree with. Nearly the last time I saw her, her first grandchild, a splendidly democratic outgoing young Canadian, was chatting to her grandmother in her hospital bed, during her last illness, sure that the close bonds established between them long ago would allow them now to communicate as ever. Joan Robinson was never to see the democratic, just and equitable society she so deeply hoped her discipline would promote. Her own nature, class and upbringing would have made it difficult for her to have been a comfortable member of it. But her immediate family and their children have the attitudes and values which are both the necessary prerequisites for creating such societies, and for living comfortably within them.

Notes

1. One was commissioned soon after her death but it never materialised. As an ultimatum to deliver by January 1994 had no effect, I decided to write one myself.
2. For a subtle and deep account of the origins of imperfect competition and of the different intentions of Sraffa, on the one hand, and of Kahn and Joan Robinson, on the other, see Marcuzzo (1994).
3. I am indebted to Miss Jacqueline Cox, the Modern Archivist at King's College, Cambridge, for her help and advice on this and other matters. Professor Yoshihiko Hakamata of Chuo University, Tokyo, has kindly allowed me to see his extremely detailed analysis of the making of Kahn's dissertation – there are four different versions of it in Kahn's papers in the King's Archives – and of the correspondence between Kahn, Austin and Joan Robinson concerning Kahn's work and Joan Robinson's book.
4. In *The General Theory*, Keynes described the method as follows: 'The object of our analysis is not to provide a machine, or method of blind manipulation, which will furnish an infallible answer, but to provide ourselves with an organised and orderly method of thinking out particular problems; and, after we have reached a provisional conclusion by isolating the complicating factors one by one, we then have to go back on ourselves and allow, as well as we can, for the probable interactions of the factors amongst themselves. This is the nature of economic thinking.' (p. 297).
5. Jan Kregel (19 December 1994) tells me I am wrong to blame the *procedure* because it is the *problem* which is intractable.

6. That Joan Robinson posed the two different questions so clearly and sharply may owe something to Dennis Robcrtson's criticism of her earlier formulation, see Robertson (1957: 95–6) and Joan Robinson (*CEP*, vol. 2, 1960: 130). I am indebted to Bruce McFarlane for this comment.

7. Jan Kregel has pointed out to me (19 December 1994) that this could well be another sign of Kalecki's influence on Joan Robinson for he was arguing much the same thing for Poland at this time.

8. '"The Philosophy of Prices" was written after some discussion with Soviet economists. They would not accept it', Joan Robinson (1974b: xii).

9. Peter Nolan told me that the leading Chinese economist Dong Fureng (who talked to Joan for a day in the 1970s) wrote a tribute to her after she died, stressing how important she was to Chinese economic thought. Sadly, the only copy was lost in the post between China and the United Kingdom.

10. I have discussed elsewhere, see Harcourt (1990), the nature of the major influence which Piero Sraffa had on the development of Joan Robinson's thought from when they first met in the late 1920s.

11. I have discussed the details of her arguments in, for example, Harcourt (1990: 55–7).

12. As President of the American Economic Association, John Kenneth Galbraith used the one piece of patronage of the presidency to choose Joan for the Ely Lecture. As he told Marjorie Turner (1989: 165), 'I never had any hesitation. I immediately chose Joan'. (Galbraith's 'failing whom' was Myrdal.) See also Galbraith (1983).

13. She also, as Luigi Pasinetti (19 December 1994) reminded me, had very wide-ranging views, the nature of which may be gauged, for example, by reading her 'beautiful work', *Economic Philosophy* (1962b).

References

Annual Report (1984) King's College, Cambridge, 32–4.

Araujo, J. A. T. R. and G. C. Harcourt (1993; 1995) 'Maurice Dobb, Joan Robinson and Gerald Shove on Accumulation and the Rate of Profits', *Journal of the History of Economic Thought*, vol. 15, Spring, 1–30; reprinted as a longer version in Harcourt (1995).

Arrow, K. J. (1989) 'Joan Robinson and Modern Economic Theory: An Interview', in Feiwel (1989), 147–85.

Berg, M. (ed.) (1990) *Political Economy in the Twentieth Century* (New York, London: Philip Allan).

Bhaduri, A. and J. Robinson (1980) 'Accumulation and Exploitation: An Analysis in the Tradition of Marx, Sraffa and Kalecki', *Cambridge Journal of Economics*, vol. 4, 103–15.

Chakravarty, S. (1983) 'Joan Robinson: An Appreciation', *Economic and Political Weekly*, vol. 18, 1712–6.

Coase, R. (1937) 'The Nature of the Firm', *Economica* (N.S.), vol. 4, November, 386–405.

Cohen, R. (1983) 'Address' at the Memorial Service in King's College, Chapel, 29 October.

Dobb, M. H. (1954) *On Economic Theory and Socialism. Collected Papers* (London: Routledge & Kegan Paul).

Eatwell, J., M. Milgate and P. Newman (eds) (1987) *The New Palgrave. A Dictionary of Economics*, vol. 4 (London: Macmillan).

Feiwel, G. R. (ed.) (1985) *Issues in Contemporary Macroeconomics and Distribution* (London: Macmillan).

— (ed.) (1989) *Joan Robinson and Modern Economic Theory* (London: Macmillan).

Galbraith, J. K. (1983) 'Joan Robinson: A Word of Appreciation', *Cambridge Journal of Economics*, vol. 7, 211.

Galenson, W. and H. Leibenstein (1955) 'Investment Criteria, Productivity, and Economic Development', *Quarterly Journal of Economics*, vol. 69, August, 343–70.

Gallaway, L. and V. Shukla (1974) 'The Neoclassical Production Function', *American Economic Review*, vol. 64, 407–36.

Goodwin, R. M. (1989) 'Joan Robinson – Passionate Seeker after Truth', in Feiwel (1989), 916–7.

Gram, H. and V. Walsh (1983) 'Joan Robinson's Economics in Retrospect', *Journal of Economic Literature*, vol. 21, 518–50.

Hahn, F. H. (1972) 'Review of Joan Robinson, *Economic Heresies: Some Old-Fashioned Questions in Economic Theory*', *Economica* (N.S.), vol. 39, May, 205–6.

— (1989) 'Robinson–Hahn Love-Hate Relationship: An Interview' in Feiwel (1989), 895–910.

Harcourt, G. C. (1990) 'On the Contributions of Joan Robinson and Piero Sraffa to Economic Theory', ch. 3 of Berg (1990), 35–67.

— (1995) *Capitalism, Socialism and Post-Keynesianism. Selected Essays of G. C. Harcourt* (Cheltenham: Edward Elgar).

Harris, J. R. and M. P. Todaro (1970) 'Migration, Employment and Development: A Two-Sector Analysis', *American Economic Review*, vol. 60, March, 126–42.

Harrod, R. F. (1939) 'An Essay in Dynamic Theory', *Economic Journal*, vol. 49, 14–33.

— (1948) *Towards a Dynamic Economics. Some Recent Developments of Economic Theory and their Application to Policy* (London: Macmillan).

Howson, Susan (1988) '"Socialist" Monetary Policy: Monetary Thought in the Labour Party in the 1940s', *History of Political Economy*, vol. 20, no. 4, 543–64.

Johnson, H. G. (1951–2) 'Some Cambridge Controversies in Monetary Theory', *Review of Economic Studies*, vol. 19, 90–104.

Kahn, R. (1929; 1989) *The Economics of the Short Period* (London: Macmillan).

— (1984) *The Making of Keynes' General Theory* (Cambridge: Cambridge University Press).

Kalecki, M. (1990) *Collected Works*, vol. I (ed. Jersy Osiatynski) (Oxford: Clarendon Press).

Keynes, J. M. (1930) *A Treatise on Money*, 2 vols (London: Macmillan) (*C.W.*, vols. V, VI, 1971.)

— (1936) *The General Theory of Employment, Interest and Money* (London: Macmillan) (*C.W.*, vol. VII, 1973.)

— (1973*a*) *The General Theory and After, Part I. Preparation. C.W.*, vol. XIII (London: Macmillan).

— (1973*b*) *The General Theory and After, Part II. Defence and Development. C.W.*, vol. XIV (London: Macmillan).

— (1979) *The General Theory and After, A Supplement. C.W.*, vol. XXIX (London: Macmillan).

Klein, L. R. (1989) 'The Economic Principles of Joan Robinson', in Feiwell (1989), 258–63.

Kregel, J. A. (1983) 'The Micro Foundations of the Generalisation of *The General Theory* and Bastard Keynesianism: Keynes's Theory of Employment in the Long and Short Period', *Cambridge Journal of Economics*, vol. 7, 743–61.

Levhari, D. (1965) 'A Nonsubstitution Theorem and Switching of Techniques', *Quarterly Journal of Economics*, vol. 79, 98–105.

Marcuzzo, M. C. (1994) 'At the Origin of Imperfect Competition: Different Views' in Vaughn (1994), 63–78.

Marshall, A. (1961), *Principles of Economics*. Ninth (Variorum) Edition with Annotations by C. W. Guillebaud, vol. 1, Text (London; Macmillan for the Royal Economic Society).

Pasinetti, L. (1987) 'Robinson, Joan Violet (1903–1983)' in Eatwell, Milgate and Newman (1987), 212–7.

Robinson, J. (1932) *Economics is a Serious Subject. The Apologia of an Economist to the Mathematician, the Scientist and the Plain Man* (Cambridge: Heffers).

— (1933*a*) *The Economics of Imperfect Competition* (London: Macmillan). 2nd edn, 1969.

— (1933*b*) 'A Parable of Saving and Investment', *Economica* (N.S.), vol. 13, February, 75–84.

— (1933*c*) 'The Theory of Money and the Analysis of Output', *Review of Economic Studies*, vol. I, October, 22–6. Reprinted in *C.E.P.*, vol. I, 1951, 52–8.

— (1936) 'Some Reflections on Marxist Economics' (a review of Strachey (1935)) *Economic Journal*, vol. 46, 298–302.

— (1937*a*) *Essays in the Theory of Employment* (Oxford: Basil Blackwell). 2nd edn, 1947.

— (1937*b*) *Introduction to the Theory of Employment* (London: Macmillan). 2nd edn, 1969.

— (1942) *An Essay on Marxian Economics* (London: Macmillan). 2nd edn, 1966.

— (1949) 'Mr Harrod's Dynamics', *Economic Journal*, vol. 59, March, 68–85. Reprinted in *C.E.P.*, vol. I, 1951, 155–74.

— (1951) 'Introduction' to Rosa Luxemburg, *The Accumulation of Capital* (London: Routledge and Kegan Paul).

— (1951–79) *Collected Economic Papers*, 6 vols (Oxford: Basil Blackwell).

— (1952*a*) 'A Model of an Expanding Economy', *Economic Journal*, vol. 62, March, 42–53. Reprinted in *C.E.P.*, vol. II, 74–87.

— (1952*b*) *The Rate of Interest and Other Essays* (London: Macmillan).

— (1953) *On Re-Reading Marx* (Cambridge: Students' Bookshop). Reprinted in *C.E.P.*, vol. IV, 1973, 247–68.

— (1953–4) 'The Production Function and the Theory of Capital', *Review of Economic Studies*, vol. 21, 81–106. Reprinted in *C.E.P.*, vol. II, 1960, 114–31.

— (1956) *The Accumulation of Capital* (London: Macmillan). 2nd edn, 1965, 3rd edn, 1969.

— (1960) *Exercises in Economic Analysis* (London: Macmillan).

— (1962*a*) *Essays in the Theory of Economic Growth* (London: Macmillan).

— (1962*b*) *Economic Philosophy* (London: Watts & Co).

— (1971) *Economic Heresies: Some Old-Fashioned Questions in Economic Theory* (London: Basic Books).

— (1972) 'The Second Crisis of Economic Theory', *American Economic Review*, vol. 62, May, 1–9. Reprinted in *C.E.P.*, vol. IV, 1973, 92–105.

— (1974*a*) 'History Versus Equilibrium' (London: Thames Polytechnic), reprinted in *C.E.P.*, vol. V, 1979, 48–58.

— (1974*b*) *Selected Economic Writings* (Bombay: Oxford University Press).

— (1975) 'The Unimportance of Reswitching', *Quarterly Journal of Economics*, vol. 89, February, 32–9. Reprinted in *C.E.P.*, vol. V, 1979, 76–89.

— (1977*a*) 'Michal Kalecki on the Economics of Capitalism', *Bulletin of the Oxford Institute of Economics and Statistics*, vol. 39, February, 7–17. Reprinted in *C.E.P.*, vol. V, 1979, 184–96.

— (1977*b*) 'What are the Questions?' *Journal of Economic Literature*, vol. 15, December, 1318–39. Reprinted in *C.E.P.*, vol. V. 1979, 1–31.

— (1980, 1985) 'Spring Cleaning', Cambridge, mimeo. Published as 'The Theory of Normal Prices and the Reconstruction of Economic Theory' in Feiwel (1985), 157–65.

— (1981) *The Arms Race* (The Tanner Lectures on Human Values) (Logan, Utah: University of Utah).

— and Morison, Dorothea (1951) 'Beauty and the Beast', *C.E.P.*, vol. I, 1951, 225–33.

— and Naqvi, K. A. (1967) 'The Badly Behaved Production Function', *Quarterly Journal of Economics*, vol. 81, November, 579–91. Reprinted in *C.E.P.*, vol. IV, 1973, 74–86.

Samuelson, P. A. (1989) 'Remembering Joan' in Feiwel (1989), 125–43.

Sen, A. K. (1960) *Choice of Techniques. An Aspect of the Theory of Planned Economic Development* (Oxford: Basil Blackwell).

Shove, G. F. (1944) 'Mrs Robinson on Marxian Economics', *Economic Journal*, vol. 54, 47–61.

Solow, R. M. (1975) 'Brief Comments', *Quarterly Journal of Economics*, vol. 89, February, 48–52.

Strachey, J. (1935) *The Nature of Capitalist Crisis* (London: Victor Gollancz).

Swan, T. W. (1956) 'Economic Growth and Capital Accumulation', *Economic Record*, vol. 32, 334–61.

Tahir, P. (1990) 'Some Aspects of Development and Underdevelopment: Critical Perspectives on Joan Robinson'. Unpublished PhD dissertation, Cambridge University Library.

Turner, M. (1989) *Joan Robinson and the Americans* (Armonk, New York: M. E. Sharpe).

Vaughn, K. I. (ed.) (1994) *Perspectives on the History of Economic Thought*, vol. X: *Method, Competition, Conflict and Measurement in the Twentieth Century* (Aldershot: Edward Elgar).

7
Lorie Tarshis, 1911–1993: In Appreciation*

I

Lorie Tarshis died in Toronto on 4 October 1993. By his death the profession has lost an eminent member, one who was an independently-minded, enthusiastic, original and lucid Keynesian. Tarshis was reared on the *Treatise of Money* by Wynne Plumptre at the University of Toronto. He attended the lectures by Keynes in the 1930s at which *The General Theory* took shape; and in his Cambridge PhD dissertation, Tarshis (1939a), he saw the required connections between the imperfect competition revolution contained in Joan Robinson's 1933 book and Richard Kahn's lectures on the economics of the short period (to which he went), on the one hand and the systemic analysis of *The General Theory*, on the other.

Lorie Tarshis was born in Toronto on 22 March 1911. His father, Dr Saul Singer, was a general practitioner and the city coroner. During a typhoid epidemic in Toronto in 1915, he contracted typhoid, possibly because of the post, and died, leaving Lorie's mother, Ella, a widow at 22 with two small children and a third on the way, a son who died in infancy. She soon married again. Her second husband was Joseph Tarshis, a retailer and wholesaler,

* Originally published in *The Economic Journal*, vol. 105, September 1995, 1244–55. I am most grateful to Omar Hamouda, Joan Harcourt, Susan Howson, Peter Nolan, Walter Salant, Tibor Scitovsky, Hans Singer, Inga Tarshis, Bob Wallace and Gavin Wright for their comments on a draft of this essay. I hope they will forgive me for not taking on board all their suggestions.

of whom Lorie was very fond and whose name he took. Lorie was educated at Huron Primary School, the University of Toronto School and, as mentioned above, the Universities of Toronto and Cambridge.

Tarshis taught at Tufts before the Second World War, served in the US army and, with his great friend George Housner, 'liberated' Rome (and met Inga-Maria Rappaport, who later became his second wife. His first marriage was to Elizabeth Kent in 1937. There was an amicable divorce in 1949. Lorie remained on excellent terms with their three children and their grandchildren. Lorie and Inga have a much loved daughter, Tanya.)

After the war Tarshis went to Stanford and stayed for over twenty years – I recount below the memories and tributes of his colleagues of the time. In 1971, sickened by the Vietnam war and the growing illiberalism of the United States, he returned to Canada as Chairman of the Division of Social Sciences of the newly formed Scarborough College of the University of Toronto. The economics department contained a wonderful group of (mostly) young people with whom I had the privilege of being a colleague (if not young) on two occasions (1977, 1980). Tarshis 'retired' in 1978, going, first, to the Ontario Economic Council to direct research (he continued to teach Keynes at Scarborough), then, in 1980 he returned to teaching, at Glendon College, York University in Toronto, where he became Professor and Acting Chair. At Glendon he worked closely with a mutual friend, Omar Hamouda, and was as respected and loved as ever by his colleagues and pupils. He taught into his 80th year. The last two years of his life were dogged by serious illness. He is desperately missed by all who knew him; yet no one would have wished on Lorie, always an active person mentally and physically (he played excellent squash well into his 70s), continuation of such a non-life.

II

At Toronto Tarshis was well-trained in the schemas of the *Treatise on Money* by Wynne Plumptre, who had recently returned from Cambridge. Having grown up in a small open economy, Tarshis especially appreciated the international aspects of the analysis. He also came from a tradition in which Canadian economic history was interpreted through the writings and teaching of Harold Innis. This, together with a keen interest in politics and industrial relations, ensured that Tarshis was always aware of the roles of historical processes and factual backgrounds in economic analysis. This overall background permeated all his work. For example, his two textbooks, Tarshis (1947 (1966), 1955) are liberally sprinkled with informative tables and crucial orders of magnitude of key variables and concepts. Virtually all his writings were intended to culminate in sensible, down-to-earth, national and/or international policy proposals. In his last years he was writing papers on what to do about the debt problems of developing countries e.g. Tarshis (1988), Dore and Tarshis (1990). Prior to this he worried about and derived schemes to offset the effects of the Euro-dollar market – 'the financial San Andreas fault of modern capitalism', he called it.

Tarshis went to Cambridge in September 1932 on a Massey Scholarship to read (in two years) for a second undergraduate degree, the Economics Tripos. His college was Trinity (Plumptre thought Lorie would get the best of all possible worlds if he were to be at the college of Dennis Robertson and meet Keynes, Kahn, Shove and Sraffa at King's and at Keynes's Political Economy Club).

Tarshis went with his Canadian friend, Bob Bryce, to Keynes's lectures. They expected to hear an elaboration of the arguments of the *Treatise on Money*. Instead, the system of *The General Theory* emerged before them over the four years they attended the lectures.[1] They were given the chance to buy and read *The General Theory* the weekend before its publication. They were most surprised by the omission (a tactical mistake, as it turned out) of the sections on the cooperative, neutral and entrepreneur economies, the arguments concerning which contained the essential clue to Keynes's innovations. In particular, they highlighted the crucial roles which money played from the start of an analysis of the economic system, both as a store of value and as the means of payment, especially of the money-wage. Many years later Tarshis was to write a critique of the exposition of Keynes's discussion of Say's Law in *The General Theory* and to show that the deficiencies of Keynes's arguments could be overcome by using the analysis of the cooperative, neutral and entrepreneur economies, see Tarshis (1989).

Like, I suspect, many others, Tarshis had never been able to make sense of Keynes's argument in *The General Theory* (p. 26) that, in a Say's Law world, competition between employers ensures that activity is ultimately constrained only by the upper limit set to employment by the marginal disutility of labour: hence Keynes's arguments concerning Say's Law in *The General Theory* only established that there were a number of neutral equilibria, lying anywhere on the *coinciding* aggregate demand and supply functions. But: 'If it is supposed that management's objective in a cooperative [or a neutral] economy is to maximise ... profits, and that each firm pays its workers on the basis of predetermined shares [either in kind or in money], then there is only one position of equilibrium for each...: where its output is at capacity', Tarshis (1989, p. 41). With activity in the economy on the way there, as it were, the upper constraint in the labour market will bite – full employment equilibrium will be attained. But this is not so in an entrepreneur economy where the aggregate demand function has a separate life of its own.[2]

Tarshis not only absorbed the message of the newly emerging macro theory, he also responded to the other revolution in theory of the time, imperfect competition. He was especially influenced by the writings of Piero Sraffa (whose 1926 paper and contributions to the 1930 symposium on the representative firm he had already taken on board as an undergraduate in Toronto), and also by Joan Robinson's 1933 book and related articles, and by Richard Kahn's lectures in the early 1930s on 'The economics of the short period'.[3]

Tarshis obtained a First in 1934 in a year remarkable for its Firsts and received a scholarship from Trinity to do a PhD. In his doctoral dissertation, 'The determinants of labour income', Tarshis (1939a), Tarshis saw the link between the two developments. He started with the firm as the basic unit of analysis – a starting point for analysis which he kept for the rest of his life. For example, it was a feature of the framework of his 1947 textbook. The specific question which he addressed in the dissertation was: what determines the course of real wages and the share of labour over the cycle? Purely competitive price-taking had only a preliminary role in his analysis. He mostly emphasised imperfect competition *à la* Kahn and Joan Robinson and, in the later stages of his analysis, the modifications implied by the writings of Berle and Means and others.[4] Starting from individual marginal cost curves, he analysed in great detail the conditions needed for correct aggregation up to the overall marginal cost of production in the economy as a whole. This laid the foundations for what I believe to be his single most important contribution, his chapter on the aggregate supply function in the *Festschrift* for Tibor Scitovsky, Boskin (1969). Tarshis always insisted that expositions of Keynes's system emphasise aggregate supply as well as aggregate demand, a feature which was lacking in most expositions in the early postwar period and which, I believe, was to have serious consequences in the 1970s and 1980s, see below.

As Luigi Pasinetti (1994) has recently argued, Tarshis's paper is the most profound exposition of the essential nature and purpose of the aggregate supply function since Keynes introduced it in *The General Theory*. The irony is that already in his dissertation Tarshis had built up to aggregates from an imperfectly competitive base; yet it is only in the 1980s that this approach has become fashionable in the profession at large. There is a fine survey of these developments by Huw Dixon and Neil Rankin (1991) and the two-volume collection on *New Keynesian Economics* edited by Gregory Mankiw and David Romer (1991), especially Vol. 1. Robin Marris's 1991 book is the culmination of *his* profound thinking on these matters since the 1940s on. Had Tarshis's dissertation been published in the 1940s, had his textbook been at least co-equal in numbers with Samuelson's, had Sidney Weintraub's writings had more impact and had Michal Kalecki's version of *The General Theory* (in his review of Keynes's *magnum opus*) been published in English instead of Polish, see Kalecki (1990) and Targetti and Kinda-Haas (1982), 40–50 years may not have to have gone by before the profession again explored this approach.

With such a topic for his PhD, it was no accident that Tarshis's dissertation should be an independently discovered version of Kalecki's macro theory of distribution – a coincidence which they recognised and about which they were delighted when they met in the late 1930s. In the Preface, Lorie acknowledged the early 1930s writings and/or lectures of Keynes, Joan Robinson and Kahn and of others – Kalecki, Dunlop – engaged 'during the past two years' on similar problems, the latter coinciding with Lorie finishing his 'rough' first draft in January 1938. Tarshis's aim was 'to deal with certain problems of functional distribution in a way consistent with recent findings in those two fields of economics ... to bridge the gap that exists between [them]' (1939a, p. i). Though the empirical findings of the dissertation were published, see Tarshis (1938, 1939b), the work as a whole never entered the public domain – as it should have done. The one publisher to whom it was sent rejected it on the advice of a contemporary who knew a superior rival when he saw one.[5]

I recently reread the dissertation and, surprise, surprise, it is sometimes hard going and obscure in places. But had it been published then, its importance could have been recognised and simpler versions, much in the mode of Kalecki's expositions, could have found their way into the literature and have been properly influential.[6]

What must be said, first, is that from the start of his professional life Tarshis never succumbed to the worst of the modern heresies: analysing systemic behaviour by the use of one representative agent. In 1979, Tarshis commented at the first ever session on Post Keynesian economics at an AEA meeting (it was held in Atlanta, Georgia). He had wise remarks to make (in Tarshis (1980)) about the fallacy of treating aggregates, e.g. flow of funds statements or even balance sheets for economies as a whole, as though they mimicked individual behaviour, were totals from which meaningful averages could be derived, rather than net outcomes of very disparate behaviour by the components e.g. those in credit lending to those in debit, or in liquidity preference theory, determining the overall rate of interest by achieving a balance at the margin, albeit often an uneasy truce, between the disparate views of bulls and bears.

What is unexpected for modern readers – this one anyway – is the great emphasis given by Tarshis in the dissertation to Keynes's concept of user cost. Christopher Torr (1994) has recently written a masterly exposition of the role of the concept in *The General Theory*, emphasising how it affects individual prices through being a crucial component of short-term marginal costs and also, as a consequence, of the general price level (even though user costs net out in the aggregate when the national income is constructed). Tarshis makes the same point in great detail (it was in a PhD dissertation after all).

Tarshis arrives at a key formulation for the overall share of wages in value added which is at least a first cousin to Kalecki's. The 'degree of monopoly' concept, suitably aggregated, is absorbed within it, not as an identity but as a deduction from assuming, as a first approximation, that firms are profit-maximisers – an assumption which is modified later on when the implications of Berle and Means's findings and oligopolistic structures are discussed. Tarshis has a sophisticated and systematic discussion of the nature of time periods and economic decisions, of when various costs may be regarded as variable rather than as fixed, and of what exactly it means to say that 'profits are to be maximised'. In this he shows much curiosity about the detailed facts of production, investment decisions and the like and their expression in economic theories and models. He has as much an eye for detail in an economic argument as did Richard Kahn, for example, without being a fuss pot about it all for himself, or for others.

Tarshis was awarded his PhD in 1939. His examiners were J. R. Hicks and Marjorie Tappan-Hollond, both of whom were, according to Tarshis, more nervous than the candidate at the viva (which spread over most of the day). Remembering how shy John Hicks was even in his later years, he may have been wary of a candidate who had some sharp criticisms to make, especially of Hicks's parallel work at the time.

Tarshis had to return from the United States for the viva, as he was already teaching at Tufts. There he was an influential member of the colony of 'bright young things' in Cambridge, Mass., who brought Keynes to Harvard. Tarshis was also one of the authors of the influential pamphlet, *An Economic Program for American Democracy* (1938), the arguments of which had an impact on Franklin Roosevelt's budget in 1938.

III

After the war Tarshis returned to Tufts before taking up his post at Stanford in 1946.[7] I have, see Harcourt (1993, pp. 79–80), discussed the frenetic making of his first textbook *The Elements of Economics* (1947) in those years and the disgraceful way in which Tarshis and his book were treated by the American right, led by the anti-new dealer Merwin K. Hart and, later, William Buckley Jnr., and implemented through Rose Wilder Lane's pre-McCarthyite pamphlet. Keynes and the 250 or so pages on Keynesian economics in Tarshis's book were the principal targets of the attack.

It is extraordinary, reading Tarshis's book today, to imagine that this could ever have happened. Tarshis explicitly claimed at the time that economic principles, including those of Keynes, were independent of political ideology (except, I suppose, of the very broadest sort that it would be wise to save capitalism from itself, if possible).

'The economist can give advice, but the businessman, the union leader, the congressman, the voter will take the final decision'. Tarshis (1947: x).

Tarshis returned to this episode in the Preface of his other text-book, Tarshis (1955). There he says:

> Since an earlier effort of mine was most strongly, and I believe unfairly, attacked (from outside the profession), I must make my position or point of view perfectly clear. [Tarshis] ... intended to teach one thing – a method, call it economic analysis – and not a conclusion ... There is one mold into which [he would like to think] all students of economics would comfortably fit ... an eagerness to apply the clearest and most objective thinking possible to economics problems ... 'right answers' are urgently needed, [only obtained] when minds as intelligent and as free from prejudice as possible are set to work [– the] only indoctrination to which [Tarshis] should like to contribute.
>
> (p. vi)

This is a most mild-tempered understatement, considering what had happened to him.

Tarshis's close friend, contemporary and colleague at Stanford, Tibor Scitovsky, captures the atmosphere of the period when he writes (25 January 1994):

> [Lorie] and I came here at the same time, in 1946, and we immediately became close friends, not only because we were the Department's youngest members and its only postwar recruits, but also, because we were its only revolutionaries, believers in macroeconomics and employment theory, the Keynesian revolution. No non-economist and no economist of later generations can imagine how revolutionary a revelation Keynes's book was to us, who were graduate students at the time. It was as obsessive as a political revolution or a religious conversion, and made us feel superior to unbelievers and anxious to convert them. I was only an enthusiastic convert; but Lorie, a student and true disciple of Keynes, participated in the making of that revolution, wrote the first and best introductory textbook on the subject; and his Stanford lectures gave this University the distinction of being the

first West of the Mississippi and one of the first in the whole country, to teach its students up-to-date economics. And Lorie's introductory lectures were delivered with all the passion appropriate to a revolutionary doctrine.

Revolutionaries, however, are usually attacked as subversives; and Lorie was not immune to that. Indeed, I suspect that the attacks on him were more violent and vicious than any on Keynes himself. But Lorie, unlike Galileo, stood up for his beliefs; and I am glad to add that the Department's chairman, and the University's president, stood up for Lorie and repudiated the pressures that he be dismissed.

By the late 1960s, perceptions had changed though Lorie still had to be careful about inessentials. In Jonathan Pincus's absorbing memoir (1994) of his 1967 Summer teaching with Lorie at the Robert Louis Stevenson School for Boys, Del Monte Forest, California, he recounts how 'Tarshis dressed more conservatively than usual [for] an afternoon tea for the local sponsors to meet the teachers'. Though Pincus knew that Tarshis's textbook 'had been red-listed by some conservatives, [the students] did not think of Tarshis as anything other than a bright, scholarly, somewhat conservative gentleman. ...Stanford economics was regarded as progressive ... because Paul Baran was employed there'.

Of his 1947 textbook itself: its features include a splendid blend of fact and theory and an integration of the interrelationships of micro and macro elements into the accounts of systemic behaviour. Significantly, the book is subtitled: *An Introduction to the Theory of Price and Employment.* Each is, of course, exposited separately – simultaneity can only go so far – but the reader is continually reminded of the to and fro between the two aspects. As I have already mentioned, the basic organising unit is the firm, refreshingly not the individual consumer, the fiction which bedevils so many textbooks and journal articles. The driving force of the economy is rightly seen as the managerial entrepreneurial 'agent', anticipating sales, setting (or initially, accepting) prices, offering employment and planning all aspects of accumulation. Not only does this way of proceeding make the firm and industry come alive, especially when it is allied with Tarshis's admirable knowledge of institutional detail and industrial differences, it also leads the student/reader readily into the formation of the national accounts and the relationship between the main aggregates – *C*, *I*, *G*, *X*, *M et al.* – as the modern theory of employment is unfolded.

Reflecting, in effect, on what he was trying to achieve then, Tarshis in his 1948 *American Economic Review* paper sets out a succinct summary of the still novel Keynesian system. He relates it to the classicals (in Keynes's sense) and makes the surprising claim that the *Treatise on Money* was perhaps the more revolutionary book, certainly much less (neo) classical, than *The General Theory*:

> A good case can be made for the assertion that the doctrine of *The General Theory* was mothered by the *Treatise* [*on Money*] and fathered by neoclassical economics. If so, we should have to admit that the child suffered from an extreme Oedipus complex.
>
> (p. 262)

In the article, Tarshis highlights the crucial role of investment and its determinants as being ultimately responsible for the possibility of underemployment rest states.

The attack by the illiberal forces in the United States, who loathed Keynes as much as Roosevelt, combined to stop Tarshis's book being widely used in Colleges and Universities. His book took the full force of this disgraceful gale; by the time the first edition of Paul Samuelson's Introductory text was published in 1948, the gale had just about blown itself out.

Samuelson's book was affected by the residual force but this did not stop it from being to American economics (and elsewhere) what J. S. Mill's *Principles* had been for British readers in the decades prior to Alfred Marshall's *Principles*. Thus the Keynesian cross and *IS* and *LM* (through Hicks and Hansen) became the two most preferred ways in which students 'learnt' Keynesian economics. In the 1960s this allowed a vulgarised version of the Phillips curve to be grafted on to the presentation, soon to be identified *as* Keynesian economics, so setting up a straw person for the monetarists and new classical macroeconomists to knock down. It also submerged Keynes's own and Tarshis's emphasis on the equal importance of the aggregate supply function with the aggregate demand function. Such an emphasis on the aggregate supply function would have made the effects of the oil price shocks and the stagflation episodes much easier to comprehend and to do something effective about them – and it may have prevented the monetarists and new classical macro-economists from so dominating theory and policy in the 1970s and 1980s.

Tarshis himself never wavered in the face of the initial and subsequent onslaught. He always emphasised the equal role of the aggregate supply function in his teaching and after he retired from teaching at 'Scarberia', he published in an appendix to Tarshis (1984) his basic approach to the determination of the level of activity, its accompanying general price level and the distribution of income between profits and wages. This is a refined and thoroughly thought through exposition of the original system building which he started in his doctoral dissertation.

Nor did he neglect the open economy and monetary aspects of the workings of modern capitalism. Initially with Paul Baran, who subsequently withdrew because of other commitments, Tarshis wrote a sound textbook, *Introduction to International Trade and Finance* (1955), on international matters which concerned the micro, macro and monetary aspects of trade and capital movements. The presentation was lucid, clear, and systematic. There is a judicious blend of theory, empirical illustrations and policy recommendations. In the latter, as ever, Tarshis's essential humanity combines well with his dispassionate understanding of both the economic and political aspects of the issues being discussed. Lorie was by nature an optimist and he believed that the characteristics of people in high places included good will as well as intelligence. So the tone of the book reflects Keynes's own last expressed wish that the wisdom of the old – read Adam Smith – and the discoveries of the new – read Keynes and his colleagues – would have a beneficial impact on the lot of ordinary men and women everywhere by the implementation of sensible policies through democratic national and international institutions.

In his last years Tarshis turned his attention to the debt crisis of developing countries. Starting from Keynes's analysis of the German reparations problem in the 1920s and 1930s, he outlined, once in the company of M. H. I. Dore (1990), 'a monetary solution to a monetary problem'.[8] Dore contributed the prisoners' dilemma aspects of the analysis. They argued that: 'It is time to forget a bad mistake made by the creditors as well as by the debtors' (p. 464).

Basically the Dore and Tarshis scheme required debt forgiveness in order to make the operations of the developing countries weighed down by debt more manageable, with the Central Banks of the developed countries taking enough debts off the hands of the commercial banks in their countries to ensure the latter's viability. There would be a reasonable penalty involved, spread over time, and the transactions would form part of the base on which the money supply in the developed economies could be erected. Safeguards could easily be designed if the money supply was thought to be growing too fast. There also would be incentives such that all banks in the developed economies would be treated equally within a given time span. The proposed plan was designed to allow trade and capital movements to rise in an ordered and enlightened way for both developing and developed countries.

IV

Lorie Tarshis had a fine original mind. Everything that he wrote was clear, deep and serious. But it was Lorie Tarshis the person who really made the greatest impact on those who knew him. An old-fashioned teacher *par excellence*,[9] a warm supportive colleague, a devoted husband and father, a cultured, witty companion, a doughty opponent on the squash court,[10] all these traits are testified to by his colleagues and/or former students from e.g. Stanford, the University of Toronto and Glendon College.

Bob Wallace, who first introduced me to Lorie at Stanford in the summer of 1965, writes (November 1994) of a key feature – his commendable earthiness and commonsense. In teaching his graduate class in 1964(5), he asked them to visualise that (i) they lived in 1948 on a 1948 salary [$x], (ii) they lived in 1964 on the same nominal income – so [there were] no corrections for the substantial inflation. [Lorie asked them to] choose which you prefer [they all chose 1948 of course].

He then put into circulation the 1948 Sears Roebuck catalogue and the (then) current 1964(5) catalogue. They had thousands and thousands of items. He ... asked [the students] to choose again. They got the point. Bob adds:

Like you I recall Lorie, as a most dignified courteous person – unreasonably modest, given his great contributions. Like you I found it a great pleasure to be with him. He had a calming influence, reflecting his own serenity.

I reproduce below the tribute of the late Professor Burnham Campbell, who was Lorie's student at Stanford[11] and who was at the University of Hawaii's East West Center.

Lorie Tarshis was one of many stars and stars[12] to be at Stanford just after WWII. 'Sitting at the feet' of this galaxy of the famous in our profession were perhaps a dozen or so graduate students. For most it was a very difficult situation. Lorie was a friend of this small group of graduate students, taking time for their questions, discussing economics (and life) with them and serving as a mentor in many, many ways. The Stanford faculty was exceptional in many things, but Lorie was one of the few who was exceptional in his empathy for his students as well.

Lorie was low key in the hot house Stanford atmosphere, teaching industrial organisation and international economics (a strange combination in retrospect) in his quiet but very intensive manner. He guided the department's then largely graduate student undergraduate teaching crew first through the intricacies of his pioneer 'Keynesian' introductory text and then his widely used text on international economics, both widely used at Stanford. When it became his turn to Chair the department, he proved not terribly efficient as an administrator and encountered problems that partly explain his later decision to leave. However, I remember more that he was the first Chair to recognise the unmet concerns of the graduate students and take action to make them participants in rather than spectators at the on-going Stanford intellectual circus.

In the company of some exceedingly bright people, Lorie came across as a consummate intellectual, a sophisticate whose interests, knowledge and understanding went far beyond the parochial concerns of his profession. He knew good wine, good food and could walk you through an art exhibit or talk you through a play or a book or even a political [crisis] with a seemingly inexhaustible fund of knowledge. All this is not really surprising given his earlier inclusion in Keynes'[s] inner circle, but his urbanity stood out in the Stanford of the fifties. But most of all, he [is] remembered by those of us who studied with him for his humanity and generosity.

(Phrases in non-square brackets are in the original)

The following extracts from some notes which Omar Hamouda (22 December 1994) sent me reinforce Campbell's account (except on Lorie's ability, or not, to run a whelk store):[13]

Lorie Tarshis joined the department of economics at Glendon College as chairman in January 1985. He occupied that position until June 1988 at which time he continued to lecture until June 1990. Lorie was a dream chair [;] he commanded respect and treated everybody ... the same. He made the department run smoothly and efficiently and had an extraordinary way of getting things done without offending or burdening anyone. For students he had unlimited time, patience and devotion. He liked young people and always wanted to help. The door of his office was open to anyone who wanted to talk to him.

In a span of a few years Lorie created an atmosphere of excitement at Glendon. Perhaps in his mind he wanted to recreate a vivid image of the experience he went through as [a] young man in Cambridge in the early thirties. There, he [had] been welcomed by Keynes and Robertson and [had] immediately been thrown, together with other young students, into the arena of the professionals of that time.

V

I was fortunate to know Lorie Tarshis for nearly 30 years. He was an inspiring role model as teacher, colleague and citizen. He and his wonderful, courageous wife, Inga, similarly inspired as partners, parents and friends. Like his mentor, Keynes, Lorie's objective was always to tame the dark forces of ignorance and uncertainty so as to allow people to achieve their potential, just as he, despite those cruel setbacks, fully achieved his own.

Notes

1. Tarshis's lecture notes were the leading species of the genus of those which Tom Rymes used to put together his representative student's notes of the lectures, see Rymes (1989).
2. Tibor Scitovsky has recently written a brilliant explanation of Keynes's essential insights about the possibility of a sustained lack of effective demand in terms of the hoarding of money and other assets. Significantly, the article is entitled 'Towards a theory of second-hand markets', Scitovsky (1994).
3. These were based on Kahn's 1929 dissertation for King's which was published in English only after his death in 1989, Kahn (1989). An Italian translation was published in 1983 through the good offices of Marco Dardi, Kahn (1983).
4. Strangely, Chamberlin does not rate a mention.
5. Tibor Scitovsky (29 November 1994) tells me that the account in the text 'is either completely new to [him] or the correct version of something [he] knew but in an incorrect form'. He had believed that Lorie had submitted an article based on part of his dissertation to an American journal, that it was rejected and that the main idea appeared soon afterwards in a book by the contemporary mentioned in the text, who must have read it as a referee. I originally heard the story from Lorie in 1980, see Harcourt (1993, pp. 75–6).
6. Or would they? Look what happened to Kalecki's contributions and, later, to Sidney Weintraub's.
7. He had had a 'good war', mostly working as a boffin advising on bombing raids and other puzzles. From their experiences, he and George Housner learnt an important methodological lesson: if you ask a silly question, you get a silly answer.
8. Omar Hamouda (11 December 1994) reminds me that the Dore and Tarshis paper was the last in a long line of papers on the issue, mostly unpublished, which Lorie wrote in the late 1970s and in the 1980s.
9. Perhaps because of this, as Omar Hamouda (22 November 1993) remarks, while Lorie 'wrote a lot, [he] somehow never persevered to publishing most of his ideas. Lorie's CV was always a most haphazard affair and there is no complete list of his publications.
10. I must also mention, as Omar Hamouda (11 December 1994) reminded me, Lorie's great love of all things Italian – Italian food, Italian wine, above all, Italian art.
11. I am grateful to Professor John Power for sending the tribute to me. Sadly, Professor Campbell died in October 1994.
12. Tarshis, Arrow, Houthakker, Reder, Goldberger, Scitovsky, Abramovitz, Chenery, Phelps, David, Hickman, Haley, Shaw, for starters. This is Campbell's list. Gavin Wright added Baran, Enthoven, Gurley, Nerlove, and Uzawa.

13. See also the entry on Lorie written by Hamouda and Price in Arestis and Sawyer (1992: 571–8).

References

Arestis, P. and M. C. Sawyer (1992) *A Biographical Dictionary of Dissenting Economists* (Cheltenham: Edward Elgar).

Boskin, M. J. (ed.) (1979) *Economics and Human Welfare. Essays in Honour of Tibor Scitovsky* (New York: Academic Press).

Dixon, H. and N. Rankin (1991) 'Imperfect Competition and Macroeconomics: A Survey', Warwick Economic Research Papers, November, 1–52, i–vi.

Dore, M. H. I. and L. Tarshis (1990) 'The LDC Debt and the Commercial Banks: A Proposed Solution', *Journal of Post Keynesian Economics*, Spring, vol. 12, 452–65.

Hamouda, O. F. and B. B. Price (1992) 'Lorie Tarshis (born 1911)', in Arestis and Sawyer (1992), 571–8.

— and J. N. Smithin (eds) (1988) *Keynes and Public Policy after Fifty Years*, vol. 2, *Theories and Methods* (Aldershot: Edward Elgar).

Harcourt, G. C. (1993) *Post-Keynesian Essays in Biography* (London: Macmillan).

— and P. A. Riach (eds) (1997) *A 'Second Edition' of The General Theory*, 2 vols (London: Routledge).

Kahn, R. (1989) *The Economics of the Short Period* (Basingstoke: Macmillan). The 1983 Italian translation is *L'Economia del Breve Periodo* (Turin: Bogingheri).

Kalecki, M. (1990) *Collected Works*, Vol. I, *Capitalism, Business Cycles and Full Employment*. Edited by Jersy Osiatynski (Oxford: Clarendon Press).

Keynes, J. M. (1930) *A Treatise on Money*, 2 Vols (London: Macmillan), *Collected Writings*, Vols V and VI, 1971.

— (1936) *The General Theory of Employment, Interest and Money* (London: Macmillan), *Collected Writings*, Vol. VII, 1973.

Mankiw, N. G. and D. Romer (eds) (1991) *New Keynesian Economics* vol. 1, *Imperfect Competition and Sticky Prices*, vol. 2 *Coordination Failures and Real Rigidities* (Cambridge, Mass: MIT Press).

Marris, R. (1991) *Reconstructing Keynesian Economics with Imperfect Competition* (Aldershot: Edward Elgar).

Pasinetti, L. L. (1994) 'The Principle of Effective Demand', Milano, mimeo (draft of a chapter for Harcourt and Riach, vol. 1, (1997)).

Pincus, J. J. (1994) 'With Lorie Tarshis at the Robert Louis Stevenson School for Boys, Del Monte Forest, Summer 1967. A Memoire by J. J. Pincus', mimeo, Adelaide.

Robinson, J. (1933) *The Economics of Imperfect Competition* (London: Macmillan).

Rymes, T. K. (1989) *Keynes's Lectures 1932–35. Notes of a Representative Student* (London: Macmillan).

Scitovsky, T. (1994) 'Towards a Theory of Second-Hand Markets', *Kyklos*, vol. 47, 33–52.

Sraffa, P. (1926) 'The Laws of Returns under Competitive Conditions', *Economic Journal*, vol. 36, December, 535–50.

— (1930) 'A Criticism' and 'A Rejoinder' in 'Increasing Returns and the Representative Firm: A Symposium', *Economic Journal*, vol. 40 (March) 89–92, 93.

Targetti, F. and B. Kinda-Hass (1982) 'Kalecki's Review of Keynes's *General Theory*', *Australian Economic Papers*, vol. 21, December, 244–60.

Tarshis, L. (1938) 'Real Wages in the United States and Great Britain', *Canadian Journal of Economics and Political Science*, vol. 4, August, 362–76.

— (1939*a*) 'The Determinants of Labour Income', unpublished PhD dissertation (Cambridge: Cambridge University Library).

— (1939*b*) 'Changes in Real and Money Wages', *Economic Journal*, vol. 49, March, 150–4.

— (1947) *The Elements of Economics. An Introduction to the Theory of Price and Employment* (Boston: Houghton Mifflin), 2nd edition, 1966.

— (1948) 'An Exposition of Keynesian Economics', *American Economic Review*, vol. 48, May, 261–72.

— (1955) *Introduction to International Trade and Finance* (New York: John Wiley; London: Chapman & Hall).

— (1979) 'The Aggregate Supply Function in Keynes's *General Theory*', in Boskin (1979), 361–92.

— (1980) 'Post-Keynesian Economics: A Promise that Bounced?' *American Economic Review*, vol. 70, May, 10–4.

— (1984) *World Economy in Crisis. Unemployment, Inflation and International Debt* (Toronto: James Lorimer).

— (1988) 'The International Debt of the LDCs', in Hamouda and Smithin (1988), 183–93.

— (1989) 'Keynes's Co-operative Economy and the Aggregate Supply Function', Chapter 2 of John Pheby (ed.), *New Directions in Post-Keynesian Economics* (Aldershot: Edward Elgar), 1989, 35–47.

— *et al.*, (1938) *An Economic Program for American Democracy*. Vanguard Press.

Torr, C. (1994) 'User Cost', Pretoria, mimeo (draft of a chapter for Harcourt and Riach, vol. 1 (1997)).

8
Edward Austin Gossage Robinson, 1897–1993*

I

Austin Robinson was born on 20 November 1897 at Farnham in Surrey, the eldest child of 'an impecunious clergyman', Albert Robinson, who read mathematics as a scholar of Christ's College, Cambridge and became a wrangler. He was ordained at the age of twenty-four, and spent the next eight years as a curate. Austin's mother, Edith Sidebotham, was the daughter of a clergyman who was the vicar at Bourne near Farnham in Surrey for thirty-three years.[1] As Alec Cairncross (1993: 4) has told us, it was a very happy marriage. The Robinsons had four children: three boys and a girl. The children had a happy childhood, even though their father was a remote and distant figure so that their mother did the lioness's share of their upbringing. The upbringing itself fostered self-reliance, fun and games as well as providing an introduction to a sense of duty and the practical application of Christian principles.

Scholarships were necessary for Austin's education and he duly obtained them, first to Marlborough and then to Christ's (he came top of the St John's/Christ's group of Cambridge Colleges). Classics was Austin's subject. He was 'rigorously drilled' in its grammar by an eccentric schoolmaster, A. C. B. Brown. This allowed him to jump all the necessary hurdles but it dimmed his enthusiasm, so that his heart was never completely captured. It did ensure that Austin wrote in a distinctively agreeable style in his books, articles, reviews and

* Originally published in *Proceedings of the British Academy*, vol. 94, 707–31.

letters – he was a prolific writer of letters which were noted for their lucid elegance as well as for their substance.

Austin obtained his scholarship to Christ's in late 1916. Before taking it up, he joined the Royal Naval Air Service to train as a test pilot of seaplanes, an occupation which he loved. His 'most military' activity was to chase but never catch a Zeppelin (Cairncross 1993: 11). The war itself was a deeply significant and traumatic event in his life. In his autobiographical essay (Austin Robinson 1992: 204) he wrote: 'In the modern world, deeply concerned with the dreadful threat of a nuclear war, it is too often forgotten how terrible was the mortality of that pre-nuclear conflict. Of the twenty senior boys in the "house" into which I had gone ... in 1912, thirteen were dead before I got to Cambridge in the summer of 1919'. He came up to Cambridge 'a very different person'. Though never a pacifist in 'the technical sense', like hundreds of others who had seen war at first hand, 'almost all of [his] generation of Cambridge undergraduates', he was determined to try to make a world in which war was never again used to settle its problems. 'Naive we may have been, but we were nonetheless sincere' (Austin Robinson 1992: 204).

Austin spent his first fifteen months at Cambridge reading classics – his college 'was unsympathetic to [his] view that [he] should use a classical scholarship to be taught the more professional aspects of designing aeroplanes' (Austin Robinson 1992: 204). He duly obtained a First. He then went with relief to economics. A major influence on this decision was hearing Maynard Keynes give a lecture in the course of lectures which became *The Economic Consequences of the Peace* (1919). C. R. Fay, who then taught economics at Christ's, persuaded the college to allow Austin to make the switch and he lent Austin the Marshalls' *Economics of Industry* and Tawney's *Acquisitive Society* to start him off. Austin read them, Taussig's *Principles* and Marshall's *Principles* during the day in the summer of 1921, while working each evening as 'poor-man's lawyer' in the dockyards of Liverpool, getting 'a remarkable education regarding the life and problems of the poor' (Austin Robinson 1992: 205). Austin found Fay an enthusiastic supervisor who was sublimely uncomprehending of the economic theory to be found in Marshall (much as Fay worshipped Marshall himself). This led to furious arguments in supervisions, forcing Austin to make explicit and coherent theoretical arguments in order to drive out misunderstandings and incoherence. When Fay left Christ's for

Canada, Austin went to Dennis Robertson and Gerald Shove. Though he felt he was well-instructed by powerful minds, his supervisions never again had the same magic.[2]

Austin graduated with a First in 1922 (the same year as Maurice Dobb who also obtained a First). He began to research in economics at Corpus Christi, which was then renowned for its unique brand of High Church, high Toryism. Having to argue with intelligent colleagues who took very different views on economic and social matters was of inestimable value to Austin, especially after he became a Fellow in 1923 and had to teach as well as to argue and understand. To understand for Austin was to act, he was always a 'hands on' political economist. By 1925 he had moved from lecturing on Money, Credit and Prices, with which he was never happy, to what was and remained his favourite subject, Industry (Cairncross 1993: 17–18).

II

In 1922 Joan Maurice came up to Girton to read economics, having read history at St Paul's Girls School. She 'graduated' in 1925; she and Austin, whose pupil she had been, married in 1926 (thus releasing Austin from being the one unmarried Fellow resident in Corpus Christi).[3] Soon after they married, the Robinsons went to India where Austin was to tutor the young Maharajah of Gwalior, then aged about ten. Cairncross tells a graphic tale of Austin's experiences there, how he combined an increasing knowledge of British India and the Princely States with involvement in the complex intrigues of the court, and especially in clashes with the strong-willed and all but impossible mother of his pupil. As far as Austin's future career was concerned, not only did the visit in a general way kindle his love for the subcontinent and its peoples but it also introduced him to the problems of economic development in a very practical way. He contributed a first-class piece of applied political economy to *The British Crown and the Indian States* (1928). He drew on inadequate statistics and showed judgement and imagination in estimating fiscal flows to and from the Princely States to British India.

The Robinsons were in India for nearly two years.[4] Austin returned to Cambridge to start afresh his long academic career there; it was only seriously interrupted by his distinguished service in Whitehall during the Second World War. He became a University Lecturer in 1929 and a Fellow of Sidney Sussex in 1931. (Joan became a University Assistant Lecturer in 1934.) Austin had known Keynes since his undergraduate days – he had quickly been admitted to Keynes's political economy club where, early on, he read a paper which made a big impression.[5] In 1934 Keynes invited him to become assistant editor of the *Economic Journal* with the consequence that Austin was eventually to write more reviews probably than any other economist before or since. The appointment also marks the start of his long association with the Royal Economic Society (RES) itself, editor for thirty-six years, secretary for twenty-five years (from which post he retired in 1970), and sixty years service in all to the society.[6]

III

Dennis Robertson asked Austin to write the book on *Monopoly* for the respected 'Cambridge Economic Handbooks' series. Austin ended up writing two books (1931, 1941) as he cleared the ground for *Monopoly* by writing on *The Structure of Competitive Industry*, a project which became a book in its own right. Its *Economic Journal* reviewer, Philip Sargant Florence (to whose lectureship Austin had been appointed when Sargant Florence went to the Chair at Birmingham), rightly praised it as the potential classic it was to become – 'a most original contribution ... lively style ... obvious ... fund of industrial experience to back it [up] –' (Sargant Florence 1932: 66). He was as complimentary about *Monopoly* when nearly a decade later he was again the *Economic Journal* reviewer (perhaps as review editor, Austin wanted to see how Sargant Florence reacted second time around?). Sargant Florence gave the first book both high praise and stringent criticism. The praise was for the excellent structure of the argument which gave outstanding unity to the book. Austin looked at the optimum size of firms from a number of points of view – techniques, management, product(s), marketing, for example – then brought all these aspects together, reconciled in the size of a real firm. The criticism related to a fuzziness of definition, that in much of his argument, it was not clear whether Austin was referring to plants' 'scale of operations' or to firms' 'scale of organisation'. Nevertheless, Austin's work essentially established in an excellent way in Cambridge what we now call industrial organisation. He blended together a judicious mix of theory, facts, and policy – always his approach to economic issues – thus deserving 'the gratitude of all who wish to bring description closer to theoretical economics' (Sargant Florence 1932: 69). His reviewer had one main criticism of the second volume, that Austin confused the difficulties of creating a monopoly and circumventing competition with those of controlling an established monopoly. Despite this, Sargant Florence felt the author managed 'to pack in most of the real world of monopoly while arguing all the time patiently from first principles' (Sargant Florence 1941: 483).

Austin's Christianity and his interest in development came together when in the 1930s he took part in two major studies of African problems, the first of which required him to visit what is now Zambia. The Archbishop of York asked Pigou in 1932 to suggest someone to join a commission of enquiry under the auspices of the International Missionary Council, to spend six months in Africa analysing the impact of copper mining on indigenous society. Cairncross (1993: 51) says Austin's chapters in *Modern Industry and the African* 'constitute one of the first attempts by an economist to arrive at a view of what makes for successful economic development in a backward country'. There, he used the new ideas that were emerging in Cambridge as Keynes moved from *A Treatise on Money* (1930) to *The General Theory* (1936), spurred on by the criticisms and suggestions of the 'circus', of which Austin was a key member.[7] They gave him the rudiments of a national accounting framework in which to think about structures and imbalances as between rural and urban sectors, overseas trade and development, and the impact of government expenditure and taxation on economic systems.

Austin was also always interested in individuals as such (and their groupings); so, as he thought about rural underemployment and poverty, he was keen to use the potential skills and aspirations of people *where they were*, rather than advocate large migrations or the creation of huge urban concentrations. In his letters he wrote much about the characteristics of the Africans with whom he came into contact, using as his *numeraire* the various groupings of Indians he had known and/or observed in the 1920s. He wrote reflecting first impressions: 'In India where servants are perfect we say "This is evidently a servile race. They can't rule themselves". In South Africa we say "These people can't even lay a table. How can they run a country?"' (Cairncross 1993: 55). For him, economic development had to build on the characteristics of the people as they were, or would become, and he was what we would call now very much a 'horses for courses' person. He was always suspicious of all-purpose general theories and their accompanying models which were thought to be applicable regardless of time or place. In fact he said of the Cambridge developments of those years associated with Keynes and his colleagues:

> It was ... a great step forward in economic thought when Keynes insisted that we should have ... a theory that was valid not only with full (or near-full) employment, but also with unemployment – and that we should know quite clearly which of the propositions of economics were universally valid, and which were valid only in conditions in which it might be true that an increase of one activity was possible *only* at the expense of another activity.
>
> (Austin Robinson 1947: 44; emphasis in original)

His other work on Africa in the 1930s did not require him to go there but it was nevertheless a major contribution, two long chapters, 157 pages in all, in Lord Hailey's *African Survey* (1938). Austin spent the vacations of the three years 1934–7 working in Chatham House on the chapters. The *Survey* itself was set up in response to an appeal by General Smuts in 1929 – he called for a survey of Africa's affairs as a whole, reviewing developments in each country and to what extent they were affected by and gained from modern knowledge. Austin drew on the work of S. F. Frankel on capital investment in Africa and Charlotte Leubuscher on African foreign trade for the external aspects (chapter 19), and on Hailey's own 'immensely conscientious' notes for the internal aspects (chapter 20). The quality of Austin's chapters was such as to give the 'chapters a place amongst the classics of economic literature' (Noel Hall, quoted by Cairncross 1993: 73).

Austin increasingly assimilated the new lessons Keynes was developing, so much so that he was to review *The General Theory* (1936) for *The Economist* (29 February 1936), the only ever signed review in that journal (and then it was initials only, E.A.G.R.). Evidently the paper gave Austin's review a title of which he disapproved (it was misleadingly – because far too narrow – called 'Mr Keynes on Money') and also may have altered the emphasis and balance by editorial cuts. When Austin complained to Keynes of this, Keynes said it served him right for publishing in the yellow press. The review was perceptive and accurate, as to the essential nature of the new theory. It could be read with profit today by modern students to allow them both to get the essence of the theory and of how the advanced world still works. Austin's classical training was in evidence. In commenting on Keynes's polemical passages, Austin wrote: 'Like Horace's schoolmaster, Mr Keynes whips his pupils into agreement, where modest reasonableness, many will feel [not Austin, though], would better have achieved this end' (Austin Robinson 1936: 472).

What is illuminating, considering the muddled debates that were to occur, was that Austin had a clearer view of the meaning of the equality of saving and investment and the roles which it played in the analysis than perhaps even the author himself. He refers also to Keynes's masterly and clear style in previous writings and deplores its comparative absence in *The General Theory*: 'Many will sigh for the earlier Keynes who possessed in unusual bounty the gift of translating theoretical ideas into realities and conveying them in words of one syllable' (Austin Robinson 1936: 472). Austin himself uses plain language to good effect both to describe the existence of the underemployment rest state and the process by which it may (or may not) be reached in the economy as a whole. His keen sense of industrial organisation is evident when he explains that the non-profitable levels of output as a whole away from the rest state mean that the positions are not sustainable, even in the short term.

IV

Austin spent the war years in Whitehall, working in two different sections. He went first to the Offices of the War Cabinet, subsequently joining the Economic Section when it, and what became the Central Statistical Office, were set up. Austin came to Whitehall much impressed by Keynes's talk to the undergraduate Marshall Society in Cambridge on the issues contained in Keynes's booklet, *How to Pay for the War* (1940). It also convinced him of the fundamental need for reliable estimates of national income and expenditure on a continuing basis. These were to be provided by Austin recruiting James Meade 'to get the logic right' and Richard Stone for 'his remarkable familiarity with British economic statistics' (Cairncross 1993: 79). Cairncross tells us that Austin 'always regarded [getting] the annual national income accounts on a consistent basis as his chief contribution to the war' (Cairncross 1993: 79). In February 1942 Austin became the Economic Advisor and Head of the Programmes Division in the Ministry of Production. The lessons he learnt in these two sections he regarded as the most important elements in his long apprenticeship as an economist (Austin Robinson 1992: 219).

His wartime tasks and experiences reaffirmed his belief that macroeconomic analysis without simultaneous attention to the microeconomic details of firms and industries, supplies of specific types of labour and capital goods, and of infrastructure, is seriously flawed. As someone who had absorbed Marshall very deeply, Austin always connected together the long-term development implications of short-term changes and vice versa.

After the war in Europe ended, Austin went to Germany as a member of a small committee on how Germany should be treated in the postwar era. Austin kept a diary which was 'remarkably lucid, coherent and perceptive [conveying] a remarkable picture of the contrasts between town and country, occupiers and occupied, movement on the roads and inertia elsewhere, devastation and disorder on the grand scale but some things still working normally and in good order' (Cairncross 1993: 91). In a letter to Keynes of 16 June 1945 Austin wrote: 'Fact, cold hard fact, is almost certainly different [but he] preferred [his] stories, and as the theologians say when pressed too hard, the story may convey the picture without being literally true' (Austin Robinson 1986a: preface, no page number.) Austin went on to Russia where he emphasised perceptively 'the complete ascendancy of defence over opulence in the mind of the Communist government – an ascendancy that continued throughout the postwar years in a measure unequalled anywhere else' (Cairncross 1993: 94).

Austin drew on his wartime experiences twenty years later when in his Marshall Lectures of 1965, *Economic Planning in the United Kingdom: Some Lessons* (published in 1967), he set out what is still a blueprint for policy-making in a free society which is nevertheless determined to employ all its citizens and direct its overall development in the long term as well as in the short term. He returned to the same themes in his review article (Austin Robinson, 1986b) of Alec Cairncross's account of the transformation from war to peace (Cairncross 1985). As well as playing a key role in manpower planning during the war, Austin was also involved in the determination of the import needs and export possibilities of the United Kingdom in the postwar period. Though he applauded his general approach, Cairncross thought he was too pessimistic about the possible outcomes in his detailed estimates of what was possible and needed.

Austin was never persuaded on this and as late as 1986 pointed out that the original estimates, made in 1943, were made on the assumption that the war against Japan after Germany was defeated would be a long, drawn-out affair, eighteen months to two years or more. Dropping the atomic bombs in 1945 drastically shortened the relevant time period and brought forward the beginning of the transition. Austin argued that they had identified the main problems: the balance of payments where exports were no more than 28 per cent of their 1938 volume. There were shortages of steel, timber, coal and energy generally, and also of certain labour skills. Cairncross summed up: '…when the risks are high, as they were in 1947, it is not the outcome that is the best measure of a man's judgement but how the risks seemed to good judges at the time, and there were few who foresaw a future materially more fortunate than [Austin] did' (Cairncross 1993: 108).

Austin returned to university life after the war, feeling that he was not 'tough enough to carry on indefinitely under the pressure [he] had worked during the [war] years' (Austin Robinson 1992: 218). (He certainly fooled us all!) His reputation was such that Whitehall and the Government would not let him go completely. Twice for extended periods he was called back at Stafford Cripps's insistence. He spent a year in London helping to draft the *Economic Survey for 1948* and the *Economic Survey for 1948–52*, six months in Paris with the Office of the European Economic Community (OEEC) ensuring that the Marshall Plan could go through. He chaired 'the committee that drafted the collective report to Congress, showing that we collectively had plans that would make us viable' (Austin Robinson 1992: 219). With that task done, his 'long apprenticeship' ended, he was on 'the threshold of a subsequent forty years as an academic' (*ibid.*). Nevertheless, he kept his links with Government and Government service for many decades afterwards; he served on selection boards for the Civil Service and through the National Institute of Economic and Social Research (NIESR) and development agencies, he influenced advice given and personnel chosen. His scholarly contributions were recognised by his election as a Fellow of the British Academy in 1955.

V

Increasingly in the postwar period, Austin was drawn towards the problems of developing countries. He was an indefatigable founder of and worker for the International Economic Association (IEA), of which he was Treasurer (1950–9), President (1959–62) and General Editor (1950–80). Austin edited or co-edited twelve volumes of its conferences, world and small. The bulk of them were concerned with development issues. To them all Austin made lucid, carefully considered contributions.[8]

Cairncross (1993) cites the IEA volumes either edited by Austin or to which he contributed chapters in his bibliography of Austin's writings. A selection of the titles alone indicate the breadth of Austin's interests and knowledge: *The Economic Consequences of the Size of Nations* (1960), 'Foreign Trade in a Developing Economy', a chapter by Austin in Kenneth Berrill (ed.), *Economic Development with Special Reference to East Asia* (1964); *Problems in Economic Development* (1965); *The Economics of Education* (edited with John Vaizey, 1966); 'The Desirable Level of Agriculture in Advanced Industrial Economies', a chapter in Ugo Papi and Charles Nunn (eds), *Economic Problems of Agriculture in Industrial Societies* (1969); *Backward Areas in Advanced Countries* (1969); *Economic Growth in South Asia* (edited with Michael Kidron, 1970); *The Economic Development of Bangladesh* (edited with Keith Griffin) (1974); *Appropriate Techniques for Third World Development* (1979).

His commentaries were always clearly expressed, he combined optimism tempered with caution, and he tried to delineate clearly the boundaries within which academic economists could speak with (relative) authority and outside of which they were trespassing without good reason. Thus in the 1960 volume (which arose from a conference held in 1957 – as with the effects of changes in the quantity of money, the publication of IEA volumes is subject to uncertain and variable lags), he wrote that it was 'not for us, as a group of academic economists, to reach political conclusions, and we made no attempt to do so' (xxi). The subject of this particular conference – the relation of size to economic prosperity – had, its editor wrote, received very little discussion in the 180 years since the publication of *The Wealth of Nations*. Typically, Austin started by getting definitions straight and asking why the concept of a nation was relevant for economic analysis. He found the answer in the dis-continuities which the boundary of a nation provides – some natural, some institutional, for example, tariffs, limits on the move-ment of labour. In our day (Austin's then), the nation had renewed itself because it had become the unit for government action and economic activity. (Are we now leaving this era?)

Austin pointed out that the definition of size differed according to the purpose in hand. At the conference they examined the USA (a rich country), Switzerland, Belgium, and Sweden (which were excep-tions to the size rule). Austin noted that Switzerland achieved neces-sary economies of scale by relying on export markets, while Belgium achieved high living standards by concentrating on the unfashion-able factors of industrial efficiency and hard work (both dear to Austin's heart). He pointed out that with few exceptions technical economies are exhausted by firms of quite moderate size. He also formed the impression that most of the major industrial economies of scale could be achieved by a relatively high income per capita country with a population of fifty million. Foreign trade could provide an escape (from size) but a precarious one and the economic arguments for further integration of nations, so as to create wider markets, were not overwhelmingly conclusive – the political argu-ments were, of course, another matter, a topical conclusion in 1996. Size was obviously useful for defence but not exclusively for any-thing else.

Austin's chapter on foreign trade in developing countries in Kenneth Berrill's 1964 IEA volume started with a list of intellec-tual debts: Ragnar Nurkse, Harry Johnson, Berrill himself, David Bensusan-Butt, Hla Myint, and Phyllis Deane. He first identified two impacts of international trade on the development process. The first was positive: by aiding specialisation and accumulation in those activities in which productivity is highest, the process of development may be accelerated. The second, which was negative, arose because often the propensity to import runs ahead of the power to export, so imposing constraints associated with threatening balance of payments difficulties. If higher rates of interest are used, for example, to protect foreign exchange reserves they may lead to an uneasy equilibrium characterised by underloading of the economy and a slow rate of development. Though the ratio of exports to imports reflects in the very long term the size of country concentration and range of endowments, the exports to income ratio is the ultimate constraint, a point which Austin illustrates by reference to the historical experience of the United Kingdom and Japan. A typical Austin emphasis is that the better use of resources may often have been more important than a slightly higher rate of accumulation.

He lists five channels of causation whereby a rise in the exports to income ratio may contribute to the acceleration of growth: by a transfer of resources from low to high productivity areas; by ridding any industry of dependence solely on home markets (but if this is achieved by foreigners' investing and producing the benefits to the home country may be minimal); by the spread of higher industrial efficiency first introduced through international trade; by what we now call the demonstration effect, knowledge of new products or products not previously known in the country leading to increased desires to produce them and for increased incomes to purchase them. The most important aspect for Austin though is that a high level of trade and possible imports provides a means of escape from both major and minor errors of planning and production. He illustrated these principles by looking at the experiences of India and Pakistan. An important emphasis that emerged was that he was sceptical of the potential of price changes, for example, devaluations, as opposed to the power of income and quantity changes.

In his opening address to the Second World IEA Congress in Vienna in September 1962, the subject of which was the problems of economic development, Austin said that the topic was chosen deliberately, adding: 'Just as in the 1930s almost all schools of economists were concerned with problems of economic fluctuations … today [they were] mostly concerned with attempting to understand the causes of economic growth' (Austin Robinson 1965: xv). Austin expressed the wish that these developments would help to eliminate poverty which does so much damage to human happiness and that they would help to close rather than to widen the gap between the poor and the rich nations. He referred to the profound difficulties associated with defining and measuring the stock of capital goods in a world of continually changing prices and technologies, adding that even more insoluble problems arise when we try to define and measure stocks of scientific and engineering knowledge or of freedom of opportunity – all variables which complement one another in the development process.

He criticised Rostow's (then) attempts to generalise historical experiences of rapid growth in more advanced economies and to apply this directly in policies for 'backward countries'. For Austin (as for Marshall) change is continuous, not abrupt, that is to say, in general there is no 'take-off'. Nevertheless, to increase the speed of development attention must be paid as much to creating the right institutions and economic framework as to potential supplies of capital. Especially vital is education to allow developing countries to absorb knowledge and skills. Reflecting the influence of Keynes and his followers, Austin referred to the need to understand the causes of fluctuations in the prices of primary products and to devise schemes to reduce them. Austin returned to the role of foreign trade in development, to export-led growth and balance of payments constraints. He stressed the need to model interrelationships between countries, taking explicit note of the sizes of price and especially of income elasticities of exports and imports. He urged that, in order for small emerging countries to escape from the penalties of smallness, markets be opened to both their traditional and newly emerging exports, even manufactures – still a tract for our times.

The quantity and quality of the population of nations was always a foremost concern of Austin's. He gave explicit voice to it in the volume on *The Economics of Education* (1966) which he edited with John Vaizey, a pioneer of the subject in the United Kingdom. In the introduction, Austin itemised the conceptual difficulties and the deficiencies of the available statistics. He was also careful to show that education was gravely misconceived if viewed solely (or even at all) as a consumption good. In these days of consumer sovereignty in all things, it is refreshing to be reminded that investment and production are vital aspects of economic and social life as well, and that while a balance must be struck, neglect of any is detrimental to human welfare. Austin has wise things to say about taking into account the future effects on activity of the stocks of educated persons as well as analysing the current flows; and that in our statistics, we neglect the collection of data on the educational attainments of immigrants and emigrants at our peril.

In 1969 Austin edited a volume on backward areas in advanced countries. All advanced countries have such areas; one reason why they persist is because individual entrepreneurs cannot be expected to take into account all the factors which from a national point of view are relevant for the location of industries. Austin was (and remained) an unrepentant interventionist. He argued that with the possible exception of the USA, people were not indifferent to where they live or have lived. It followed that the principles of international trade rather than the analysis of a single country were appropriate for considering backward areas and what may be done about them.

Appropriate Technologies for Third World Development (1979) was a topic especially suited to Austin's humanitarianism and 'nuts and bolts' philosophy. All his working life he emphasised that development on the spot using already established communities was most to be preferred. Promoting the appropriate technologies for such a process had been hampered by artificially cheap capital facilities, tax holidays, and similar measures. He also stressed that there are appropriate products as well as methods of production, very much a close-to-the-ground view which reflected his frustrated engineer side – as did his emphasis on the crucial role which the ability to provide adequate maintenance of machines plays in the process of development.

Other volumes which he edited relate to developing countries such as Sri Lanka and Bangladesh, on which we comment below. Austin also wrote many reports on development themes. His biographer, Alec Cairncross, has singled out for special praise a report for the United Nations Development Programme, which Austin wrote in the mid-1970s at the request of I. G. Patel (who had been his pupil in the 1940s). Cairncross regards it as the single best and most impressive account of the principles of development to come from Austin's pen. We discuss now its main features, features already present in embryo in his 1920s work in India and 1930s work in Africa.[10]

His focus was on 'the massive underemployment and unemployment in many developing countries'. Austin asks why they are so persistent and he sets out six constraints on a policy of increasing demand to draw these workers into employment and allow incomes to rise.

The usually dominant constraint is the failure of domestic food production to match expanding incomes, so that import demand rises. Unless exports match this, expansion is constrained by balance of payments problems. Austin's orders of magnitude for a typical developing country with population growth of 2.5 per cent a year and a target growth rate of 7 per cent a year is that the constraint will bite if agricultural output does not grow by 5 per cent a year. Top priority must therefore be given to overcoming this constraint by creating the necessary agricultural surplus.

Austin also stressed that the 'weakness in the exchange mechanism between town and country was sometimes the main constraint'. Undernourished farm workers consumed the additional food so that the demands of the urban population, swollen by an inflow from rural areas, went into imports: hence the need for effective organisation for buying, financing, transporting, and distributing the agricultural surplus needed in the city. As befits an economist of the same university as Malthus, Austin also recognised the need to limit the import content of consumer goods, not least 'luxury' goods.

The fourth limitation was inadequate accumulation due to low saving rates, inefficient methods of finance and also the high import content of investment.

The fifth and sixth constraints are associated with the limitations of skills available – administrative as well as productive, especially in industry where education systems may not be geared to produce them. Austin thought it may be necessary to create '"small-scale low-capital-intensive occupations" with "very large numbers of small craftsmen, traders, entrepreneurs starting successful small business"' (151) in order to bypass the problem.

Strangely, Austin does not mention cultural factors which could be an important part of the explanation of differences between countries, for example, acceptance of discipline in the industrial sector: strange, because, as we have seen, his letters from India and Africa are full of details on just these characteristics of the local populations.

Austin then discussed the dual economy aspect of development – the contrast between modern sectors and traditional sectors, and the choice this raises of whether to go for rapid development through faster growth and lower capital inputs per jobs, or a gradual transition and the consequent need to 'revitalise and reinvigorate the traditional economy'. He had advocated the latter advance in the 1930s.

Finally, he recognised fully the problems associated with rapid population growth which in some cases meant absorbing 'as much as three quarters of all national investment ... in merely standing still' (152).

We may illustrate Austin's approach, in particular, his well developed sense of relevant orders of magnitude in the simple macro development models which he carried in his head, by briefly examining the arguments of his Kingsley Martin Memorial Lecture, 'The economic development of Malthusia' (Austin Robinson 1974), which was given in Cambridge on 6 March 1974. There, he used Bangladesh as his example. He started by stating the question which was asked '[o]ne hundred and seventy five years ago [by] a shy young Fellow of Jesus'. The question is 'whether economic development was possible, or whether it would be frustrated by the growth of population' (Austin Robinson 1974: 521). To say that 'Malthus has been discredited by subsequent history' is, says Austin, 'a very dangerous half truth', for while the advanced countries have broken through the Malthusian barrier into cumulative growth, the rest of the world has not; it 'continues to live under conditions of near stagnation, little above the subsistence level, in very much the conditions that Malthus envisaged' (Austin Robinson 1974: 521).

Austin worked out two scenarios for the next twenty years in Bangladesh according to whether it continued with Malthusian-type birth and death rates, or with European-type through which it had broken out of the Malthusian trap. He relates these statistical exercises to the actual plans then being proposed in Bangladesh. His sense of the interrelationships of the broad aspects of the economy is beautifully done. He shows that in the most favourable scenario, a considerable proportion of the problems of unemployment, underemployment and poverty would be overcome by the end of the period; while with the other scenario, Malthus's worst fears would have been realised and an opportunity available now (1974) would have been lost for ever. It is pleasing to report in 1996 that Austin's 'waking hopes' (Austin Robinson 1974: 532) are nearer to being achieved than his worst fears realised (see, for example, Reddaway (1996)).

VI

In the Faculty of Economics and Politics itself, Austin not only taught but also played a major role in its administration. The building which now bears his name (it was so christened at the party in honour of his ninetieth birthday) is very much the outcome of his enthusiasm and persistence. Austin was appointed to a Chair in 1950. As well as lecturing and supervising, Austin had long spells as Secretary of the Faculty Board and also as its Chairman. The clashes between the Keynesians and the Robertsonians were fierce and unyielding in the postwar years. Austin did his best to bring peace and maintain cohesion. James Meade, who came to Cambridge in the late 1950s and who was witness to some of the toughest debates, thought that Austin tried hard to be fair and obtain principled compromises, even if often in practice they favoured one side more than the other. In any event, Austin was faced with a virtually impossible task in a faculty where consensus is defined as agreeing with whoever is speaking.

In September 1965 Austin retired from his Chair (he was succeeded by Joan). He was to have nearly thirty years more of extremely active life. He was physically frail towards the end – he was knocked off his bicycle by a motorist about ten years before he died and injured his back. It continued to trouble him despite the efforts of a renowned osteopath who ministers, usually most effectively, to the underworld of the back sufferers of Cambridge, including the present writer. Nevertheless, some of his best papers were written in his eighties and early nineties. The editors of the *Cambridge Journal of Economics* often used him as a reliable, critical, but fair-minded referee. In a book published in 1984, *Economics in Disarray*, Austin's contribution, a comment on Peter Wiles on the full-cost principle, stands out for its clarity and deep economic intuition. It reflects his knowledge of firms, his exchanges in the 1950s with the full-cost theorists of Oxford, and his experiences from his years as a Syndic of the Cambridge University Press. And, of course, he wrote his superb autobiographical essay. 'My Apprenticeship as an Economist' for Szenberg's 1992 volume on *Eminent Economists*, which, together with his obituary of Keynes in the March 1947 *Economic Journal*, most typically reflect Austin's great strengths as an economist, perceptive human being, and elegant stylist.

VII

Austin was elected to a Fellowship in Sidney Sussex in 1931. From then on the college was a central focus of his life, especially after Joan died in 1983 and Austin moved from the house in Grange Road to a flat opposite the college itself. Roger Andrew, a former Bursar of Sidney who was close to Austin, writes: '[Austin's] enthusiasm for the College and his concern for it [are] known only to those within its framework. The ideal for College life is the City State of Plato in which like minds administer and further the affairs of the establishment. Austin filled this position admirably... His philosophy was to guide and to bring those other members by persuasion to a similar belief'. His daughter, Barbara Jeffrey, writes that 'he also felt it was important to college life that people should be able to get on well with one another'.

In his address at the Memorial Service for Austin in November 1993, Alan Hughes, Austin's colleague and an economics Fellow of Sidney, spoke of Austin's role as an active mender of the investments committee responsible for the management of the stockmarket portfolio set up in the 1960s, of his many gifts of, for example, silver plate and carpets for public rooms and of the 'exceptionally generous bequest to Sidney to further education and research'. He described Austin in retirement 'as a familiar figure in college, especially in the continuation of his life-long association with the chapel. His interest in sport ... meant that any other fellow with a similar interest in following [horse racing, and rugby] on TV would often find an agreeable companion in Austin', not least because of the wine he provided to offset the bitter reaction to an Oxford try on 'a gloomy mid-winter Tuesday'.

VIII

Austin had a long life, worked extraordinarily hard, and was associated with a breath-taking number of institutions in academia,

Government, and internationally. Of all these institutions he was, in his own words, a willing 'slave'. As with many of his generation, he found delegation difficult and this caused clashes and misunderstandings, sometimes leaving Austin feeling hurt and unappreciated by other officers of the organisations for which he worked so hard and, overall, served so well.

I wrote to a selection of people from these and other institutions who knew Austin, asking for their impressions and evaluations. What emerged is the respect and affection in which he was held in so many spheres: respect for his outstanding abilities, affection for him as a person even though his stature and personality were such that I do not think my correspondents felt they were able to get really close to him, much as they may have wished to.

I start with Gavin Reid (14 September 1993) who came to know Austin when at Darwin on a sabbatical in 1987–8. Reid 'was impressed with his willingness to extend courtesy to an academic transient', and he thought that Austin set 'very high standards' which nevertheless were achievable by 'mere mortals'.

Robin Matthews (6 March 1994) worked closely with Austin in the 1940s, 1950s and 1960s in the Faculty and also on the *Economic Journal* when Matthews was review editor. He singled out Austin's contributions to economics, emphasising the *range* of topics to which he made original contributions. Though Austin did not keep up to date with the literature, he 'had a knack of identifying what was important'. Matthews identified four fields: firm and industry, development economics, 'practical macro' from the viewpoint of the economic advisor (all predictable), and the economics of R&D; not so predictable, but just as impressive. Matthews concluded that Austin was a most serious and optimistic economist who 'believed that economics was capable of doing good'.

Frank Hahn's views (6 June 1994) are, as ever, complementary to those of Matthews.

Austin was a born 'mandarin' … impatient of theory which abstracted from the 'real world'. His aim was to improve the world whether it was the small world of Cambridge, the Indian subcontinent or the Royal Economic Society. His memoranda … were perfect instances of what such writings should be: lucid, precise, and brief.

Referring to Austin's many years as Secretary of the RES, Hahn high-lights Austin's role 'as the moving force getting Keynes' writings col-lected and edited', a judgement which is echoed by several other economists who knew the background story to the Keynes papers. Hahn concluded:

> Austin was socially a cut above many of his more recent col-leagues. He had enormous self-confidence, and spoke in upper-class Cambridge English. He was also apt to favour those he knew – especially in Cambridge – when it came to jobs and honours. This was not really a sign of the 'old school tie' syndrome. He simply took it for granted that the best minds, and indeed the morally most reliable minds, were to be found in Cambridge. After that he would allow some merit to Oxford and London, but not much beyond that. This was a failing, but one found it hard to blame him for being faithful to beliefs formed when England and its Universities were very different from what they are now.

Hahn's conclusion is, I believe, accurate, revealing of both writer and subject, stating things which ought to be stated but which could only be done by someone with Hahn's insight and self-confidence.

Austin was long associated with the NIESR. Two former Directors, Bryan Hopkin and David Worswick, sent me recollections of Austin's role there and much else besides. Bryan was a pupil of Austin's at Cambridge in the 1930s, David was an Oxford graduate. Their appraisals naturally differ, at least on the surface but not on fundamentals if read carefully between the lines, especially Worswick's. Worswick tells an amusing tale of how, at Robert Hall's prompting, he concocted a seventy-and-over rule to rid the Executive Committee of Austin and one other 'old man' (which soon took off Hall himself). To their credit, 'both departed gracefully ... without enquiring too closely into the origin of the rule'. Worswick then described his personal experiences of working with Austin when Worswick was President of the RES and in the IEA, when he often remembered that rule. He could not condone Austin treating the edition of the Keynes papers and the IEA as 'personal fiefdoms'. His reason told that it would have been better if Austin had brought in more and younger people to take over some of his responsibilities. Yet, Worswick concluded, Austin 'was so good at what he did … that [he was] not so sure!'

Hopkin (5 June 1994) reported on Austin's massive contributions during Hopkin's time as Director (1952–7). Austin 'took a detailed interest in all the work … going on, [gave] wise and informed counsel …' and personal support to Hopkin. Austin was the ideal person to fill such a role because he knew and was respected by so many people, he criticised work incisively but gently, and was well behaved even in the most difficult circumstances.

I turn now to American evaluations, starting with Paul Samuelson's (7 July 1994), and then Bob Solow's (17 June 1994). When President of the IEA, Samuelson 'was most content to have [Austin] run me and all in sight'. He thought that, as an economist, Austin was original and lucid, that he had good judgement which was not affected by dislike or personality. He considered it remarkable that he 'never heard [Austin] utter a sour criticism of any in the Cambridge menagerie'. Solow praised Austin's role in the IEA, highlighting the length of the conferences under Austin's guidance, which enabled serious discussion of papers, and that Austin's force of character made sure that authors wrote the papers that the conference needed. Solow liked Austin, not least for his plain speaking, which contrasted with '[a] lot of Cambridge conversation [which struck Solow] as a move in a game (whose rules and objectives [he did not] know)'. I wish to emphasise the importance of the views of Samuelson and Solow – both liked Austin 'a lot' – because another distinguished American economist felt that Austin did not like Americans and that he was, in a thoughtless English way, anti-Semitic – as well as being imperious and overbearing on occasions.

In the body of the essay I tried to give due weight to Austin's contributions to development economics. One person who knew of these at first hand is Esra Bennathan. In a letter of 18 July 1992 to Alec Cairncross (which they kindly let me see), Bennathan mentions that after being interviewed by Austin for the Civil Service in 1961 he discovered that an 'admired colleague' at Birmingham regarded 'Austin with the utmost suspicion, a dangerous figure of the Establishment, a duplicitous nature hiding behind an ascetic and saintly face'. Bennathan's long experience of Austin was 'totally different'. His lengthy letter is concerned not only with Austin's crucial gifts as an economist but also with his practical Christianity, especially in helping academics in what became Bangladesh both to escape persecution and to build up their libraries and laboratories.

Bennathan summed up his idea of Austin's 'private and instinctive' approach to development issues: '[Austin] work[ed] through and for people ... [He] ... measur[ed] his effectiveness by his effect upon them, their actions and their progress ... [Austin] nurtur[ed], encourag[ed] and sponsored those he [thought] promising, without expecting too much'. Bennathan found this totally impressive and sympathetic.

Finally, Bennathan quotes the oral tradition that Keynes regarded Austin as 'his brightest student'. [Bennathan] had 'never heard a clearer explanation of Ramsey's social utility function, and the asymptote to Bliss, than that given by Austin in the Diamond Hotel, Poona, surrounded ... by very actively loving American couples relaxing from meditative exertions in Rashneeshi's Ashram just round the corner'.

I. G. Patel (5 July 1955) knew Austin as a supervisor (1946–9) and then 'in many capacities' – visits to India (sometimes as a family guest), IEA conferences, consultant to UNDP, Council of the RES. His first impression of him was 'of a very generous and rather shy and self-effacing person'; his final summing up: 'Generous, self-effacing and deeply committed'.

Hans Singer (4 October 1994) also paid tribute to Austin's generosity and first-rate intelligence. Austin was the secretary of 'a small committee at Cambridge' set up in the early 1930s to help two German refugee students of whom Singer was one. Though not Singer's PhD supervisor, Austin gave him 'invariably helpful' advice on some problems in his dissertation. Austin's 'empirical approach and clear language were a great help to a new arrival, bewildered ... by the incomprehensible lectures and papers by Wittgenstein and Piero Sraffa [as well as] by the intricacies of liquidity preference'. Always 'young Singer' to Austin, 'up to shortly before his death people ... from Cambridge [carried] greetings from [Austin] to "young Singer"'.

Perhaps Susan Howson (3 October 1994) may be allowed a last word: 'I have a great admiration, as well as love, for Austin, who always struck me as one of the most sane members of our profession'.

IX

To the end of his life, Austin remained mentally rigorous and alert. During the alarm a few years ago about the impact on health of certain French cheeses, Austin was asked at lunch in Sidney Sussex by a Fellow in his late eighties whether they should eat them. Austin said: 'It is only dangerous for pregnant women and old people – and we do not belong to either category'. Austin had a fine sense of humour which was often combined with sharp, even wicked end lines about his contemporaries, delivered with a twinkle. He enjoyed gossip and barbed, but not malicious comments in private, for he was, first and foremost a kindly man, who nevertheless was realistic about, and comforted by the fact that foibles as well as achievements characterise the human condition.

Though Austin is on record as saying that the optimum length of time to see a grandchild is half an hour, both he and Joan were proud and fond of their five grandchildren and had, especially after the arrival of grandchildren, excellent rapport with their daughters and their respective husbands, who in turn appreciated the love and support they could depend upon. In May 1993, Austin had a bad fall and was taken to Addenbrookes Hospital in Cambridge. He died peacefully on the morning of 1 June, having heard some of his favourite Bible readings and prayers the night before.

Austin Robinson was the role model *par excellence* for the aspiring applied political economist. At his Memorial Service in Sidney Sussex Chapel on 20 November 1993, one of the readings was the parable of the talents. Some thought this a peculiar choice; but a close friend who knew Austin intimately thought it peculiarly appropriate because Austin could not abide those who did not use their talents to the full. For Austin economics was a 'hands on' subject – the sole object of theory was for it to be applied to explanation and then to policy proposals: 'no economist is more dangerous than the pure theorist without practical experience and instinctive understanding of the real world that he is attempting to analyze, seeking precision in a world of imprecision, in a world he does not understand' (Austin Robinson 1992: 221). His Christian upbringing, in which works were emphasised even more than faith, and his wartime experiences led him to a life of service to his discipline and to humanity, and especially to those least able to help themselves, victims of both oppression and the malfunctionings of social systems.

Note

I especially thank, but in no way implicate, Marjorie Chibnall, Phyllis Deane, Alan Hughes and Barbara Jeffrey for their comments on a draft of the memoir. In writing it I have drawn extensively on Alec Cairncross's 1993 biography of Austin and on Austin's 1992 autobiographical essay in Szenberg (1992). Finally I am most grateful to the economists who responded so willingly to my request for their recollections of Austin and their evaluations of his contributions.

Notes

1. Austin's father was the Rector of Toft in Cambridgeshire but his mother went to her family home for the birth of their first child.
2. Shove, who later became renowned as a teacher (see Kahn, 1987), was shy and ill at ease with returned servicemen because he felt they despised people who had been conscientious objectors during the war. Austin and Shove became firm friends as colleagues in the 1930s.
3. The Maurices were a formidable and numerous clan whom Austin found 'a trifle frightening' (Cairncross 1993: 19).
4. Joan returned before Austin and may have helped to draft parts of the report in the United Kingdom (Tahir 1990: 21).
5. It was applauded: 'a most unusual tribute' (Cairncross 1993: 15).
6. In a letter (22 November 1988) to Aubrey Silberston, who was then secretary of the RES, Austin set out his future agenda for both the society and journal. He wanted the society to speak for the profession as he felt it had in Keynes's day and the journal to be the 'journal of the profession as a whole'.
7. The 'circus' was a group of young economists – Austin and Joan Robinson, Piero Sraffa, Richard Kahn, and James Meade – who met to discuss the *Treatise on Money*. Their deliberations were usually reported to Keynes by Kahn who then conveyed Keynes's reaction to the 'circus' members, see Austin Robinson (1985) and Richard Kahn (1985) for their recollections.
8. Ken Arrow and Tony Atkinson (July 1994) have written that Austin thought that the small conferences generated the most valuable discussions but in order to guard against exclusiveness he urged the need for regional conferences. 'As General Editor, he wielded his pencil forcefully' – the pay-off was the academic quality of the conference volumes.

9. I should also mention that Austin was at the 1975 S'Agaro Conference on the Microeconomic Foundations of Macroeconomics which I chaired. I expected we would jointly edit the volume of the same title (1977), but after I sent Austin a draft of the introduction he generously suggested that I do it alone.
10. This section is based on the 1996 Kingsley Martin Memorial Lecture (Harcourt, 1998; this volume Chapter 22). The page references (150–2) are to Alec Cairncross's discussion of the report (Cairncross 1993).

References

Berrill, K. (ed.) (1964) *Economic Development with Special Reference to East Asia* (London: Macmillan).

Cairncross, A. (1985) *Years of Recovery: British Economic Policy 1945–51* (London: Methuen).

— (1993) *Austin Robinson. The Life of an Economic Advisor* (London: Macmillan; New York: St Martin's Press).

Davis, J. M. (ed.) (1933) *Modern Industry and the African* (London: Macmillan; new edn., London: Frank Cass, 1967).

Hailey, Lord (ed.) (1938) *African Survey* (Oxford: Oxford University Press; reprinted 1945).

Harcourt, G. C. (ed.) (1977) *The Microeconomic Foundations of Macroeconomics* (London: Macmillan).

— (ed.) (1985) *Keynes and his Contemporaries* (London: Macmillan).

— (1998) 'Two Views on Development: Austin and Joan Robinson', *Cambridge Journal of Economics*, vol. 22, 367–77.

Kahn, R. (1985) 'The Cambridge "Circus" (I)' in Harcourt (1985), 42–51.

— (1987), 'Shove, Gerald Frank (1888–1947)' in J. Eatwell, M. Milgate and P. Newman (eds) (1987) *The New Palgrave. A Dictionary of Economics*, vol. 4 (London: Macmillan), 327–8.

Keynes, J. M. (1919) *The Economic Consequences of the Peace* (London: Macmillan) *C.W.*, vol. II, 1971.

— (1936) *The General Theory of Employment, Interest and Money* (London: Macmillan) *C.W.*, vol. VII, 1973.

— (1940) *How to Pay for the War. A Radical Plan for the Chancellor of the Exchequer* (London: Macmillan) *C.W.*, vol. XXII, 1978, 40–155.

Reddaway, B. (1996) 'The Bangladesh Economy in a World Perspective', in A. Abdullah and A. R. Khan (eds), *State, Market and Development: Essays in Honour of Rahman Sobhan* (Dhaka: University Press), 289–304.

Robinson, E. A. G. and others (none explicitly named) (1928) *The British Crown and the Indian States* (London: P.S. King).

— (1931) *The Structure of Competitive Industry* (Cambridge: Cambridge University Press; rev. edn. 1953).

— (1936) 'Mr Keynes on Money', *The Economist*, 24 February, 471–2.

— (1941) *Monopoly* (Cambridge: Cambridge University Press; reprinted 1956).

— (1947) 'John Maynard Keynes 1883–1946', *Economic Journal*, vol. LVII, 1–68.

— (1960) 'The Size of the Nation and the Cost of Administration', in E. A. G. Robinson (ed.), *The Economic Consequences of the Size of Nations* (London: Macmillan), xiii–xxii.

— (1964) 'Foreign Trade: Foreign Trade in a Developing Country', in Berrill (1964), 212–32.

— (ed.) (1965) *Problems in Economic Development* (London: Macmillan).

— (1967) *Economic Planning in the United Kingdom: Some Lessons* (Cambridge: Cambridge University Press).

— (1969) 'The Desirable Level of Agriculture in Advanced Industrial Economies' in U. Papi and C. Nunn (eds), *Economic Problems of Agriculture in Industrial Societies* (London: Macmillan), 26–50.

— (mid-1970s) *Future Tasks for UNDP: Report to the Administrator of the United Nations Development Program.*

— (1974) 'The Economic Development of Malthusia', *Modern Asian Studies*, vol. 8, 521–34.

— (ed.) (1979) *Appropriate Technologies for Third World Development* (London: Macmillan).

— and J. E. Vaizey (eds) (1966) *The Economics of Education* (London: Macmillan).

— and M. Kidron (eds) (1970) *Economic Development in South Asia* (London: Macmillan).

Robinson, A. (1984) 'Comment', in Wiles and Routh (1984), 222–32.

— (1985) 'The Cambridge "Circus" (2)', in Harcourt (1985), 52–7.

— (1986a) *First Sight of Postwar Germany May–June 1945*, private circulation (printed by Brian Allen, The Cantelupe Press, Great Abington, Cambridge).

— (1986b) 'The Economic Problems of the Transition from War to Peace: 1945–49', *Cambridge Journal of Economics*, vol. 10, 165–85.

— (1992) 'My Apprenticeship as an Economist', in Szenberg (1992), 203–21.

Sargent Florence, P. (1932) 'Review of *The Structure of Competitive Industry* (1931)', *Economic Journal*, vol. XLII, 66–70.

— (1941) 'Review of *Monopoly*', *Economic Journal*, vol. LI, 481–3.

Szenberg, M. (ed.) (1992) *Eminent Economists. Their Life Philosophies* (Cambridge: Cambridge University Press).

Tahir, P. (1990) 'Some Aspects of Development and Underdevelopment: Critical Perspectives on Joan Robinson' (Cambridge: unpublished PhD dissertation).

Wiles, P. and G. Routh (eds) (1984) *Economics in Disarray* (Oxford: Basil Blackwell).

9
Karl Marx, 1818–83*

with Prue Kerr

Overview

Because some of the tendencies which Marx identified (and his critics mistakenly interpreted as predictions) have not in fact occurred, he must rest content instead, as the late Ronald Meek told us (1967: 128), with being 'just another genius'. Marx was the most profound interpreter of the capitalism of his age, arguably of any age. He bequeathed to us a set of methods with which to approach issues of high theory, historical and philosophical analysis, and policies embracing *Realpolitik* in the social sciences. We concentrate here on these aspects of his contributions. His views on the operation of socialism and of its transformation to communism are on a different plane, often approaching in naivety those of Utopian Christian Socialists – hence the *non sequitur* involved in supposing that the overthrow of the USSR and Eastern European regimes discredits Marx's most enduring contributions, Baroness Thatcher notwithstanding.

Personal background

His personal story, because it is so familiar, may be quickly told. Born in 1818 in Trier, on the river Moselle, into a respected

* A slightly revised version of the entry on 'Marx, Karl Heinrich (1818–1883)' in M. Warner (ed.), *International Encyclopedia of Business and Management* (London: Routledge, 1996), 3388–45. We thank but in no way implicate Peter Nolan, Renée Prendergast and Malcolm Warner for their comments on a draft of the essay.

middle-class Jewish family which nevertheless had been forced to assimilate, Marx went to university first at Bonn and then at Berlin. There, he abandoned romanticism for Hegelianism which dominated Berlin at the time. He became involved in liberal journalism. When the state authority closed down the paper for which he wrote he moved to Paris. There, Marx became a communist and met Friedrich Engels for the first time. He was expelled from Paris, went to Brussels for three years and then to London in 1849. He was to stay for the rest of his life with his wife and growing family. In 1843 Marx had married Jenny von Westphalen who lived next door to him as a child; it was a deeply devoted union which survived poverty, illness, the deaths of two of their five children and Marx's infidelity with their unpaid maid, Lenchen. Marx worked as a scholar, a journalist – and a political revolutionary (after all, he and Engels published *The Communist Manifesto* in 1848). Though not as poor as he liked to make out, especially when he wanted further hand-outs from Engels, Marx and his family did experience poverty, insecurity and recurring bouts of bad health which eventually prevented him bringing out all three volumes of *Capital* in his own lifetime.

As Robert Heilbroner's excellent chapter on Marx in *The Worldly Philosophers* (1991: 149) suggests, Marx was *not* an admirable person. Possibly he was the victim of both his age and class – he would not allow his daughters to meet Engels' working-class mistresses and he did not think any of his sons-in-law were good enough for his daughters, for instance. Whether he was or was not an anti-semite as well is, at best, *not proven*, see Wheen (1999: 55–57) for a most balanced assessment. He could be crass, insensitive and grossly unfair to his critics and his predecessors, yet all this is ultimately beside the point: the principle that he evolved, of soaking himself in historical facts and figures and in the writings of those who came before him, initially criticising them from within their own texts and then developing his own alternative theory and approach, incorporating and expanding and often changing profoundly what he had criticised and discarding what was misleading, incoherent or just plain wrong, is surely the right way to do original work in social science.

Major works

Marx, K. and F. Engels (1848) *Manifest der Kommunistischen Partei*; in English, *Manifesto of the Communist Party*, in *Marx: The Revolution of 1848* (Harmondsworth: Penguin, 1973).

Marx, K. (1858) *Zur kritik der Politischen Ockonomie*; in English, *Contribution to the Critique of Political Economy* (London: Lawrence & Wishart, 1970).
Marx, K. (1867) *Das Kapital*, Band I; in English, *Capital*, Vol. I (Harmondsworth: Penguin, 1976).
Marx, K. (1885) *Das Kapital*, Band II, published by Engels; in English, *Capital*, Vol. II (Harmondsworth: Penguin, 1978).
Marx, K. (1894) *Das Kapital*, Band III, published by Engels; in English, *Capital*, Vol. III (Harmondsworth: Penguin, 1981).
Marx, K. (1905–10) *Theorien über der Mehrwert*, published by Karl Kautsky; in English, *Theories of Surplus Value* (Moscow Progress Publishers, 1963).

Method of analysis

Marx came to political economy from philosophy, trained especially in German philosophy and crucially influenced by the philosophical views of Hegel and the principle of dialectical change. The use of a dialectic led him always to look for internal contradictions both in systems of thought and in the working out of social processes. His organising concept when he came to political economy was the notion of *Surplus* – how it was created, extracted, distributed and used in different societies. Marx looked at human history as succeeding epochs of different ways of surplus creation *et al.*; he was determined to find by analysis of the power patterns of each, the seeds of both their achievements and their internal contradictions and eventual destruction and transformation as, through the endogenous processes thus discovered, one form gave way to the next. The jewel in his crown was his analysis of capitalism. Maurice Dobb (1946) has given us a detailed historical analysis from a Marxist viewpoint of how feudalism gave way to capitalism. Here we concentrate on Marx's views on capitalism itself.

Marx's method of analysis may be likened to an onion. At the central core which underlies the overlapping outer layers of skin is the pure, most abstract yet fundamental model of the mode of production (Marx's phrase) being analysed. All fossils from the past, all embryos of what is to come, are abstracted from this. The system is revealed in its purest form. Yet the aim is to show that the fundamental characteristics and relationships thus revealed are robust – that they survive intact the complications provided by adding back (in analysis) the inner and outer layers of skin of the onion, that they still remain the ultimate determinants of what is observed on the surface. Thus, if we may illustrate from the transition from Vol. I to Vol. III of *Capital* (the latter was written before Vol. I but only published after Marx's death, edited by Engels): though there is little explicit mention in Vol. I of the (near) surface phenomenon of prices of production of Vol. III, yet the links from the underlying labour values of Vol. I are always at the forefront of Marx's intention – not in the mainstream sense of providing a theory of relative prices (the neoclassical interpretation of what the labour theory of value (LTV) is about) but in making explicit the link as a necessary part of the story of production, distribution and accumulation in capitalism.

Labour theory of value

Having mentioned the dreaded phrase, LTV, let us say what we understand by it. As we have said, the principal task Marx set himself was to explain the creation *et al.* of the surplus in capitalism. Naturally, he linked this in capitalism with an explanation of the origin of profits and the determination of the system-wide rate of profits in this mode of production. He identified in previous modes the role of classes in each, one dominant, one subservient, with reference to the creation of wealth and so social and economic power, and the connection of their relationship to the creation *et al.* of the surplus by a process of explicit exploitation of one class by another. For example, in feudalism the process was obvious: its institutions and laws ensured that the lords of the manor could physically extract from the serfs part of the annual product, either by making serfs work for set periods on the lords' lands or because the serfs were tenants, requiring them to 'hand over' part of the product of the land which their labour had brought forth.

When we get to pure *competitive* capitalism such a process seems impossible. For one aspect of capitalism, purified in modern theory to become price-taking behaviour by all agents with prices set by the impersonal forces of the market, in classical and Marx's times more robustly specified as a wide diffusion of power amongst *individual* capitalists and *individual* wage-earners, seems to make it impossible for individual capitalists to coerce free wage-earners into doing what they do not wish to do. They could always leave one and work for another, just as any one capitalist and his capitals could leave or enter any activity – hence the *tendency* for rates of profit to be equalised in all activities and the need to explain what determined the origin and size of the systemic rate of profits to which their individual values tended. Moreover, each free wage-labourer was paid a definite money wage for all the hours he or she worked. Under these conditions, how could exploitation occur or a surplus arise, and where *did* profits come from?

Marx answered this in terms of the distinction between necessary and surplus labour time associated with the class relations of capitalist society. Capitalists *as a class* (subset into industrial, commercial and finance capital) had a monopoly of the means of production and finance. Workers *as a class*, having only their labour power to sell, had to do as they were told in the workplace. As propertyless, landless but free wage-labourers, the proletariat whose creation was the byproduct of feudalism giving way to capitalism, they had but one choice – *either* to work under the conditions established by the capitalist class, *or* to withdraw from the system entirely, and starve. Therefore the working day could conceptually be split into two parts: the hours needed with the existing stock of capital goods, methods and conditions of production to produce wage goods – necessary labour; and the rest – surplus labour – which was the source of surplus value in the sphere of production, and of profits in the sphere of distribution and exchange. Marx adopted the classical idea, strictly Ricardo's, that all commodities had an embodied labour value to explain how labour services, a commodity saleable just like any other in capitalism, would tend to sell at their values. But human labour had the unique property that it would create more value – produce more commodities – than was needed for its own reproduction and this was embodied in the commodities corresponding to this surplus labour time.

A subsidiary part of the story was that the actual operations of capitalism resulted in the waxing and waning of the reserve army of labour (RAL) – a much more suitable euphemism for the unemployed than the modern description of the same phenomenon as flexible labour markets – causing actual wages to tend towards (or fluctuate around?) their natural values (a purely classical story). But the main story was that while the surface phenomenon seemingly reflected fairness and efficiency – people paid fully for what they did and all the hours they worked – this masked the underlying exploitation process arising from the situation of class monopoly. In the sphere of production there was a tendency to equality in the length of the working day (week, year) and intensity of work too. In the sphere of distribution and exchange, abstracting from actual (market) prices, there was a tendency for the prices of production to be such that a uniform rate of profits was created (the first great empirical generalisation of classical political economy) and for the profit components of the prices of production to be such as to constitute uniform rates of return on total capitals, similarly measured, in all activities.

Circuits of capital

The total capitals consisted of two parts – advances of wages to the wage-earners, variable capital (v) (variable because this component *alone* created more value than it started off with); and constant capital (c), 'dead' labour embodied in durable assets from previous rounds – circuits – of surplus labour, surplus value and profit-creation and reinvestment. Marx famously pictured the capitalist process as the circuit of capitals: $M \rightarrow C \rightarrow C' \rightarrow M'$, where M and M' were money quantities with M' hopefully $> M$, and C and C' were commodities encompassing wage goods and services of constant capital which were transformed, again, hopefully, through the production process into commodities (C) saleable at a profit $M' - M$. On the way to creating *The General Theory*, Keynes applauded Marx for this insight.

Value and price

Many have come to see the 'transformation problem' relating the underlying embodied labour values of commodities to their prices of production as a sterile exercise and debate. Yet viewed in this way it makes sense, both in explaining a fundamental characteristic of capitalism and in illustrating the power of Marx's method and approach. In order to show that anything classical political economy could do Marx could do as well and better, it was necessary to reconcile the pure theory of the origin of profits in the capitalist mode of production with the other major 'finding' of political economy – the tendency to a uniform rate of profit in all activities – and also to 'explain' what determined the size of the system-wide rate of profits. (Piero Saffra, who had a deep knowledge of and admiration for Marx's work, always spoke of the rate of profits, indicating that it *was* the system-wide concept which needed to be explained within the classical and Marxist system. As Luigi Pasinetti said of his own modern variant of the theory of the rate of profits: 'It is macro-economic because it could not be otherwise', Pasinetti, 1974: 118.)

The various conundrums arise because, while competition would ensure a uniform rate of exploitation (s/v, where s = surplus labour and v = necessary labour) in all industries because, as we have seen, free wage-labourers can always move from one occupation to another, there is nothing obvious or even not obvious in the forces of competition and their impact on technical progress to ensure that the corresponding organic compositions of capital (c/v) (with some licence, the capital–labour ratios) should also tend to equality. But since a well-known Marxist result is that $r = s/v$ $(1 + c/v)$, when all variables are measured in terms of abstract socially necessary labour time, *if* the LTV meant that commodities exchanged in proportion to their embodied labour amounts, there would not be a tendency, not even a long-run one, to equality of rates of profit (so measured) in all activities. Therefore it became necessary to explain the deviations of the prices of production with their uniform profit components around the underlying labour values, at the same time requiring the explanation to embrace the magnitudes of surplus value *et al.* in the sphere of production.

This step is what the various proposed 'solutions' of the transformation problem were meant to establish – Sraffa's is the most satisfying as Ronald Meek pointed out in his 1961 review article of *Production of Commodities*. The fact that Marx's own solution was wrong and that Engels would not part with the promised prize to those who got it right (even when they did) is beside the point, Böhm Bawerk and *Karl Marx and the Close of his System* (1889) notwithstanding. It also allows us to comment on another modern controversy arising from consideration of the transformation problem – Ian Steedman's argument (1975, 1977) that including joint production techniques in a model of value, distribution and accumulation stopped the Fundamental Marxist Theorem (FMT, as Michio Morishima dubbed it) going through. The FMT is the proposition that the necessary and sufficient condition to observe a positive rate of profits in the sphere of distribution and exchange is to have positive surplus labour (and value) in the sphere of production. Steedman argued that it was possible in a joint production system to have *negative* surplus labour and value in the sphere of production associated with *positive* profits in the sphere of distribution and exchange.

But, as a number of economists soon showed (for example, Miroshima 1976), this is not so if Marx's sturdy intuition is specified appropriately in the model. Again, this is not just esoteric game-playing in order to fill out (or up) CVs, but an excellent example of making precise sense of a major insight which still has relevance today. For while the RAL no longer pushes *all* wage-earners' incomes down to subsistence levels, nevertheless recent macro-economic policy has unwittingly been drawing on Marx's insights to create a potential surplus for greater profits and accumulation by creating cowed and acquiescent workforces whose necessary labour time has been much reduced. Of course, the policy-makers have forgotten another Marxist insight that there are internal contradictions present in each mode of production. In modern capitalism, as in the capitalism of Marx's time, the policies used to create a potential surplus may simultaneously so dampen and depress the 'animal spirits' of the decision-making and accumulating class, that the potential surplus may remain largely unrealised by actual accumulation and actual investment expenditure – the initial $C \to C'$ in the circuit above. Marx also recognised that industrial, commercial and finance capital must advance in tandem and that when they do not, crises occur. Hilferding (1910) was one of the first major writers on this theme. The dominance of industrial and commercial capital by financial capital has been a major cause of the instabilities in world capitalism of the past 20 years or more.

Schemes of reproduction

We now move on to lessons from Vols II and III, especially the role of the Schemes of Reproduction which played such an important part, often unrealised by the people employing them, in both the Keynesian/Kaleckian revolution and the immediate prewar and postwar theories of growth. As Claudio Sardoni (1981) has made clear, to interpret the schemes of reproduction as precursors of steady-state growth models is to misunderstand what Marx was doing. What Marx's three departmental schemas – wage goods, luxury goods, capital goods – were meant to make explicit were the consistency conditions needed to ensure, period by period, that total demands and total supplies, as well as their compositions, matched. Satisfying the conditions period by period did not imply steady growth over 'time' though it was, of course, a possibility. There is no suggestion in Marx, just as there wasn't in Joan Robinson's (1956) 'Golden Ages' (nor, to be fair, in Solow's original 1956 neoclassical growth model), that this was descriptive economics. Indeed, in the first two instances, the principal objective was to show just how very special the conditions of the various inter- and intra-departmental purchases and sales had to be, so as to make it a complete fluke if capitalism left to itself with its myriad of decision-makers doing their own thing collectively brought such conditions about. Moreover, if they were not satisfied in fact, the authors went on to show how this could precipitate possibly a crisis and certainly serious malfunctioning. As Joan Robinson pointed out, Roy Harrod (her contemporary), in complete ignorance of a predecessor, discovered this all over again when he discussed the unstable nature of the warranted rate of growth. If the economy was on it, well and good, but if it was not, the system gave out signals which took the economy farther and farther away from it – and this, quite regardless of whether or not the warranted and natural rates of growth were coinciding. In a not unrelated manner, Rosa Luxemburg (1913) argued that c/v would tend to increase to a point where the consumption of wage goods would be insufficient to absorb their production, that is she raised the spectre of underconsumption, to be initially resolved by the courting of external markets through imperialism and sales of armaments.

Endogenous technical change and crises

Finally, in Marx's work we have one of the first systematic attempts to provide a theory of endogenous technical progress. He attempted to show that the capitalist system would experience deeper and deeper crises, principally by changing methods of production in each cycle such that a tendency to a falling rate of profits was produced. (It was common to all economists up to and including Marx that there was such a tendency, it was over the explanation that they differed.) A falling rate of profits would in the times when Marx was writing stifle both the desire and the ability to accumulate (have things changed that much?). Because real wages tended to rise in the upswing and boom as the RAL shrank, labour-saving innovations would be induced and embodied in the stock of capital goods by current accumulation. It was sensible, indeed essential, for each individual capitalist to so respond, in order to try to survive in a fiercely competitive environment (just as it was sensible for them always to try to weaken the power of the wage-earners on the workshop floor); but the systemic result was to swell on trend the RAL and reduce the fund of living labour from which surplus labour and surplus value could be extracted for future accumulation. Thus falling realised profits would reduce both the desire and ability to accumulate – the fundamental contradiction of capitalism was to tend to induce just the sort of technical progress which ultimately would tend to destroy the system itself.

We know now that the details of the argument meant that this was only a *possibility*, not an inevitable result as Marx tended(!) to believe. The point is that looking at events in Marx's way leads us to concentrate on the appropriate variables and processes to be used and analysed respectively.

Conclusion

Marx's writings on economics generated a tradition of study combining economic history with classical political economy. Confrontation or class struggle had occurred in every mode of production both as an economic and a social/political confrontation. The development of successive forms and forces or modes of production is the process of historical materialism. Capitalism is that phase in this history at which labour-power has become a commodity. Starting from the concept of embodied labour Marx explained the exploitation in capitalism of the direct producers through both the relations of production and the appropriation of the surplus by the class which purchased their labour-power. Struggle over the conditions of its sale and the production, distribution and use of the surplus it produced become part of the contradictory conditions which, through a dialectical process, resolved into new forms or, ultimately, new social relations or forces and so new modes of production. Marx saw final events as resolutions of already existing but conflicting features of the economic system. Value, therefore, is primarily an historically relative category, specific to capitalism. The measurement difficulty arising from reconciling labour-embodied values with prices of production can be regarded as no longer a problem if the labour theory of value is seen as a conceptual argument about the origins of the surplus and of expanded reproduction and change.

Marx recognised the drive for capital accumulation. He also recognised the contradictory tendencies present in this pursuit, demonstrating some possibilities in the circuits of capital. He was therefore inconclusive about the exact nature of the collapse of capitalism.

References

Böhm-Bawerk, E. von (1889b) *Zum Abschlus des Marxschen Systems*; translated P. Sweezy (ed.), *Karl Marx and the Close of his System*; including reply by R. Hilferding, *Böhm-Bawerk's Criticism of Karl Marx* (New York: Augustus M. Kelly, 1949). Claimed to have found a fundamental inconsistency between the theory of value and distribution in Vol. I and that of Vol. III of *Capital*.

Dobb, M. H. (1937) *Political Economy and Capitalism: Some Essays in Economic Tradition* (London: Routledge; reprinted Westport Conn.: Greenwood Press, 1972). A modern statement of the strengths of Marxian analysis.

— (1946) *Studies in the Development of Capitalism* (London: Routledge). Dobb's writing has stimulated a tradition in Marx's method of historical materialism. He saw the LTV not as a measure of relative prices but as a fundamental principle in explaining expanded reproduction and change.

Heilbroner, R. (1953, 1991) *The Worldly Philosophers* (Harmondsworth: Penguin Books), 6th edn. Best introduction to the lives and contributions of the great economists ever written.

Hilferding, R. (1910) *Das Finanzkapital*; translated T. Bottomore (1981) *Finance Capital* (London: Routledge & Kegan Paul). A treatise on the need for finance, commercial and industrial capitals to move in tandem to avoid crises.

Luxemburg, R. (1913) *Akkumulation des Kapitals*; translated by Schwarzschild with introduction by J. Robinson (1951) as *The Accumulation of Capital* (London: Routledge & Kegan Paul). Luxemberg argued that while Marx rejected Say's Law he was unclear that desired saving did not necessarily equal desired investment. Therefore she argued that he had not foreseen the possibility that domestic market demand may fall short of supply: external markets and the development of imperialism were one solution.

Meek, R. L. (1961) 'Mr Sraffa's Rehabilitation of Classical Economics', *Scottish Journal of Political Economy*, vol. 8, 119–36; reprinted in Meek (1967). Brilliant review article of Sraffa's classic, making explicit the relationship of Sraffa's analysis to classical and Marxist thought.

— (1967) *Economics and Ideology and Other Essays. Studies in the Development of Economic Thought* (London: Chapman and Hall). Measured and balanced essays on classical and Marxian political economy, past and present.

Morishima, M. (1987) 'Positive Profits with Negative Surplus Value – A Comment', *Economic Journal*, vol. 86, 599–603. Refutation of Steedman's claim that joint production systems could exhibit negative surplus labour and value with positive profits.

Pasinetti, L. L. (1974) *Growth and Income Distribution. Essays in Economic Theory* (London: Cambridge University Press).

Popper, K. (1945) *The Open Society and its Enemies*; 2 vols (London: Routledge). The second volume attacks Marx's claim for scientificity. It is impossible, Popper argues, for a theory of dialectical materialism to be demonstrated as true or false.

Robinson, J. (1956) *The Accumulation of Capital* (London: Macmillan). Joan Robinson's *magnum opus*, attempting 'to generalise *The General Theory* to the long period' (with Classical and Marxian overtones).

Rubin, I. I. (1928) *Essays on Marx's Theory of Value*; Moscow. English trans (1972) (Detroit: Black & Red). Deeply insightful essays on the core of Marx's theoretical system.

Sardoni, C. (1981) 'Multi-Sectional Models of Balanced Growth and the Marxian Schemes of Expanded Reproduction', *Australian Economic Papers*, vol. 20, 383–97. Definitive interpretation of the purposes of the Marxian schemes of expanded reproduction.

Solow, R. M. (1956) 'A Contribution to the Theory of Economic Growth', *Quarterly Journal of Economics*, vol. LXX, 65–94. The seminal paper on neo-classical growth theory, written independently but published at the same time as Trevor Swan's 1956 classic *Economic Record* paper on the same subject.

Sraffa, P. (1960) *Production of Commodities by Means of Commodities. Prelude to a Critique of Economic Theory* (Cambridge: Cambridge University Press). Both a critique of the conceptual foundations of neoclassical theory and the provision of a formal structure of the classical surplus approach.

Steedman, I. (1975) 'Positive Profits with Negative Surplus Value', *Economic Journal*, vol. 85, 114–123. Attempts to show that in joint production systems it is possible to have negative surplus labour and value associated with positive profits.

— (1977) *Marx after Sraffa* (London: NLB). A systematic discussion of the implications of the analysis in Sraffa's (1960) book for the main propositions of Marx's system.

Sweezy, P. M. (1942) *The Theory of Capitalist Development* (New York: Monthly Review Press). Develops Marx's theory of crisis into the new forms of capitalism characterising the twentieth century.

Wheen, F. (1999) *Karl Marx* (London: Fourth Estate). Most readable and fair account of Marx's life and contributions.

10
Keynes, John Maynard*

John Maynard Keynes, the eldest child of John Neville and Florence
Ada Keynes, was born into a professional middle-class English
household on 5 June 1883 in Cambridge. There were three children,
all gifted and destined to make their own mark, but Maynard
Keynes excelled. He was his parents' favourite and modern students
of sibling rivalry no doubt could have a field day analysing the consequent impact on his brother, Geoffrey, and sister, Margaret. John
Neville was a university lecturer in the Moral Science Tripos when
Keynes was born (in the year that Karl Marx died). He was to be the
author of two 'minor classics', *Studies and Exercises in Formal Logic*
(1884) and *The Scope and Method of Political Economy* (1891). He was
also a colleague of Alfred Marshall, whose pupil Maynard Keynes
became. He subsequently became the Registrary of the University, in
1910.

Maynard Keynes went to Eton, where he excelled intellectually
and socially, and then to King's, to read mathematics. He seems to
have spent as much time on philosophy as on mathematics and he
continued his hectic social and intellectual life. He was elected to
the Apostles, spoke at the Union, and made lifelong friends in
King's and Trinity. His tripos result – 12th Wrangler – was
respectable but disappointing for such a gifted person. He stayed on
in Cambridge to read for the civil service examinations in 1906, so
having his first contact with economics. He was supervised by

* Originally published in Thomas Cate (ed.), *An Encyclopedia of Keynesian
Economics* (Cheltenham, Glos: Edward Elgar, 1997), 278–81.

Marshall, who quickly realised that he had a genius on his hands. Characteristically, in effect, Marshall said, 'We old men must kill ourselves' – the usual mixture of grudging admiration and envy which characterised this great economist and awful person. Nevertheless, Keynes's lowest mark in the civil service examinations was in economics (presumably, he said, because the examiners knew less about the subject than he did) and, as he came second in the examinations as a whole, he had to settle for the India Office rather than his first love, the Treasury. While in the civil service, Keynes started work on a fellowship dissertation for King's (it became *A Treatise on Probability* in 1921). He was elected in 1909, at his second attempt. He had already returned to Cambridge in 1908 to become a lecturer in economics, paid for by Marshall out of his own pocket (here he *was* generous). Keynes was primarily interested in monetary theory and policy, though he lectured on a wide range of topics.

His social life kept on apace, as he was a core member of the Bloomsbury Group and a friend of many of the up and coming artists, theatre people and, subsequently, psychoanalysts – Keynes was vitally interested in the cultural and intellectual developments of his time, especially, of course, the philosophical developments associated with G. E. Moore, Bertrand Russell, Frank Ramsey and Ludwig Wittgenstein.

During World War I, Keynes worked in the Treasury (to the disgust of many of his friends who were pacifists and conscientious objectors). Keynes thought the war was an unspeakable crime but that, if the United Kingdom had to be in it, the war effort should be guided by rational and humane principles provided by intelligent and educated people who accepted 'the presuppositions of Harvey Rd' (Keynes's birthplace) as Harrod put it. Keynes was one of Lloyd George's advisors at Versailles; he was so appalled by the vindictive and destructive provisions of the Treaty that in the end he resigned and wrote *The Economic Consequences of the Peace* (1919), which made him world famous. In doing so he changed from being just an extraordinarily clever but often superficially flip and cynical young man into a serious maturity which can only be described as admirable. His beautifully written polemic is still worth reading for its passionate anger, power and application of theory in its best sense to explanation and policy.

Keynes returned to Cambridge in the 1920s, resigning his lecture-ship but maintaining his fellowship in King's (of which he was now senior bursar) and the editorship of the *Economic Journal* (to which he was first appointed in 1911). He performed an enormous number of roles – speculation, journalism, director of an insurance company, bibliophile, patron of the arts, theatre and ballet (in 1925, he was to marry Lydia Lopokova, the Russian ballerina, a mutually supportive partnership based on love and laughter) – all while he 'settled down' in order to write the three books which were to make him an immortal: *A Tract on Monetary Reform* (1923), *A Treatise on Money* (1930) and *The General Theory of Employment, Interest and Money* (1936). (We should also mention *Essays in Persuasion*, 1931 and *Essays in Biography*, 1933).

Initially Keynes worked on monetary matters within the Marshallian paradigm as he saw it, yet reacting to his teacher by concentrating more and more on happenings in the short run for policy recommendations. His most famous line – '*In the long run* we are all dead' – is to be found in a passage where he exhorts econo-mists to live and work and advise on the here and now. But he put the general price level at the centre of what was to be influenced by monetary policy and he had not yet arrived at a coherent theory of an integrated monetary production economy where both the general price level and activity were entwined – *that* was to come with the writing of *The General Theory*.

Keynes's marriage in 1925 marked a major sea change in his per-sonal life. Prior to this Keynes had been actively gay, as Skidelsky tells us in graphic detail in his Vol. I (1986), repairing the deliberate omission of this aspect of Keynes's life by Roy Harrod in the first 'official' biography in 1951. The happiness associated with his mar-riage had, it may be conjectured, a crucial impact on his creativity and understanding, so that his *magnum opus* was both a true work of genius and the work of a contented man, who was therefore all the more passionately angry about a system which brought mass unem-ployment and poverty to others. Keynes was also supremely confident that he could teach us why these evils happened and what we could – and should – do about them.

In 1937, he had the first of several severe heart attacks and the next two years or so were wiped out – relatively; that is to say, he only did what normally clever people would have done. In particular, though he replied to those he considered the most important of his critics in some important articles, including a summary restatement of his theory in the *Quarterly Journal of Economics* in 1937, he never did write those 'footnotes' to *The General Theory* which he told Ralph Hawtrey in August 1936 he was intending to do. Then came World War II in which (reluctantly at first, because of his health) Keynes became more and more involved. Not only did he 'generalise' *The General Theory* to tackle the inflationary problems of wartime scarcities, but he also took a larger and larger role in the actual running of the wartime economy and in the design of institutions to make the postwar world better and more just – Bretton Woods and all that.

Keynes literally killed himself for his country and the world by his efforts. His last major task was to get the British government and people to accept the harsh conditions of the American loan: his speech to the House of Lords on this issue was crucially important for the acceptance of the conditions. Exhausted, he returned to his country home, Tilton, in Sussex (in 1942, he had become Baron Keynes of Tilton) and on Easter Monday 1946 he had his last and this time fatal heart attack, dying far too young, at 62. Yet, as Austin Robinson told us, those whom the Gods love die young – 'a great economist and a very great Englishman', as *the Times* obituarist put it, a man whose life and works provide a resounding 'yes' to the Moorean puzzle with which Keynes and his contemporaries grappled: is it possible both to *be* good and to *do* good?

Reference

Skidelsky, R. (1986) *John Maynard Keynes*, vol. 1, *Hopes Betrayed, 1883–1920* (London: Macmillan).

Part III
Tributes

11
George Shackle: A Tribute*

Everyone who knew George Shackle inevitably said what an exceptionally kind and generous person he was. My introduction to this aspect of George's make up happened when I was a young lecturer in Adelaide in the late 1950s. We had there a very bright second-year undergraduate, Richard (Dick) Blandy (who is now Director of a Research Institute at the University of Melbourne, akin to the NIESR and the DAE combined). Dick had found a subtle mistake in one of Shackle's books, something to do with potential surprise, if I remember correctly, and had written to Shackle about it. Shackle replied, thanking him in a most gracious way, and in the reprint of the book – or perhaps it was in another book which covered the same topic – there was a two-page discussion of the point attributed, with much emphasis and praise, to Mr Richard Blandy of the University of Adelaide. I remember our then youthful Professor, Peter Karmel, showing this to all and sundry in the Department, enthusiastically mingling pride in Dick's achievement with admiration for Shackle's generosity of spirit.

Another aspect of George's personality and contributions which virtually everybody who wrote about him also inevitably commented on was his exquisite, and effective, use of English to convey his thoughts, not least his deep analytical insights. Here is an example of late Shackle (8 September, 1991).[1] It comes from a letter which George dictated to Catherine in reply to Jack

* Originally published in the *Review of Political Economy*, vol. 5, 1993, 272–3.

Gilbert (who had sent George a manuscript, 'Shackle and Keynes's economics'). George writes:

> Catherine has just read aloud to me a copy of your manuscript 'Shackle and Keynes's Economics'. I am intensely delighted by it. I should like to think that it will come to the notice of everyone who is touched in their deep feelings when Keynes's influence in economic theory is discussed ... Keynes released economics from the belief that businessmen wait until money-savings have accumulated in their own or others' bank accounts and then decide to use them to pay for the building of premises, vehicles, ships and all kinds of productive equipment including houses. On the contrary the investment comes first and helps to produce income. One of my articles was called 'Levels of Simplicity in Keynes' Theory of Employment'. Keynes'[s] insistent theme is the importance of looking at economic life as something creative, a new ship, dock, warehouse or electricity generating station, and all such tools are the result of enterprise, of businessmen's decisions to embark their funds in imaginatively conceived businesses. Investment is the driving force of business life. I think this idea is insistently and powerfully present in your paper. In this respect Keynes was a worthy and intensely successful follower of Marshall. Indeed Marshall's *Principles*, Knight's *Risk, Uncertainty and Profit* and Keynes'[s] *General Theory* show their respective authors as together constituting a powerful engine for driving economic theory forward. It is their work which has carved the path of advance for economic theory and been its inspiration in our century. Your paper most admirably thrusts this idea into the reader's mind so that he can as it were feel the vibrations of the rails on which our science runs and from which indeed it derives its value and effective power.

I need say no more.

Note

1. I am indebted to Victoria Chick for bringing this letter to my notice and to Catherine Shackle for allowing me to quote it here. The manuscript referred to by Jack Gilbert is 'Shackle and Keynes's Economics', *Review of Political Economy*, vol. 5, 1993, 165–80.

12
What Josef Steindl Means to My Generation*

I realise the title is pretentious for I cannot speak for a generation. But I can speak for myself; so I shall try to set out what Josef Steindl means to me.

I started economics at the University of Melbourne in 1950, in a Faculty that was very Keynes and Cambridge orientated. However, we were also introduced to the classical political economists and to Marx, both directly and through the writings of Maurice Dobb and Paul Sweezy. We read a lot of Kalecki as well in our honours years and also Hayek. As an undergraduate I discovered Kurt Rothschild's marvellous 1947 *Economic Journal* paper, 'Price theory and oligopoly' – it was probably the single most important paper that I read as an undergraduate.

Again, as an undergraduate, once I got J. R. Hicks *Value and Capital* (Part I) out of my system, I became most interested in employment and trade-cycle theory – as a result of studying Keynes, Kalecki and Schumpeter. I was also fascinated by imperfect competition – Joan Robinson (1933), Edward Chamberlin (1933), Robert Triffin (1940), Nicky Kaldor (1934; 1935) – and especially by oligopoly theory. Naturally, I wanted to see how I could bring these interests together and I first tried to do this in my undergraduate dissertation in 1953. I am still trying to do so today, see Harcourt (1992) (in Arestis and Sawyer, 1992). Naturally also, with this set of

* Originally published in the *Review of Political Economy*, vol. 6, 1994, 459–63.

mentors and these interests, I had to discover Josef's work. I was immediately enthralled by it and I have remained an enthusiastic fan ever since.

Josef Steindl has told us how great an influence Kalecki was on him. He first met Kalecki in Oxford in 1940 at the Oxford Institute of Statistics where he was its

> inspiration and [Steindl's] Guru. [Kalecki] had, independently of Keynes and before him, created economics anew, unburdened by the traditions of the subject and inspired by the department scheme of Marx, unaware until the publication of the *General Theory* in 1936 that the same kind of revolution was taking place in Cambridge. Kalecki had a penetrating mind and a passionate interest in what was going on in the world. He continuously absorbed, analysed and discussed the daily flow of events ... and his judgement almost always proved right.
>
> (Steindl, 1984: 7)

The traits that Josef so admired in Kalecki and his work I found, expressed in Josef's own unique manner, in him and his work too. One of the truly great plusses of the International Summer School at Trieste in the 1980s was to meet Josef in person and to hear him lecture to the students. Of all the people who were there, you could be certain that he would give a lecture that was highly relevant and topical, presented in a lucid, economically analytical form, with absolutely no frills in the presentation. Moreover, his lectures were (are) on political economy in the best sense; he identified the villains and heroes (and the innocent victims) – and did not pussy-foot around when saying so. There would be a sense of righteous anger when injustice or even escapable foolishness, was exposed and proper contempt when hypocrisy or silly-clever sophistication was criticized. 'Economists have tried to throw out all relevant material from the field of economics as if it were stones, and to leave in nothing but the principle of rationality. But this principle is empty as long as you do not know what people expect, nor how their manifold wishes, fears and doubts continue to produce a one-valued decision. To reduce them to a maximum of utility or profit is just begging the question, an infertile kind of *a-priorism*' (Steindl, 1984: 10). Although the purposes of the lectures were always serious ones, there would be an overlay of wry humour, definitely his own yet with overtones of which I feel sure Kalecki could have approved.

Josef and his work are splendid role models for many reasons. Let me try to set out some of them. First, and I think most importantly, he is a political economist who *insists* that the *raison d'être* of economics – political economy, that is! – is the application of its principles to the explanation of the malfunctioning of the body politic and economic, and the provision of policies with which to tackle the causes of the malfunctioning. In 1984 he asked: 'What might be done to overcome the sterility of today's economics? The first condition, [he said] is that we go back to the great tradition of the classics, Kalecki and Keynes whose work was rooted in the economic policy problems of their time, and derived its relevance from them. They asked what should be done and how. Economic policy is the main inspiration of economic theory' (Steindl, 1984: 13–14). Such policies have to be politically and socially realistic to be effective – he despises mechanical crank handlers who grind out instruments for targets while ignoring the political and social realities of the situation to which they are meant to apply. Yet, strange as it may seem, an increasing number of modern economists get angry if Josef's justification for our discipline – it is mine, too – is made explicit. They really do think that intellectual curiosity – the desire and ability to jump intellectual hurdles – is sufficient reason for our existence. What poppycock! Of course I applaud intellectual curiosity – would that more of our present-day students had it! – and I admire analytical ability in general. But they are not enough for a social science (certainly not for a branch of moral philosophy), and they would not have been thought so by our founding mothers and fathers.

Because Josef Steindl is a social scientist, he is very conscious of time and place, of situation-specific models. He has no time for grand, all embracing, universal systems, independent of time and place. Instead, he lets the world tell him what is happening, so avoiding what is, until very recently anyway, the mainstream blinkered and question-begging view – there *must* be an equilibrium out there (or several) and they must be (locally or globally) stable. Secondly, he deplores the Balkanisation of our subject into specialist sub-sets because this loses, often irretrievably, insights and understanding. 'Instead of evolving towards fundamental multidisciplinary combinations of various fields in the social sciences, so urgently needed by the nature of our problems, economics has gone the diametrically opposite way ... has split up into parts which are becoming alienated from each other ... specialisation leads to fragmentation with all its drawbacks', (Steindl, 1984: 6–7). Like Kalecki – and he like Marx – Josef Steindl always has, at the back of his head, the complete system of interrelationships for the issues in hand and he systematically fills in the details on each part before fitting them all together. Again – like Marx, Kalecki and Keynes – the simple but profound insight that the whole may be more than the sum of the parts, that the macroeconomic foundations of microeconomics are as important as the microeconomic foundations themselves, informs his approach. The ability starkly to reveal the major factors at work, to produce robust results, both analytically and empirically, is a noted characteristic of his work.

His two major books, *Small and Big Business* (1945) and *Maturity and Stagnation in American Capitalism* (1952: 1976), as Nina Shapiro (1992) so cogently reminds us, were respectively about the microeconomic and macroeconomic aspects of the processes at work in monopoly *cum* oligopoly capitalism. The first was concerned with how large and small firms could survive together side by side; the second was concerned with the inherent tendency to stagnation in an investment environment dominated by oligopolistic market structures. The latter implies an ever-present possibility of excess capacity emerging, as 'rational' behaviour at the micro level creates 'irrational' macroeconomic outcomes.

Thirdly, Josef *is* a good mathematician, so that any mathematics that he uses is always his servant, never his master. Having no reason to show off – indeed, it is not in his nature to do so – and because he is in complete control of his chosen tools, what mathematics he does use is chosen because it is appropriate for the economic issues being discussed, not, as is so often the case, and to the great detriment of the discipline, the other way around. Josef comments wryly on this deplorable aspect of modern developments:

[A]t a certain period I also had great optimism with regard to the possibilities of mathematics. Kalecki warned me of that, and he also warned me of the computer: He suggested that both were ideally suited as a scientific cloak to cover the lack of economic substance. Whatever the potentialities of mathematics, with regard to the use which was actually made of it he was dead right. [Its role in] economics has been a most unfortunate one. Instead of being a tool ... it has developed a life of its own. Rather than looking for methods to suit [their] economic problems, [students ask their teachers] to set [them] problems which suit the formal problems [they have] learned.

(Steindl, 1984: 8–9)

Fourthly, Josef believes in good old-fashioned empirical work: understand the meaning, strength and limitations of the data, do not use fancy techniques for their own sake, but rather choose those which are appropriate for the nature of the data which are being used. Sometimes, this involves the use of sophisticated techniques in order to extract the utmost from the data, sometimes it involves the use of very simple techniques, for a scatter diagram and a regression line, or even a well set-out table, may be all that is needed to focus on the economic intuition involved. Like Tinbergen, Josef knows that diminishing returns set in very quickly in the application of our techniques because of the essential nature of the subject matter of our discipline. But again, this time, like Frisch, Josef would never shirk from making use of difficult techniques and analysis if they were thought to be appropriate for tackling an issue, or an aspect of the issue in hand.

Josef Steindl has a most real sense of relevance and a tremendous seriousness of purpose, to which he has been true all his life. Because he is acutely aware of the terrible economic problems which still plague us (had more notice of his advice been taken in the past these problems would have been considerably less), he has very strict standards concerning what we should and should not work on in our discipline. I am not at all sure he would approve of me having written this tribute.

In conclusion, may I say how much I wish our greatly loved, mutual friend, the late Krishna Bharadwaj, were here to join in the celebrations and tributes? Long may Josef remain a splendid and a principal source of inspiration, keeping us straight and, as ever, guiding us.

References
Arestis, P. and M. Sawyer (eds) (1992) *A Biographical Dictionary of Dissenting Economists* (Aldershot: Edward Elgar).

Chamberlin, E. H. (1993) *The Theory of Monopolistic Competition* (Cambridge, Mass.: Harvard University Press).

Harcourt, G. C. (1992) 'G. C. Harcourt (born 1931)', in P. Arestis and M. Sawyer (eds), 232–41.

Hicks, J. R. (1939; 1946) *Value and Capital* (Oxford: Oxford University Press).

Kaldor, N. (1934) 'The Equilibrium of the Firm', *Economic Journal*, vol. 44, 60–76.

— (1935) 'Market Imperfection and Excess Capacity', *Economica*, vol. 2, 33–50.

Robinson, J. (1933) *The Economics of Imperfect Competition* (London: Macmillan).

Rothschild, K. W. (1947) 'Price Theory and Oligopoly', *Economic Journal*, vol. 57, 299–320.

Shapiro, N. (1992) 'Josef Steindl (Born 1912)', in P. Arestis and M. Sawyer (eds). 549–55.

Steindl, J. (1945) *Small and Big Business: Economic Problems of the Size of Firms* (Oxford: Basil Blackwell).

— (1952; 1976) *Maturity and Stagnation in American Capitalism* (Oxford: Basil Blackwell).

— (1984) 'Reflections on the Present State of Economics', *Banca Nazionale del Lavoro Quarterly Review*, March, 3–14.

Triffin, R. (1940) *Monopolistic Competition and General Equilibrium Theory* (Cambridge, Mass: Harvard University Press).

13
A Left Keynesian View of the Phillips Curve Trade-Off*

I

I only met Bill Phillips four times. The first time was in the mid-1950s when he was the selected 'heavy' of the host economics department (LSE) who spoke at the Cambridge–London–Oxford research students seminar. As far as I can remember he gave a paper on feedback mechanisms in Marshallian supply and demand analysis. It was refreshingly lacking in respect for Marshall in particular and economists in general. Not that he was a show-off, it was just that he said what he thought and backed up any critique with hard-headed analysis of the sort he was accustomed to use for engineering problems. That was one of his greatest strengths.

The second time was in Adelaide in the late 1950s where he gave a paper on an Australian Phillips Curve (chapter 28 of Leeson, 2000), having recently published *the* Phillips Curve itself (Phillips, 1958, chapter 25 of Leeson, 2000). His paper was only a first draft but it was so criticised and dissected by Eric Russell in particular that it never saw the light of day in the public domain. In this instance his engineering background was a weakness, for he seemed inclined to take economic statistics as gospel, that is, that they actually meant something really *precise*. Eric, of course, knew the Australian statistics on wages, employment and prices intimately and was able

---

* Originally published in R. Leeson (ed.), *A. W. H. Phillips. Collected Works in Contemporary Perspective* (Cambridge: Cambridge University Press, 2000) 304–7.

to show that the data were so non-homogenous as to make completely unsound any attempt to fit a curve to them. Even if there were to be an underlying relationship to be teased out of the figures, they were just not in a form, and nor could they be put in one, to allow this procedure to occur. Moreover, Eric doubted that there *was* a stable relationship waiting to be found. Bill Phillips took all this on board with good grace and, of course, while Eric's logic was remorseless and compelling, he was such a courteous and fine person that, as ever, as Al Watson once put it, his criticisms left no bruises.

I think I also saw Bill twice in Canberra when he was at the ANU, once before his dreadful stroke when he spoke enthusiastically about renewing his interest in China. The other time was after his stroke when he was very much knocked about. He told me about how he came to be captured by the Japanese during the Second World War. He was on a cliff and had to decide whether to jump and risk being killed either by the rocks or by drowning in the river below, or being captured on the top of the cliff. The moment of indecision led to the last occurring. He said that even the simple act of coming down stairs now brought the same feelings back to him. Bill was a most attractive, likeable and unassuming man and I found both Conrad Blyth's and Robert Leeson's obituary essays on him unbearably moving.

II

What though of a Left-Keynesian's view of the Phillips Curve trade-off itself? I have always regarded as an intellectual and political disaster the fact that the Phillips Curve trade-off came to be identified with Keynesianism, both as a view of how the world 'worked' and as a basis for policy. It was an intellectual disaster because there is no way that the Phillips Curve trade-off, as usually interpreted, may be found in either *The General Theory* or in Keynes's writings generally. Nor is it in anyway consistent with Keynes's views on the nature of economic theory or method, or on how economies work, or on how econometric work may or should be done. It was a political disaster because the stagflation episode allowed not only the Phillips Curve trade-off itself to be discredited but also Keynesianism itself. This was unjust and illogical, for no one who understood either Keynes or *The General Theory* – or the world and how it works – could have been surprised at the emergence of stagflation. But because the coupling was made, not least by Samuelson and Solow, this played into the hands of those who invented monetarism and its accompanying abhorrent anti-wage-earners, anti-the-poor and defenceless policies in so many countries. I cannot condemn too harshly those who did this – and those who allowed it to happen, or provided intellectual rationalisations for the policies, hired prize-fighters indeed.

III

Why cannot the Phillips Curve trade-off be found in *The General Theory*? First, because Keynes would have been horrified by the argument that a stable, dependable, *long-term* relationship between $\dot{p}$ (or $\dot{w}$) and u (and/or $\dot{u}$) could exist – horrified in the sense that it flew in the face of all his priors as to how the system worked. That is not to say that in a qualitative manner, what Arthur Brown has called an ordinal Phillips Curve relationship may not sometimes be discerned in Keynes's understanding of the world in specific situations. He did expect, for example, that higher levels of activity would in general be associated with higher price levels and, near full employment, with higher money-wage levels. But to go further and postulate a stable dependable relationship between *rates* of change of p or w and levels of unemployment was alien to his thought forms. What would be the specific historical association between $\dot{p}$ (and $\dot{w}$) and $\dot{u}$ would depend very much on specific historical circumstances – whether the particular level of u was approached from above or below and how fast were the approaches involved. Such a situation-specific approach means that stable relationships with stable parameters can never be expected to be present.

IV

As to the stagflation episode, had Keynes's own aggregate demand and supply analysis from *The General Theory* not been largely driven out of the textbooks – perhaps it would be better to say that it never really got into them – any self-respecting student would have seen immediately that an imported cost shock, for example, an oil price rise, or an autonomous increase in money-wages, would have effects on the aggregate *supply* function which would tend, *ceteris paribus*, to raise the general price level and lower the level of activity and employment of the short period concerned. That this could set off further rises in prices and money-wages and further falls in activity and employment, emerge as distinct and plausible possibilities. The policy implication, therefore, was not to try to choose an *à la carte* mix of $\dot{p}$ and u by moving up or down a stable long-term relationship, but, rather, to try to devise a package deal of policies which included a permanent incomes policy consistent with the history, institutions and sociological characteristics of the society concerned. The object would be to bring the rate of change of money-wages and other incomes under some sort of control while preserving levels of *employment*, although, if necessary, at lower levels of real income, or increases of real income, if there had been a permanent worsening in, for example, the terms of trade.

In many countries the package deals of policies above were never adopted because of the identification of Keynesianism with the Phillips Curve trade-off and then the subsequent onslaught on it by the monetarists (and the new classical macroeconomists) who provided the intellectual ammunition for the implementation of what Tommy Balogh called 'the incomes policy of Karl Marx', that is, smash the wage-earners by creating unemployment through harsh prolonged monetary policy, and so change the balance of economic, social and political power as between labour and capital, both nationally and internationally. Of course, in the process these people forgot – most of them never knew it – an essential characteristic of capitalism, to wit, its inherent contradictions. By creating the conditions for a potential increase in the surplus of the system, that is to say, in the amounts potentially available for accumulation, they simultaneously destroyed the incentives and the abilities of the capitalists to turn what was potentially there into actuality, to realise the surplus. For the coarse and blunt instrument of monetary policy is a sure destroyer of those animal spirits on which, in the last analysis, the desire to accumulate depends. They were destroyed not only immediately but for such long periods as to ensure that much of the potential surplus remained unrealised.

Thus do the insights of Marx, who died in the year that Keynes was born, join up with those of his successor to illuminate the inequities of the conservative reaction to the bankruptcy of the Phillips Curve trade-off.

References

Leeson, R. (ed.) (2000) *A. W. H. Phillips: Collected Works in Contemporary Perspective* (Cambridge: Cambridge University Press).

Phillips, A. W. H. (1958) 'The Relation between Unemployment and the Rate of Change of Money Wage Rates in the United Kingdom, 1861–1957', *Economica*, vol. 25, 283–99.

14
The Results of the Capital Theory Controversies and General Equilibrium Theory: Some Reflections on Concepts and History*

I

I am happy that the organisers of the conference asked me to give a paper under the rubric of the results of the capital theory controversies and general equilibrium theory. I once got into hot water with Christopher Bliss when in a draft of a paper which eventually appeared in two versions (Harcourt, 1975, 1976) (one with a title, which, in retrospect, I regret having chosen), I tried to reconcile the clash between Christopher Bliss (1970) and Pierangelo Garegnani over Garegnani's (1970) *Review of Economic Studies* article. Bliss had written a comment on it in which he expressed surprise at some of Garegnani's results because, *within an Arrow–Debreu framework*, the results were not likely to occur. Garegnani's results related to comparisons of values of relative factor prices and shares following a 'change' in accumulation which he thought were unable to be reconciled with any real-world observations. (In his PhD dissertation (1959), Garegnani had made much the same point about marginal productivity theory and had used Walras and Wicksell as his guinea pigs.) I suggested that perhaps their difference in opinion *might* be traced to the fact that Garegnani concentrated (*à la* Ricardo) on the ultimate long-period outcomes of 'changes' in the values of specific

---

* A paper given in Rome in October 1998 on the occasion of the centenary of the birth of Piero Sraffa. I thank but in no way implicate Stephanie Blankenburg, Peter Kriesler and Ajit Sinha for their comments on a draft of this paper.

variables, while Bliss had put more emphasis (*à la* Malthus) on immediate, short-period results. Bliss interpreted my comments (made in a footnote and subsequently removed) as an assertion that he did not know the difference between the short period and the long period – oh dear me! We eventually sorted out our differences and resumed our restored friendship. With the fullness of time to provide hindsight, I would like now to make a few remarks about the issues involved.[1]

Since the 1970s a number of scholars have looked at the structure and the workings of the Arrow–Debreu intertemporal model and its offshoots. Some have detected, *within its own framework*, the possibility of 'perverse' results which are akin to those of the capital theory controversies and which are at odds with the fundamental conceptual notion underlying the subjective theory of value that utility is the source of value and that price is an index of scarcity. Furthermore, though not connected directly with these contributions, there are the disquieting results of Hugo Sonnenschein (and others) which Abu Rizvi has shown, in two fundamental papers (1991, 1994), undermine the mainstream attempt to lay down microeconomic foundations of macroeconomics. Alan Kirman (1989) has also commented on these and other matters and has pointed the way towards the use of social groups rather than isolated individuals as the appropriate starting point for macroeconomic analysis, indeed economic analysis in general. So perhaps a convergent process is starting between poles-apart economists – but I would not bet on it.

As I understand Garegnani's arguments, he was attempting to show that in a situation where a tendency to equality of rates of profit in all activities was at work, both the Marshallian and Walrasian frameworks (those which Krishna Bharadwaj called the supply and demand approach) could not guarantee convergence on long-period situations where this was ensured. Or, even if it did occur, the resulting before and after comparisons of the properties of the long-period positions were such as not to be compatible with any observed 'changes' in, say, income distributions in actual economies. It was a question concerned, first, with establishing exis-tence (and uniqueness) and, secondly, with the possibility of the equilibrium, if it existed, exhibiting local and global stability. This last is a much harder task, one which the most thoughtful general equilibrium theorists seem to have conceded cannot be done unless very special and artificial, arbitrary or, dare I say it, *ad hoc* conditions are assumed. Heinz Kurz has written an especially lucid account of the existence and stability arguments in his 1985 article in *Contributions to Political Economy*; there he set out the 'critique of economic theory' implicit in Piero Sraffa's 'prelude' and, more explicitly of course, in the writings of Garegnani and other scholars.

All these expositions are a far cry from the general equilibrium model taught, for example, by Harry Johnson to his graduate students in the 1960s and 1970s, and left to us and posterity in his 1970 Yrjö Jahnsson Lectures (Johnson, 1971). There, he ensures that capital-theoretic puzzles are removed by assumption. The capital good used in the two sectors may be costlessly and timelessly removed and reshaped in response to the pull of changes in relative prices, so that except for large Giffen good effects (considered to be unlikely), prices in product and factor markets are able to do their things. Marshall's dynamical principle of substitution, seen ever at work in *both* consumption and production, dominates outcomes, which themselves confirm the neoclassical intuition that price *is* an effective index of scarcity in *all* markets, product and factor.

Finally, Avi Cohen (1989) has pointed to an incoherence in both approaches to value and distribution once we try to establish the robustness of their insights, intuitions and results outside the confines of one-, all-purpose, commodity models. In his 1993 paper he revives George Stigler's useful distinction between analytical and empirical propositions, a distinction which dates back at least to Ricardo when Ricardo conceded the effects of the durability of capital goods on the formation of relative values. (His editor, though, would not have accepted such a concession as far as pure, precise theory is concerned.)

In this paper I discuss these and other conceptual issues and argue – with hindsight – that they have become obscured at times as the debates developed over the years. As I recently wrote (Harcourt, 1997), it is far easier to put an explicit, logical and coherent structure on arguments and events after they have occurred than to be fully, or even dimly, aware of them while they are happening.

II

I started by reading again Garegnani's (1959) PhD dissertation (in English, I am ashamed to say that I have not yet the Italian to read it in its Italian book form. Indeed, when our first grandchild Caterina was born, Joan (Harcourt) responded by learning Italian, and I by learning English). There, he makes crystal clear that in Ricardo, Walras and Wicksell, despite their very different approaches to the theory of value and distribution, there is nevertheless a common source of error associated with the *meaning* (as Joan Robinson repeatedly stressed) of capital which in one dimension of the problem shows itself in its *measurement*. Garegnani argued – probably he is right – that in the classical surplus approach, in which the source of value is the difficulty or ease of reproduction (of commodities by means of commodities), the problem was solvable; but that in the supply and demand approach of Walras, Wicksell and Marshall and, as Sraffa and Krishna Bharadwaj were to argue, *all* forms of neoclassical theorising, it was not solvable.

The basic reason is that capital cannot be both an exogenous (determining) variable and an endogenous (determined) variable *at one and the same time*. Yet if we are to say that the relative prices of the services of the neoclassical factors of production are 'low' or 'high' because we have a 'lot' or a 'little' of their 'quantities' (or that more of the services of the relatively cheaper factor will be used if its relative price is 'low'), we must know what we mean by a 'lot' or a 'little' capital *before* the analysis starts. That is one reason why the mutual determination nature of general equilibrium theory, and whether Joan Robinson or Sraffa understood the nature of mutual determination (they did), is beside the point. As I said, Johnson was able to dodge this problem (and thus get 'pleasing' results) by assuming away virtually all the characteristics of capital goods (and finance capital) as we know them in modern economies.

The 'lot' or 'little' aspect was seized on by neoclassical economists as a measurement problem and therefore associated with aggregation puzzles. The latter, they argued, were the same (and as easy or as difficult to solve) for labour as for capital goods (or for the collection of heterogeneous goods which make up the national product). In a sense they were right – but about the incoherence in their own approach, not in the alternative approach. For increasingly it has been realised that, *even in general equilibrium systems*, the whole is more than just the sum of the parts, so that starting analysis from isolated individual behaviour virtually ensures that there is a *lacunae* between individual's behaviour, on the one hand, and the collective outcome of all the individuals' behaviour taken together, on the other.

This I take to be the principal thrust of Kirman's paper and of his recent review (1998) of Donald Walker's fine book (1997) on what Walras really said. Walker argues that Walras always tried to analyse processes, the formation of prices in particular, as they occurred in real-life markets even though towards the end of this life he changed his mind on what exactly they were, see also Walker (1987). Kirman argues that by a process of rational reconstruction, he and other general equilibrium theorists like him imposed an auctioneer on Walras's analysis as this was the only *logical* way to make his general equilibrium system coherent and equilibrate (in the sense of proving existence).

This observation also seems to be the crucial thrust of Rizvi's critique of the mainstream microeconomic foundations of macroeconomics programmes stemming from Sonnenschein's results about the arbitrary nature of the excess demand functions in Arrow–Debreu systems. Recently, Jan Kregel (1998) has written a subtle account of the link between the so-called New Keynesians' agenda and the fundamental reasons why the markets for labour and investment goods do not 'clear' at full employment, even when market structures are competitive. He traces these reasons back to the even more subtle arguments of Keynes about what knowledge ('information' as it is fashionable to say today) it is and is not reasonable to assume that people have when making employment and investment decisions and the implications of making these within an inescapable environment of uncertainty for the (unaided) attainment of full employment. Kregel links these arguments to similar ones to be found in George Richardson's critique of the coherency of the concept of competition (1959, 1960), to Ronald Coase's arguments for the existence of firms (1988), and so to the ultimate failure of markets to fulfil the promises its proponents claim they will deliver.

III

Many of these arguments explicitly point the way to an exciting new theme which Avi Cohen has developed in recent papers and which will be the subject of his forthcoming book on controversies in capital theory ancient and modern, appropriately subtitled *From Böhm-Bawerk to Bliss* (the person, not the state). He is convinced that the distinction between history and equilibrium lies at the heart of all the controversies, from those between Böhm-Bawerk and Fisher (and J. B. Clark), through those between Hayek and Knight, up to the modern ones which, started by Joan Robinson in the 1950s, drew fundamentally on the insights of the person, the centenary of whose birth we are celebrating at this conference. I must, of course, leave Avi to spell out the details of his argument. Suffice it to say here that the equilibrium approach will never be able to capture the essentials of the dynamic problems of accumulation with which the concept of capital is inescapably and crucially associated. (Sraffa shows that there is incoherence *even* within the confines of an equilibrium system.) All the contestants (in the ancient controversies, anyway) seem to have recognised this yet have vainly sought to find ways around it because they thought that economic theory and equilibrium must always go together.

This conclusion brings to the fore two developments which were occurring simultaneously in the postwar years, in which we know otherwise staunch allies were at loggerheads. For the critique of general equilibrium value and distribution theory by Sraffa and those influenced by him was usually carried out within structures which used the long-period method. One of the byproducts of this was to point to the retreat by modern defenders of the subjective theory of value and distribution, a retreat marked by the change in the definition of equilibrium, a move towards temporary equilibrium models and/or the Arrow–Debreu construction, see Garegnani (1990). It would then be argued, incorrectly, that Sraffa's analysis *must* be contained within this different but now universal framework, albeit as a (very) special case, as though an overlap of mathematics must automatically imply an overlap of economic conception, intuition and understanding. This movement was not only to be noted in the early Hicks but also in Hayek, who, having recognised the problem in the late 1920s, had hoped to solve it in *The Pure Theory of Capital* (1941) and so restore coherence to, he hoped, the agreeable results achieved by the traditional method – a task which he admitted he failed to carry out. Yet always his intuition (perhaps his fond desire) told him there must come out of Austrian capital theory a well-behaved, downward-sloping demand curve for the services of capital and that competitive markets, so necessary for his absolute value of freedom in society to be sustained, really did have underlying them stable patterns of relative prices which properly reflected relative scarcities. For him, Dr Pangloss, despite all theoretical and empirical evidence to the contrary, remained alive and well.

Such an act of faith was not, of course, confined to Hayek – it is also reflected in, for example, the opening paragraphs of Ken Arrow's (1973) Nobel Prize Lecture (though not in Hahn's (1973) critique of Kornai's *Anti-Equilibrium*, nor in the final summing-up in Bliss's (1975) book). Hayek himself tried to ally this belief with another, that the analysis of dynamic processes was to be the way forward, even though he himself gave up the task and concentrated on the theory of knowledge, the place of law in the good society and the absolute and ultimate value of freedom.

IV

What is the challenge for the heirs of Piero Sraffa if the general equilibrium approach is not a way forward but a dead end, even a negative achievement in Hahn's view? One thing which has clearly been exposed as misleading and unacceptable is the use of representative agent models for systemic analytic (not that their use has ceased!). They have served to suppress the attention which Keynes, for example, drew to the dangers of the fallacy of composition when analysing overall behaviour. The general equilibrium theorists thought they *could* avoid it but the weight of evidence suggests that they were wrong. Too often, too, post-Keynesians have looked at aggregate relationships and treated them as though they were representative of the behaviour of the firms throwing them up. (An early example of this criticism of post-Keynesian procedures is to be found in Lorie Tarshis's (1980) *American Economic Review* paper where he warns against viewing aggregate flows as an average when they are often the net outcome of extremely divergent behaviours.) Anyone who has pondered on liquidity preference theory realises that we must have at least two agents, a 'bull' and a 'bear', whose different desires are reconciled, at least momentarily, in an uneasy truce by the level of the rate of interest. Similarly, anyone who has even the faintest notion of what drives capitalism – the process of accumulation allied with endogenous technical progress – would need to use a model with at least an investment-goods and a consumption-goods sector with distinct social groups in each. Since I have always thought that Piero Sraffa was contributing – deeply, greatly – within a Marxian framework, I would like to think that he would have accepted this too.

Note

1. I have written the paper in a relatively unscholarly way, that is, few references and quotes, in order to set out the skeleton of the argument.

References

Arrow, K. J. (1973) 'General Economic Equilibrium: Purpose, Analytic Techniques, Collective Choice', *Les Prix Nobel en 1972* (Stockholm: The Nobel Foundation), 206–31.

Bliss, C. J. (1970) 'Comment on Garegnani', *Review of Economic Studies*, vol. XXXVII, 437–8.

— (1975) *Capital Theory and the Distribution of Income* (Amsterdam: North-Holland; New York: Elsevier).

Coase, R. (1988) *The Firm, the Market and the Law* (Chicago: Chicago University Press).

Cohen, A. J. (1989) 'Prices, Capital and the One-Commodity Model in Neoclassical and Classical "Theories"', *History of Political Economy*, vol. 21, 231–51.

— (1993) 'Samuelson and the 93% Scarcity Theory of Value', in M. Baranzini and G. C. Harcourt (eds), *The Dynamics of the Wealth of Nations. Growth, Distribution and Structural Change. Essays in Honour of Luigi Pasinetti* (London: Macmillan), 149–72.

Garegnani, P (1959) 'A Problem in the Theory of Distribution from Ricardo to Wicksell', unpublished PhD dissertation, University of Cambridge.

— (1970) 'Heterogeneous Capital, the Production Function and the Distribution of Income', *Review of Economic Studies*, vol. XXXVII, 407–36.

— (1990) 'Quantity of Capital', in J. Eatwell, M. Milgate and P. Newman (eds), *The New Palgrave: Capital Theory*. (London and Basingstoke: Macmillan), 1–78.

Hahn, F. H. (1973) 'The Winter of our Discontent', *Economica*, vol. 40, 322–30.

Harcourt, G. C. (1975) 'The Cambridge Controversies: The Afterglow', in M. Parkin and A. R. Nobay (eds), *Contemporary Issues in Economics* (Manchester: Manchester University Press), 305–14.

— (1976) 'The Cambridge Controversies: Old Ways and New Horizons – or Dead End?', *Oxford Economic Papers*, vol. 28, 25–65.

— (1999) '"The End of a Perfect Day". "Horses for Courses" and Policy Proposals', *Economic Issues*, vol. 4, 7–20.

Hayek, F. A. (1941) *The Pure Theory of Capital* (London: Routledge).

Johnson, H. G. (1971) *The Two-Sector Model of General Equilibrium*, the Yrjö-Jahnsson Lectures, 1970 (London: Allen & Unwin).

Kirman, A. (1989) 'The Intrinsic Limits of Modern Economic Theory: The Emperor has No Clothes', *Economic Journal*, vol. 99 (Conference 1989), 126–39.

— (1998) 'Review of Donald A. Walker (1997) *Walras's Market Models*, Cambridge and New York: Cambridge University Press', *Economic Journal*, vol. 108, 1184–6.

Kregel, J. A. (1998) 'Keynes and the New Keynesians on Market Competition', in R. J. Rotheim (ed.), *New Keynesian Economics/Post Keynesian Alternatives* (London: Routledge), 39–50.

Kurz, H. D. (1985) 'Sraffa's Contribution to the Debate on Capital Theory', *Contributions to Political Economy*, vol. 4, 3–24.

Richardson, G. B. (1959) 'Equilibrium, Expectations and Information', *Economic Journal*, vol. 69, 223–37.

— (1960) *Information and Investment* (Oxford: Oxford University Press).

Rizvi, S. Abu Turab (1991) 'Specialisation and the Existence Problem in General Equilibrium Theory', *Contributions to Political Economy*, vol. 10, 1–20.

— (1994) 'The Microfoundations Project in General Equilibrium Theory', *Cambridge Journal of Economics*, vol. 18, 357–77.

Tarshis, L. (1980) 'Post-Keynesian Economics: A Promise that Bounced?' *American Economic Review, Papers and Proceedings*, vol. 70, 10–15.

Walker, D. A. (1987) 'Walras, Léon (1834–1910)' in J. Eatwell, M. Milgate and P. Newman (eds), *The New Palgrave. A Dictionary of Economics*, vol. 4. (London and Basingstoke: Macmillan), 852–63.

— (1997) *Walras's Market Models* (Cambridge and New York: Cambridge University Press).

15
Investment Expenditure, Unrealised Expectations and Offsetting Monetary Policies*

Introduction

I first met Hy Minsky at the 1979 AEA Meeting in Atlanta, Georgia, the first (and only) time I have been to the Meetings. The highlights for me (apart from meeting Hy, of course) were Bob Solow's courageous Presidential Address (Solow, 1980), which caused outrage amongst the new classical macroeconomists and their clones; Tibor Scitovsky's Ely Lecture (Scitovsky, 1980); the receipt by Joe Stiglitz of the J. B. Clark Medal; the session on post-Keynesian economics at which Jim Crotty, Lorie Tarshis and Janet Yellen were the principal speakers (I commented on Janet's paper, so recording another first and only, a paper in the *American Economic Review*, albeit the May 1980 *Supplement*); and meeting over two of the largest chocolate sundaes I have ever seen, Carol Heim and Rhona Wilensky, who were then two of the best and brightest graduate students at Yale, exhausted after *n* interviews on the slave market which accompanies the Meetings.

* Originally published in R. Bellofiore and P. Ferri (eds), *Financial Fragility and Investment in The Capitalist Economy. The Economic Legacy of Hyman Minsky* (Cheltenham: Edward Elgar, 2000, pp. 69–75). I have left this essay much as it was when read at the Conference in honour of Hy Minsky, held at Bergamo in December 1998. This does *not* mean that I am not grateful for the comments I received at the Conference itself, and subsequently at seminars in Adelaide and Melbourne, and from Stephanie Blankenburg and Peter Kriesler.

I had reviewed Hy's 1975 book on Keynes in *Economica* (1977) and we arranged to meet in order to discuss the review. He also gave me his interpretation of the meaning and significance of the results of the capital theory controversies (which interpretation, I must admit, I did not understand). We then met regularly at the annual International Summer Schools at Trieste in the 1980s and the Minksys and the Harcourts became firm friends. I owe Esther and Hy a non-payable debt for, in effect, saving my life. At the conference in honour of Tom Asimakopulos at the Levy Institute of Bard College in September 1992, they twigged that I was experiencing the onset of diabetes (Hy had diabetes). They brought in his blood-sugar-level machine to test my blood-sugar level. I immediately went into the *Guinness Book of Records* with my reading – even when they checked with a reading from Hy as a *numeraire* they could not believe mine. So, Esther got me to Emergency at the local hospital quick smart. Therefore, to be asked to give a paper at the conference in honour of Hy is both a privilege which allows me to pay a tribute to a great economist and an opportunity to say a public 'thank you' from Joan and myself to Esther for her, and Hy's, perception and positive actions.

Background and starting point

My starting point is Hy's book on Keynes; for it contains a detailed analysis of the endogenous cycle arising from the intertwining of real and financial factors which Hy (generously, I think) discerned in *The General Theory*. Hy was to make this analysis the hallmark of all his subsequent writings. I ally this central departure point with Keynes's celebrated 1937 articles, Keynes (1937a, 1937b), *C.W.*, Vol. XIV, 1973: 201–23, in which he reintroduced the finance motive into his accounts of individual investment decisions and its role in systemic behaviour. These Keynesian beginnings precipitated a large post-Keynesian literature, following Tom Asimakopulos's criticism in 1983 of Keynes and Kalecki concerning the generality of the separation of investment from saving and the role of finance in the investment decision and process. I also draw on the insights in a paper by J.R. (as he then was) Hicks from the early 1950s, Hicks (1954; 1983), in which he distinguishes between 'Stickers' and 'Snatchers' in imperfectly competitive environments.

Essence of Minsky

What is the essence of Hy's analysis of the interrelationships between the real and the financial? For me anyway, it is the following: production, employment and, especially, investment decisions in firms *have* to be made on the basis of *expected* future cash flows, that is, these decisions must be taken in an all-pervading, uncertain environment (uncertain, of course, in the sense of Knight and Keynes). The decisions lead amongst other things to financial decisions which imply the locking-in of *certain, inescapable* payments of interest and principal (or their equivalents) which are reflected on the liabilities side of the balance sheets of the firms involved. Expectations generally turn out to be wrong (even though, as Keynes argued, we have to base our decisions, in order to be able to *do* anything at all, rather than to starve to death like the well-known and stupid ass of antiquity, on the convention that the future will be the same as the immediate past and present, unless there are very strong reasons for supposing otherwise). Because of the resulting discrepancies arising from the unrealised cash flows and committed payments, the consequent actions of business people turn out to be different, often vastly so, from what they would have been had their expectations been realised (in the latter case what the firms were committed to and what they actually could do would have coincided).

If cash flows turn out to be greater than expected, firms receive bonuses of extra finance, these buoy up the 'animal spirits' of investors and result in more investment and production than otherwise would have been the case. This starts a cumulative upward movement in activity over and above what real factors *alone* would have tended to bring about, at least for a while. If, however, cash flows are disappointing relative to what had been expected, there is a double bind: there is now less cash available than was anticipated because the certain inescapable payments have to be met (this is absolutely so for interest payments, within a fuzzy band for dividends). This reinforces the dampening of 'animal spirits' which the disappointing cash flows already imply – so we have an amplified downward movement for at least some time until we reach a situation where expectations are realised, or even more than realised, again.

On the basis of these insights Hy tells a story of an endogenous cycle whereby one ultimately unsustainable situation transforms itself into another equally unsustainable situation, and so on, all of which is the result of the intermingling of real and financial factors. We thus have cycles of greater amplitude and possibly deeper and longer slumps, accompanied by greater numbers of business failures and bankruptcies than would be predicted by a real multiplier-accelerator model, or indeed by the real business cycle models so beloved of our trade in modern times.

Such a set of results has been reinforced since Keynes's time by the extraordinary increase in the provision of 'credit for all', the creation of credit facilities for consumption spending. While this is clearly a private 'good', because it expands the boundaries of choice to a much greater number of people by allowing them to pay as they consume the services of consumption goods (albeit, often at an exorbitant price), systemically it is a 'bad'. For by tending to turn *all* spending into that which was traditionally characteristic of investment spending only, the traditional stability of the consumption function and consumption spending has been undermined – with the result that slumps now tend to be deeper and more prolonged and the amplitude of the cycle greater than in earlier periods of the capitalist era.

Keynes, finance and the crucial role of the banks

When Keynes wrote in the 1930s he thought of the typical characteristics of investment projects as follows: businesspeople estimated the m.e.i.s (marginal efficiencies of investment) of investment projects and then obtained short-term finance from the banks in order to implement them. If the projects turned out to be successful, in particular if they fulfilled (or at least started to fulfil) what had been expected of them, funds could be raised at advantageous (or at least not disadvantageous) terms on the capital market, through either the issue of equities or debentures, to pay back the initiating short-term bank loans. That is to say, the new issues would not have adverse effects on the values of the existing financial assets of the firms concerned.

If investment was occurring at a steady pace and level in the economy as a whole, Keynes conceived of a 'revolving fund' of bank finance and also a steady flow of new saving (associated with the multiplier process and the equilibrium condition that planned saving equals planned investment) which could be used to purchase the newly issued securities as they come onto the market. Kaldor (1939) was subsequently to set out the conditions that had to be fulfilled for this process to proceed smoothly. He identified a class of speculators whose role was to take up the new financial assets and prevent interest rates from changing (which in turn could have reduced the stream of planned investment being turned into actual investment). Keeping interest rates steady meant that the (simple) multiplier could always do its full thing without interruption. For our own purposes, the key point to note is Keynes's emphasis on the vital role that the banks play in initiating (and continuing) the process and especially in not aborting it if there should be, for example, a rise in the systemic level of planned investment. 'The investment market can become congested through shortage of cash. It can never become congested through shortage of saving. This is the most fundamental of my conclusions within this field' (Keynes, *C.W.*, Vol XIV, 1973: 222). It may, of course, be argued that Keynes was over-influenced by the United Kingdom practice of the time and that financing of investment in other economies did, and does, not follow exactly the pattern he identified. For example, folklore has it that German and Japanese banks have much longer-term stakes, through long-term loans, in industry than Keynes envisaged. The core insight that it is finance and, in particular, bank finance which is the crucial ingredient for planned investment to become actual investment does seem to me to have considerable relevance for our time, just as much as it did for Keynes and his time.

Hicksian 'Stickers' and 'Snatchers'

I turn now to Hicks's distinction between 'Snatchers' and 'Stickers'. (For moral reasons he reversed the order.) Hicks had in mind industrial firms and Roy Harrod's writings on their behaviour in imperfectly competitive market conditions. Hicks presented a period analysis of price-setting and identified when it would be 'safe' always to maximise short-period or immediate expected profits, that is to say, to snatch completely what was *immediately* available, regardless of the consequences (formally, because there were none). This situation was contrasted with one where it would be necessary to take into account the longer-term consequences of snatching now. In this case, the objective became the maximisation of *long-term* expected profits, to stick rather than snatch, so foregoing some immediate opportunities because of the possible effects of negative feedbacks on customer goodwill, for example, in future periods. I cite Hicks's article despite its antiquity (many modern economists seem to think economics began ten years ago with a moving peg) because it may be argued that commercial banks all round the world (and especially in the developed world) have behaved much more like snatchers than stickers in their lending behaviour, notably over the past twenty to thirty years. This has had disastrous consequences, not only for their customers and even themselves, but also for the performance of the system as a whole. I suppose the conventional view of bankers is that they are sound, cautious, conservative people who still, at least metaphorically, dress in sober dark suits, have butterfly collars on their shirts and wear reassuring homburg hats on their heads. But their actions in recent decades belie such a stereotype; in fact, they seem to be either overoptimistically euphoric about economic situations and lend accordingly – lots – without proper assessments of risks or creditworthiness generally; or they are unduly pessimistic and deeply depressed, calling in loans without any regard to the medium to long-term viability and soundness of their customers' situations, having been unduly influenced by the immediate situation and shaky cash-flow positions. This behaviour is not confined to banks alone, of course – it has also been characteristic of non-banking financial institutions over the same period (not least when they are advised by Nobel Prize-winners in economic science), perhaps even more so. My point is that banks play a key central role in the process of accumulation; moreover, their behaviour is contagious. The result has been that their behaviour has served to significantly reinforce the cyclical processes which Minsky identified in Keynes's system.

What is to be done?

So: What is to be done? As Minsky recognised (as did D. H. Robertson, Michal Kalecki and Richard Goodwin before him), it will never be possible to eliminate the cycle completely, despite what Gordon

Brown and his *alter ego*, Ed Balls, keep telling us in the United Kingdom. As Robertson, Kalecki and Goodwin, to name only three of the more prominent and perceptive students of capitalist processes, all showed, the cyclical nature of the growth process is inevitable. What we must try to do is not allow *controllable* financial influences to make it worse. Central banks the world over should use their influence (and accompanying sticks and carrots) to persuade commercial banks to change their natures from 'snatching' to 'sticking'. The rewards would be more stable systems, probably growing faster on average, and less bad debts and higher (and less fluctuating) profits for the banks.

Such a policy would require coordinated actions – no one commercial bank could go it alone. They need to make serious, informed assessments of the medium to long-term viability of the projects and businesses of their clients. This will require the employment of expert research staff with high-level economic and accounting as well as business skills to do the analyses required. Then, in the event of a shock or a downturn, for example, instead of mechanically and ruthlessly calling in existing loans and refusing to make new ones, actions which reflect their unduly pessimistic stances at such times, they should instead assess the longer-term prospects of borrowers past and present and, if they look reasonable, offset any immediate cash-flow problems their customers have at the present time. One bank in isolation could not expect to do this and necessarily remain viable itself. But if all behave like this, there will be a sea change in systemic behaviour. This will, of course, require central banks to back-up the banks' actions, to be prepared to help them if they in turn need short-term cash. (Mića Panić has suggested to me that the *quid pro quo* for the banks to receive such help should be compliance with a code of conduct of banking business, keep out of derivatives, for example.) In so far as the financial sectors' consequent behaviour modifies the shock to the 'animal spirits' of investors which is simultaneously occurring, we may expect planned investment in the economy as a whole to hold up more than it otherwise would have, and the banks may then play their role of helping to make plans become actuality.

In the case of the upturn or a boom, the new environment of Marshallian soberness which I have discussed, in which the long term is given equal or preferably more prominence than the immediate period when assessing investment projects and loans for them, will serve to reduce the unduly euphoric expectations of the banks at these times. This will further allow the creditworthiness of borrowers and balanced and informed assessments of risks to be made by the banks (as well also by would-be borrowers who now will know that whenever they ask for initiating loans, they are going to have to be able to pass informed and intelligent assessments of their proposals). (Sheila Dow (1998) brilliantly discusses these and other issues within the context of a comparison of the New Keynesian theory of credit with that of the Post Keynesians (and especially of Hy Minsky) and the vital distinction between New Keynesian information and Post Keynesian knowledge.)

Conclusion

No doubt there are already elements of these ideas emerging in the practice of the world banking system as it reacts to the irresponsible and horrendous events of recent years. What I am arguing for is a systematic and explicit exploration of such views and practices, and of the institutions required and the detailed accompanying incentives needed to put them securely and widely into practice. I feel sure that, had Hy been here, he would have given us much detailed good advice on all this and no doubt some very stringent criticisms of what I have and have not said.

References

Asimakopulos, A. (1983) 'Kalecki and Keynes on Finance, Investment and Saving', *Cambridge Journal of Economics*, vol. 7, 221–33.
Dow, S. (1998) 'Knowledge, Information and Credit Creation', in R. J. Rotheim (ed.), *New Keynesian Economics/Post Keynesian Alternatives* (London: Routledge), 214–26.
Harcourt, G. C. (1977) 'Review of Minsky (1975)', *Economica*, vol. 44, 306–7.
Hicks, J. R. (1954) 'The Process of Imperfect Competition', *Oxford Economic Papers*, vol. 6, 41–54, reprinted as 'Stickers and Snatchers', ch. 12 of John Hicks (1983), *Classics and Moderns, Collected Essays on Economic Theory*, Vol. III (Oxford: Basil Blackwell), 163–78.
Kaldor, N. (1939) 'Speculation and Economic Stability', *Review of Economic Studies*, vol. 7, 1–27.
Keynes, J. M. (1937a) 'Alternative Theories of the Rate of Interest', *Economic Journal*, vol. 47, 241–52; reprinted in *C.W.*, Vol. XIV (1973), 201–15.
— (1937b) 'The "Ex-Ante" Theory of the Rate of Interest', *Economic Journal*, vol. 47, 663–9; reprinted in *C.W.*, Vol. XIV (1973), 215–23.

Minsky, H. P. (1975) *John Maynard Kenyes* (New York: Columbia University Press; London: Macmillan, 1976).

Scitovsky, T. (1980) 'Can Capitalism Survive – an Old Question in a New Setting', *American Economic Review*, vol. 70, no. 2, 1–9.

Solow, R. M. (1980) 'On Theories of Unemployment', *American Economic Review*, vol. 70, no. 1, 1–11.

Part IV
Review Articles

16
Joan Robinson and the Economics Profession*

The three volumes under review are about the life and contributions of Joan Robinson. Of *Joan Robinson and the Americans*, the author, Marjorie Turner, tells us, candidly and immediately, that Joan Robinson did not think the book could be written because it would be hard for 'someone ... brought up in modern American economics [to understand her] intellectual development' (xiii). In a sense this is true – Americans (and Australians!) really do find it hard, perhaps impossible, to understand the nuances of the British way of life, especially the way of life of those earlier generations in the Ancient Universities. Yet, as I argue below, I am glad that Marjorie Turner persevered with the project.

Of the two volumes edited by Feiwel, *Joan Robinson and Modern Economic Theory* and *The Economics of Imperfect Competition: Joan Robinson and Beyond*, I have to say that though they contain many worthwhile papers, this does not excuse the insensitivity of the editor in insisting on going ahead with a project which several of Joan Robinson's closest friends and colleagues explicitly asked him not to. Why? Because Robinson would have hated to have had such a collection published in her honour and in memory of her. She had

* Originally published in *History of Political Economy*, vol. 23, 1991, 158–66, reviewing *Joan Robinson and the Americans* (M. S. Turner, Armonk, New York, and London: M. E. Sharpe, 1989, xv, 315 pp.); *Joan Robinson and Modern Economic Theory*, Vol. 1 (G. R. Feiwel (ed.), London: Macmillan, 1989. 1xvii, 927 pp.); *The Economics of Imperfect Competition and Employment: Joan Robinson and Beyond*, Vol. 2 (G. R. Feiwel (ed.), London: Macmillan, 1989. 1x, 775 pp.).

said, in effect, of many of the contributors that she wished they would stop paying her compliments and answer her questions instead. She loathed the way many of them did economics, and she abhorred the damage which she believed they had done to the discipline as she understood it.

There is considerable overlap between the three volumes, first, because Joan Robinson is their subject and, second, because some people (for example, Paul Davidson, Paul Samuelson) have contributed to both projects. Marjorie Turner has gathered together an enormous amount of evidence on Robinson's relationships – some friendly, some hostile, some ambivalent – with American economists. She has then told the Joan Robinson story chronologically, highlighting interactions with Americans and American economists, starting with her first visit in the early 1960s and closing with her last visit as a Bernhard Fellow at Williams in the autumn of 1982. Sadly, this was also to be her last period of work. Shortly after she returned to Cambridge she suffered a severe stroke from which she never recovered. She died in August 1983. The account of her time at Williams is thus moving and poignant in itself and because of what followed. The testimony of Juliet Schor and the Williams students reveals (as do many of the memoirs in the Feiwel volumes, for example, those by Paul Streeten, Harvey Gram, Vivian Walsh, Edward Nell, Richard Goodwin and Lorie Tarshis) admirable characteristics that may not always have been obvious to those who only knew the public figure. Joan Robinson always tried to respond to requests from students, and Marjorie Turner documents fully her responses in America, especially in the turbulent years of the later 1960s and early 1970s.

In the early chapters of the book we learn of her background, schooling, interests and contributions up to the end of the 1950s, by which time she already had behind her the significant work on imperfect competition, important contributions to the Keynesian revolution, the essay on Marxian economics, the major book on growth, and many articles on capital theory and the critique of the methods and results of the neoclassical theory of value and distribution. By the time she came to the United States in her late fifties, she had met Samuelson on several occasions in the United Kingdom and had already begun exchanges in the journals, in correspondence, and in person with Robert Solow. Her friendship with John

Kenneth Galbraith dated from 1937, when he came to Cambridge for a year. Their economics overlapped only on imperfect competition and Keynes – they were more political partners and great friends. When Galbraith was president of AEA in 1971 he used his one gift of patronage to make Joan Robinson the Richard Ely Lecturer. Her lecture, 'The Second Crisis in Economic Theory', was given to an audience that overflowed into adjoining rooms. Marjorie Turner describes its contents, its reception and the peculiar events at the dinner beforehand, as related by Paul Davidson (183).

Her relationship with Paul Davidson and the American post-Keynesians, Alfred Eichner, Jan Kregel and Sidney Weintraub, for example, mostly started a little later; Robert Clower's relationship with her went further back. Evidently after an enthusiastic start they grew apart intellectually, though Clower retained great affection and respect for her. He lamented that she was ill at the time of the Keynes Centenary Conference at King's in July 1983, for he felt that murder was got away with there as far as Keynes was concerned. It needed someone with Joan Robinson's seriousness, stature and 'bleak Cambridge rudeness' to make a proper gesture (I think he forgot that Nicky Kaldor *was* there). Her correspondence and contact with Clarence Ayres and Walt Rostow are also reported.

Inevitably I was most interested in the account of the exchanges between Joan Robinson, on the one hand, and Samuelson and Solow, on the other, over the capital theory issues, because I witnessed some of them when Solow (and Arrow) were in Cambridge in 1963–64, and because I have tried to chronicle them for the profession. Incidentally, if I may move to Feiwel's Vol. 1 for the moment, I must tell Andreu Mas-Colell that I was never 'a *militant* Robinsonian' (1: 505, emphasis added). My role in the capital theory debates (as it was in the antiwar movement, when Australia and New Zealand were America's only respectable allies in Vietnam) was always that of a moderate, something Robinson upbraided me for. That she herself *was* militant, seemingly inflexible, and *very* tough at any moment of time, but willing to change if convinced, comes out clearly from these volumes. For example, for years she would not accept Paul Davidson's argument that Kaldor's neo-Pasinetti theorem had a Say's Law aspect to it; but when she did accept it, she apologised – gruffly and succinctly, but an apology nevertheless (Turner, 193).

What does emerge from all three volumes is that though her American (and other) friends and adversaries liked and respected her courage and intellect, yet they maintained that ultimately while *they* understood *her* only too well, or, perhaps, perceived the nature of what they thought to be her muddles, she never completely understood them (or theirs). Not even her great intelligence could cope with the intricacies of their own great technical facilities. At least I take this to be the view of Samuelson and Solow and, in the United Kingdom, of Frank Hahn, as revealed in the interview on his love/hate relationship with Joan Robinson in Feiwel's Vol. 1. Solow occasionally was inclined to hedge, sometimes saying he did not understand at all what she was on about, or that if she really believed what she claimed, usually about him, she was completely mistaken. Kenneth Arrow demurs, considering her to be 'technically very competent [able to do] fancy mathematics' (1: 179).

I wish this had been true. She never claimed it herself, often saying that as she had never learned mathematics, she had had to think. What is correct, I think, is that Joan Robinson had great intuitive powers which would often allow her to sense that results were wrong even when it may not have been possible for her to pinpoint exactly where some purely technical argument had gone astray. This is attested to by both Richard Goodwin (1: 916), and Hahn and I think it would be generally agreed by those who knew her.

Samuelson pays her a great compliment in the Feiwel volumes:

> What I learned from Joan Robinson was more than she taught. I learned, not that the general differentiable neoclassical model was special and wrong but that a general neoclassical technology does not necessarily involve a higher steady-state output when the interest rate is lower. I had thought that such a property generalized from the simplest one-sector Ramsey–Solow parable to the most general Fisher case ... Robinson's repeated critiques of capital theory [were not] tedious and sterile naggings ... [they deepened] our understanding of how a time-phased competitive micro system works. (1: 137–9)

Of all the Americans with whom she tussled, Samuelson tried hardest to understand, to be generous and not to take personal offense. As a result he was, I am afraid, the one most harshly repelled, often as the one who paid her compliments but did not always answer her questions. It is possible to sympathise with Solow's bewilderment when in their first exchanges he thought he was backing up an argument of her 1953–54 article in *Review of Economic Studies* – to wit, that it was only under very special and unlikely circumstances that a scalar measure of heterogeneous capital goods was possible – only to find his argument interpreted as a *defense* of the aggregate production function procedure. Yet, as the debate proceeded, did he not begin to protest a bit too much, was he not trying to have his cake and eat it too, when arguing that the aggregate production function procedures have worked so well and so often in empirical work that they are justified despite their admitted lack of theoretical robustness? Or is he rather reflecting James Mirrlees's philosophy:

> If anything explains the heat of debates in growth theory, it is the difficulty thinkers in the scholastic tradition have in appreciating that, for workers in the scientific tradition, it makes sense to entertain a model and use it without being committed to it, while scientists cannot imagine why mere models should be the object of passion. (1973, xxi)?

Be that as it may – and there is much much more in the book – *Joan Robinson and the Americans* is a generous and positive book written by a sympathetically critical admirer who has tried hard to understand Robinson's critique of mainstream American economics and what she tried to put in its place. It reveals a courageous, warm, tremendously honest person who could be extremely loyal and perceptive, as well as extremely tough and frightening. Her saving grace was to be as hard on, and sometimes as unfair to, herself as she was to others. This may not have been a consolation to those directly in the firing line, but it ought to be remembered – and Marjorie Turner's book will help us to do just that.

The Feiwel volumes are mainly directed to two areas in which Joan Robinson made major contributions: the theory of imperfect competition and the theory of employment. There is a long introduction to both volumes by the editor, 'Joan Robinson inside and outside the Stream.' By itself it constitutes a short book. It is a balanced assessment of her achievements and attitudes (though it is not based on as intimate or as favourable a relation-ship between the editor and his subject as Feiwel would have us believe).

In recent years imperfect competition theory has had a new lease of life, both in its own domain and in the 'high theory' of macro behaviour and international trade. There are examples of these con-tributions here, especially in Vol. 2: for example, 'Involuntary Unemployment and Imperfect Competition: A Game Theoretic Macro Model', by John Roberts (2: 146–65), and in part 3, with papers by Ariel Rubenstein, Robert Wilson, Leonid Hurwicz, Paul Milgrom and Jean Gabszewiez and Jacques-François Thisse. There is also an outstanding paper by John Whitaker on the history of the development of the ideas which led up to the writing of *The Economics of Imperfect Competition*. He makes it clear that it was the Pigovian rather than the Marshallian form of value theory that both Piero Sraffa (whose 'pregnant suggestion' was the crucial impetus for the writing of the book) and Joan Robinson were attacking. Especially useful is his account of how the concept of the represen-tative firm, which Marshall used in order to discuss how an industry could be in equilibrium, even though its firms might be growing, declining, or in their prime, *and* increasing returns were around to be exploited, was transformed by Pigou into a subtly different concept of the equilibrium firm. The latter attained equilibrium simultaneously with the industry but at a cost of realism and a nar-rowing and tightening of analytical techniques.

Joan Robinson was first to use similar techniques (her box of tools analogy was taken from a public lecture by Pigou) but then subse-quently to refute them, describing the static method of her first book as a 'shameless fudge'. The particular application here was the notion that businesspeople could search for equilibrium profit-maximising prices by a process of trial and error without having any effect on the positions of their demand or supply curves and there-fore on the prices themselves. The economic system (in this case, a firm or an industry) was treated as an equilibrating mechanism in which the equilibrium itself was independent of the path taken to it. In recent years this assumption has been reexamined and a new class of path-dependent equilibrium models developed. As Hahn acknowledges in his interview (1: 895–910), Robinson's insights may have given impetus to this research programme, though she herself would have denied that there would be an equilibrium there to be found, even eventually, in such situations. Franklin Fisher discusses these and related issues in a helpful and revealing interview (1: 311–22), and Vivian Walsh (1: 303–10) quietly but effectively demonstrates that 'her well-known objections to "getting into equilibrium" have been vindicated'.

Joan Robinson always stressed that people should state their assumptions so that their logic could be checked, and reasons for disagreement revealed. While over the years she became more and more pessimistic about minds ever meeting, some minds anyway, even if this were to be done, I think she would have approved of Peter Hammond's paper, 'Some Assumptions of Contemporary Neoclassical Economic Theology' (1: 186–257). There he illustrates excellently and in a very modern manner the gains to be made from such a careful approach – and he does so, as she herself would have wished and as she taught him in her classes on economic theory, with 'some healthy scepticism [and] without using squiggles'.

Though the papers in the volumes are mainly concentrated in the areas of employment and imperfect competition theory, there are some contributions which illustrate the extraordinary range of Joan Robinson's own contributions. Jan Tinbergen (2: 749–68) has a thoughtful essay on what economists could contribute to the understanding of the causes and consequences of war, a sustained, passionate cause of Robinson's. When she was old and ill in 1981 she still insisted, against doctor's orders, on traveling to Utah to deliver the Tanner Lectures, choosing 'The Arms Race' as her subject. There is a sympathetic and perceptive essay on her contributions to development theory by Irma Adelman and David Sunding (1: 702–22). Robinson went to India for about two years shortly after graduating, and this kindled a lifelong love affair with the subcontinent, which she visited many times subsequently. Her interest in China is of course well-known, and indeed notorious in those quarters which disapproved of the deliberate leaven of advocacy that she brought to her writings on the Chinese experiment. She did this because she thought it might act as a counterweight to what she took to be a generally hostile attitude in the profession. Moreover, she fervently hoped that there would be created in China a society in which poverty would be vanquished and the potential of all its citizens would be realised in an environment of cooperation, hard work and mutual respect and affection – inevitably, as she was to admit, an impossible dream but no less noble for that. As Paul Samuelson puts it, '"True socialism" was her first and ever love, not the pretenders who took its name in vain'. And he continues: 'Who is to say her value judgments were wrong, or other than noble?' (1: 36).

James Galbraith, having complimented her for saying that we needed different theories and policies (though not providing them herself), then proceeds to an outline of what he thinks she may have approved of. No doubt Joan Robinson would have told him bluntly whether she did or not, while approving of his aims and approach. But I shudder to think of what she would have made – and said – of 'Steady States and Determinancy of Equilibria in Economies with Infinitely Lived Agents', by Timothy Kehoe, David Levine and Paul Romer (1: 521–44), or of 'Dynamic Optimization under Uncertainty: Non-convex Feasible Set', by Mukul Majumdar, Tapan Mitra and Yaw Nyarko (1: 545–90), or, even, of 'An Axiomatic Approach to Marxian Political Philosophy' by John Roemer (1: 833–50).

I think she would have approved of Dudley Dillard's account (2: 599–612) of the paradox of money in her economics. I know she would have approved of Lorie Tarshis's paper 'Debts, Deficits and Interest Rates' (2: 694–708), both for its crucial topical importance and for its lucid clarity and depth of analysis. It is a typical product of that first generation of Keynesians who were brought up on *A Treatise on Money* and who absorbed *The General Theory* first in lectures and then from the book itself.

I want to end on themes in pure theory and mention, first, the reactions to Robinson's 1956 magnum opus, *The Accumulation of Capital*. Lawrence Klein and, more guardedly, Robin Matthews show a special appreciation and understanding of it. Klein is especially taken by its introduction – not only an introduction to the book itself but also 'a truly masterful statement of economic principles, especially principles of macroeconomics, that would serve better than almost any other "Principles" textbook in laying bare the fundamental aspects of our subject to the beginner' (1: 258). Robinson wrote a new preface, itself never published, to the book some years after its publication. In it she set out the aims and, by implication, the structure of this difficult and complex book. She used a model of an unregulated free enterprise economy in which firms 'within the limits set by their command of finance determine the rate of capital accumulation' while members of the public constrained 'by their command of purchasing power, are free to make the rate of expenditure what they please'. The model was then used 'to analyse the chances and changes of development of an economy as time goes by'. Robin Matthews describes the model and its assumptions, 'a coherent and interesting set', and agrees that it was 'a valuable contribution to work out their consequences' (1: 913). He concludes of the book itself, however, that 'for all its merits [he would not] rate it highest amongst [her] writings' (914).

Secondly, there are papers which relate to her sustained critique of neoclassical theory, to which I have already briefly referred. Arrow (1: 147–85) takes the lack of robustness of the results obtained from one-commodity models as an established technical point, but in effect agrees with Joseph Stiglitz (2: 504 n. 3) that Robinson failed to distinguish between particular results which were shown to be faulty, and general *methods* which may be shown to survive, that is, that the conceptual basis of the theory is unaffected. Samuelson seems to agree with this when he says that Robinson never had a *theory* of distribution, unless it be a vague institutional, historical and sociological one of the relative power of capital and labour at different points of the cycle. I think that Robinson was here reflecting the views of both Keynes and Richard Kahn that a *general* theory of the determination of money-wage levels, for example, was not possible.

But I also think there is a basic conceptual divide, though Robinson may have made it too rigid and watertight. On the one hand, there is the view of the process of accumulation which comes from the classicals, Marx, Keynes and Kalecki that businesspeople and their investment plans rule the roost and all else adjusts to this. On the other hand, there is the Wicksellian–Fisherian vision whereby it is the lifetime consumption and saving plans of utility-maximising individuals that dominate, and all else – firms, stock exchange, banking system – are subordinate to them. The Bastard Keynesians (a term of which Solow approves because it suggests 'hybrid vigour') think the two views may be combined, in their respective spheres, in the neoclassical synthesis. Solow's interview (2: 537–53) is especially illuminating on this, and I think it was the late Trevor Swan's view as well. Joan Robinson would not have had a bar of it; she called it pre-Keynesian theory after Keynes. Sadly, near the end of her life, she became almost nihilistic about economic theory itself, saying she had been doing it for over fifty years and it had come to pieces in her hands. As ever, she was too hard on herself.

Obviously I have only scratched the surface – after all, the Feiwel volumes amount to nearly 1700 pages! The list of contributors almost constitutes a who's who in modern economics (though not a who's who Joan Robinson would have wished for), and the standard of the contributions is extremely high. Browsing through the contents and reading what takes your interest will be a rewarding task. Certainly the judgment of Robinson that emerges from the Feiwel volumes and Marjorie Turner's book seems closer to Samuelson's evaluation – 'Joan Robinson will be long remembered for her originality and breadth – and for the person she was' (1: 139) – than to Hahn's, that she will not 'be remembered all that much' (1: 909). Perhaps Stiglitz said it most succinctly, that 'her sense of intellectual commitment, and the passion with which she pursued economics, [had] left a lasting impression on [him]', and I. G. Patel (1: 863–65) most movingly, in his memoir of this remarkable human being as well as outstanding economist. The Nobel Prize electors still have a lot of explaining to do.

Reference

Mirrlees, J. A. (1973) 'Introduction' in J. A. Mirrlees and N. H. Stern (eds), *Models of Economic Growth* (London: Macmillan).

17
Fifty Years of Measurement: A Cambridge View*

with Michael Kitson

Introduction

Fifty Years of Economic Measurement, edited by Ernst Berndt and Jack Triplett, commemorates 50 years of distinguished work at the National Bureau of Economic Research (NBER) Conference on Research in Income and Wealth.[1] The contributions contained in the volume, which cover a range of empirical issues, are firmly based on the conceptual foundations of orthodox neoclassical economics and their implications for measurement. Our evaluation is from an alternative perspective, one which uses as its starting point the development of empirical work at the Cambridge Department of Applied Economics (DAE). The Cambridge tradition was, and is, sceptical of the relevance and explanatory power of much of neoclassical economics. It is a tradition which emphasises, rather than downplays, real world complexities and which stresses the conceptual and practical limitations of empirical analysis.

* Originally published in the *Review of Income and Wealth*, series 39, no. 4, 1993, 435–47. A Review article of E. R. Berndt and J. E. Triplett (eds), *Fifty Years of Economic Measurement: The Jubilee of the Conference on Research in Income and Wealth*, Studies in Income and Wealth, vol. 54 (Chicago and London: University of Chicago Press, 1990). We are most grateful to Lars Osberg for detailed and helpful comments on the draft version of this paper.

Economic measurement – some Cambridge contributions

The focus of applied economics at Cambridge in the postwar years has been the DAE which started in 1945 with Richard Stone as its first Director. Keynes (who gets a rather poor press directly and indirectly in the book under review, see, for example, Boskin's arguments on p. 160) was extremely significant in its founding. Cambridge economics has always been a broad church and it could be even argued that the Directors of the DAE have been patriarchs drawn from different denominations. It has had four Directors so far – Richard Stone (1945–55); Brian Reddaway (1955–70); Wynne Godley (1970–1987) and now David Newbery (1988–).[2] Despite their different approaches to economics they all have in common the desire to see the completion of thorough applied work, not only in order to explain and predict, but also in order to make contributions to policy, either immediately or ultimately. Richard Stone (who died in 1991) has given us his credo in, for example, his splendid set of essays, *Mathematics in the Social Sciences* (1966). He used mathematics in order to express theory rigorously and precisely and in a form in which it could be tested by quantitative methods, many of which he and his colleagues developed, just as they did the theory itself. Stone started from Keynes's work in macroeconomic theory and, of course, was a pioneer in developing the Keynesian framework of national accounts. His microeconomic theory had Marshallian roots but he very quickly put his own unique stamp on the developments with which he was associated. This view permeated not only his own work but also the work of the officers of the DAE while he was Director and then, when he became P. D. Leake Professor of Accounting in 1955, in the Growth Project group. The latter continued into the 1980s, led first by Stone and J. A. C. Brown, and then, after Brown had gone to Bristol and Stone had retired, by Terry Barker.

Brian Reddaway's period as Director was marked by an extremely down-to-earth approach to problem-solving. He emphasised the importance of understanding the strengths *and* weaknesses and limitations of data and the framing of questions in a manner which allowed the data to throw light on the answers. On the whole he encouraged the use of techniques which were less technical than those which were applied in the

Stone era, and afterwards. Reddaway himself liked to be given problems to solve – two of the most famous reports during his period were *The Effects of U.K. Direct Investment Overseas* (1968) and *The Effects of the Selective Employment Tax* (1973). The SET itself was the brainchild of Nicholas Kaldor who was a teaching officer of the Faculty of Economics and Politics (of which the DAE is an integral part) and who regularly had research projects in the DAE (one of the reasons for setting it up in the first place was to make this procedure possible).

In the Godley period the emphasis was very much on forecasting and short-term policy proposals, as well as on longer-term problems of structural change in a more competitive world. Godley's own group pioneered the study of macroeconomic policy within a consistent set of stock and flow relationships, reflecting in some ways and probably unconsciously, Marshall's approach to the analysis of the long period. Finally, in the Newbery era, there has been great interest in the problems of restructuring in Eastern Europe and Russia as well as work on the environment, privatisation and various microeconomic problems, the explanation of which is required, together with the design of policies which draw on the pragmatic application of received theory, often tailor-made, to the problems in hand. The last was always a feature of the theoretical aspects of the DAE's contributions. Spanning the four periods of the different Directors has been the encouragement of projects in economic history. Seminal work by Phyllis Deane, Brian Mitchell, Charles Feinstein and Robin Matthews often originated as DAE projects.

The Cambridge approach to applied economics, as nurtured by the different Directors of the DAE, stresses the limitations of much of orthodox neoclassical theory, however elegant, in explaining economic phenomena in the real world. Instead, it emphasises the importance of relevance in economics, incorporating the lessons of history, the institutional context and prevailing social and political conditions. Theory and measurement are thus mutually interdependent as robust empirical analysis is dependent on relevant theory, which in turn depends on reliable observations. Cambridge advances in theoretical[3] and applied economics have, therefore, gone hand-in-hand. Furthermore, techniques have never been allowed to obscure the analysis – the medium is not the message.

Economic measurement: some basic principles

Apart from celebrating 50 years of existence (if not uniqueness), a principal aim of *Fifty Years of Economic Measurement* is to provide a series of comprehensive survey articles on the state of the art in measurement which will be of value to graduate students in particular and to the profession generally. Accordingly there are chapters on productivity and economic growth (Dale W. Jorgenson), the measurement of capital (Charles R. Hulten), issues in the measurement and interpretation of saving and wealth (Michael J. Boskin), two papers on hedonic price indexes (one by Zvi Griliches, the other by Jack E. Triplett), the measurement of construction prices (Paul E. Pieper), data difficulties in labour economics (Daniel S. Hamermesh), demands for data induced by environmental policy (Clifford S. Russell and V. Kerry Smith) and measuring the tax burden (B. K. Atrostic and James R. Nunns), written, as can be seen, by acknowledged experts in their respective fields. The chapters are clearly and authoritatively written, comprehensive and useful. They are complemented by excellent discussion papers by other experts, taking up particular points raised, sometimes in praise, sometimes critical, sometimes extending.

The contribution of theory

A feature of virtually all of the chapters in the volume is the complacency of mainstream economists. The large body of economists working outside, or not soley within, the neoclassical paradigm either gets no mention at all, or is summarily and contemptuously dismissed. Thus those economists sceptical of the aggregation of capital goods,[4] or labour economists working within an institutionalist framework, are largley ignored. Jorgenson (p. 24) even goes so far as to attribute the discovery of reswitching, or at least the initiation of the controversy that surrounded it, to Paul Samuelson in 1962 – which is a bit rich when it is remembered that Samuelson relegated it to a footnote far on into his article.[5] The point we wish to make is that these surveys are workmanlike efforts *if* initially it is accepted that the main processes in economic life are captured in a basically Fisherian world of intertemporal consumption, saving and investment behaviour (or even a simple extension of J. B. Clark's theoretical vision to applied work) so that all the statistical data which is used may be taken as reliable quantitative expressions of the concepts of this theoretical approach. Solow (1974: 121) put this very well in his exchange with Anwar Shaikh concerning the humbug production function: 'It merely shows how one goes about interpreting given time series if one starts by *assuming* that they were generated from a production function and that the competitive marginal-product relations apply' (italics in original). *If* this is accepted, it is possible to assess how good the statistical methods are for getting reliable measures of the orders of magnitude associated with the variables and the parameters of the assumed interrelationships between them over time and place. What is missing is any discussion of whether there are ways of testing whether the statistics thrown up in the data may have been generated by entirely different economic processes to those modelled.[6] (Also, the theoretical approach taken imposes conceptual meanings on the variables in the theoretical relationships. This, in turn, raises the question whether the available statistics are suitable for matching, even at several removes, the theoretical concepts. Applied economists, even those in this volume, often forget to ask if the conceptual categories which define the measurement of statistics *are* the appropriate ones for modelling the underlying economic processes.) That all this should be so after 20 years of the Western World lurching from one crisis to another (having been preceded by the Golden Age of Capitalism which on the face of it, was the outcome of the view of 'economic processes' least likely to be considered or accepted by the authors of these surveys) is an index of the extraordinary hegemony that characterises the mainstream practitioners in the US – and, no doubt, elsewhere as well.

Again, in their seemingly comprehensive, historically detailed and critical survey of measuring the tax burden, Atrostic and Nunns make no mention (p. 344) of John Burbidge's (1974) critique of the neoclassical theory of tax incidence as set out in, for example, Mieszkowski (1969), to whom they *do* refer. (Burbidge's critique was contained in his prize winning PhD dissertation on theories of taxation incidence.) Nor do they refer to Burbidge's paper (with the late Athanasios (Tom) Asimakopulos), 'The Short-Period Incidence of Taxation' which was published in *The Economic Journal* in June 1974. Asimakopulos and Burbidge criticised the (then) 'recent work on the incidence of taxes' for being 'largely carried out on the basis of neoclassical assumptions [in pre-Keynesian models] ... [R]eal wages are determined in the labour markets ... full employment [is] automatically achieved through price and wage flexibility. Investment is ... determined by saving out of full employment income' (1974: 267). As a result in the short period the legal and economic incidence of taxes coincide. Asimakopulos and Burbidge obtain different results by using a model from an alternative frame-work which is based on the work of Keynes and Michal Kalecki. One of its appraisers, Carl Shoup, could have told them of the existence of Burbidge's dissertation and even the most dyed-in-the-wool Chicago person would have at least have heard of *The Economic Journal*.

It would be wrong, of course, to imply that there is complete harmony and no discord within the mainstream boundaries themselves. Jorgenson's chapter, for example, continues his long crusade to show that the approach to the measurement of the contributions to the growth of productivity and economic growth generally by, for example, Solow and Denison is basically wrong-headed; that by properly measuring productive inputs, which means correctly allowing for their 'improved' quality over time, nothing (much) is (or should be) left for 'explanation' by 'the measure of our ignorance', which soon the contribution of tech-nical progress came to be called. Even Jorgenson and Griliches, though they are well-known collaborators, can fall out over fun-damentals. Ernst Berndt, the discussant of Hulten's chapter on 'The Measurement of Capital', tells a delightful story of a clash between these two giants, plus one other, Larry Lau, who played the role of Adam Smith's impartial spectator:

> As a young economist just out of graduate school, I once had a privilege of listening to an exchange among three very wise men ... – Dale Jorgenson, Zvi Griliches, and Larry Lau. Based on his recently completed research ... Dale Jorgenson provocatively summarised his findings by saying ... [in effect], 'I do not believe value added exists'. Looking towards Dale's bookshelf containing works by John Kendrick, Jack Faucett, Ed Denison, and others, Zvi Griliches scratched his beard and responded, 'Of course value

added exists. There's a whole set of value added measures on that bookshelf.' And Larry Lau smiled. (p. 152)

Discord within the neoclassical paradigm is also to be found in the work on tax incidence surveyed by Atrostic and Nunns, where they draw attention to a crude misspecification error within a mainstream framework. It concerns the illegitimate combination of a long-period substitution process between capital and labour, modelled by CES functions, with a short-period non-substitution process in the use of intermediate products, modelled by a Leontief fixed-coefficent matrix. As their discussant, Martin H. David, comments, 'This weakness can and should be remedied' (p. 414).

Throughout the volume, it is evident that the underlying models employed are predominantly supply-side – as though (if we may be completely old-fashioned) Harrod's natural rate has been the guiding spirit of the processes which have generated the statistics to be used, the raw data, rather than them being the outcome of an interplay between the warranted rate and deviations from it and the consequent feedback effects of these on the size of the natural rate, the sorts of processes analysed so effectively and illuminatingly over the years by John Cornwall, (see, for example, Cornwall, 1972, 1977 and 1990). A typical example is on p. 162 where Boskin argues as if saving is the necessary condition for investment, providing the necessary funds for the latter to occur. But for most of the period covered by his statistics, saving was created by investment which itself was constrained, first, by the 'animal spirits' of American and foreign businesspeople – their confidence, basic drive, and initiative and so on – and secondly, by their access to funds from financial intermediaries at home and abroad. Saving itself is a decision not to spend – period. It is only when the economy is fully employed that, for *extra* investment to occur, extra saving is needed to release resources for the production of the investment goods to occur. Even then extra finance is necessary as well. In any other situation a free lunch is usually possible – we may have extra investment and extra consumption at the same time.

Of course Boskin may well be right that, given the restructuring needs of the US economy, even at full employment the saving ratio (however defined) may be too low to release the resources to increase capacity and stimulate structural change. If this is what he means when he is discussing the genesis of saving and its purposes and meanings in the United States he should say so. As it stands, it is a confused discussion as it is unclear whether the model of the economy which he has in mind is capacity or demand constrained. It may be that the USA has followed the disastrous British path where the long-term lack of investment has reduced the growth potential of the economy so that the effective constraints on production are the capital stock and the balance of payments rather than the workforce. If so, the inflation barrier is met long before the workforce is fully employed. Thus a higher domestic saving rate is a necessary, although not sufficient, condition to break the bottleneck to allow a higher level of activity and (sustainable) rate of growth to be achieved. Also required are mechanisms to channel the released resources into productive purposes – the British experience suggests that the market cannot achieve this alone.

The scope of measurement

In his 1984 Nobel Memorial Lecture Richard Stone (1986, p. 5) noted that 'the three pillars on which an analysis of society ought to rest are studies of economic, socio-demographic and environmental phenomena'. In many ways this reflects the Cambridge tradition in empirical work which analyses economic processes within a broad framework. The thrust of this volume is narrower in scope and although it would, of course, be churlish to expect a collection of essays to comprehensively cover all areas, there are a number of notable omissions. There is little discussion of the immense problems in measuring activity in the service sector[7] and the area of constructing reliable historical data is largely ignored. Of the remaining two pillars of Stone's measurement edifice, socio-demographic phenomena are not directly considered but the issue of data and environmental policy is addressed in the chapter by Russell and Smith.

In discussing Griliches's chapter, Robert E. Lipsey comments:

> as we become more interested in the output and productivity of the service sector, and if we are more skeptical about the official measures, as I am, we will be compelled to think more seriously about the meaning of output and input in service industries and

about the relationships between service industry inputs and outputs ... I suspect that there is more to be learned about the mysteries in recent productivity developments along these lines than in pursuing that picture of the continuous process plant producing a single output from labor and capital inputs.

(p. 205)

The service sector is by far the largest in developed western economies but, if British experience is a typical yardstick to go by, we remain seriously ignorant of its development and growth. Indicators such as the volume of labour input and deflated wage bill measures provide little guidance to changes in activities producing increasingly sophisticated outputs, where product differentiation and customisation are particularly important. The British Central Statistical Office observed that 'there is at present no satisfactory treatment of quality changes in the service industries' (CSO, 1985: 40)[8] – perhaps a *prima facie* case for the use of hedonic price indexes, so thoroughly discussed by both Triplett and Griliches in this volume.

The lack of historical national income data is an important oversight. Recent extensions and revisions to historical data have done much to enlighten debates in economic history.[9] Furthermore, a rigorous evaluation of historical phenomena is necessary to understand the processes of economic growth and development. Many current economic problems are well-rooted in historical processes. In the British case, understanding slow and erratic growth, poor trade performance, short-termism, lack of investment in skills and so on, demands a thorough analysis of British economic history.

An important chapter in the volume is by Russell and Smith on 'Demand for Data and Analysis Induced by Environmental Policy'. They identify clearly the large gaps in the data, gaps which need to be filled in order to fulfill the needs of the emerging environmental policy agenda. They observe that 'When compared with the effort and experience devoted to the conventional topics considered under the auspices of the Conference on Income and Wealth, the record of empirical analysis of public policies for the management of environmental resources is quite limited' (p. 322). Russell and Smith identify four areas of immediate policy concern: environmental risk, air quality, water quality and stock pollutants and global climate change. 'The great need here is for data-gathering and model-building efforts to reflect the demands for policy analysis. Identifying the need is a great deal easier than meeting it, for the required interaction has all the difficulties of interdisciplinary research' (p. 323). This must surely be the case in an area dominated by the moral issue of whether the current generation has the right to irreversibly damage the environment that will be inherited by future generations.

Data and data manipulation

The effectiveness of extending the scope of economic measurement will ultimately be constrained by the reliability of raw data and the careful construction of economic indicators. These factors are of increasing importance as economies grow, as this increases the fragmentation of markets – greater product differentiation and a wider range of skills and functions in labour markets – and products and services become more sophisticated.

A number of chapters in the volume seek to shed light on the difficulties of collecting and constructing reliable data. Hamermesh considers 'Data Difficulties in Labor Economics'. He argues that some studies of labour market behaviour have been based on data that are inappropriately disaggregated, unrepresentative and uncharacteristic of current structures (p. 291). Furthermore, and counter to most of the other studies in the volume, he identifies the demand side of the labour market as an area of importance which is in need of improved data. He suggests the increased use of labour market surveys and the deployment of more resources towards the production of disaggregated data. 'Rather than rely on inappropriate data, those of us interested in empirical research in labor economics outside the narrow and decreasingly fertile area of labor supply must adopt some of the sociologists' willingness to generate new sets of data' (p. 291). This is an admirable objective although it would also be desirable to construct models of labour market behaviour that adopt some of the sociologists' willingness not to rely on a narrow range of economic, mainly price, variables.

The importance of collaboration between government and academia in improving economic measurement is demonstrated in the chapter by Pieper. In 'The Measurement of Construction Prices: Retrospect and Prospect' he reviews the past 40 years of development of the price indexes used by the US Bureau of Economic

Analysis. He concludes that there is no single best method for deflating construction as each approach has its strengths and weaknesses. More tellingly, he observes that 'progress in construction deflation has been made in the past when there has been interaction between government statisticians and the academic profession' (p. 260).

The resistance of statistical agencies to change is discussed in the chapter by Jack Triplett. He contributes a masterly survey of the use and abuse of, and conceptions and misconceptions about, hedonic price indexes – all you ever wanted to know but were too afraid to ask. He concludes that the conceptual issues have mostly been resolved and should no longer pose any barrier (p. 228). 'The data problems remain formidable' (p. 228) but the statistical agencies could crack them if they were convinced that the hedonic methods would improve price indices. They would be hard put to argue otherwise after Triplett – but, as indicated in the chapter by Russell and Smith, just because a cause is just does not mean it will triumph.

As Berndt, the discussant of Hulten's chapter, notes, the author has written a useful and readable chapter on applied theory and practical issues in the measurement of capital. It remains true that precise, exact and rigorous definitions of capital (and profits) only exist in Golden Age conditions far removed from the actual world. Golden Ages were originally called so in order to indicate their mythical quality. Yet measurement has to be done if applied work is to get off the ground. Berndt makes the fundamental point that how you measure depends upon what you want the measure for. Like Hulten he distinguishes at least three possible uses in this context: to help to explain and predict investment in producer durables and non-residential structures; to help to measure productive capacity; and to help to measure *multifactor productivity growth*. Putting the question first clears the mind as to what exactly is needed (Reddaway would approve).

Hulten highlights the major difficulties associated with the measurement of capital, that much of the data comes from accountants' procedures and is greatly affected by their conventions, which, in turn, have been considerably modified over the years for which the figures are reported as, for example, the profession (and their employers) have reacted more and more to living in a world of continuing (but changing rates of) inflation. Secondly, because markets for used capital goods are notoriously thin, the valuation of capital goods in use is an extremely tricky problem of indirect imputation. In tackling this problem, it is vital to be clear whether the problem being addressed concerns productive capacity, actual or potential, or the value of the quasi-rents expected to be received for the remaining lives of the assets, where the lives themselves are endogenous variables, the values of which have to be determined as well. One subtle point which Berndt emphasises is that mere passage of time is not necessarily an accurate measure of asset life unless constant utilisation is assumed. This is often an incorrect assumption, for example, car-owners reacted to oil price rises by using their cars far less. Hulten has a careful section in which he relates patterns of decline in the physical productivity of durable assets to the conventional methods used by accountants to reckon depreciation. These have wide-ranging implications not only for assessing potential productivity but also for making measures of profitability which mean 'something'.

In his chapter on 'Hedonic Price Indexes and the Measurement of Capital and Productivity: Some Historical Reflections', Griliches disclaims any originality concerning hedonic price indexes. 'What was impressive about ... [Griliches, 1961] is that it took the idea seriously, did a lot more work with it and showed that something interesting can be accomplished [so having] a significant impact on the subsequent literature' (p. 186), itself huge. Griliches takes a splendidly pragmatic approach, arguing that what is being estimated by the use of hedonic price indexes and the like 'is the locus of intersections of the demand curves of different consumers with varying tastes and the supply functions of different producers with possibly varying technologies of production' (p. 189). It would be foolish therefore to expect to be able to push back futher to the underlying utility and cost functions, especially, we might add, if they may not even be there to be found.

Very succinctly, Griliches sets out his objections to available capital measures, *viz*, that they are 'over deflated and over depreciated ... items with different expected lives [are] ... added together in [the] ... wrong way, and ... no allowance [is] ... made for changes in the utilization of such capital' (p. 192). His criticism that the observed depreciation rate in secondhand markets contains a large obsolescence component induced by the rising quality of new machines is well taken as is his comment that, while it is a valid subtraction from the Present Value of a machine in current prices, it is not the right concept to be used in the construction of a constant quality notion of the flow of services from the existing capital stock in 'constant prices'.

Griliches reports on the exchanges between Jorgenson and himself with Denison in 1972, in which they conceded to Denison the weakness of their treatment of utilisation, with the result that their 'explanation' of productivity growth shrank from 94 per cent to 43 per cent and with it also their 'claim to "do it all" (without mirrors)' (p. 193). He still believes that they were right to 'explain' rather than 'just measure' and that this required expanding their framework further to allow for R&D and other expenditures, increasing returns to scale and other disequilibria! (p. 194).

Griliches makes a distinction between the amounts of the services of labour and capital goods actually used rather than just paid for (the latter involve expectations of sales and cost-minimisation proportions so that remunerations and expected marginal products match). He readily admits that many of the differences stem from 'the failure of the assumption of perfect competition that is the basis for much of the standard productivity accounts' (p. 195). This makes life hard but, he argues, it is an admission of failure to switch over to a model of the world where market power is not evenly distributed but concentrated in the hands of a few decision-makers who have considerable discretion as to the prices they charge for their products (and, in labour markets, the prices paid or, sometimes, charged for services).

The comments which Griliches makes on the slow-down of US productivity are extremely interesting. Though he said that it was the neglect of education, investment in research and economies of scale which hindered his work with Jorgenson, he argues that the recent slow-down is not due to a slow-down in technical progress but to misguided macroeconomic policies associated with the oil price shocks and fear of inflation – the 'Germanisation' of the United States' (and other countries') bourgeoisie. He argues that we should not use data from those years for long-term studies. What is happening inside the production possibilities frontier does not give us clues as to how (and why) the latter is moving out over time (p. 198). Again we have common sense and deep economic intuition associated with an inappropriate framework. We also have the implied acceptance of the legitimacy of distinguishing the factors responsible for the cycle from those responsible for the trend (and those responsible for their theoretical cousins, existence and stability), so ruling out the work of, for example, Richard Goodwin and Kalecki on the indissolubility of trend and cycle and much modern work on path dependent equilibria (or even no equilibria at all).

Use and misuse

The concluding chapter in the volume is a 'Policy User Panel' which contains observations and comments by Charles L. Schultze, Rudolph G. Penner, Ian A. Stewart and a summary by Roger B. Porter. Schultze considers the problems of organising statistical material in the US and recommends the creation of a chief statistical office to help coordinate the federal government's statistical activities. Penner considers the problems of producing reliable preliminary data. He believes 'that forecasting the past may occasionally mean actually ceasing the prediction of data that do more to confuse than enlighten' (p. 429). This strikes a painful cord in recent British economic history. In the mid-1970s initial estimates of the British fiscal deficit for 1976–77 were put at £11.2 billion. The perception of a major fiscal crisis led to the arrangement of an IMF loan, controls on public expenditure and the introduction of monetary targeting. For many observers the disastrous British monetarist experiment started here and not with the election of Mrs Thatcher in 1979. As for the fiscal deficit for 1976–77, it turned out to be a far more manageable £8.8 billion, more than 20 per cent below the initial estimate; with more reliable initial figures, 15 years of economic mismanagement may have been avoided. Stewart's contribution emphasises the need to extend measurement beyond purely economic issues. In some ways echoing the approach of Stone, he argues for an extension of national accounts to 'portray aspects of society and policy issues, such as the health system, the education system, the work system, all of which have aspects about them which are beyond the narrowly economic and whose policy issues entails research issues that are certainly beyond the narrowly economic' (p. 433).

The policy users remain reasonably optimistic about the political manipulation of data. Schultze cites a remark attributed to Winston

Churchill: 'When I call for statistics about the rate of infant mortality, what I want is proof that fewer babies died when I was prime minister than when anyone else was prime minister' (pp. 422–3). Schultze does not, however, believe that policy-makers behave this way. The view from this side of the Atlantic is less sanguine. Throughout the 1980s, the definition of the major British economic curse, unemployment, has been continuously revised, virtually always leading to lower estimates.[10] A former Government minister responsible for employment has acknowledged that his job seemed to be not to address the unemployment problem but to devise ways of reducing the figures (Clark, 1993). Similarly, British politicians continue to be highly selective in the use of economic data. When discussing economic *growth* they focus on the *level* of national income. Continually – at least prior to the present slump – we hear of a 'record level of output' as if this is a unique phenomenon. In fact since 1855, from when we have reliable figures, we could speak of a 'record level of output' in five out of every six peacetime years. Since 1979, this has fallen to four out of six years. The reluctance to discuss growth rates perhaps reflects poor recent performance, particularly in comparison to the much berated period of Keynesian demand management in the 1950s and 60s. We can only hope that the bombardment, through the media, of the general public with statistics and indicators will raise economic literacy to the level where the 'wheat' can be more easily distinguished from the 'chaff'.

Conclusions

This volume is an articulate celebration of orthodox empirical economics. There is, however, little acknowledgement of the existence, let alone importance, of alternative approaches to applied work. Very occasionally the cracks in the facade appear. Hamermesh, for example, notes that 'The cultural imperialism of American empirical economics should not blind us to the possibility that the structure that describes a relationship in the U.S. may not be representative of some (any?) other economies' (p. 274). The neoclassical approach is *a* way of doing economics, it is not *the* way. The Cambridge approach is one alternative; an approach, however imperfect, which tries always to place great emphasis on the complexities of the real world. Reliable measurement is dependent on relevant theoretical hypotheses. The neoclassical approach, displayed in this volume, provides clarity and internal consistency. An alternative Cambridge approach, sceptical of the ability of markets to clear, would more readily accept that individual and collective actions are affected by institutions and political and social forces. The resulting picture of the world that emerges may be less-defined but also perhaps less distorted.

As we have been critical, perhaps harshly so, it seems appropriate to close by paying a warm tribute to the sheer professionalism, technical intelligence and sheer hard work contained in this volume. We may not recognise the world as depicted in many of the chapters; nevertheless, the editors are to be congratulated for bringing together such a splendid set of economists and so providing a volume which will more than 'do' until the next fifty years are up and we celebrate 100 years of economic measurement.[11]

Notes

1. A most amusing section of the volume is the report of the speeches at the Luncheon in honour of the founding fathers (there do not seem to have been any mothers) – Roy Blough, Solomon Fabricant, Milton Friedman, Robert Nathan and Carl Shoup. Friedman could not make lunch but his message is included. He was an early research assistant of the 'natural patron saint of the conference', Simon Kuznets. Fabricant remembers Friedman as 'the first secretary of the conference and the first editor of the conference volume ... a remarkably good editor, the best [he had] ever encountered ... if [Friedman] had only stuck with that he might have amounted to something!' (p. 10).
2. Alan Hughes more than held the fort as a most capable Acting Director in the interim. He is now Director of the Cambridge University Centre for Business Research, an interdisciplinary organisation which undertakes research into business behaviour and performance and the Margaret Thatcher Professor of Enterprise Studies.
3. The other tradition which influences our assessment is an amalgam of the work of the Classical Political Economists (including Marx) with the work of Keynes, Michal Kalecki and Piero Sraffa. These were amongst the principal influences on modern Cambridge economists such as Joan Robinson, Richard Kahn and Nicholas Kaldor who, of course, made outstandingly original contributions of their own (see Hamouda and Harcourt, 1988 and 1992).
4. Even when the capital theory controversies are mentioned (see Hulten, p. 119) the basic criticism is misunderstood. The principal critique related to the meaning of capital rather than its measurement and this was associated with a different view of the accumulation and distribution processes in modern capitalist economies (see Harcourt and Whittington, 1990: 199–206).

5. Samuelson was attempting to provide a rationale for Solow's theoretical work on neoclassical growth models and his pioneering empirical work on technical progress using the same simple models. Both of these approaches were criticised by Joan Robinson, Kaldor and Sraffa. Robinson and Kaldor were simultaneously developing the Classical–Marxian *cum* Keynesian–Kaleckian approach to growth and distribution, while Sraffa was attempting to revive the conceptual framework of Classical Political Economy and Marx.

6. We recognise that this is much easier said than done, see, for example the rather rueful comments on this, and other issues, in Pesaran and Smith (1992). They cautiously conclude that 'it seems unlikely that economic theories can be tested. [Yet] ... within an agreed procedure for inference it may be possible to judge whether the conditional predictions of a particular model ... do in fact match the data better than those of a rival model' (p. 17).

7. Nevertheless the NBER Conference on Research in Income and Wealth has made important advances in this area, see, for example, Fuchs (1969) and, more recently, Griliches (1992).

8. Of perhaps greater concern in the British data is the subjective treatment of the public and private sectors. For education and health services, 'the indicators used for the public sector elements cover employment and capital consumption ... In the absence of suitable alternatives, the private sector elements are also covered by arbitrary series or employment indicators, *with arbitrary adjustments for changes in output per head*' (CSO, 1985: 44, italics added). So an arbitrary productivity term is added to the private sector element, but not the public sector. There can be no justification for such a biased approach; data should be treated in a consistent manner and not according to dogma. By and large, within the confines of their theoretical perspective, the authors in this volume have done just that.

9. The Conference on Research in Income and Wealth has made important contributions in this area, for example, NBER (1960), NBER (1966) and Engerman and Gallman (1986).

10. Of the 30 changes made to the definitions of unemployment by the UK Department of Employment in the 1980s all but one reduced the jobless total. This raises the issue of the independence of statistical agencies. The British decentralised system lacks formal independence from government whereas countries such as Canada, Australia and Holland provide their statistical agencies with statutory protection from political pressure.

11. British readers will recognise the significance of scoring 100.

References

Asimakopulos, A. and J. B. Burbidge (1974) 'The Short-Period Incidence of Taxation', *The Economic Journal*, vol. 84, 267–88.

Burbidge, J. B. (1974) 'The Incidence of Profits Tax', unpublished PhD dissertation, McGill University, Montreal, Quebec, June. (Awarded First Prize, doctoral dissertation competition of the National Tax Association–Tax Institute of America, 1975.)

CSO (1985) *United Kingdom National Accounts: Sources and Methods*, 3rd edn (London: HMSO).

Clark, A. (1993) *Diaries* (London: Weidenfeld & Nicholson).

Cornwall, J. (1972) *Growth and Stability in a Mature Economy* (New York: John Wiley).

— (1977) *Modern Capitalism: Its Growth and Transformation* (London: Martin Robertson).

— (1990) *The Theory of Economic Breakdown: An Institutional-Analytical Approach* (Oxford: Basil Blackwell).

Engerman, S. and R. E. Gallman (eds) (1986) *Long-Term Factors in American Economic Growth*, NBER Studies in Income and Wealth, vol. 51 (Chicago and London: University of Chicago Press).

Fuchs, V. R. (ed.) (1969) *Production and Productivity in the Service Industries*, NBER Studies in Income and Wealth. vol. 34 (New York: Columbia University Press).

Griliches, Z. (1961) 'Hedonic Price Indexes for Automobiles: An Econometric Analysis of Quality Change', in *The Price Statistics of the Federal Government*, NBER Staff Report No. 3., General Series No. 73, NBER, New York, 173–96.

— (ed.) (1992) *Output Measurement in the Service Sectors*, NBER Studies in Income and Wealth, vol. 56 (Chicago and London: University of Chicago Press).

Hamouda, O. F. and G. C. Harcourt (1988) 'Post Keynesianism: From Criticism to Coherence?' *Bulletin of Economic Research*, vol. 40, January, 1–33. Reprinted as Chapter 10 of C. Sardoni (ed.) (1992) *On Political Economists and Modern Political Economy, Selected Essays of G. C. Harcourt* (London: Routledge), 202–32.

Harcourt, G. C. and G. Whittington (1990) 'Income and Capital', in Creedy, John (ed.), *Foundations of Economic Thought* (Oxford: Basil Blackwell), 186–211.

Mieszkowski, P. (1969) 'Tax Incidence Theory: The Effects of Taxes on the Distribution of Income', *Journal of Economic Literature*, vol. 7, 1103–24.

NBER. (1960) *Trends in the American Economy in the Nineteenth Century*, Studies in Income and Wealth, vol. 24, Conference on Research in Income and Wealth (Princeton: Princeton University Press).

— (1966) *Output, Employment, and Productivity in the United States After 1800*. Studies in Income and Wealth, vol. 30, Conference on Research in Income and Wealth (New York: NBER).

Pesaran, M. H. and R. Smith (1992) 'The Interaction Between Theory and Observation in Economics', *The Economic and Social Review*, vol. 24 (1), 1–23.

Reddaway, W. B. (and others) (1968) *The Effects of U.K. Direct Investment Overseas*, University of Cambridge, Department of Applied Economics Occasional Paper No. 15 (London: Cambridge University Press).

— (in collaboration with S. J. Potter and C. T. Taylor) (1973) *The Effects of the Selective Employment Tax*, University of Cambridge, Department of Applied Economics Occasional Paper No. 32 (London: Cambridge University Press).

Samuelson, P. A. (1962) 'Parable and Realism in Capital Theory: The Surrogate Production Function', *Review of Economic Studies*, vol. 29, 193–206.

Solow, R. M. (1974) 'Laws of Production and Laws of Algebra: The Humbug Production Function: A Comment', *Review of Economics and Statistics*, vol. lvi, no. 1, 121.

Stone, R. (1966) *Mathematics in the Social Sciences and Other Essays* (London: Chapman and Hall).

— (1986) 'The Accounts of Society', Nobel Memorial Lecture 1984, *Journal of Applied Econometrics*, vol. 1, 5–28.

18
The Kaldor Legacy*

Causes of Growth and Stagnation in the World Economy is in a profound sense Nicky Kaldor's last will and testament to our profession. The book arises from his 1984 Raffaele Mattioli Lectures which he had not finished preparing for publication when he died in September 1986. Subsequently, Ferdinando Targetti and Tony Thirlwall (his biographers), and Carlo Filippini, were asked to prepare the manuscript for publication, together with the account of the discussion of the lectures and reprints of Thirlwall's splendid memoir of Kaldor (which was originally published in the *Proceedings* of the British Academy, Thirlwall (1987)), and Targetti's *Bibliography of the Works of Nicholas Kaldor*, Targetti (1988). The book is beautifully produced, worthy of its subject and the distinguished series in which it has been included.

There are five lectures: (1) Equilibrium Theory and Growth Theory; (2) Alternative Approaches to Growth Theory; (3) The Problem of Intersectoral Balance; (4) The Effects of Interregional and International Competition; and (5) Policy Implications of the Current World Situation. They allow Kaldor to have a final say on what he found wrong in orthodox theory, of which he had been a

* Originally published in *Journal of International and Comparative Economics*, vol. 5, 1997, 341–57. Reviewing Nicholas Kaldor, *Causes of Growth and Stagnation in the World Economy* (Cambridge: Cambridge University Press, 1996). I thank but in no was implicate John McCombie and Tony Thirlwall for their comments on a draft of the essay.

critic all his working life, first as a distinguished insider, then, in postwar years, increasingly as an outsider, see Harcourt (1988, 1993) for an account of the three phases of Kaldor.

Having found orthodoxy wanting, Kaldor then outlined the alternative approach which he had developed, inspired by his teacher Allyn Young, and aptly described by the title of the 1983 Okun lectures which he gave towards the end of his life, *Economics Without Equilibrium*, Kaldor (1985). From Young (and, of course, Gunnar Myrdral) he took the process of cumulative causation as being most representative of the processes actually to be found occurring in real-life markets, economies and, ultimately, the world. (No doubt if Nicky had lived he would not have confined himself to the world but would have gone on to include the universe; no one was ever less constrained – I should say more unconstrained – in all dimensions than Kaldor, which, no doubt, is one reason why he sloughed off his original neoclassical skin.) Taking the approach so characteristic of him, especially in the postwar period, his final lecture presents an integrated set of policies with which to tackle the deep problems he identified in the world economy at the time he presented the lectures in Italy. The lectures are thus a fitting summing up of all his endeavours during a busy, exuberant lifetime. For, as Tony Thirlwall so rightly says, Nicky Kaldor 'was a dominant influence in economic debates on the world stage for over fifty years, and hardly a branch of economics escaped his pen' (1987: 145). 'Kaldor lived life to the full both as a professional economist and as a family man' (*Ibid.*: 146).[1]

II

Before the Second World War Kaldor mainly wrote on theoretical issues – he made important contributions to the new theories of imperfect and monopolistic competition, to capital theory, to the 'new' welfare economics and, of course, to the Keynesian revolution. His finest article under this last rubric and indeed overall, both in his own view and in the view of informed Kaldor watchers including Hahn and Hicks, was his 1939 *R. E. Studs* paper, 'Speculation and Economic Stability'. With it may be coupled his Keynesian model of the cycle, Kaldor (1940), in which investment drives and income and saving respond.[2]

As a result of his wartime and immediate postwar experiences when he worked in Geneva at the newly created Economic Community for Europe (ECE) and wrote with his own, handpicked team, the first and subsequent *Economic Surveys of Europe*, as well as other influential documents on enlightened policy for the postwar world (166), he increasingly insisted on doing applied work as well. (This was to be of great value to him when he had spells in the 1960s and 1970s advising the Wilson and Callaghan Labour Governments in the UK.) Of course, innovative theoretical ideas still continued to flow from his pen. Indeed during his early phase as a growth theorist, Bob Solow pictured him as a rotund Sputnik circling the earth and dropping a new growth model on it before previous ones had even reached the ground. As far as the present volume is concerned, his most important article from the interwar years (apart from the 1939 article) was published in the first-ever issue of *R. E. Studs*. Disarmingly titled 'A Classificatory Note on the Determinateness of Static Equilibrium', Kaldor (1934), in it is set out clearly the essential principles of path dependent models which are now so fashionable – and relevant. From the 1939 article we may take a deep analysis of the workings of markets in which stocks dominate flows and expectations and speculators' views of the expectations of other transactors play major roles in the determination of prices and activity.

Kaldor is always associated with the term 'stylized facts' – broad empirical generalisations which hold, in a rough and ready way, often for long runs of historical time and require situation-specific theories and accompanying models to explain them. It was Kaldor's particular genius to discern more of these than probably any other economist of the century. In the present set of lectures the 'stylized fact' that stands out most strikingly and in need of explanation – for the inferences of orthodox theory do not, in his view, predict them – is the extraordinary volatility of the prices of raw materials in recent times, especially of those materials most often thought of as providing the real world counterparts of products with the appropriate characteristics to be found and traded in competitive markets, for example, wheat as foodstuffs, cotton or copper as industrial materials. He refers specifically to the role of dealers ('jobbers') which is to equate flows of demand and supply by judicious use of price quotes and stock additions or run downs. He does not think their job well done – 'these are the sectors with the least satisfactory features of capitalist market economies ... prices [go] regularly up and down like a yo-yo, even when differences between the rates of production and consumption are relatively small' (13). The source of instability is how weak a belief there is in a normal price based on 'normal' cost of production (11). Like Keynes and Arthur Okun, Kaldor always stressed the need for the establishment of 'norms' in order to give stability to the workings of economic systems, the modern counterpart of the role which natural prices and prices of production respectively played in the classical and Marxian systems, and normal prices and quantities played in Marshall's *Principles*.

To read these lectures is to absorb the mature reflections of a great intellect on the development of economic theory from the Physiocrats and Adam Smith to the present day, together with lively summaries of some of the principal episodes in the history of capitalism and its reactions with the rest of the world. Few people in our trade could approach Kaldor in his ability to sum up epochs by using well-chosen orders of magnitude and a striking narrative. Kaldor also had a remarkable ability to pick out the gist of others' insights and systems and to integrate them into his own, always original and stimulating, views of the world and its issues and problems. This is as true of his interpretations of our founders – the Physiocrats, Smith, Ricardo, Malthus, Marx, Marshall – as it is of the moderns – Young, Sraffa, Harrod, Joan Robinson, Samuelson, Solow, Arrow, Debreu and, of course, most importantly, Kalecki and Keynes. Even his lack of mathematical techniques – he always said he was too impatient to take the time to acquire them – did not debar him from absorbing the strengths and weaknesses of modern economic theory. He sometimes made mistakes on details – for example, in the present volume I suspect he has been too harsh on the limitations of stability analysis in modern general equilibrium theory – but his criticisms of the cores of the theories and his intuitions are almost invariably spot on. And, of course, he presents his own contributions vividly and persuasively, showing the sort of open mind and willingness to scrap own intellectual capital which only supremely confident, highly intelligent free spirits such as Keynes and Kaldor are capable of. For example, in the discussion of the lectures, Kaldor cheerfully admits, on the basis of subsequent empirical evidence, that the argument in his Inaugural Lecture at

Cambridge in 1966, Kaldor (1966), that 'the absence of labour reserves ... was an important factor in limiting production of manufactures and exports [in the UK]', was 'quite wrong' and that, no doubt, if he were to be tackled five years on concerning his confidently stated propositions in this set of lectures, he would be as willing to admit that he had changed his mind on them too (107–8).

III

Kaldor classifies the evolution of our subject, or rather the issues on which we mainly concentrate, into two: first, the static resource allocation, Pareto optimum properties of competitive markets which reached their finest theoretical expression in the Arrow–Debreu model of general equilibrium. The latter is said to be driven by Smith's original conjecture (as read through neoclassical eyes, I would argue) that a group of greedy people left to fend for themselves in a competitive environment would bring about a sort of social optimum. Kaldor does not mention the reservations of the most subtle of general equilibrium practitioners, for example, Frank Hahn (not always noted for being subtle) that in setting out the conditions necessary for Smith's alleged conjecture to be true we find out why it is not true, or likely to be true, of the world as we know it. Rather, Kaldor interprets the Arrow–Debreu model as descriptive analysis at a high level of abstraction, a first approximation, which, as scaffolding, will progressively be removed to reveal a durable building which *could* encompass descriptive analysis. In Kaldor's view, this cannot happen: in fact, more and more axioms and special assumptions have had to be added and whenever its practitioners have tried to introduce inescapable characteristics of the real world – increasing returns, imperfect competition, unforeseen technical progress, that prices are no longer exclusively information providers concerning relative scarcity, for example (Hahn would have added money) – the scaffolding bursts asunder and the building itself collapses.

The other set of issues is the causes and consequences of growth, their relationship to the process of distribution and the accumulation decision which includes an account of endogenous technical change, what Baumol called many years ago the 'magnificent dynamics'. Kaldor feels that the first set of issues has for too long dominated research and teaching, that it is a mistake to think that developments within them may be effectively used to analyse the second set of issues, even though this is just what, first, neoclassical growth theory and now the new endogenous growth theory have tried to do. Apart from the technical critique and his assessment of its contributions – strong on proving existence, weak on explaining how it comes about and how economies may move from one equilibrium to another – Kaldor objects to its abstract axiomatic nature. Like the classical political economists, Marx and also Marshall, Kaldor prefers to start from empirical generalisations about systemic behaviour and the behaviour of decision-makers and then to build on them theory and accompanying models and see if the inferences deducible from the latter match in a general way the observations to be explained. There are many examples of Kaldor doing this within his own framework in the present volume.

Kaldor can be funny as well as biting. When discussing the Arrow–Debreu model with complete markets, having explained that all events from now to Kingdom Come are predetermined from period 1 on, he adds: 'From period 2 on, life must become very boring!' (7). If ever there was a person unsuited to dwell in a neoclassical world it was Kaldor. He despised an approach which argued that (even expected) satisfaction was maximised at the point of the chaste kiss of the budget line with the indifference curve cheek, as Axel Leijonhufvud remarked long ago. But what really stuck in his gullet, as far as neoclassical economics is concerned, was its inability to take account of increasing returns (in the form first set out by Smith and then applied to more modern conditions by Allyn Young). It was not so much Cournot's and Marshall's worry that increasing returns were incompatible with competition when analysed in a static setting – after all, Marshall admitted in Appendix H that the irreversibility of the long-period supply curve struck at the logical foundations of the heart of the *Principles*, Book V on the determination of the long-period normal equilibrium of demand and supply – but the basically blind eye that was turned to the most obvious fact of life of capitalism: that it created a social environment in which technical progress and accumulation went together. This was recognised by Smith and Marx. Smith further saw the connection between the size of the market and the extent of the division of labour in a mutually determining process. Marx had seen that individual survival in a competitive environment fostered innovation and investment even though what, in his view, was rational, indeed essential, for the individual capitalist entrepreneur to do, namely to install labour-saving machines, led to irrational behaviour at the level of the system as a whole. For this tended to dry up the source – living labour – of future accumulation possibilities. Kaldor, too, often identified perverse systemic behaviour (though he never bought this one of Marx). For example, on p. 61, he criticises the unreal assumptions of Ricardo's account of comparative advantage and the universal benefits of free trade, that they depend on the existence of competition, constant returns to scale and the maintenance of full employment of labour before and after trade. He then develops a model which explains Friedrich List's attachment to tariffs and accounts for the destruction of the Portuguese textile industry in the 18th Century as a result of the Methuen Treaty with Portugal of 1704.

Nevertheless, Kaldor was much influenced by Marx, not with regard to the theory of value on which Kaldor was more a pragmatic Marshallian together with his own oligopolistic *cum* price-leadership theory of price, but with regard to Marx of the schemas of reproduction. Marx asked the question: what conditions must be fulfilled period by period, in order that both aggregate demand and aggregate supply, *and their respective compositions*, match? This is not the same thing as proposing a steady-state growth model – rates of growth could vary from period to period yet there still could be conditions which allowed both aggregates and their compositions to match, see Sardoni (1981). Marx himself used three sectors (departments) – wage goods, capital goods and luxury goods – and worked out the conditions which ensured that each could take in their own and the other sectors' washing, as it were. By establishing how special the conditions had to be, Marx highlighted the distinct possibility of imbalance, resulting in instability and often crises in the real world. Kaldor follows the same strategy but concentrates, not on aggregate demand and supply within a closed capitalist economy, but on balances and sources of imbalance and its consequences as between rural areas and towns, as between primary products and industrial goods (where the former are associated with rural areas, the latter, with towns), extending this dichotomy to international trade and so, painting on a yet more broad canvas, to the growth of the world economy.

These commodity balances and imbalances may be thought of as the supply-side aspects of his story, in some ways analogous to Marx's sphere of production (these are not completely overlapping sets). The demand side of the story emanates from Keynes's *Treatise on Money* (1930) and Kalecki's basic model of income distribution and the level of employment and is more analogous to Marx's sphere of distribution and exchange with the theory of effective demand made explicit and coherent. Kaldor used these ideas initially for his 'Keynesian' macro theory of distribution, Kaldor (1955–56). This was a long-period theory and assumed full employment of labour, so that the investment-saving nexus determined the distribution of income rather than the level of income and employment as in Keynes's *General Theory* (1936). It is usefully thought of as asking how the potential surplus available in the sphere of production, itself the outcome of the conditions of work, past accumulation and the present state of the class war, whereby wage-earners working with existing equipment are able to produce more than their own wage-goods, may be realised as an actual surplus by the forces of aggregate demand, in particular those parts of it which are exogenous to the production of wage-goods. In Kaldor's model (in contrast to the classical and Marxian models), the accumulators get first bite of the cherry, and the residual is then available for the wage-earners, an unrealistically passive lot (until recently anyway).

If we think of a closed economy in which only wage – consumption – goods are produced, even if the wage-earners spend all their wages, wage-good producers as a class will at best cover their variable costs. (In the economy as a whole intermediate purchases of raw materials net out.) If wage-earners save – a point which Kaldor considers in the light of the rise in institutional saving in recent decades – not even this is so.[3] Therefore we need expenditure and production from elsewhere to create wages (and other incomes) to be spent on consumption goods and to provide a source of profit over and above wage-costs. This insight is contained in the 'fundamental equations' of *A Treatise on Money* and was spelt out by Kaldor in his writings of the 1950s and early 1960s. Kalecki independently and earlier than Kaldor produced a similar mechanism but without confining himself to either full employment or the long period.[4] Given the level of investment, the productivity of labour in both the consumption goods and investment goods sectors and the mark-ups on costs used by businesspeople, there is a unique level of employment in the consumption goods trades which will allow the production of consumption goods for these wage-earners and for those in the investment goods sector. The economy will tend to settle at this level where there will be just enough profits created to allow saving to match investment. In Kaldor's version, given long-period full employment output, there is a unique distribution of that income which gives a share of saving from it to match the exogenously given share of investment in income. Though Kaldor refers continually in the text to saving financing investment, in the discussion on pp. 129–30 he makes explicit the vital importance of the banking system in providing finance to allow investment to occur in the first place, so to create the profits from which the saving may come.

Kaldor originally used his approach to offer his solution to the Harrod/Domar problem. (Harrod himself would never admit that he and Domar were the same.) Harrod thought his central contribution was to find the instantaneous rate of growth of accumulation – his warranted rate of growth, g_w – which if implemented would through the multiplier provide enough aggregate demand to match the ensuing aggregate supply so that, after the event, decision-makers would find that not only were their investment plans fulfilled but also the plans themselves were justified by the rise in sales being exactly what had been expected when the plans to enlarge capacity were made.[5]

There was, of course, no reason why this particular value of g_w should coincide with the natural rate of growth, g_n. Kaldor showed that if we feed the value of $\bar{I}/Y_f$ which allows growth of g_n into his model, Π/Y_f would settle at the level which allows S/Y_f to equal $\bar{I}/Y_f$, and so g_w to equal g_n. Thus a variable S/Y_f due to variations in the distribution of income does in Kaldor's model what variable K/L and K/Y ratios do in the Swan–Solow model.

By the time he came to give the Mattioli Lectures (indeed long before), Kaldor was no longer satisfied with these particular arguments. He now thought that the problems of steady growth arose, not from the saving, investment balance, but from the difficulty of keeping the growth of the availability of primary products in line with the growth of the absorptive capacity of the industrial sectors of the world. He argued that both the Keynesian and the neoclassical growth models were in essence single sector and so could not handle the basic *complementarity* of an integrated world. The latter requires a multi-sector model to do it justice, to tackle the mutual interdependence of different sectors where the development of each depends on and is stimulated by the development of the others.

Kaldor sets out the characteristics of the traditional classification into primary, secondary and tertiary activities. The first are 'land-based' activities; the second are associated with transforming raw materials through long chains of processes in manufacturing industries; and the third sector takes in transport and the distribution of the products of the first two sectors as well as activities such as medical, educational and so on – services rendered by persons and not (primarily) through material products. It is usually said that the relationship of the three sectors to each other measures the degree of development attained. Once a surplus emerges in agriculture, manufacturing, 'the engine of growth', may take-off and provide major advances in human knowledge which are reflected in new products and industries and in transforming and enlarging preferences. Its productivity increases with the size of the market – a unique characteristic. It is, Kaldor stresses, hard to disentangle the prior changes in technique which induce increased demand by making products relatively cheaper from the changes which occur because of the rising demand itself. Services use up an increasing proportion of resources but are characterised by low increases in productivity because their typical market structure results in excess capacity. With the exception of agriculture, imperfect or monopolistic competition are universal and this has far-reaching consequences for the mode of operation of markets. Prices are set by sellers not by market-making middlemen. Owing to economies of scale in manufacturing we tend to have 'competition amongst the few'; in the tertiary sector the strength of demand in the economy influences the number of companies which are viable by raising or lowering 'break-even' points.

IV

Kaldor uses a simple two-sector model of agriculture and industry in order to bring 'to light aspects of the economic problems that tend to be neglected both in micro- and macro-economics' (41). There is dual interdependence between the sectors, each being a market for the other's product and a supplier of the means necessary for the other's production. The industrial sector needs material inputs as its means of production and wage goods – 'food' – for its employees; the primary sector depends on the industrial sector for capital goods. Technical progress is 'land-saving' in agriculture. There is assumed to be a stream of innovations, the adoption of which requires additional investment for their realisation. The agricultural sector produces 'corn', industry, 'steel' (capital goods). Kaldor abstracts from the production of consumption goods in the industrial sector and from investment goods such as irrigation or larger herds in agriculture. He assumes a community with surplus labour, most of which is attached to agriculture, so that industry may hire workers in unlimited numbers at a wage in 'corn' sufficiently above real earnings in agriculture to induce whatever migration is needed.

While both sectors accumulate capital by saving part of current income, there is an important difference: in agriculture saving requires a decision to refrain from consuming part of 'corn' output. The 'corn' so released is sold on the market in exchange for the capital goods which the introduction of new accumulation requires. Its rate of accumulation is therefore determined by the amount of corn so saved and the rate of exchange – terms of trade – between corn and steel. In industry, investment comes first, it creates the profits from which saving then comes (a third commodity, money, has yet to be introduced). Steel producers accumulate capital by retaining a proportion of their current output in order to expand their own capacity and sell the remainder on the market. Their costs consist of the payment of wages (fixed in corn) so that the total amount of corn sold by agriculture determines total employment. If steel output per worker is given, the total output of steel is given irrespective of the price of steel. Its minimum price is wl, where w is the wage in terms of corn and l is the labour requirement per unit of steel, below which no steel is produced. At prices above wl we have a relationship between the degree to which price exceeds costs and the proportion of steel reinvested, with the resulting profits being just sufficient to provide the saving to match the investment undertaken.

Kaldor has a neat diagram (44) which has the price of steel in terms of corn (*p*) on the vertical axis and the associated rate of growth of each sector (*g*) on the horizontal axis (Figure 18.1). The cheaper the agricultural sector can obtain steel the faster it can grow for a *given* saving ratio but because of diminishing returns the g_A curve would shift inwards unless this is offset by 'land-saving' innovations which *ceteris paribus* shift it out. The g_I curve slopes upwards because the cheaper is corn the more labour for making steel can the sector buy and the more of its own output it may invest, and so the faster it may grow.

The price is written as $p = wl(1 + \pi)$, where π is the mark-up. (The g_I curve shifts when either the real wage or labour productivity, $1/l$, changes.) At the point p^*, g^*, where the two curves intersect, we have rates of growth in both sectors and terms of trade between sectors which allow the supply and demand of agricultural and industrial goods to balance.

In telling the stability stories – convergence on the intersection of the two curves – Kaldor emphasises that the steel producers are quantity adjusters, acting so as to bring the growth in capacity in their sector in line with sales, whereas competition between agricultural producers tends to bring the price of corn in terms of steel to a

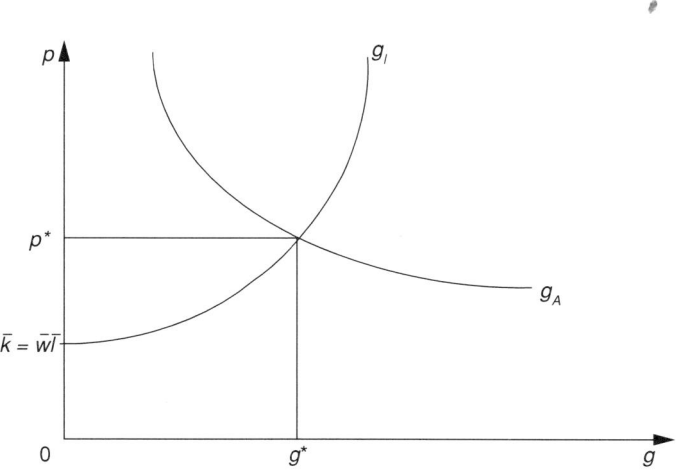

Figure 18.1

point where the growth rates are equal and, more fundamentally, demand and supply match.

An important feature of the model is its dependence on the persistence of 'land-saving' innovations which in the model keeps the system growing at a constant rate as long as growth is not hampered by scarcity of labour in the world as a whole. Kaldor says that we are nowhere near such a problem, that unemployment is a growing problem even though, he argues, the rate of growth of world population had passed its peak (when he wrote 17 years ago).

Kaldor then uses his model to illustrate the effects of 'labour-saving' innovations in steel (associated with Verdoorn's Law and the induced rise in the rate of growth of productivity in the economy as it grows) and to consider the destabilising effects of the inherent instability of both curves due to, for example, weather, a non-steady rate of technical innovations in both sectors and the different pricing behaviour as between the sectors.

Suppose we bring in money so that corn is sold for money which *can* be used to buy steel. We consider the effect of a new super crop which shifts the g_A curve to the right by a 'large' amount. We suppose that the price of corn also falls by a 'large' amount because the market-making middlemen are unwilling to increase their commitments until the price falls to abnormally 'low' levels. Steel producers find their sales restricted by 'effective demand' and emerging surplus capacity unleashes a downward spiral which is both contractionary – investment plans are revised downwards – and deflationary.

If both corn and steel had had the *same* regime for marketing, this 'absurd' result would not have occurred because the price of one commodity could not have fallen so much as to reduce the producers' purchasing power over the others. The remedy is to reduce the large fluctuations in the prices of primary products by the use of buffer stock schemes, *not* to go back to market-determined prices for manufactures (as the modern world increasingly seems to have done and to have been told by economists to do). Buffer stock schemes actually do what the market-making merchants are supposed to do. Kaldor points out that the great slump of 1929–32 had many of the features of his examples and concludes that: 'in a well-functioning world economy it is the availabilies of primary products which should set the limit to industrialisation – the expansion possibilities of which are limitless, or rather are only limited by demand – and not the other way round' (54).

V

When we come to the 1970s Kaldor discerns another set of causes of deep troubles which he discusses in his fourth lecture on the spatial aspects of the economic problem. He regards primary products as land-based commodities which are geographically spread while industrial activities are concentrated in urban areas, so that exchange between primary products and manufactures is also an exchange between the products of town and country. Industrial producers devote only a part, if any, of their activities to their own consumption. The greater part is obtained by exchange. Agricultural producers could produce *only* for their own consumption while industrial producers can operate *only* in a social setting with activities dependent on demand from others through the market, their success or failure depending on the strength of this demand.

We then come to a typical Kaldorian generalisation and insight: that the world may be divided into relatively rich and relatively poor areas and that this is a matter of relatively recent occurrence, reflecting persistent differences in rates of growth over the past 2–3 centuries. The basic cause is neither differences in resource endowment nor a reward for virtuous thrifty behaviour (as opposed to spendthrift expenditure); rather, it results from the process of industrialisation and its 'fall out' in terms of political and educational institutions. Industrial activities are not self-sustaining but depend upon demand for goods coming from outside the industrial sector, the ultimate causal factor which accounts for all other activities. It involves a sort of multiplier process. Industrial activities are concentrated in urban areas because of the growth of marketing activities and the social economies gained by division and sub-division of the making of articles into a number of separate operations (on p. 58 Kaldor quotes a well-known passage from Allyn Young on this). He also mentions the advantage of having highly specialised workers in close proximity to one another together with small and specialised firms. He cites the Italian industrial districts (Kaldor always knew how to flatter a host) and Marshall's analysis of a similar phenomenon, engulfing the static and dynamic economies of large-scale production *and* the economies of large production.

The existence of increasing returns makes a large difference to the way markets develop and competition operates – the remarkable thing, says Kaldor, is only why its consequences are so largely ignored. Businesspeople, unlike our trade, would never ignore the existence of diminishing costs. With increasing returns a rising market share means success, but a falling one – failure. In a growing market a business can never stand still, indeed it must grow if it is to survive (64). Kaldor comments that only Marx fully recognised this in the nineteenth century – in neoclassical theory each firm has an optimum size so that the number of firms has to increase when the industry grows. (Marshall tried to have it both ways with the analogy of trees in a forest and the concept of the representative firm; Pigou undermined him by turning the latter into the equilibrium firm.) So we move on to success meaning more success, failure meaning more failure – Gunnar Myrdal's 'principle of circular and cumulative causation' (64) which became the hallmark of Kaldor's later work.

Having earlier on shown the very special circumstances in which free trade benefits all, Kaldor now argues that free trade in the field of manufacturing goods allied with the process of cumulative causation begets a process of polarisation which inhibits growth of such activities in some areas while concentrating them in others. In a nutshell this is what happened during the industrial and transport revolutions of the nineteenth century. He reviews the history of UK manufactures and their export and the role of tariffs when other countries industrialised. The successful ones were discriminating in their use of tariffs, as were Japan and then the NICs in the postwar period. The Latin American countries made indiscriminate use of them and the resulting costs of their products in terms of primary products made them too expensive to enter world markets successfully.

Thus Kaldor is led to the key role of export-led growth in successful development and to the ultimate constraint imposed by the value of the import income-elasticity of demand. He uses Harrod's foreign trade multiplier analysis of three years *before The General Theory* which was brought to fruition in the postwar period in the work of John McCombie and Tony Thirlwall (1994). The balance of payments is seen as the effective constraint on growth, the rate of which will be higher, the greater is the export income-elasticity and the lower is its import counterpart, reflecting differences in non-price competitiveness.

Kaldor recognises that price-elasticities are important for trade in traditional goods like texiles and shoes where the newly developed countries may copy the latest technical advances in other countries and have huge advantages because of the lower price of labour services. Kaldor quotes with approval Hufbauer's classification of 'low wage' trade and 'technological lead' trade (69). But, in the large picture, it is income – quantities – not prices which are the basic clue to the nature of growth processes and the success or otherwise of development.

VI

As befits such a 'hands-on' allrounder as Kaldor, his last lecture is concerned with the policy implications of the current world situation (then the mid 1980s but not *that* different from the mid 1990s, say his editors). Kaldor starts with a nutshell description of the 'long boom' – 1948–73, the most rapid, most widespread and most even growth ever recorded,[6] the strength of which was as unexpected as was its end in 1973. Kaldor contrasts what actually happened to growth – overall, food, manufactures – and productivity with what turned out to be the pessimistic predictions of even such a wise and seasoned campaigner as the late Arthur Lewis. After 1973 the falls in rates of growth of developed countries were remarkably uniform and were paralleled by falls in productivity, themselves blessings in disguise as unemployment rates, instead of being merely disgraceful, would have been catastrophic. For example, in the USA Kaldor argues they would have been over 20 per cent and in Europe three times as high as were actually experienced.

Why did the 'long boom' last so long? Kaldor argues that sustained growth is only possible if the growth in primary products is in line with the requirements of industrial production. This does not imply that they must grow at the *same* rate (though this is an implication of Kaldor's little model. While he says that it is not an essential result I have not been able to see how *in his model* he could get any other, but see Thirlwall (1986)). In the real world, with the exception of oil, primary products grew at considerably lower rates than those of secondary and tertiary production as fabrication, transport and distribution took up a steadily growing proportion of the final price of the average commodity. These differentials were partly due to differences in pricing behaviour which is encapsulated by the effects of technical progress under the rubric of the 'Prebisch Effect' – the benefits are passed on in lower prices in primary products, but are retained as higher wages and profits by the producers of manufactured goods.

Up to the first oil price shock in 1973, the terms of trade between primary products and manufactured products remained relatively stable. This was not due to flows but to the handling of surplus stocks by public agencies which first absorbed them at maintained prices, then, from the mid 1960s on, unloaded them via 'soft food loans' combined with enforced acreage restrictions in the developing countries. Raw material and energy flows kept pace with requirements until the end of the 1960s and prices were stabilised by strategic stockpiling. The 'long boom', Kaldor sums up, was due to continuous growth in demand for manufactured goods in all the main industrial countries and the consequent 'important spill-over effects on the growth of services in housing and construction, as well as on demand for primary products' (76).

As far as the conscious contribution of the USA was concerned, it was not its fiscal policy (except in the Kennedy years) but its stress on institutional arrangements for restoring liberal capitalist systems – steady liberalisation of trade, reduction in tariff barriers, restoration of currency convertibility (on current transactions) and generous financial aid from the USA itself and through the Bretton Woods institutions. In the UK, because of Keynes's lasting influence on the state budget, there was a conscious effort to match overall demand to the expected growth of productive potential – but the policy makers were too pessimistic about the latter, so that a golden opportunity may have been missed. France with its series of indicative five-year plans achieved a rate of growth of 5 per cent per annum. West Germany, Italy and Japan too were not driven by conscious fiscal policies but by strong rates of growth of their exports, rates of over 10 per cent per annum for nearly 20 years. This enabled Germany to absorb several million Germans expelled from East Germany and then a stream of 'guest workers' (sending them back when blips occurred), while France and Italy had substantial reserves of labour in their agricultural sectors.

Kaldor attributes a primary role to the US dollar as the *de facto* international reserve currency. The USA had unlimited borrowing power and its increasing deficits on 'basic transactions' gave other countries additional reserves, so allowing them to expand without hitting balance-of-payments constraints. Until 1971 the USA was in deficit almost every year; this implied an addition to the demand for goods and services in the world outside. But the seeds of destruction were planted from the very beginning of the era. As countries obtained more and more dollars and the USA's official liabilities came to exceed its gold holdings by several times. countries became increasingly less willing to hold dollars, especially when the deficit assumed large dimensions during the war in Vietnam.

The Bretton Woods agreement collapsed in 1971 but the world economic system still continued to boom. Commodity prices rose as bad harvests in Russia and China and ensuing purchases emptied US grain reserves for the first time in 40 years. Stocks of non-ferrous metals went down and their prices rose, not least because of speculative activity in commodities because of an assumption of general inflation, following the suspension of the convertibility of the US dollar into gold. All these factors were reinforced by the sharp rise in the rate of increase of money-wages in industrialised countries from 1968–69 on, rupturing well-established 'norms' to which the stability of the various economic systems was anchored. Prices of manufactured goods rose at 5 per cent per annum from 1969 on.

The actions of OPEC at the end of 1973 started the era of stagflation. The change in the distribution of the incomes of the world that they implied and the inability of the OPEC countries to spend immediately their rise in incomes resulted in a large contraction in world income. From 1980 on there was a new wave of recession, mainly confined to Western Europe. Kaldor blames Mrs Thatcher (as she then was) who came on stream (steam?) at much the same time as North Sea oil. Her monetarist policies produced a huge slump in manufacturing output (a fall of 15 per cent); they destroyed much of the UK's industry and required its oil revenues to be used more for paying the unemployed than to allow the required restructuring of the economy through imports of investment goods from other countries who would have bought North Sea oil.

Instead of which, monetarism spread in the UK and in the USA – 'the incomes policy of Karl Marx' as Kaldor's contemporary Thomas Balogh had it – reversing the shift in economic, social and political power from capital to labour by recreating the reserve army of labour to try to control inflation. In effect, after the failure of monetarism, a failure which was generally acknowledged by the end of the 1980s, there emerged, in Kaldor's view, a complete paralysis of policy making at the international level, while no one country (with the possible exceptions of USA now and the UK in 1980–82) could go it alone any more.

Kaldor concludes by outlining the necessary policies for recovery, policies which would need worldwide agreement. First, there would need to be coordinated fiscal actions which used a set of balance-of-payments targets and 'full employment' budgets. (When Kaldor gave the Mattioli Lectures, most 'full employment' budgets were restrictive with government expenditure less than the taxation which would have been raised at the level of full employment, exactly the opposite of what was – is – required.) Kaldor regards trade liberalisation, even though it was a positive influence during the years of expansion, as a serious obstacle to recovery in a period of prolonged stagnation. Groups of countries need to set agreed import to export ratios and coordinate their overall policies if expansionary policies are not to be brought to a halt by balance-of-payments crises. Then there is no reason why full employment should not be restored through expansionary policies, preferably directed by the expansion of state investment in much needed social infrastructure.

Real interest rates should be brought down as far as possible and as much as possible. (In the past 20 years or more we have had extended periods with real interest rates at levels which Keynes in his wildest dreams would not have thought any even remotely sensible government and central bank could have allowed.) If the USA will not agree to this, Kaldor suggests that European countries impose an interest-equalisation tax to make it unattractive for their nationals to hold money in US dollar balances.

The most important requirement is to prevent the volatility of commodity prices. Kaldor would do this by creating buffer stock schemes directly out of a newly created international currency acceptable to participating governments just as SDRs were used (then) to settle claims. SDRs themselves should be issued to an international commodity corporation which would use them to pay for commodity purchases so that the cost of holding stocks would not fall on the tax payers of such nations but be a 'backing' or 'cover' for a reserve currency convertible into national ones. Kaldor wanted the system to start gradually and when there are low prices and recession so that it would be desirable and possible to stimulate future production and investment in an environment of stable prices. He would have us start with food grains and non-ferrous metals and gradually extend the net in order to bring in all sorts of commodities.

Like Keynes, Kaldor also seems to leave unresolved (unresolvable?) the chronic tendency for inflation to accelerate under conditions of full employment. He attributes this mainly to the process of setting wages by collective bargaining agreements and he identifies three major objectives of wage-earners which are incompatible with one another: a desire to maintain relativities, a desire to have a 'fair' share of any increase in companies' profits and a reluctance to allow any encroachment on achieved standards of living due to unfavourable events which may be external. Because productivity increases at different rates as between industries and as between firms in the same industry, the second objective conflicts with the first so that money-wages tend to grow faster than effective productivity. Successful oligopolists compound this tendency by not cutting prices and by paying wages above normal market rates in order to try to secure good industrial relations for themselves. Kaldor cannot see any way out of this impasse short of a system of continuous consultation between social partners to secure social consensus concerning a 'fair' distribution of income, reasonably full employment and monetary stability. He cites certain periods in the postwar period in Austria and West Germany as success stories of this nature.

This is rather a lame way for him to end. I was surprised he did not refer to the work of Wilfred Salter (1960, 1965) and Kalecki (1943) whereby adjusting nominal incomes for overall productivity plus prices greatly enhances the chances of economies establishing high-productivity scenarios. These in turn offer real gains in return for money incomes restraint, so providing a chance to overcome the basic dilemma that Kalecki discerned in the difference between *getting* to full employment and *sustaining* it, see Harcourt (1997). I was also surprised that Kaldor did not advocate the use of some variant of the Tobin tax in order to dampen down the systemically harmful effects of speculation by Marshallian/Pigovian carrot and stick measures, see Harcourt (1995). But then there is only so much that may be expected, even from such an undoubted Colossus as Nicky Kaldor.

Notes

1. As first Kaldor's PhD student (in the 1950s) and then his colleague and friend (from the 1960s on), I can confirm the soundness of this judgement.
2. This model still makes more sense of cyclical fluctuations in capitalist economies than do its modern rivals.
3. Kaldor's analysis of the deflationary and contractionary effects of institutional saving is akin to Keynes's discussion in *The General Theory* of the effects of 'financial prudence', whereby fixed assets were 'written off' long before they were due to be replaced, so necessitating that much extra current investment expenditure to offset the extra leakages created, see Keynes (1936, 98–104).
4. I was always surprised that Kaldor was not more enthusiastic about Kalecki's writings for it seemed to me that they were kindred spirits analytically, if not in personality – Kalecki was rather severe and austere but also *very* funny.
5. If we suppose that planned and actual saving *always* equal their investment counterparts in the short period, accumulation plans are always realised. But it is only on g_w that people are glad, after the event, that they made those plans in the first place. Harrod's insight may be summed up by saying that by assuming that planned saving is always equal to planned investment in the short period, he was able to bring out starkly the unstable consequences of them not being equal (at a level of income matching *expected* sales) in the long period – hence Joan Robinson's remark that Harrod had rediscovered Marx, Vols II and III.
6. John McCombie (22 May 1997) reminds me that Nicky may have been too sweeping at this point, that there were substantial disparities in the rates of growth of advanced economies over this period.

References

Harcourt, G. C. (1988) 'Nicholas Kaldor, 12 May 1908–30 September 1986', *Economica* vol. 55, 159–70, reprinted in Harcourt (1993).
— (1993) *Post-Keynesian Essays in Biography* (Basingstoke, Hants: Macmillan).
— (1995) *Capitalism, Socialism and Post-Keynesianism. Selected Essays of G. C. Harcourt* (Cheltenham: Edward Elgar), ch. 3.

— (1997) 'Economic Policy. Accumulation and Productivity', in J. Michie and J. Grieve Smith, *op. cit.*, 194–204.

Harrod, R. F. (1933) *International Economics* (London: Macmillan).

Hufbauer, G. C. (1966) *Synthetic Materials and the Theory of International Trade* (London: Duckworth).

Kaldor, N. (1934) 'A Classificatory Note on the Determinateness of Static Equilibrium', *Review of Economic Studies*, vol. 1, 122–36.

— (1939) 'Speculation and Economic Stability', *Review of Economic Studies*, vol. 7, 1–27.

— (1940) 'A Model of the Trade Cycle', *Economic Journal*, vol. 50, 78–92.

— (1955–56) 'Alternative Theories of Distribution', *Review of Economic Studies*, vol. 23, 83–100.

— (1966) *Causes of the Slow Rate of Economic Growth in the United Kingdom.* Inaugural Lecture at the University of Cambridge (Cambridge: Cambridge University Press).

— (1985) *Economics without Equilibrium,*(New York, Armonk: M. E. Sharpe).

Kalecki, M. (1943) 'Political Aspects of Full Employment', *Political Quarterly*, reprinted in Kalecki (1971).

— (1971) *Selected Essays on the Dynamics of the Capitalist Economy 1933–1970* (Cambridge: Cambridge University Press).

Keynes, J. M. (1930) *A Treatise on Money*, 2 vols (London: Macmillan), *C.W.*, vols. V, VI, 1972.

— (1936) *The General Theory of Employment, Interest and Money* (London: Macmillan), *C.W.*, vol VII, 1973.

McCombie, J. S. L. and A. P. Thirlwall (1994) *Economic Growth and the Balance of Payments Constraint* (London: Macmillan).

Michie, J. and J. Grieve Smith (eds) (1997) *Employment and Economic Performance: Jobs, Inflation and Growth* (Oxford: Oxford University Press).

Robinson, E. A. G. (ed) (1965) *Problems in Economic Development* (London: Macmillan).

Salter, W. E. G. (1960) *Productivity and Technical Change* (Cambridge: Cambridge University Press) 2nd edn 1966.

— (1965) 'Productivity Growth and Accumulation as Historical Processes'. In: Robinson, 266–291.

Sardoni, C. (1981) 'Multi-Sectoral Models of Balanced Growth and the Marxian Schemes of Expanded Reproduction', *Australian Economic Papers*, vol. 20: 383–397.

Targetti, F. (1988) 'Nicholas Kaldor', *Teoria e politica economica di un capitalismo in mutamento*. Società Editrice II Mulino S.p.A. Bologna.

Thirlwall, A. P. (1986) 'A General Model of Growth and Development on Kaldorian Lines', *Oxford Economic Papers* 38: 199–219.

— (1987) *Nicholas Kaldor 1908–86. Proceedings of the British Academy LXXIII.*

Young, A. (1928) 'Increasing Returns and Economic Progress', *Economic Journal*, vol. 38: 527–542.

Part V
Survey

19
Post-Keynesian Thought*

> To me, the expression *post-Keynesian* has a definite meaning; it
> applies to an economic theory or method of analysis which takes
> account of the difference between the future and the past.
>
> Joan Robinson (1978: 12, emphasis in original)

Introduction

The approaches to political economy which reflect post-Keynesian
thought are there partly for historical reasons and, partly, because of
logical associations. Post-Keynesianism is an extremely broad church.
The overlaps at each end of a long spectrum of views are marginal,
reflecting little more than a shared hostility towards mainstream neoclassical economics and methodology, *IS/LM* Keynesianism and the
'fix-price' Keynesianism of the 'New Keynesians' and certain French
economists. Some post-Keynesians are working actively towards a synthesis of the principal strands. Others regard the search for a synthesis,
for a general all-embracing structure, as a profound mistake; to quote
Joan Robinson, a founding mother, a misguided attempt to replace
'one box of tricks' by another. Post-Keynesianism should be a
situation-and-issue-specific method of doing political economy, a

* Not previously published. I draw heavily on a joint paper with L. D. Spajic,
'Post-Keynesianism', in Shri Bhagwan Dahiya (ed.), *The Current State of
Economic Science*, Vol. 2 (Rohtak, India: Spellbound, 1999) 904–34. I am
grateful to Sheila Dow and Guiseppe Fontana for their comments on a
draft of the essay.

'horses for courses' approach, itself an all-embracing structure at the methodological level.

In this essay we first discuss the historical origins of post-Keynesian thought and then deal with the approaches to a number of fundamental issues that political economists (and even economists) have tackled at least since the time of the Physiocrats and Adam Smith. They include theories of value and distribution, price-setting, accumulation, growth and the cycle, and the role of money and financial intermediaries, especially the debates associated with whether money is endogenous or exogenous. Most importantly, post-Keynesian thought belongs to the tradition that the *raison d'être* of our discipline is its bearing on policy. Thus great stress is put on the role of institutions in determining economic and political processes, the political philosophies of the post-Keynesian economists concerned and the policies which follow from their theories. This echoes what Keynes wrote when summarising the system of *The General Theory*:

> Our present object is to discover what determines at any time the national income of a given economic system and ... the amount of its employment ... Our final task might be to select those variables which can be deliberately controlled or managed by central authority in the kind of system in which we actually live.
>
> (Keynes, 1936, 1973a: 247)

All of these issues are intertwined, as are the methodologies that are implied in them and the particular 'vision' of the economy associated with each strand. This essay therefore concentrates on origins, pioneers and issues. For a full cast-list of players, readers could consult, for example, Eichner and Kregel (1975), Hamouda and Harcourt (1988), Arestis (1992) and Lavoie (1992).

Classical roots

Keynes's theory has no trouble reaching back over the 70 or so years of neoclassical economics which preceded it to join up with the preoccupations and approaches of our classical forebears. In the process much that was integral to Keynes's system, especially its Marshallian offshoots, was jettisoned, at least by those post-Keynesians who were (are) sympathetic to the viewpoints of the original classical economists and Marx. This rules out two of the most prominent American post-Keynesians, the late Sidney Weintraub and Paul Davidson whose structures are amalgams of Marshall and Keynes and who are hostile to the writings of Marx, Michal Kalecki and Piero Sraffa.

One of the most important aspects of classical economics for post-Keynesian thought is the organising concept of the surplus – its creation, extraction, distribution and use. It is the core of their system and of its modern counterpart. The concept dovetails logically with a view of economic processes as evolving, progressing organic systems, a dynamic view of the nature of our discipline as opposed to the more static allocative one which characterised neoclassical economics until the emergence of the neoclassical theory of growth in the 1950s. Linked with the concept is the notion of society as made up of broad classes, sometimes people, sometimes income classes, sometimes overlapping. The different classes perform different functions. They are treated for the purpose of analysis as homogenous, so that there is no need to start from the isolated individual economic agent of modern economic analysis. (Lorie Tarshis made a coherent case for starting with the firm as the basic unit of analysis. This has been integrated with class analysis. Tarshis thus avoided the modern heresy of analysing systemic behaviour in terms of a representative agent model.)

Also associated with the concept of the surplus is the concept of the long-period position, containing the centres of gravitation of the system (natural prices in Smith, prices of production in Marx, long-period normal equilibrium prices (and quantities) in Marshall). With these concepts goes the view that *general* theory may only relate to an examination of the interrelationships of the dominant and persistent forces at work in society. Its modern counterparts are Sraffa's work on value and distribution and Garegnani's long-period interpretation, together with those of Eatwell, Milgate and Rogers, of the nature of the Keynesian revolution.

The Marshallian–Keynesian roots

Turning to the Marshall–Keynes connection, we note the historical process through which Keynes liberated himself from Marshall's system of thought as he understood it, on which he had been brought up and within which he perceived himself as operating up to the publication of *A Treatise on Money* in 1930. The basic ingredients were the dichotomy between the real and the money, an emphasis on the long period, and the logically prior need to have a Say's Law long-period equilibrium position of the economy as a prerequisite for the Quantity Theory of Money to be a theory of the general price level. Until Keynes liberated himself from these aspects of his upbringing, he was not able to write the theory of a monetary production economy which comprises the system of *The General Theory*.

Effective demand is the point of intersection of the aggregate demand and aggregate supply functions, a position which usually implies some involuntary unemployment. The money rate of interest rules the roost (it is the price which clears the money market, not the market for saving and investment). Uncertainty is a permanent environment for the most important economic decisions, especially those concerning investment and the holding of financial assets for speculative and other purposes. The consumption function is relatively stable, the investment function is relatively volatile, and the two of them are combined by the Kahn-Meade multiplier. Finally (this is an aberration for most post-Keynesians), the general price level is explained by a short-period Marshallian analysis at the level of the economy as a whole. For the American post-Keynesians in particular, all this is the jumping-off point for their own contributions.

Keynes's theory of accumulation

All theories of accumulation under our rubric either start from or incorporate the ingredients of Keynes's own theory. The details of his analysis are usually stringently criticised; the recipes which emerge use the same ingredients, but mix them together in different, more acceptable ways. Even within its own framework Keynes's theory was not acceptable. Keynes confused the stock and flow aspects of accumulation by naming his principal concept the marginal efficiency of capital (*MEC*). For capital is a stock, and it was investment, a flow, and so the marginal efficiency of investment (*MEI*) with which he was mainly concerned.

Keynes's arguments as to why a higher rate of accumulation would be associated with a lower value of the *MEI* so that short-period flow equilibrium would be achieved when $MEI = i$, where $i =$ the rate of interest, were either far-fetched or non-clinching. Keynes assumed rising marginal costs of production in all industries and (usually) marginal-cost pricing. As we consider higher and higher values of accumulation in a given situation, there would higher and higher supply prices and thus lower and lower values of the *MEI*. But this assumes that all the individual free competitors have, in effect, rational expectations so that it is *as if* they use in their calculations, not the market price of capital goods (which they know) but the *eventual equilibrium price*. Otherwise, their combined actions will *not* bring about that overall rate of production of capital goods which establishes the appropriate supply price and the value of the *MEI* equal to *i*.

Secondly, Keynes argues persuasively that because we do not know the future, we adopt the convention of projecting the present into the future unless there are good reasons for not doing so. In his schema, higher levels of investment are associated with higher sales, prices, profits, output and employment, yet Keynes's analysis of investment assumes that the expected longer-period demand curves for the products concerned remain stable – given – while the future short-period supply curves associated with various possible levels of investment now move further and further to the right. This implies lower expected prices of the products and therefore lower expected quasi-rents for the investment projects now, so again bringing about lower *MEI* values. But if Keynes were to be true to himself, the expected demand curves would move too. The predicted lower values of prices *et al.* then would not *necessarily* follow. Keynes has used a static analysis to analyse an essentially dynamic process, a set of criticisms first made by Kalecki in 1936 in his review in Polish of *The General Theory* (see Targetti and Kinda-Hass, 1982, for the first English translation of Kalecki, 1936) and subsequently by Joan Robinson and Tom Asimakopulos.

They reacted by setting out the two-sided relationship between accumulation and profitability – that actual investment is a major determinant of current profits while current profits are a major determinant of expected profits which in turn determine planned accumulation in situations of given financial conditions and long-term expectations. This is the basis of Kalecki's theory of distribution, accumulation, growth and the trade cycle and of Joan Robinson's analysis of the same phenomenon in her famous banana diagram, Robinson (1962: 48). We discuss them below, following our account of theories of value, distribution and pricing.

Pasinetti (1997) remained true to Keynes's original formulation. He points out that, very quickly, the *MEI* became identified with the marginal product of capital so that investment was treated as a process of 'deepening' in response to different values of *i*. Pasinetti argues that Keynes made no such claim – that he only argued that in a given situation, a lower value of *i* would make more of the existing stock of investment *projects* seem to be profitable *regardless of the ordering of their implied capital-intensities*. Davidson (1972), too, accepted Keynes's analysis but followed Keynes's alternative presentation of his theory in terms of describing investment projects by their net present values (*NPV*) at the ruling *i*(s), and used Keynes's spot, forward and futures analysis to go from investment possibilities – demand prices greater than supply prices in existing conditions – to determine the equilibrium flow per period.

Post-Keynesian theories of value, distribution and price-setting

We now examine the post-Keynesian theories of value and distribution and of price-setting at the level of the, usually, oligopolistic price-leader firm. Both sets of theories of value and distribution – especially of distribution – arise from dissatisfaction with the supply and demand theories of neoclassical economics. The theories criticised and those put forward as alternatives are macroeconomic theories. They arose because one of the first empirical observations *cum* theoretical deductions of classical political economy was that, in a world of free competition, there would be a tendency to create of a uniform rate of profit in all activities. The analytical questions then arose: what is the origin and what determines the size of the system-wide rate of profits (Sraffa's usage) to which the individual rates of profit tend to be equal? The most explicit and refined answers in the classical tradition are given by Marx. In the process it is emphasised that the ultimate source of value is the difficulty of reproduction in a system characterised by production of commodities by means of commodities (as opposed to utility and scarcity in the alternative tradition). (Avi Cohen, 1989, provides a 'plague on both your houses' analysis of these two traditions outside one commodity 'worlds'.) A reconciliation is needed between the embodied labour values of commodities which arise in the sphere of production and their prices of production in the sphere of distribution and exchange. The latter contain the overall rate of profits as one of their ingredients and are the centres of gravitation of the system.

The other major alternative theories of distribution to the neoclassical marginal productivity explanation of the returns to capital and labour and the share of wages and profits in the national income are those Kaldor (1955–56) called Keynesian theories of distribution. He was not the first to set forth such a theory. Kalecki (1971: 78–9) had long before, arguing that 'capitalists may decide to ... invest more in a given period than in a preceding one, but they cannot decide to earn more ... therefore, their investment ... decisions ... determine profits ... not vice versa'. Kaldor himself located its origins in the widow's cruse story of *A Treatise on Money* [1930]. Nevertheless, Kaldor's version is the best-known in the literature. All versions have as common features different saving behaviour at the margin as between wages and profits (and/or wage-earners and profit-receivers) and the Keynesian/Kaleckian proposition that investment leads and saving responds, rather than the other way around, as in the neoclassical tradition. In Kaldor's theory, the mechanism is, paradoxically, long-period and relates to a fully employed economy. Kaldor argued, never completely coherently, that a growing economy must be a fully employed one in the long-period sense. Then planned saving may be brought to equality with planned investment (and its share of full employment income) if the distribution of income is such that the matching amount and proportion of saving are forthcoming.

The process by which the equality is brought about depends upon Kaldor's (claimed) empirical observations that while in the short term money prices and money-wages are sticky, so that changes in income are needed to make saving equal investment, there is a tendency for prices to be *more* flexible than money-wages in the longer term, and these differential changes continue until the equality is secured. This implies that wage-earners in modern situations have real wage levels so far above the subsistence levels of the classicals and Marx that within a wide range of possible shares they passively accept what remains for them after the capitalist profit-receivers have had first bite of the cherry: exactly the opposite of the older scenarios in which wages had to be met and the surplus available for profits (and thus accumulation and rentier consumption) is what is left, potentially only in a non-Say's Law world.

Virtually all the other theories under this heading concern the short period and are not constrained to be at full employment. We thus have a class of models in which saving is brought to equality with investment by changes in the level of activity *and* the distribution of income as profit margins change relative to wage costs, a rest state which in general exhibits involuntary unemployment. (In the most developed models there is a role for both the government and the overseas sectors.) As we mentioned, Kalecki was one of the first to advance such a theory. Joan Robinson provided a most lucid account of his theory in the 1977 issue of the Oxford *Bulletin* in his memory. Consider the simplest case of no consumption by rentiers, no saving by wage-earners and no overseas or government sectors. Then profits (II) must be exactly equal to investment (I), with causation running $I \rightarrow II$.

The most rigorous presentation of the modern classical theory is in Sraffa's 1960 *Production of Commodities by Means of Commodities*. Sraffa uses a model which has formal similarities to Leontief's input – output model but the *conceptual* interpretation is very different. When there is production with a surplus and both the wage rate (w) and the rate of profits (r) are explicit, Sraffa shows that we must know from outside the value of one of the distributive variables. The classical economists and Marx chose w, Sraffa himself finally settled for r:

> The rate of profits, as a ratio, has a significance which is independent of any prices, and can well be 'given' before the prices are fixed. It is accordingly susceptible of being determined from outside the system of production, in particular by the level of the money rates of interest ... the rate of profits will therefore be treated as the independent variable.
>
> (Sraffa, 1960: 33)

He demonstrated how the pattern of the prices of production and the value of the other distributive variable are simultaneously determined. The prices of production are the centres of gravitation of the system in the particular circumstances of the time, around which market prices fluctuate – or perhaps on which they converge, it is not clear which is the dominant interpretation. (Moreover, some modern work suggests that they do not necessarily do *either*.)

Sraffa starts with a circulating, single-use commodity model, then takes us all the way through non-renewable and/or addable to resources (land and rent) and joint production (in order to analyse durable capital goods rather than Marshall's wool and mutton). He closes with a discussion of the choice of techniques in the investment decision. The last shows the possibility of reswitching, destroying the conceptual foundation of a well-behaved demand curve for 'capital' in the alternative tradition.

The size of the mark-up

There are many variants of the theory of the size of the mark-up, the most widely known (apart from Kalecki's 'degree of monopoly' version) being the version of the late Alfred Eichner (1976). He related its size to the investment plans of firms in oligopolistic industries and their financial requirements. There is a flaw in his definition of the investment function (it is basically Keynes's investment function), so we present here the long-period model of Adrian Wood (1975) as representative of this class of models. Wood's model is a steady-state model of a firm in an oligopolistic industry, steady-state in the sense that expectations of the values of all relevant variables are assumed to be realised. It is a partial analysis – the level of aggregate demand is given so it shows a firm striving for what it regards as its optimum share of demand for the industry's products at the expense of other firms in the industry.

The firm is assumed to be motivated by a desire for its sales revenue to grow as fast as possible subject to two constraints, formalised as an opportunity frontier and a finance frontier. The opportunity frontier reflects the fact that in a given situation, there is eventually a trade-off between the size of the profit margin on turnover and the rate of growth of sales revenue, so that to increase the latter requires that the former be squeezed either by a price cut or a rise in sales costs (or both). Assuming only one best-practice technique to invest in and given external financial conditions, each possible rate of growth of sales requires a particular profit margin to finance the capacity that will make it possible. Where the two frontiers intersect defines the margin associated with highest possible rate of growth. Introducing the possibility of a choice of techniques defines a family of interacting frontiers, one for each technique. Because the opportunity frontier moves out at a decreasing rate – greater investment per unit of sales lowers costs at a decreasing rate while the finance frontiers fan out proportionately – a locus of margins and rates of growth lie along a concave curve which contains a maximum margin, rate-of-growth combination.

Wood's analysis is in Golden Age logical time; an attempt to set the problem in historical time, using Salter's vintage analysis (1960, 1966), may be found in Harcourt and Kenyon (1976; Sardoni, 1992). The principal result is to show that setting the price which serves to finance the accumulation programme simultaneously shows what accumulation is needed to satisfy expected future sales and what existing capacity will still be profitable (in the sense of covering its variable costs) and so able to contribute towards production to satisfy future sales. Frederic Lee (1998) tells the story of post-Keynesian price theory from the earliest times to the present day.

Post-Keynesian accumulation: Moses and the profits

The stage is set now for an examination of the characteristics of post-Keynesian theories of accumulation. Historically, they were stimulated by Harrod's immediate pre- and post-Second World War pioneering contributions towards a dynamic economics. In retrospect, we see that Harrod (without realising it) rediscovered within a Keynesian framework the systemic instabilities of capitalism which Marx had pointed to through his schemas of reproduction analysis. Marx asked: what conditions had to be satisfied in his three department schema, period by period, in order that both aggregate demand and aggregate supply, and their compositions, always match. This threw up the impossibility of these being brought about by individual decision-making capitalists doing their own things with regard to production, employment and accumulation.

Harrod essentially obtained the same result. He brought out the *long-period* destabilising effects of a momentary gap between planned saving and planned investment when the *short-period* stabilising effects had been abstracted from by assuming that the investment that was planned each short period was immediately achieved. This raised the possibility that even though plans were achieved, the level and rate of growth of income which allowed planned saving to equal planned investment may have been such that if businesspeople had known in advance what they were to be, they would not have planned those levels of investment in the first place. The saving and investment functions were so related to each other that excess demand situations were to the right of the equilibrium position, and excess supply situations to the left, so that the system gave exactly the wrong signals as to what to do next. Unless the system were growing at the warranted rate (g_w) in the first place it would always tend to move away from it. All this was regardless of whether or not g_w coincided with the natural rate of growth g_n.

Solow and Swan interpreted Harrod as imposing a fixed capital–output ratio on the system, and wondered whether this was responsible for his disturbing results. So, as pioneering Keynesians, they assumed an all-wise government to take care of effective demand puzzles. They then asked whether in a long-period sense, Marshall's 'dynamical principle of "Substitution" ... seen ever at work' would allow a competitive price mechanism to give out appropriate relative price signals, causing the methods of production chosen by accumulators to be such as to lead g_w to approach g_n (itself exogenously given by the growth of the labour supply and autonomous technical progress). The answer is 'yes', at least in the simplest one, all-purpose commodity models.

Naturally these results and more complicated versions of them attracted the attention of the Cambridge, UK growth theorists, who, already suspicious of smooth continuous substitution possibilities, wished to bring in the more realistic 'book of blueprints' approach. (This approach had long been 'at home' at MIT and elsewhere within a different context and approach.) The Cambridge UK theorists were also loathe to leave the concepts of aggregate and effective demand out of the picture. Their writings remained, for the most part, within the confines of steady-state growth models, learning to walk before they ran, except Kaldor who used his distribution mechanism to ensure the equality of g_n and g_w.

Kalecki, Steindl and Goodwin followed a different path, one which eventually became congenial to both Kaldor and Joan Robinson. Kalecki originally developed trendless cycles but by the time he published his last paper (1968) on these themes, he argued that the trend and cycle were indissolubly mixed: 'the long-run trend [is] but a slowly changing component of a chain of short-period situations ... [not an] independent entity' (Kalecki, 1971: 165).

This view of life had been developed independently by Goodwin from the 1940s on, reaching maturity in his paper, 'A Growth Cycle', in the 1967 Dobb *Festschrift*. He used the Volterra prey – predator model whereby the analogy of 'the symbiosis of two populations – partly complementary, partly hostile – is helpful in ... understanding ... the dynamical contradictions of capitalism, especially when stated in a ... Marxian form' (Goodwin, 1967, 1982: 167). He analysed the fight over wages and profits and the feedback on real variables – and spawned a literature which is still expanding.

Goodwin, though, was not satisfied. He needed to integrate effective demand and production interdependence into the model. The two lines of thought came together, as an impressive whole, in Goodwin and Punzo (1987). The work is extremely eclectic; the influence of Marx, Schumpeter, Keynes, von Neumann, Joan Robinson, Sraffa and Kalecki may all be discerned. So, too, may the developments of catastrophe theory and the concept of 'bifurcation', together with the older biological analogy drawn from the Volterra prey–predator model. Goodwin concentrated on the nature of evolutionary structures which experience from time to time large jumps and breaks, which he regarded as the key to the cyclical development of economies characterised by production interdependencies.

Joan Robinson (1962a) synthesised some of these ideas in her banana diagram. From Kalecki's theory of distribution she derived a relationship between actual accumulation and achieved profitability; from Keynes's theory she derived the 'animal-spirits' function which related desired accumulation to expected profitability, itself a function of achieved profitability, in a situation where financial conditions and long-term expectations are givens. With plausible conjectures about the shapes and positions of the two curves, she showed that an iteration procedure took the economy to a stable intersection point where what was expected and desired was achieved, her version of Harrod's g_w. But this is not a solution of Harrod's or Domar's problem, for there is no reason why g_w should coincide with g_n. Nor are there any mechanisms in the model to cause it to seek a path to g_n. Moreover, even if the economy did attain g_w, there is nothing to ensure that it will not be driven away from it at future points in time, for neither of the two relationships can be expected to remain stable over time.

When Joan Robinson discussed *The General Theory* 25 years after its publication, she signalled the change of method which lay behind her analysis in 1956 and 1962a (she was not always true to herself as Tom Asimakopulos pointed out on several occasions):

> The short period is here and now, with concrete stocks of the means of production in existence. Incompatibilities in the situation … will determine what happens next. Long-period equilibrium is not at some date in the future; it is an imaginary state of affairs in which there are no incompatibilities in the existing situation, here and now.
>
> (Joan Robinson, 1962b: 690)

Summing up, the developments constitute an attack, first, on the procedure of setting up theoretical issues as a search for existence and uniqueness, themselves determined by a set of factors which are largely independent of those responsible for the second aspect, stability, local and global. Similarly, the applied procedure of separating trend from cycle with largely independent factors again responsible for each is also discarded. This is an excellent jumping-off point for the discussion of post-Keynesian methodology and methods.

Post-Keynesian method

There are two main views on method within post-Keynesian thought, when post-Keynesianism is defined historically. Increasingly, commentators tend to put the so-called neo-Ricardians in a class of their own. I do not agree with this tendency. The Sraffian critique of neo-classical economics and Sraffa's positive contributions are integral parts of both the historical and the logical developments. Especially is this so when his underlying Marxism is recognised as it always was by, for example, Maurice Dobb, Ronald Meek and Krishna Bharadwaj. It is true that the neo-Ricardians take a distinct stance on method and theory, a stance (on method) which they identify as common to all strands of political economy until the 1920s when neoclassical economists, including Hayek, started to recognise the incoherence associated with the concept of the marginal product of capital and its relationship to the long-period method. They reacted, it is argued, by changing the questions and the method to the temporary equilibrium analysis of, for example, J. R. Hicks in *Value and Capital*. The essential point of the neo-Ricardians is that *general* theory can only be written about the characteristics of long-period positions which reflect the ultimate outcomes of the relationships associated with the dominant and persistent forces at work in economies. The economist's role is to identify these and to make rigorously explicit their relationships with each other. This method, they argue, was common to Smith and Marx and also to Marshall who fitted the 'new' supply and demand theories into the old method, so making long-period equilibrium normal prices and quantities the heart of the *Principles*. The corollary was, as we mentioned earlier, that for Keynes's revolution be to a true revolution, his theory of underemployment equilibrium must be a long-period one. Garegnani, Eatwell, Milgate, Rogers and Krishna Bharadwaj refer to various passages in *The General Theory* which they argue support this viewpoint. There is no corresponding role for short-period theory in its own right as opposed to situation-specific analysis at different levels of abstraction.

In contrast, Kalecki, Kaldor and Joan Robinson and their followers, and Paul Davidson and his (though the *theories* differ considerably), argue that the long-period method is a non-starter for *descriptive* analysis. (For doctrinal debates even Joan Robinson who was the most insistent proponent of the alternative viewpoint granted it a role. If a conjecture or concept could be shown to be incoherent under ideal conditions at a high level of abstraction, this was a legitimate critique of an approach, its conceptions and intuitions, as well as of its theories and theorems.) For descriptive analysis, though, we have to start from a given short period with its inherited historical circumstances and accompanying expectations. Long-term expectations and factors are then relevant for some of the decisions that will be made now – for example, investment, pricing – while short-term expectations and factors are relevant for production and employment decisions which again have to be made now. The story then unfolds as we move on from one short-period to another. (We have simplified for if we use a short-period analysis, some of the current activity is the result of decisions taken in the past, and some of the current decisions will be relevant for activity in future short periods – a view which led to Keynes abandoning period analysis because he despaired of ever finding a determinate time unit into which could be fitted *all* the relevant interrelationships occurring.) There is an element of convergence in the discipline recently because such a philosophy surely underlies modern work on path-dependence even when the *theory* is unambiguously neoclassical. The writings of Richard Goodwin and Hyman Minsky, on the one hand, and of Brian Arthur and Paul David, on the other, may all be classified under this description.

These new developments link back to old approaches as far as method is concerned. Keynes, following Marshall, always pointed out that which variables (or relationships) were regarded as endogenous (determined) and which were regarded as exogenous (determining) were on any absolute criteria arbitrary. The crucial decider was the issue in hand. Here is his description of 'the nature of economic thinking':

> The object of our analysis is, not to provide a machine, or method of blind manipulation, which will furnish an infallible answer, but to provide ourselves with an organised and orderly method of thinking out particular problems; and, after we have reached a provisional conclusion by isolating the complicating factors one by one, we then have to go back on ourselves and allow, as well as we can, for the probable interactions of the factors amongst themselves. This is the nature of economic thinking.
>
> (Keynes, 1936, 1973a: 297)

Thus the Marshallian/Keynesian method consists of looking at parts of the economy in sequence, holding constant or abstracting from what is going on, or least the *effects* of what is going on elsewhere, for the moment. In this way Marshall hoped we would get definite, if partial, results and that, if we went right round the economy, we would eventually be able to bring all our results together to give a full, overall picture. That the procedure was inconsistent with his deeper vision that economic processes were akin to systemic interrelated biological processes he seems to have forgotten. This *may* be one of the reasons why ultimately both Marshall and Joan Robinson thought that they had failed – not from realising that by following the procedure, they were attempting the impossible, but because the *procedure* itself was at fault. (Jan Kregel argues that it is not the *procedure* but the *problem* which is intractable.)

Sheila Dow (1991) stresses the unifying methodological aspect of post-Keynesian thought, which justifies diversity of method. In doing so, she recalls to mind Keynes's own views on method and theorising – that there is a continuum of languages which runs all the way from poetry and intuition through lawyer-akin arguments to formal logic and mathematics. Each has its rightful role depending upon the issues, or aspects of issues, in economics being discussed. This emphasis in Keynes's approach had no greater champion than the late George Shackle whose favourite example was Keynes's most effective use of the word 'sentiment' in economic analysis. Though it could not be defined mathematically, it nevertheless gave insights, conjured up atmosphere, invoked the environment of the situations under analysis. In a classic article in 1976 Kregel identified in *The General Theory* three different models of actual economic reality of differing degrees of complexity. The most complex was the model of shifting equilibrium. He argued that the methods were common to Keynes *and* the post-Keynesians when modelling decision-making in an uncertain environment.

While the post-Keynesians who follow on from Goodwin, Kalecki and Joan Robinson eschew the Marshallian (or even Keynesian) method, there are others who manage to combine a similar 'vision' of society with an explicit use of the Marshallian/Keynesian method or even earlier, the implicit method of the classical economists. The outstanding examples include Pasinetti whose work of over 20 years on a multisectoral growth model came to fruition in 1981 in *Structural Change and Economic Growth* (with a simple exposition in 1993). Pasinetti integrated the macro aggregates of Keynes with the production interdependence of the classicals, Marx and Sraffa. In both books he outlines in careful detail the consistency conditions required for maintaining full employment growth in a multisector model in which the demands for commodities over time follow their respective Engels curves, technical progress occurs and, in the later stages of the analysis, the economy is an open one, trading with and borrowing from or lending to the rest of the world. (The resemblance to the procedure of *Capital*, Vols II and III is not fanciful.) The most widely-known exposition of his insights is his 1962 *R. E. Studs* paper in which he obtained the 'remarkable result' that $r = g/s_c$. This result has proved extremely robust as complications have been added – international trade, government, financial intermediaries, endogenously determined saving ratios – and some commentators have attempted, unsuccessfully, to destroy or play down the generality of the result.

Another major contribution which is relevant here is Marglin's contribution to the conflict inflation literature (1984). (Rowthorn, 1977, earlier and independently came up with the same results.) Marglin has a Keynesian–Marxian outlook on life but is resolutely Marshallian in method. His central aim is to establish long-period 'equilibrium' relationships – long-period crosses which are approached on the way by short-period stations and which stay 'put' until and after they are reached. His principal result is that sustained rates of inflation are the means by which the disappointed aspirations of wage-earners and capitalists are shared between them in an uneasy but sustainable truce.

Post-Keynesian thought aims to start from real world observations, one set of which has been made famous by Kaldor's description of them as 'stylised facts'. These are broad empirical generalisations which hold, in a rough and ready way, often for long runs of historical time and require situation-specific theories and accompanying models to explain them. Kaldor himself pioneered the theory of cumulative causation, a deep idea which he first learnt of from his teacher, Allyn Young (and also from Gunnar Myrdal); Young further alerted Kaldor to the pervasive existence of dynamic increasing returns in economic life. He exploited these illuminations, together with his stress on inter-regional relationships, to analyse the outcomes of various specific periods of economic history.

The contrast between mainstream axiomatic, equilibrium theory, on the one hand, and post-Keynesian cumulative causation theory, on the other, may be illustrated by the analogy of a wolf-pack. The first approach thinks of a wolf-pack running along. If one or two wolves get ahead or fall behind, powerful forces come into play to return them to the pack. The second, though, identifies powerful forces which make those who leave the pack get further and further ahead or fall further and further behind, at least for long periods of time – hence the rejection of the use of the concept of equilibrium and especially of long-period equilibrium as being of any use in descriptive analysis.

Endogenous money

There is evidence that Keynes, both before and after *The General Theory*, was an endogenous money person. That is to say, he argued that the demand for money, and especially for credit, played a significant role not only in determining the rate of interest but also in determining the supply of money overall. Was then his stance in *The General Theory*, where he has been interpreted as regarding the money supply as exogenous and the rate of interest as the price which allowed it to be voluntarily held at any moment of time, an aberration? The most convincing answer (given most recently by Sheila Dow, 1997) is that he took the supply of money as *given* not *exogenous* for the particular arguments he was making in *The General Theory*. Certainly, by 1937 he had reverted to type when in his discussion of the finance motive for holding money (read, demanding credit), he had the banks initiating credit creation in response to demands from the private sector for finance for investment projects. This is one of the bases from which the post-Keynesian debates on the demand and supply of money and credit starts.

Within the post-Keynesian discussions, there are claims that the money supply is entirely demand-determined, as opposed to supply-determined, summarised in the phrase, Horizontalists versus Verticalists, see Moore (1988). Moore's, though, is an extreme position. Most writers, while they reject the verticalist interpretation, a stance which they attribute to much mainstream theory, do allow important roles to be played by credit rationing and rising interest rates in the determination of the outcomes in the money market and the market for financial assets in general. What is almost universally argued is that it is the meeting of demand for funds, principally for investment expenditure but now in the brave new world of credit for all, for some forms of consumption expenditure as well, which creates deposits in the first place. This is contrasted with the mainstream view whereby the deposits of present and past saving initiate the provision of potential lending by financial intermediaries The former view was most fervently expressed by Keynes who stated: 'The investment market can become congested through shortage of cash. It can never become congested through shortage of saving. This is the most fundamental of my conclusions within this field' (*CW*, Vol. XIV, 1973b: 222). This view was independently arrived at by Kalecki and most post-Keynesians have followed on from here, responding to new institutional developments as they occurred and refining and extending the analysis in various ways. In doing so they reflect the major change in an outlook which James Meade attributed to Keynes: that Keynes changed us from looking at the world as a dog called saving which wagged a tail called invest-ment to one in which the investment dog wagged a saving tail. Meade maintained this stance to the end of his life, both with regard to the domestic economy and to the international economy. Would that the bulk of the profession had stayed with him!

Within this particular set of discussions, some have stressed the stock aspects of money and financial assets generally, others the flow aspects of credit as a source of finance for important flow expenditures. Associated with this distinction is the group of post-Keynesian economists who have concentrated on one period only in their analysis of money – the accomodationists. They have been contrasted with another group, the structuralists, who stress a period-by-period analysis in the manner of the Kalecki's mature views, and also those of John Hicks. The upshot has been the preser-vation of the significance of Keynes's theory of liquidity preference in an explanation of the demand for money and other financial assets, of the level and pattern of interest rates, and of banks extend-ing credit guided by their own state of liquidity preference, so that not all demand is necessarily accommodated; see Cottrell (1994).

Policy

The connection between post-Keynesian analysis and the real world extends to a healthy preoccupation with policy. By and large, the policy proposals of the mean post-Keynesian match those of the mean Bastard Keynesian – a slightly left-of-centre package deal of monetary policy, fiscal policy and incomes policy. These are com-bined with a longer-term commitment to freer trade while preserv-ing protective positions until 'the time is ripe' and a preference for a system of fixed exchange rates (with institutional means to allow orderly realignments to be made every now and then). Revamping the structures of Bretton Woods, in order to try to remove the built-in contractionary biases of the modern world, guides suggestions on the international stage. The international deregulation of financial markets and the 'freeing up' of exchange rates have unleashed an era of instability to follow the more tranquil experience of 'the Golden Age of Capitalism' that preceded it. This has led in turn to attempts to curb the excesses of speculative movements in the principal markets involved – foreign exchange markets, the stock exchange, property markets – of which the Tobin tax on transactions is the best-known.

Where post-Keynesians feel they have the upper hand in these arguments is in their argument that cumulative causation processes as opposed to equilibrating processes characterise the workings of many of the most important markets and indeed whole economic systems. If such processes operate it is much harder to make a case for beneficial systemic effects of speculation – that it reduces fluctuations and gets the market (system) to the underlying long-period equilibrium values (positions) more quickly than otherwise would be the case. For if there are not such underlying values or positions, speculation will almost certainly make matters worse. We are thus led inevitably to middle way programmes, somewhere between ruthless *laissez faire* (but not that competitive) capitalism, on the one hand, and authoritarian, inefficient, centrally planned economies on the other. Heinrich Bortis has developed the philosophical, political and economic aspects of these developments most profoundly. He has synthesised the three majors strands of post-Keynesianism: the neo-Ricardian approach to capture the longer-term aspects of development of economies, the Kaleckian – Robinsonian their cyclical aspects, and the American post-Keynesians the short-period behaviour in product and money markets under uncertainty. To this he has allied a democratic socialist platform replete with philosophical foundations and a comprehensive outline of policy, nationally and internationally, see Bortis (1997). Another stalwart has been John Cornwall. Over the years he has not only developed his original theoretical critique of Harrod for supposing that the warranted rate and natural rate could be regarded as independent of each other, but he has also supplemented his original analysis of the implications for growth of systemic supply and demand interdependence with a steady stream of down-to-earth and humanely enlightened recommendations for institutional reforms, again national and international; see Harcourt and Monadjemi (1999) for an evaluation of his contributions.

Both Bortis and Cornwall have been much influenced by Kaldor's writings. In Kaldor's last book (1996), he set out his mature views on how the world works. In the last chapter he outlined his policy proposals. He has long emphasised the importance of increasing returns in industry and the different pricing behaviour with regard to the (export) products of primary producing countries, on the one hand, and those of the countries producing industrial goods, on the other. This led him to combine his policies for relative stability in exchange rates worldwide with international buffer-stock schemes for primary commodities. The latter could serve the dual purpose of reducing the fluctuations in prices and incomes which so damage the economies of the countries that produce these commodities (and those that buy them), while at the same time providing worldwide liquidity for trade and capital movements. Such a provision would be free of the disadvantages which arise when one major country's currency performs this role, as happens now.

References

Arestis, P. (1992) *The Post-Keynesian Approach to Economics* (Aldershot: Edward Elgar).

Bortis, H. (1997) *Institutions, Behaviour and Economic Theory. A Contribution to Classical-Keynesian Political Economy* (Cambridge: Cambridge University Press).

Cohen, A. J. (1989) 'Prices, Capital and the One-Commodity Model in Neoclassical and Classical "Theories"', *History of Political Economy*, vol. 21, Summer, 231–51.

Cottrell, A. (1994) 'Post-Keynesian Monetary Economics', *Cambridge Journal of Economics*, vol. 18, 587–605.

Davidson, P. (1972) *Money and the Real World* (London: Macmillan).

Dow, S. (1991) 'Keynes's Epistomology and Economic Methodology', in O'Donnell (1991), *op. cit.*, 144–67.

— (1997) 'Endogenous Money' in Harcourt and Riach, *op. cit.*, vol. 2 (1997), 61–78.

Eichner, A. S. (1976) *The Megacorp and Oligopoly: Micro Foundations of Macro Dynamics* (Cambridge: Cambridge University Press).

— and J. A. Kregel (1975) 'An Essay on Post-Keynesian Theory: A New Paradigm in Economics', *Journal of Economic Literature*, vol. XIII, 1293–314.

Goodwin, R. M. (1967) 'A Growth Cycle', in C. H. Feinstein (ed.), *Socialism, Capitalism and Economic Growth* (Cambridge: Cambridge University Press).

— (1982) *Essays in Dynamic Economics* (London: Macmillan).

— and L. F. Punzo (1987) *The Dynamics of a Capitalist Economy: A Multi-Sectoral approach* (Oxford: Basil Blackwell, Polity Press).

Hamouda, O. F. and G. C. Harcourt (1988) 'Post-Keynesianism: From Criticism to Coherence?' *Bulletin of Economic Research*, vol. 40, January, 1–30.

Harcourt, G. C. and P. Kenyon (1976) 'Pricing and the Investment Decision', *Kyklos*, vol. 29, fasc. 3, 449–77.

—and M. S. Monadjemi (1999) 'The Vital Contributions of John Cornwall to Economic Theory and Policy', in M. Setterfield (ed.) (1999), *Growth, Employment and Inflation. Essays in Honour of John Cornwall* (London: Macmillan).

— and P. A. Riach (1997) *A 'Second Edition' of The General Theory*, 2 vols (London: Routledge).

Kaldor, N. (1955–56) 'Alternative Theories of Distribution', *Review of Economic Studies*, vol. 23, no. 2, 83–100.

— (1996) *Causes of Growth and Stagnation in the World Economy* (Cambridge: Cambridge University Press).

Kalecki, M. (1936) 'Some Remarks on Keynes' Theory', in J. Osiatynski (ed.) (1990) *Collected Works of Michal Kalecki*, Vol. I (Oxford: Oxford University Press), 223–32.

— (1971) *Selected Essays on the Dynamics of Capitalist Economies 1933–70* (Cambridge: Cambridge University Press).

Keynes, J. M. (1930) *A Treatise on Money*, 2 vols (London: Macmillan), *C.W.*, Vols. V, VI, 1971.

— (1936, 1973a) *The General Theory of Interest, Employment and Money* (London: Macmillan), *C.W.*, Vol. VII.

— (1973b) *The General Theory and After: Part II, Defense and Development* (London: Macmillan), *C.W.*, Vol. XIV.

Kregel, J. A. (1976) 'Economic Methodology in the Face of Uncertainty: The Modelling Methods of Keynes and the Post Keynesians', *Economic Journal*, vol. 86, June, 209–75.

Lavoie, M. (1992) *Foundations of Post-Keynesian Economic Analysis* (Aldershot: Edward Elgar).

Lee, F. S. (1998) *Post Keynesian Price Theory* (Cambridge: Cambridge University Press).

Marglin, S. A. (1984) *Growth, Distribution and Prices* (Cambridge, Mass.: Harvard University Press).

Moore, B. J. (1998) *Horizontalists and Verticalists: The Macroeconomics of Credit Money* (Cambridge: Cambridge University Press).

O'Donnell, R. M. (ed.) (1991) *Keynes as Philosopher-Economist* (London: Macmillan).

Pasinetti, L. L. (1962) 'Rate of Profit and Income Distribution in Relation to the Rate of Economic Growth', *Review of Economic Studies*, vol. 29, no. 1, 267–79.

— (1981) *Structural Change and Economic Growth: A Theoretical Essay on the Dynamics of the Wealth of Nations* (Cambridge: Cambridge University Press).

— (1993) *Structural Economic Dynamics. A Theory of the Economic Consequences of Human Learning* (Cambridge: Cambridge University Press).

— (1997) 'The Marginal Efficiency of Investment', in G. C. Harcourt and P. A. Riach (eds), *A 'Second Edition' of The General Theory*, Vol. 1 (London: Routledge), 198–218.

Robinson, J. (1956) *The Accumulation of Capital* (London: Macmillan).

— (1962a) *Essays in the Theory of Economic Growth* (London: Macmillan).

— (1962b) 'Review of H. G. Johnson, *Money, Trade and Economic Growth*', *Economic Journal*, vol. 72, September, 690–2.

— (1977) 'Michal Kalecki on the Economics of Capitalism', *Oxford Bulletin of Economics and Statistics*, vol. 39, February, 7–17.

— (1978) 'Keynes and Ricardo', *Journal of Post Keynesian Economics*, Fall, vol. 1, 12–18.

Rowthorn, R. E. (1977) 'Conflict, Inflation and Money', *Cambridge Journal of Economics*, vol. 1, 215–39.

Sardoni, C. (ed.) (1992) *On Political Economists and Modern Political Economy. Selected Essays of G. C. Harcourt* (London: Routledge).

Sraffa, P. (1960) *Production of Commodities by Means of Commodities. Prelude to a Critique of Economic Theory* (Cambridge: Cambridge University Press).

Targetti, F. and B. Kinda-Hass (1982) 'Kalecki's Review of Keynes's *General Theory*', *Australian Economic Papers*, vol. 21, 244–60.

Wood, A. (1975) *A Theory of Profits* (Cambridge: Cambridge University Press).

Part VI
General Essays

20
Critiques and Alternatives: Reflections on Some Recent (and Not So Recent) Controversies*

In 1980 (or thereabouts), I was asked to reflect on the major issues in the capital theory controversies, together with the critique of neoclassical theory and the alternative approach(es) that were then being developed as a consequence of the critique. This was a tall order; I tried to fulfill the brief by setting down some general reflections on the issues. In the event, the paper was never published. As I said in Harcourt (1995a), it 'was thought to be in poor taste, unprofessional and unfair'. I added that 'looking back [in 1995] I thought it was spot on' (245), so I am delighted that Paul Davidson has allowed me to publish it here, together with an addendum in which I may retract and/or add to my then-views. What follows is the original script (with a bit of necessary supporting scholarship added). Please read on.

I start with a piece of casual empiricism that has impressed itself on me as a result of spending the first six months of 1980 in North America, and then coming back to my old haunts in Cambridge, England, for the remainder of 1980. I refer to the rise of what James Tobin and Robin Matthews (the latter in his lectures to the Preliminary Year to Part II of the Economics Tripos at Cambridge) have aptly christened Monetarism, Mark II (or Wave II). This comprises the theoretical and empirical contributions of the rational expectations school, associated especially with Barro, Lucas, Sargent and Wallace, and the great attraction that they have for the

* Originally published in the *Journal of Post Keynesian Economics*, vol. 19, Winter 1996–97, 171–80.

brightest (if not the best) of the young North American economists today (and for some of their UK counterparts as well).

In the 1920s and 1930s, when people such as Joan Robinson and James Meade, those who became the first generation of Keynesians, were starting their careers as economists, they came to our discipline principally because they were appalled by poverty and by the waste and misery associated with unemployment. They wanted to find out why these things happened and what could be done about them. Their counterparts today, when they observe similar if not yet as drastic situations, are concerned also to find out why. Their next reaction, however, is drastically different – namely, to explain not what can be done about them but why, for example, the levels of unemployment we observe now (and observed in many of the inter-war years too) are the outcome of voluntary choices, that is, that people are in preferred positions. There are not, it seems, too many of Marshall's 'young [people] with cool heads but warm hearts' (Pigou, 1925: 174) around these days. Their heads are cool but their hearts are cold; we, all of us, are on our supply curves where what we do is what we wish to do. The ideological backlash against intervention has arrived with a vengeance.

Friedman (Monetarism, Mark I) marshalled his theoretical and empirical evidence over the decades to argue that, even if the world left to itself did not work perfectly (partly because it has been tinkered with for so long), it certainly worked better, and would do so again, especially within those constraints on action that are needed to make the world safe for free people, than if there were continuous intervention. This was principally an empirical judgment. Monetarism, Mark II – the new Classical Macroeconomics – goes much further. It argues in effect that it may be shown theoretically that the world left to itself must work perfectly (or be viewed 'as if' it does), and that, in any event, intervention is bound to be harmful, or, at best, ineffectual, unless we make the obviously absurd assumption that people in general are stupid.

Now, in outlining this piece of casual empiricism, I do not wish to deny that there are aspects of the growth of bureaucracies and of the power and influence of policy-makers that are disquieting, to say the least. Keynes' optimism that 'the presuppositions of Harvey Road', whereby disinterested and highly intelligent persons desire the common good more than their own good (except indirectly by obtaining satisfaction from making the world more rational and just than they found it), has not always been borne out. The structures of many government departments – the hierarchies, the motions that have to be gone through for promotion, the drive and ruthlessness needed in order to reach the top – are not necessarily the ideal incentives or channels for ensuring that altruistic, charitable and tolerant people (as well as intelligent ones) make it to the top. Bureaucratic empires built for their own sakes, rather than to serve useful social purposes, are also not unknown. Those who favour intervention, as I do, and a flourishing public sector must seriously come to grips with these problems.

Nevertheless, having said this, it is still necessary to deplore the swing away from altruism, from enlightened policies, and the cynical acceptance of unacceptable levels of unemployment, the waste of people's lives, the appeal to prejudice and self-interest that characterises much of what passes for economic analysis and policy these days. It probably leads to self-fulfilling prophecies. It is no accident, I believe, that many economists who are now at the end of their careers argue that they would not be attracted to economics as it is today: If they were given the choice of a career again, or were young people about to choose a career, they would not choose economics as their discipline. And it is sad to see other fine scholars and compassionate human beings in the later years of their professional lives despairing that everything they have stood for and have tried to build in the past is continuously under attack, indeed, is in danger of being routed. I think here particularly of the American Keynesians – Tobin, Solow, Samuelson, the late Arthur Okun, Walter Salant – who seem to me to be beseiged (though they still fight vigorously against rather overwhelming odds). It is a shame that the Post Keynesian school has not been prepared, except in isolated instances – for example, when Sidney Weintraub welcomed Okun, Solow, Tobin and others on board his TIP schemes, to form a united front with these, their more orthodox brothers and sisters, against the powerful forces of reaction. (Of course, the PKs may argue that it takes two to tango.) Similarly, in the United Kingdom, Keynesianism is at a heavy discount. The only policy groups who, to my mind, made much sense – the National Institute of Economic and Social Research (NIESR) in London and, especially, the Cambridge Department of Applied Economics (DAE) Policy Group led by Godley and Cripps, as well as Nicholas Kaldor, a group by himself – are isolated and more often than not despised or, at best, neglected, by the bulk of the United Kingdom profession. While, as I shall argue, there are fundamental differences between the American Keynesians on the one hand, and the Post Keynesian school, including its Sraffian branch, on the other, they have enough common cause to draw together on the immediate and pressing problems facing Western capitalist countries today, in particular, to rid us of the suicidal deflationary and contractionary policies we are currently being asked to endure. Indeed, I think they should welcome the very telling attacks that Frank Hahn, for example, has made in recent years on the theoretical foundations of Monetarism, Marks I and II. (This has occurred, in at least one instance, when Hahn and Robert Nield came together to attack the theoretical foundations of Friedmanism.)

Turning again, for the moment, to Monetarism Mark II, of course they have some wise comments to make especially concerning the learning processes of humans locked into social organisms to which man-made policies are applied so that the stability of the structural parameters of the systems themselves are suspect. (This, after all, was Keynes's principal criticism of Tinbergen's early econometric work, and it is also in the spirit of Trevor Swan's remark about the ineffectual nature of econometric investment functions, that they cannot capture the effects of those animal spirits that refuse to be bottled.) However, this view does not logically lead to a *laissez-faire*, leave-well-enough-alone stance – rather, it should persuade us to return to the common sense position implied by viewing economics as a moral philosophy, and policy as an art whereby policy-makers must fly by the seat of their pants, must sniff the air in any given situation, rather than mechanically follow the predictions and/or forecasts of small or large models of the economy. That is to say, there is still, as there always has been, a role for judgment and 'feel', and it is these characteristics rather than technical virtuosity that in the final analysis separate the good economists from the also-rans. So what's new? We have known all this at least since Keynes's biography of Marshall, where, in describing the characteristics that an economist ought to have – and suggesting that they were largely there in Marshall, though not always in the correct proportions – he was in fact describing himself (Keynes, 1972: 173–4). So let us keep separate from their ideological presuppositions the contributions of these talented and clever people, because the latter are not the logical implications of their technical arguments.

I turn now to the perhaps more fundamental issues of high theory, and in particular to the nature of the critique of orthodoxy emanating from the Cambridge, England, School, especially from Piero Sraffa and his followers on the one hand, and Joan Robinson and her followers on the other. The first general point to make is that the whole span of Sraffa's work – the 1925 and 1926 articles, the great edition of Ricardo's work with the careful and profound introduction (written in collaboration with the late Maurice Dobb, 1951) and the 1960 classic, *Production of Commodities* – must be seen as intended to reestablish the approach to political economy found in the classical political economists and in Marx. I refer, of course, to the concept of the surplus, the notion that human economic activity should be analysed from the viewpoint of the creation, extraction, distribution and use of the surplus over and above the necessities required for its creation, in a setting of dynamic reproduction and expansion. This conception has been forgotten for much of the past 110 years because of the rise and then dominance of the alternative approach associated with neoclassical economics, whereby the choice and allocation aspects also to be found in the works of the founding fathers, especially Smith, have been explored and developed. I suppose the most balanced, fair and good-humoured statement of these fundamental contrasts is to be found in Walsh and Gram's splendid *Classical and Neoclassical Theories of General Equilibrium* (1980), where they show that these are fundamentally different approaches – one, a dynamic analysis of the surplus in all its aspects, the other, a static analysis of utility maximising by individual economic agents under constraints, agents who start with given preferences and an arbitrary set of initial endowments – despite the fact that, at times and places, lemmas and theorems may overlap in the analytical aspects of the two theories. They, together with Milgate (1979), show that the concept of equilibrium also has undergone a fundamental change, as the neoclassical approach to the theory of distribution via supply and demand concepts ran into logical difficulties in dealing with a uniform rate of profits and in discussing the characteristics of the long-period positions of the economy. Thus, a change in question and in the definition of equilibrium occurred in the process, starting with Hayek (1928) and coming to fruition in Hicks's *Value and Capital* (1939).

To go to both ends of the spectrum, we may argue that the modern classical approach builds its model from the standpoint of the sphere of production and of the social relationships that characterise it and the sphere of distribution and exchange, so that, in some versions at least, there is still at the deepest layer of analysis a role for the labour theory of value (perhaps Maurice Dobb's arguments in the first chapter of *Political Economy and Capitalism* (1937) are among the most fundamental and persuasive for this particular point of view). Accumulation and profit making are ends in themselves. The neoclassical orthodox approach comes from the other end of the spectrum – the isolated individual agent, the maximisation of whose utility under various constraints is the driving force of the system, and demand and supply functions the appropriate apparatus. Even Marshall, who hoped to be a (*the*) halfway house between the two, was forced more towards the latter – witness the real costs that underlie his supply curves and the almost tautological nature of the various functions – what is received is what is needed in order to induce the efforts, demands, waiting, otherwise they would not be forthcoming. (We are here almost at one with the Monetarism Mark II school, according to which everyone is voluntarily on their supply curves, come what may. The natural rate of unemployment at any moment is whatever the *actual* rate is at any moment.)

With modern (as with ancient) classical analysis, because the surplus is the principal concept, we are led in the analysis of capitalism to show that accumulation and profit receiving are ends in themselves, imposed on the capitalist class by the very nature of the system, by its mode of operation. This view is clearly in Marx's work and, in a rather muddled way, also in Keynes' work – muddled because of the vestiges of neoclassical Marshallian thought that were ramified 'into every corner of [his mind]' (Keynes, 1973: xxiii). This differs fundamentally from the viewpoint of neoclassical analysis and is one reason why even the new microeconomic foundations of macroeconomics associated with Malinvaud and his colleagues seem rather to be skirting the central issues by concentrating on disequilibrium, fix-price, non-perfectly competitive market structures, quantity adjustments, and the like. These are important features that will eventually have to be captured in our models. Insofar as they help to provide a backlash to the more facile conclusions of the Mark II Monetarists, they are welcome, at least at a tactical level. But they do not allow us to come to grips with the most fundamental critique, the difference in 'vision', that is involved. It is not possible satisfactorily to capture the accumulation process characteristic of capitalism, ancient or modern, as long as we are committed to utility-maximising individuals, to a theory of saving and investment that derives from psychological time preference and investment opportunity lines, together with the markets for money loans, rather than from a class division of the surplus extracted by the workings of the system (or potentially there to be extracted) from the wage-earning class in the first place.

It is at this point that Kalecki and the groups he has inspired, notably the Robinsonians, and also Kaldor and Goodwin enter the picture. Kalecki, starting from the Marxist base of schemes of reproduction, spent a large part of his life attempting to provide a satisfactory model of the indissolubly mixed trend and cycle, in which the macro-interrelationships of accumulation, spending and the distribution of income among broadly defined classes were integral features. In the process, of course, the realisation problem – the problem of effective demand, in Keynes's terms – was identified and explained. Kalecki also provided micro foundations with his emphasis on the pricing practices of the oligopolistic sector, as opposed to the more Marshallian characteristics of the raw materials sector – foundations that have had to be independently rediscovered by the American economists, such as Okun and Nordhaus, as well as by Hicks, with his fix-price/flex-price dichotomy which has now found its way into the works of Malinvaud and others of the French school.

Also associated with Keynes's contributions is the work of the American Post Keynesians, especially Davidson, Eichner, Kregel, Minsky and Weintraub. Minsky and Davidson have drawn our attention to the monetary aspects of Keynes's thought, reminding us that while Keynes may have scrapped the fundamental equations of *A Treatise on Money* (1930), he did not scrap the rich analysis of money and its accompanying institutions when he moved into *The General Theory* (1936/1973) (nor, it should be added, his analysis of the determinants of the general price level in which the money-wage plays the key role). Minsky indeed has argued that embedded within *The General Theory* is a theory of the cyclical development of capitalism, the outcome of the interaction of real and monetary forces. The uncertain future, which Keynes showed was an inescapable fact of life of a monetary production economy characterised by interconnected sequences, with most production done in anticipation of sales, imposes itself particularly through the concepts of expected and realised cash flows. These together have important implications for the structure of balance sheets (the matching of assets and liabilities) that project cumulative forces into the workings of the real economy. Davidson, too, has used Marshallian demand and supply analysis to illuminate the connections between spot and forward markets, especially in the production of durable assets, to show how fluctuations occur and are the natural workings of capitalism. At a deeper level, Joan Robinson has argued that these sorts of developments, especially Kalecki's, whereby the long period has no independent existence in time but is the outcome of a sequence of short periods, are the rudimentary beginnings of analysis in historical time rather than the logical time that characterises the neoclassical general equilibrium approach.

Here, it must be said, a fundamental disagreement arises within the ranks of the critics of orthodoxy with regard to methodology. The followers of Sraffa are inclined to argue that the methodology of the classical political economists was intimately associated with the concept of centres of gravitation – the natural prices of Smith and Ricardo, the prices of production of Marx, the long-period positions of the economy. To discover the characteristics of these centres of gravitation, which are themselves the outcome of sustained, persistent and dominant forces, and to make comparisons among them, is the essential nature of economic analysis. Thus, they argue, the revolutionary nature of Keynes's contribution must have been to provide a theory of the *long-period* levels of overall employment and activity in a capitalist economy and to show that they were not necessarily full employment ones. Had he but shown that there are lapses from full employment in the short run, even lapses that may be sustained for considerable periods of time, this would not have constituted a *revolutionary* contribution. Only if he could show that, if we abstract from the effects of accumulation (except upon employment), a capitalist economy tends to oscillate around a sustained rest state of considerable unemployment, could he be said to reach back to the contributions of the founding fathers, over the aberrations of the neoclassicals in the interim, adding a theory of the long-period level of output to their theories of natural prices, wages, profits, and so on.

Opposed to this point of view, we have not only Kalecki and the Robinsonians, Minsky, Davidson and Weintraub, but also the work of Tobin and his school. Tobin, more than anyone else, has used the *LM/IS* construction effectively to analyse the interaction between the flow equilibria of the goods, financial and labour markets of *The General Theory*, and the impacts on stocks of real and financial assets and liabilities that result from the flows and which, in turn, feed back into the flows; to spell out these processes in detail and to ask where the economy tends, in particular whether it tends ultimately to a full employment equilibrium (which in general it does not). These, though, are more of the nature of arguments within the family, as it were. I would argue that there is enough common ground for all to gather for an assault on the arguments of those whom I identified at the beginning of these reflections. They, too, are classical in the sense of concentrating on the long-period position of the economy; but they differ vitally from their forebears and their critics by their arguments to the effect that we are almost always actually there, that the forces making for stability are extremely powerful and fast-working, and that intervention is doomed to failure, to be suboptimal, as well as unacceptable for political, ideological and philosophical reasons.

Addendum, February 1996

So, sixteen or so years on, what would I retract and what would I add? I still stand by the general thrust of the argument. However, since I first wrote the essay, I have been stimulated to rethink where I stand on the long-period interpretation of *The General Theory* by several readings of Heinrich Bortis's remarkable manuscript (1997), soon to be published by Cambridge University Press, and by the chapter by Colin Rogers (1997) in a 'second edition' of *The General Theory* (Harcourt and Riach, 1997). Rogers shows, at a high level of abstraction, how a theoretical argument for a long-period underemployment rest state may be set out in a context consistent with the approach of both Marshall and Keynes. I have also been comforted by reading Frank Hahn and Bob Solow's *Critical Essay* (1995). These two neoclassical Keynesians (Hahn and Solow, 1995: viii), having had at the same time a reaction like mine to 'the economics of Dr Pangloss' (2), now provide counterarguments that produce Keynes-type results and support Keynes-type remedies. Three cheers for the dynamic duo, say I.

Thus, I now see signs of convergence not only on theory but also, indeed especially, on policy, among those who could be called Keynesians of any persuasion and any favourite chapter of *The General Theory*. They (we) seem to have regained their (our) confidence, as well as coming back into favour with a greater part of the profession (if not with those who hand out Nobel prizes!), not least because the real-world happenings I described as then beginning have now been with us for so long, and with such cumulatively disastrous consequences, especially for those least able to protect themselves. Unfortunately, the moods of electorates have changed as well, often for the worse, so that attempts to devise sensible policies[1] are hemmed in by a combination of the disillusionment and the powerlessness of a large number of citizens on the one hand, and by the reactionary attitudes of a substantial number, probably a majority, of citizens who overall have done well in the short to medium term out of the policies imposed, on the other. There is, therefore, a long way to go before the effects of our generation's 'madmen in authority ... distilling their frenzy from [our] academic scribbler[s]' have been overcome, and ideas, this time derived from my heroes and heroines, become 'dangerous for good or evil' (Keynes, 1973: 383–4).

Note

1. My current views and proposals on policy may be found in the first three chapters of Harcourt (1995b), and in the companion volume to this selection of essays (2000), Chs 16, 17, 18 and 19.

References

Bortis, H. (1997) *Institutions, Behaviour and Economic Theory* (Cambridge: Cambridge University Press).

Dobb, M. H. (1937) *Political Economy and Capitalism* (London: Routledge & Kegan Paul).

Hahn, F. and R. Solow, (1995) *A Critical Essay on Modern Macroeconomic Theory* (Oxford: Basil Blackwell).

Harcourt, G. C. (1995a) 'Recollections and Reflections of an Australian Patriot and a Cambridge Economist', *Banca Nazionale del Lavoro Quarterly Review*. vol. 47, 225–54.

— (1995b) *Capitalism, Socialism and Post-Keynesianism. Selected Essays of G. C. Harcourt* (Aldershot: Edward Elgar).

— (2000) *Selected Essays on Economic Policy* (London: Macmillan).

Harcourt, G. C. and P. A. Riach (eds) (1997) *A 'Second Edition' of The General Theory*, 2 vols (London: Routledge).

Hayek, F. A. (1928) 'Das Intertemporale Gleichgewichtssystem der Preise und die Bewegungen des Geldwertes', *Weltwirtschaftliches Arhiv*, July, 33–79.

Hicks, J. R. (1939) *Value and Capital* (Oxford: Clarendon Press).

Keynes, J. M. (1930) *A Treatise on Money*, 2 vols (London: Macmillan), In *Collected Writings of John Maynard Keynes*, Vols V, VI (London: Macmillan, 1971).

— (1933) *Essays in Biography* (London: Macmillan), in *Collected Writings of John Maynard Keynes*, Vol. X (London: Macmillan, 1972).

— (1936) *The General Theory of Employment, Interest and Money* (London: Macmillan), In *Collected Writings of John Maynard Keynes*, Vol. VII (London: Macmillan, 1973).

Marshall, A. [1885] (1925) 'The Present Position of Economics', in A. C. Pigou, *Memorials of Alfred Marshall* (London: Macmillan), 152–74.

Milgate, M. (1979) 'On the Origins of the Notion of Intemporal Equilibrium', *Economica*, vol. 46, 1–10.

Pigou, A. C. (1925) *Memorials of Alfred Marshall* (London: Macmillan).

Rogers, C. (1997) '*The General Theory*: Existence of a Monetary Long-Period Unemployment Equilibrium', in G. C. Harcourt and P. A. Riach (eds), *A 'Second Edition' of The General Theory*, vol. 1 (London: Routledge), ch. 19.

Sraffa, P. (1925). 'Sulle Relazioni fra Costo e Quantità Prodotta', *Annali di Economia*, vol. 2, (1), 277–328.

— (1926) 'The Laws of Returns under Competitive Conditions', *Economic Journal*, vol. 36, 535–50.

— (1960) *Production of Commodities by Means of Commodities. Prelude to a Critique of Economic Theory* (Cambridge: Cambridge University Press).

— (ed.) with the collaboration of M. H. Dobb (1951–73) *The Works and Correspondence of David Ricardo*, Vols. I–XI (London: Cambridge University Press).

Walsh, V. and H. Gram (1980) *Classical and Neoclassical Theories of General Equilibrium, Historical Origins and Mathematical Structure* (New York: Oxford University Press).

21
Mrs Robinson and the Classics*

with Prue Kerr

Joan Robinson came to economics at Cambridge in the early 1920s from her schooldays' study of history because she wanted to know why poverty and unemployment existed. (She did not feel she received satisfactory explanations from her teachers.) So from the start she was predisposed to be interested in classical political economy and the issues it was most concerned to tackle, as opposed to the more bland issues of resource allocation and the determination of relative prices in neoclassical economics.

She was, of course, trained in Marshallian economics at Cambridge. Though from the start she was critical of it (and him), she nevertheless absorbed his approach and methods, using them herself in her first major book, *The Economics of Imperfect Competition* (1933), a use which she was later to repudiate vehemently as 'a shameless fudge'. She absorbed Marshall's static methods (Dennis Robertson and Gerald Shove did not think she always understood them properly) and she was also sympathetic, increasingly so, to his 'vision' of an evolving, growing society modifying its 'rules of the game' from time to time and resembling more a biological system evolving over time than a static (or even dynamic) neoclassical system, seeking out or returning to long-period normal equilibrium positions. Yet she felt increasingly that there was an inconsistency in Marshall's writings, to which he never properly faced up and

* Originally published in Heinz D. Kurz and Neri Selvadori (eds), *The Elgar Companion to Classical Economics, L–Z* (Cheltenham: Edward Elgar, 1998) 324–8.

which he certainly never resolved or overcame. It was between his formal analytical structure (with which he had a lifelong love–hate relationship) and his, in her view, more deep and accurate 'vision' of economic development. Recognising this relatively early on prepared her for her later absorption in classical issues and analysis.

But, first, there was the Keynesian revolution in which she took a notable part from her role in the 'circus' on. Significant for this aspect of her development was the start of her intellectual association and personal friendship with Piero Sraffa. His 'pregnant suggestion' in his 1926 article helped to create her 1933 book. His editorship of, and introduction with Maurice Dobb to, the Ricardo volumes and his development of what was to become *Production of Commodities* ... in 1960 (both of which had lengthy periods of gestation) were also to be crucial influences on her own thought and development. This was not confined to the postwar period. There is evidence that Joan Robinson and other Cambridge friends and colleagues of Sraffa became increasingly aware of the ideas and critiques ultimately to be set out in *Production of Commodities...*, that there were discussions of some of the issues in the 1930s, even though they were usually met with incomprehension or even exasperation on both sides – witness, for example, the letter in October 1936 from Sraffa to Joan Robinson about what was meant by 'capital' by an economist and a gardener. The insights in the letter were only fully understood by Joan Robinson in the postwar period.

Of perhaps even greater moment in this context is the simultaneous beginning of her friendship with Michal Kalecki and her awakening interest in Marxian analysis. The latter began with her review (1936) of John Strachey's 1935 book and reached its fullest expression in her 1942 essay on Marxian economics. The latter was written in the aftermath of the publication of *The General Theory*, her realisation that Kalecki had independently discovered the principal propositions of *The General Theory* and her first systematic reading of Marx himself. Thus when, in the postwar period following the publication of Harrod's two classics (1939, 1948), Joan Robinson and the other Cambridge economists set themselves, in the wake of the Keynesian revolution, to examine what William Baumol (1951) called the 'magnificent dynamics', almost all the necessary building blocks were in place in the public domain. By the time she published *The Accumulation of Capital*

(1956) (Joan Robinson had also prepared herself for this task by writing the introduction to the English version of Rosa Luxemburg's (1951) volume of the same title), the Introduction to the Ricardo volumes was out and only *Production of Commodities* ... remained to be published. That the 1956 book was self-consciously classical economics in the post-*General Theory* world is made explicit in the Preface:

> In recent times the centre of interest has returned to classical problems of the over-all growth of the economy ... The revival of interest in the classical questions brings a revival of classical theory ... [she] did not herself arrive at these ideas by studying the Classics. The problem presented itself ... as the generalisation of the *General Theory* ... [she] was very much illuminated by Piero Sraffa's Introduction to Ricardo's *Principles*.
>
> (1956: vi)

When she followed the 1956 book with her 'footnotes' to her *General Theory* in 1962 (1962a), Sraffa's book had been published and reviewed by Joan Robinson (1961). Moreover, the introduction to the Ricardo volumes had really set her alight, as she told us in the three remarkable essays of 1953 (*On Re-reading Marx*) in which both her analytical approach and her 'vision' were rapidly coming into focus.

She found wanting the neoclassical method (as she saw it) of using differences (comparisons of equilibrium positions) to analyse changes (processes in actual time). Moreover, she could not find in the neoclassical tradition a satisfactory theory of profits (and interest), not even in the writings of the more realistic Marshall and the painfully honest Wicksell. This realisation came to her fully during her search for a theory of the choice of technique at the level of the economy as a whole. (She went mostly to Wicksell.) She wanted to integrate this, to her, more secondary theory into the more fundamental theory of accumulation, but her criticisms of it, soon to be reinforced by Sraffa's, meant that she wished to discard the aggregate production function as a means of explaining both distribution and accumulation (itself seen primarily as a process of deepening). She found that, in the classics, and especially in Marx, their concept of the surplus provided a more satisfactory way of explaining where profits ultimately came from. And she took from Kalecki and Keynes (and also Marx, to some extent) the principle of effective demand as the most effective way of showing how the potential profits implied by the potential surplus in the sphere of production could be realised in full or, more realistically, in part, depending upon the strength of animal spirits, and so the level and composition of aggregate demand, in the sphere of distribution and exchange. Finally, she would graft onto all this the contributions of Wilfred Salter (1960) which she admired and never for a moment thought of as neoclassical. (We think she was wrong about this; and so did Salter and Trevor Swan.) Salter's work allowed her to use vintage analysis to explain the embodiment of technical progress through accumulation into the existing stock of capital goods. It also allowed her to complete her critique of Marshallian long-period analysis. Though vague as ever, Marshall does suggest that, in the long-period normal stock and flow equilibrium position, *only* the current best-practice techniques are embodied by past accumulation in the optimum stock of capital goods. Yet this theoretical concept is of little use in interpreting the world as we know it, for it is at odds with the observation that old machines work happily side by side with the newest in actual industries and economies.

In the end, Joan Robinson was to agree wholeheartedly with Kalecki's final view on the illegitimacy of separating the trend and cycle: 'In fact the long-run trend is but a slowly changing component of a chain of short-period situations; it has no independent entity' (Kalecki, 1968; 1971: 165). Kalecki's view is obviously consistent with Joan Robinson's critique of the Bastard Keynesians in 1965: 'The short period is here and now, with concrete stocks of the means of production in existence. Incompatibilities in the situation ... will determine what happens next. Long-period equilibrium is not at some date in the future; it is an imaginary state of affairs in which there are no incompatibilities in the existing situation, here and now' (1962b: 690). Thus she took from the classics and Marx their overriding interests in growth, accumulation and technical progress, and in institutional forms, in both developing and developed countries. And, as we have said, she completed the story by allying with their role in the sphere of production the Marx/Keynes/Kalecki macroeconomic theories of distribution in the sphere of distribution and exchange.

She did, however, run into a dilemma as far as method is concerned, for Sraffa used the long-period method and position in *Production of Commodities* ... rigorously to theorise about distribution and the formation of relative prices of production in production-interdependent systems. Moreover, Sraffa, and especially his followers, claimed to have revived not only the 'vision' and concepts of the old classics (with which she agreed) but also their method (with which she did not). To the end of her life she struggled with this dilemma, partly in continuing arguments with Pierangelo Garegnani, partly and more positively with Amit Bhaduri (1980), trying to find a way around it. She argued that Sraffa's thought experiments allow us to get basic concepts clear, precise and right (as well as to show the incoherence in core neoclassical concepts, such as price as an index of scarcity); while through Kalecki's revolution we may analyse in a properly descriptive way movements through historical time of actual economies in the spirit of Smith, Ricardo and Marx.

This attitude characterized her in her more positive moments. More pessimistic, even nihilistic, was her mood in 'Spring Cleaning' (1980). There she seemed to want us to scrap the lot, even Sraffa's thought experiments, and start again (see Harcourt, 1990). As we have often remarked, she was too hard on herself (and others). It is becoming clear that she has outlined an approach which absorbs the gist of both the approach of the classics (especially Marx) and that of Keynes and Kalecki and that, together, they give us a positive, useful 'engine of thought' for incisive analyses of modern problems.

References

Baumol, W. J. (1951) *Economic Dynamics* (London: Macmillan).

Berg, M. (ed.) (1990) *Political Economy in the Twentieth Century* (New York: Philip Allan).

Bhadhuri, A. and J. Robinson (1980) 'Accumulation and Exploitation: An Analysis in the Tradition of Marx, Sraffa and Kalecki', *Cambridge Journal of Economics*, vol. 4, 103–15.

Bradford, W. and G. C. Harcourt (1997) 'Units and Definitions', in G. C. Harcourt and P. A. Riach *op. cit.* Vol. 1.

Feiwel, G. R. (ed.) (1985) *Issues in Contemporary Macroeconomics and Distribution* (London: Macmillan).

Harcourt, G. C. (1990) 'On the Contributions of Joan Robinson and Piero Sraffa to Economic Theory', in M. Berg, *op. cit.*

— and P. A. Riach (eds) (1997) *A 'Second Edition' of The General Theory*, 2 vols (London: Routledge).

Harrod, R. F. (1939) 'An Essay in Dynamic Theory', *Economic Journal*, vol. 49, 14–33.

— (1948) *Towards a Dynamic Economics. Some Recent Developments of Economics and their Application to Policy* (London: Macmillan).

Johnson, H. G. (1962) *Money, Trade and Economic Growth* (London: Allen & Unwin).

Kalecki, M. (1968) 'Trend and Business Cycles Reconsidered', *Economic Journal*, vol. LXXVII, 263–76.

— (1971) *Selected Essays on the Dynamics of the Capitalist Economy 1933–70.* (Cambridge: Cambridge University Press).

Keynes, J. M. (1936) *The General Theory of Employment, Interest and Money* (London: Macmillan).

Luxemburg, R. (1951) *The Accumulation of Capital* (London: Routledge).

Robinson, J. (1933) *The Economics of Imperfect Competition* (London: Macmillan).

— (1936) 'Some Reflections on Marxist Economics' (review of Strachey, 1935), *Economic Journal*, vol. 46, 298–302.

— (1942) *An Essay on Marxian Economics* (London: Macmillan).

— (1951) 'Introduction' to Luxemburg (1951).

— (1953) *On Re-Reading Marx* (Cambridge: Cambridge Students' Bookshop Ltd.).

— (1956) *The Accumulation of Capital* (London: Macmillan).

— (1961) 'Prelude to a Critique', *Oxford Economic Papers*, vol. 13, 53–8.

— (1962a) *Essays in the Theory of Economic Growth* (London: Macmillan).

— (1962b) 'Review of Johnson (1962)', *Economic Journal*, vol. 72, 690–2; reprinted in *Collected Economic Papers* (1965), vol. III, 100–2.

— (1980) 'Spring Cleaning', mimeo, Cambridge; reprinted as 'The Theory of Normal Prices and Reconstruction of Economic Theory', in G. R. Feiwel (1985).

Salter, W. E. G. (1960) *Productivity and Technical Change* (London: Cambridge University Press), 2nd edn 1966.

Sardonl, C. (ed.) (1992) *On Political Economists and Modern Political Economy. Selected Essays of G. C. Harcourt* (London: Routledge).

Sraffa, P. (1936) 'Letter to Joan Robinson 27.10.1936', Modern Archives, King's College, Cambridge.

— (ed.) with the collaboration of M. H. Dobb (1951–73) *The Works and Correspondence of David Ricardo* (Cambridge: Cambridge University Press).

— (1960) *Production of Commodities by Means of Commodities. Prelude to a Critique of Economic Theory* (Cambridge: Cambridge University Press).

Strachey, J. (1935) *The Nature of Capitalist Crisis* (London: Gollancz).

22
Two Views on Development: Austin and Joan Robinson*

I first met Austin and Joan Robinson in 1955 when I came from Melbourne University to King's College, Cambridge to do a PhD. Though neither supervised me, I came to know them both well, first as teachers, then as colleagues and admired and loved friends. Joan was one of my mentors; the principal intellectual reason why I returned to Cambridge in the early 1980s was to document the contributions of Joan and her circle. In recent years, therefore, I have been reading or re-reading her books and articles and her papers in the King's Archives, and I have written a number of essays around this principal theme. I also came to know Austin over the years and to re-read or read for the first time his many contributions to our discipline. At the moment I am preparing the essay on him for the *Proceedings* of the British Academy (Harcourt, 1997). So, though I have no claim to be a development economist – I understand that

* Originally published in the *Cambridge Journal of Economics*, vol. 22, 1998, 367–77. This is a revised version of the 1996 Kingsley Martin Memorial Lecture which I gave in Cambridge on Tuesday 21 May 1996. In preparing the lecture I was much helped by reading the splendid biography of Austin Robinson by Alec Cairncross (1993) and the incisive studies of Joan Robinson's writings on development by Pervez Tahir (1990a, 1990b). I am responsible for all errors and misinterpretations. I am also grateful to two anonymous referees for their comments and criticisms, to which I have tried to respond while, at the same time, trying to preserve the structure and wording of the original lecture.

those at the pinnacle of our trade feel that there is no such animal anyway (I beg to differ) – I thought, nevertheless, that it might be of interest to have the impressions of a general economist of the insights, similarities and differences which these two great economists and human beings brought to our thinking on the problems and processes of development.

II

Austin was six years older than Joan and was already a young don at Corpus Christi College when Joan Maurice came up in 1922 to read economics, having read history at St Paul's Girls' School. Austin initially read classics and then, after hearing one of Keynes's lectures from what was to become *The Economic Consequences of the Peace* (1919), economics. Keynes's inspiration and subject married with Austin's resolve (which arose from wartime experiences that 'burned deep') 'to make the world a better place and find a way of settling its problems without resort to war' (Cairncross, 1993: 12–13). Both Austin and Joan came from not dissimilar niches in the intricate strata which constituted then (as now) the British class system, itself a source of great mystery and amusement in equal measure to colonial outsiders like me. Austin's father was an 'impecunious clergyman', his mother was the daughter of a clergyman. Joan's father was a professional soldier, well-known for his role in the infamous Maurice debates of 1918, who subsequently became an academic administrator, the head of what became Queen Mary College. Her great grandfather was Frederick Maurice, the Christian Socialist, who was an important influence on the young Alfred Marshall (see Keynes, *CW*, Vol. X, 1972: 167). Her mother was the daughter of the Professor of Surgery at Cambridge, who was also Master of Downing College. Though certainly a fiery, passionate seeker after truth, Joan was never religious in the conventional sense. I suspect she thought all organised religions a load of mumbo-jumbo. Austin was; his extraordinarily hard-working life was driven by his sense of duty and understanding of what faith with works entailed. At his Memorial Service some thought it odd that one reading was the parable of the talents; but a friend who knew Austin very well thought it 'spot on' because Austin could not tolerate those who did not use their potential to the full.

The Robinsons married in 1926 and went to India for a two-year spell (Joan returned a little earlier than Austin). Austin was tutor to the young Maharajah of Gwalior, the offer of which tutorship Alec Cairncross (1993: 19) says Austin found 'irresistible'. Their stay in Gwalior began their lifelong love affair with the subcontinent and interest in development problems. Austin was to make his interest explicit earlier than Joan. He was a principal author of the section on fiscal transfers in a report on the princely states and their relationship with the British Raj, an early piece of work which had his characteristic approach to applied analysis firmly stamped on it, though some of the phrases and sentences were characteristically Joan's, as she helped prepare the report for publication when she came back to the UK (see Tahir, 1990a; 12–21). Austin went to Africa, to what is now Zambia, for six months in 1932 with a commission of enquiry into the impact of copper mines on local society, set up by William Temple, then Archbishop of York. In the postwar years he edited 12 International Economic Association (IEA) volumes, most of which were on development problems. He also wrote reports and took part in consultancies in, for example, Taiwan, Bangladesh and Pakistan, as well as regularly visiting India on business and pleasure – his brother, Christopher, was a Bishop in India, 'first of Luknow and then of Bombay' (Cairncross, 1993: 4). Cairncross argues that Austin's mature views reflected the fact that he had contact with development issues in countries which had horrendous problems before he encountered those which were relatively prosperous and dynamic – Taiwan, for example.

In the postwar years, Joan started on her many visits to mainland China and to India (in later life she spent part of each year in Kerala State at an economics institute directed by Professor K. N. Raj). Her postwar work on growth and distribution theory, inspired initially by her friendship with Kalecki, her wartime writings on Marx and by Harrod's pre- and postwar contributions, spilt over into her concern about the terrible problems of the Third World, the plight of the wretched of the earth. As Pervez Tahir (1990a: 93–4) points out, she is credited with being the first to use the phrase 'disguised unemployment' (in 1936), though it was its occurrence and causes in advanced capitalist economies that she analysed. Nevertheless, she was to analyse it in the same year (1943) as that in which Rosenstein–Rodan named disguised unemployment in less-developed countries. Joan more literally and accurately referred to the phenomenon as surplus labour, pointing out that the persons involved could, if there were the employment opportunities available, take them up without any adverse effects on current levels of production. She allied this insight with a discussion of Marxian unemployment – persons without productive jobs because inadequate rates of accumulation meant that there were not the complementary supplies of capital goods for them to work with. In the context of advanced economies, she had argued that the cause was different – a lack of effective demand overall, so that persons were forced to do things which with free choice and adequate demand they would not have needed to do.

III

Joan died in August 1983 and Austin nearly 10 years later, in June 1993. Both were incredibly active into the last years of their lives. Both were, in their own unique ways, idealistic (Joan was asymptotically Utopian), and both were democrats in theory. In practice, Austin could be imperious and Joan autocratic – breeding will out! As economists, they had some mentors in common – Smith, Marshall, Pigou, Keynes – but then they parted company absolutely. Joan went back to the classical economists and Marx and, in the end, had her framework of thought on industrial capitalism, socialism and the process of development itself dominated by Kalecki's approach to the issues. I stress framework, for Joan was too strong a character, too original and critical, too intellectually independent, ever to be a precise clone of anyone. Austin was much influenced by the original Keynesian revolution, but remained virtually untouched by the post-war critique of neoclassical value, distribution and growth theory associated with Joan, Richard Kahn, Nicholas Kaldor and Piero Sraffa in Cambridge. (He often asked me, what *exactly* was it all about and was there anything of *any* practical substance in it?) He was essentially a hands-on economist, as Alec Cairncross concluded, an ideal economic adviser, the role model for an applied economist *par excellence*. I believe he thought that what he had worked out for himself as an undergraduate from reading Marshall (and Pigou and Shove) and, later, from the writings of, and association with Maynard Keynes, was a sound and adequate foundation on which to build the theoretical structures he would use for the many specific tasks he took on.

Austin always sought or constructed appropriate statistics from which to construct the relevant orders of magnitude for the specific models he developed, and for the projections he inevitably tried to make. He had a very keen sense of how reliable the data sources were and what weight, if any, could be put on them. Austin was also, in many ways, a frustrated engineer; he loved the nuts and bolts aspects of thinking about firms and industries, agricultural and industrial processes. He always began by considering concrete situations, letting common sense and acute, detailed observations play the key roles which simple axioms play in the writings of Debreu and modern mathematical economists. It was no wonder that Austin spent a lot of his time, and thoroughly enjoyed himself, on projects which required collaboration with engineers and an understanding of the nitty-gritty of production runs, administrative set-ups and back-ups, raw material feed-ins and trading outlets, and so on.

Joan had a different frame of mind. She made acute (if not always balanced) observations on institutions and power structures. (Austin understood these, too, especially in practice. I think he was a much more successful political operator, whether in the civil service, the Faculty of Economics and Politics or international organisations and consultancies, than Joan ever was.) She had a more sociological-type interest in social groupings and their interrelationships. Though she felt that Pigou had refined Marshall's analysis into a static formal structure which she ultimately repudiated (having first turned it into *The Economics of Imperfect Competition*, 1933), she was nevertheless much more at home with abstract analysis than Austin was or ever wanted to be. His controversies were usually about factual details and judgements. Joan's were much more about abstract concepts, ideology, logical incoherence, faulty assumptions. Both were prolific writers. Austin left diaries, wrote letters – to Joan, to Keynes – which vividly described what he was seeing in Africa in the 1930s and in Germany after the war, full of local details yet ordered by a first-class mind which instinctively wanted to set observations within a coherent structure. Not that he lacked interest in psychological and sociological matters. Cairncross has recorded extracts from Austin's letters from Africa in which he compares and contrasts the characteristics of the Africans he is meeting with those of the Indians he had known in the 1920s, in terms which by today's standards are often non-politically correct. They are, of course, leavened by his basic kindness and humanity. Goodness only know what the views of the average contemporary ex-pats were: probably very close to those described in Doris Lessing's first volume of autobiography, *Under My Skin* (1994).

Although Austin started out as what we would now call a microeconomist, or perhaps more accurately an industrial organisation specialist – his first two books (1931, 1941) are classics in this area – he did play a significant role in the development of what we now call macroeconomics, through participation in the 'circus' which argued out Keynes's *Treatise on Money* (1930) and discussed and criticised Keynes as he moved towards the publication of *The General Theory* (1936). This experience, and his subsequent collaboration with Keynes as colleague and co-editor of the *Economic Journal*, and his wartime experience, especially as a manpower planner, were crucial for all Austin's later work. It led him always to look for proper balances between broad sectors in an economy and also in the relationship of home markets to abroad, and in borrowing and lending. Though Austin was to criticise the development of Keynesian economics after Keynes for being overly concerned with aggregates, too little concerned with regions, industries, firms, social infrastructure, and supplies of different types of labour and materials, he always appreciated what he had learned from Keynes as the latter wrote *The General Theory*. The single most important lesson, he consistently maintained, was to be clear when the economics of full employment was appropriate and when it was not – the sorts of propositions and policies at both systemic and microeconomic levels which ceased to be appropriate because the economy was caught in an underemployment position:

> It was ... a great step forward in economic thought when Keynes insisted that we should have a *general* theory – a theory that was valid not only with full (or near-full) employment, but also with unemployment – and that we should know quite clearly which of the propositions of economics were universally valid, and which were valid only in conditions in which it might be true that an

increase of one activity was possible *only* at the expense of another activity.

(Austin Robinson, 1947: 44, emphasis in original)

Austin believed that

in the Cambridge thought of [his] time ... no single forward step [had] been so important [, that it had] gone right to the heart of the method of estimation of the opportunity costs of doing any-thing. Before, [they believed] the paradox that it might be profitable to a society to allow resources which might have pro-duced something to stand idle. [They] came to see why that paradox was, in fact, untrue.

(*Ibid.*: 44–5)

This lesson was to serve him well when he moved to the different scenarios in which Marxian unemployment dominated.

He took from Marshall a thorough understanding of the interplay of the forces of demand and supply in markets, and of the role of time – the market period, the short period, the long period – in economic analysis, but he was never afraid to consider practical measures to match up demand and supply in the different periods, especially in developing countries. He did not have his mentor's faith (hope?) that competitive forces would tend quickly to establish stable balances which would be maintained. So he consistently designed the appropriate nudges needed to provide what the market alone may not; or, indeed, as Joan, too, often pointed out, it may bring instead undesirable fluctuations in prices and quantities and therefore incomes of people who are far too close to subsistence to survive these ups and downs.

As I mentioned, Austin wrote many reports and was associated with a large number of IEA volumes on development themes. His biographer, Alec Cairncross, has singled out for special praise a report for the United Nations Development Programme, which Austin wrote in the mid-1970s at the request of I. G. Patel (who had been his pupil in the 1940s). He regards it as the single best and most impressive account of the principles of development to come from Austin's pen. Let us take a brief look at its main features (fea-tures which were already present in embryo in his 1920s work in

India and 1930s work in Africa). (The page references, 150–2, are to Cairncross's discussion of the report in Cairncross, 1993.)

His focus was on 'the massive underemployment and unemployment in many developing countries'. Austin asks why they are so persisent and he sets out six constraints on a policy of increasing demand to draw these workers into employment and allow incomes to rise.

The usually dominant constraint is the failure of domestic food production to match expanding incomes, so that import demand rises. Unless exports match this, expansion is constrained by balance-of-payments problems. Austin's orders of magnitude for a typical developing country with population growth of 2.5 per cent a year and a target growth rate of 7 per cent a year is that the constraint will bite if agricultural output does not grow by 5 per cent a year. Top priority must, therefore, be given to overcoming this constraint by creating the necessary agricultural surplus.

Austin also stressed that the 'weakness in the exchange mechanism between town and country was sometimes the main constraint'. Undernourished farm workers consumed the additional food so that the demands of the urban population, swollen by an inflow from rural areas, went into imports: hence the need for effective organisation for buying, financing, transporting and distributing the agricultural surplus needed in the city.

As befits an economist of the same university as Malthus, Austin recognised the need to limit the import content of consumer goods, not least 'luxury' goods.

The fourth limitation was inadequate accumulation due to low saving rates, inefficient methods of finance and also the high import content of investment.

The fifth and sixth constraints are associated with the limitations of skills available – administative as well as productive, especially in industry where education systems may not be geared to produce them. Austin thought it may be necessary to create '"small-scale low-capital-intensive occupations" with "very large numbers of small craftsmen, traders, entrepreneurs starting successful small businesses"' (p. 151) in order to bypass the problem.

Strangely, Austin does not mention cultural factors which could be an important part of the explanation of differences between countries, for example, acceptance of discipline in the industrial sector: strange, because his letters from India and Africa are full of details on just these characteristics of the local populations.

Austin then discussed the dual economy aspect of development – the contrast between modern sectors and traditional sectors, and the choice this raises of whether to go for rapid development through faster growth and lower capital inputs per jobs or a gradual transition and the consequent need to 'revitalise and reinvigorate the traditional economy'. He had advocated the latter advance in the 1930s.

Finally, he recognised fully the problems associated with rapid population growth, which in some cases meant absorbing 'as much as three quarters of all national investment ... in merely standing still' (p. 152).

It is appropriate at this point to illustrate Austin's approach, in particular, his well-developed sense of relevant orders of magnitude in the simple macro development models which he carried in his head, by briefly examining the arguments of his own Kingsley Martin Memorial Lecture, 'The Economic Development of Malthusia' (Austin Robinson, 1974), which was given in Cambridge on 6 March 1974. There, he used Bangladesh as his example. He started by stating the question which was asked '[o]ne hundred and seventy five years ago [by] a shy young Fellow of Jesus' [Malthus] – made even more appropriate, I suppose, as the present lecture was given by a shy [*sic*] old Fellow of Jesus. The question is 'whether economic development was possible, or whether it would be frustrated by the growth of population' (p. 521). To say that 'Malthus has been discredited by subsequent history' is, said Austin, 'a very dangerous half truth', for while the advanced countries have broken through the Malthusian barrier into cumulative growth, the rest of the world has not; it 'continues to live under conditions of near stagnation, little above the subsistence level, in very much the conditions that Malthus envisaged' (p. 521).

Austin worked out two scenarios for the next 20 years in Bangladesh, according to whether it continued with Malthusian-type birth and death rates, or with European-type, through which it had broken out of the Malthusian trap. He relates these statistical exercises to the actual plans then being proposed in Bangladesh. His sense of the inter-relationships of the broad aspects of the economy is beautifully done. He shows that in the most favourable scenario, many of the problems of unemployment, underemployment and poverty would be overcome by the end of the period; while with the other scenario, Malthus's worst fears would have been realised and an opportunity available now (1974) would have been lost for ever. It is pleasing to report in 1996 that Austin's 'waking hopes' (p. 532) are nearer to being achieved than his worst fears realised (see, for example, Reddaway, 1996).

IV

Joan always said she went to China to learn, not to teach, but she was not always true to herself! In her papers in the King's Archives there are the notes of three lectures which she gave in China in the 1950s. They are remarkable in that they contain in skeleton outline the policies which, broadly, the Chinese authorities are implementing now – a pragmatic, gradualist, trial and error mix of the market, openness and central control. Much of the flesh was put on the skeleton in her 1960 *Exercises in Economic Analysis*, a do-it-yourself manual for students and teachers alike. The first lecture of the 1950s trio was concerned with interdepartmental flows which planners in less-developed countries would need to have at the back of their heads – and the forefronts of their minds. The inspiration for these came, I suspect, from Marx's schemas of reproduction via Kalecki's influence – he had used Marx's schemas when he independently established the principal propositions of Keynes's *General Theory*. The sectorial flows concern both monetary and real productive flows and the conditions for balance between sectors and between the totals and compositions of broad demands and supplies.

The organisation is classical – very – as the surplus – its creation, extraction, distribution and use – is the core concept of the analysis. The analysis was brought up to date by the use of the national accounting framework associated with the development of Keynesian analysis, but the classical Marxian emphasis on the sphere of production where work and production are organised and occur is never lost sight of. And, when discussing the process of accumulation itself, she always stresses the difference between finance and the real process of accumulation, on the one hand, and finance and the process of saving, on the other – a principal lesson which she derived from the capital theory debates of the 1950s and 1960s and which she thought had been lost sight of in the neoclassical approach to growth and accumulation. In the light of the resurgence of saving determines investment models in recent years, especially in the discussion of international accumulation, she may not have been that far off the mark now (though I am also sure that Bob Solow and Trevor Swan were well aware of the distinction she was making).[1]

The second lecture is concerned with the choice of techniques of production to be embodied in accumulation in a labour-aburdant, less-developed country. The analysis here reflects two strands – her then preoccupation with Wicksell's account of the choice of technique, to which she had returned in the context of her precipitation of the capital theory debates at about this time and of her writings on growth theory where, she argued, these were the most difficult but not the most important issues she needed to deal with. The other strand was the debate associated with Maurice Dobb (1954), Walter Galenson and Harvey Leibenstein (1955) and Amartya Sen (1960) on this issue in less-developed countries. Here she felt that Dobb and Sen were inclined to rationalise a Stalinist emphasis on heavy industry, even at the expense of employment-creation and gently rising standards of living for citizens in the present. She argued for a compromise, a middle way, which allowed something to be done for both employment and current living-standards, even if it meant that the surplus extracted for accumulation was less overall and the degree of mechanisation in embodiment less than in the Dobb–Sen analysis. Here, and elsewhere, she always stressed the central role of the size of the real wage (or its equivalent in non-wage societies) – how it helped to determine how many people a given surplus of commodities would employ and also how it affected the sort of investment goods it was best for them to make at any moment of time.

In the same set of lectures she discussed the role of the price mechanism in developing countries. Her published views on this are in her difficult but profound essay, 'The Philosophy of Prices' (1960b, Vol. II: 27–48). Joan Robinson consistently argued that to understand an economy we must start from its history, institutions and 'rules of the game', especially when we are trying to influence the forms which the last two should take. Here, however, she grappled with the inescapable facts of life of any society in which commodities are exchanged, having been produced by labour and commodities, and a price mechanism rules: that there is a two-way interchange between incomes and prices and that the appropriate price structure for the desired development of the economy may not throw up for significant sections of the population incomes which are consistent with society's perception of what is a decent, acceptable and humane standard of life. This problem is made even more complicated by the fact that in one form of (pure) price system, incomes arise from prices which are related to commodities produced by specific factors, while in the other form of pure price system which she identifies, factors are not specific and can operate in any sector.

She also touched on the thorny problem of population, its role and its control. Though in later writings she was to argue that generalisations about the relationship between population growth and potential prosperity were pretty wonky propositions, she did argue that in the case of China some systematic measures to reduce family size were needed. Indeed, she was most consistent on this, arguing that population was a variable which any enlightened society would try to influence, otherwise – here she echoes Austin – so much of current accumulation would have to be taken up in the process of merely standing still. As Pervez Tahir (1990a: 103) has pointed out, her views date from observing the effects of overpopulation in India in the 1920s; this even led her to argue against Harrod for a declining population independently of stages of development or the particular form of economic and social system, a view which, she also points out, was neither that of the pioneering development economists nor that of the Marxists 'who have always brushed overpopulation aside as a capitalist bogey' (Joan Robinson, 1949: 64).[2] She added that now Communism was about to commence in a country with potentially Malthusian problems, how its rulers reacted to the issue could prove decisive!

The general principles that she drew on here continued to guide her for the rest of her life. In 1978 she published a book on *Aspects of Development and Underdevelopment* in which she spelt out in detail the approach she developed in the 1950s and earlier. Though one of her colleagues tried to dissuade her from publishing it, for fear of what it would do to her reputation, in fact it has stood the test of time remarkably well. She is as usual too starry-eyed about how the Chinese (and the North Koreans) do particular things and too harsh on how the Americans do things at home and abroad. (She always said that as empires go – went – the British Empire was not all that bad; she is highly critical of certain episodes in British history, but she is nevertheless more kindly disposed towards its performance than towards that associated with American hegemony in the postwar period.) She also argued that accumulation would inevitably be faster, if not more efficient, in a planned economy regime than in capitalism, a judgement that has not stood the test of time, though the legacy from the 1980s of unused office blocks in down-town areas of many advanced capitalist countries is not an index of rationality in accumulation decisions either.[3] Generally, the pages are filled with a mixture of acute analysis, usually well-chosen empirical examples, and a feel for what ought to be done, coupled often with realistic analysis containing *Realpolitik* but also influenced by her growing pessimism about what was likely to happen. At the end, she concludes:

> While population is still growing, though at a slightly decelerating rate, the arms race is continuing at an accelerating rate [this was a major reason for her pessimism in later life] and the spread of commercialism is destroying human values everywhere, it is not easy to take an optimistic view of the situation of the Third World today. All that economic analysis can hope to contribute is to remove some illusions and to help whoever is willing to look to see what their situation really is. (1978: 143)

As we noted earlier, the structure of her thought increasingly came from Marx's schemas of reproduction through Kalecki to her own interpretation of it. The latter was set out most perceptively in her tribute to Kalecki in the Memorial Issue for Kalecki of the *Bulletin of the Oxford Institute of Economics and Statistics* (Joan Robinson, 1977). There, she divided the economy into two sectors: the wage goods sector and the investment goods sector. She showed how activity, employment and distribution in the short term were determined by the rate of accumulation, the differing saving behaviour of the wage-earners and profit-receivers and the pricing policies of the wage goods (more generally, consumption goods) sector.

Employment would tend to settle at a level where there were sufficient consumption goods produced to provide the wages of wage-earners in the investment goods sector as well as those of wage-earners in the consumption goods sector itself. Given the rate of investment and the employment required for the production of capital goods to meet it, the prices of consumption goods, the money-wage rate, and the productivity of the wage-earners in the consumption good sector between them would determine the surplus per person in the consumption goods sector available for wages in the investment goods sector, and so the required level of employment overall.

This framework led naturally, in the context of development, to a discussion of the sorts of land reform that would best serve to raise productivity and therefore the potential surplus in the agricultural sector. In the late 1970s, Joan was still uncritical of the Chinese experience. Having pointed out that the drawback of small holdings was that each family had to produce a range of products so that land would not be specialised to its best use, she argued that the then Chinese system of large communes divided into small teams combined the advantage of intensive use of labour with control over the use of land in large units. She felt that this provided a strong incentive for teams to put in extra work to improve their land in schemes organised on an appropriate scale because they collectively share in any improved income that resulted (1978: 52–3). She comments wryly on land reform in parts of Latin America which was intended to save the peasants from exploitation' but had 'been turned into a more efficient, because less brutal, method of exploiting them' by making them wage-labourers on commercial farms (1978: 54).

For capitalist systems it was easy to show in this framework that full employment was unlikely to occur. But this was not inevitable in the context of development, which would also have to take into account foreign exchange constraints associated with trade and lending and borrowing, and the Kaleckian view that the workers must have some extra jam today rather than wait for a tomorrow which in reality often never came. It was within such a framework that Joan commented on different institutional forms, actual and ideal, the roles and limitations of government, and what behaviour could and would be expected of citizens at work and in their own community.

V

Let me conclude. In Austin and Joan Robinson the profession has been well-served by a provision of role models. Both were often difficult people to work with, for largely different reasons; but both also had that combination of first-class intelligence, keen powers of observation, a passionate desire to know how things worked and how to make them work better, especially for those least able to defend themselves, and that ability to structure and communicate in a clear and intelligible way a usable system of thought which characterises the greatest members of our trade. It was a great shame that after the 1930s they ceased to interact with each other's work, for many of their respective gifts would have been useful complements to the other's. Nevertheless, if I have been able to stimulate you to read their writings, and, having sifted out limitations associated with their personalities, class and age, to draw on their wisdom and insight, I shall feel satisfied.

Notes

1. Both Solow and Swan made explicit their *bona fide* Keynesian credentials in their famous 1956 articles on long-period growth. Thus Solow wrote: 'Everything above is the neoclassical side of the coin ... All the difficulties ... which go into modern Keynesian economic analysis have been shunted aside ... not [Solow's] contention that these problems don't exist, nor that they are of no significance in the long run' (1956: 91). Similarly, Swan (1956: 335, emphasis in original) wrote: 'Effective demand is so regulated (*via* the interest rate or otherwise) that all savings are profitably invested, production capacity is fully utilized, and the level of employment can never be increased merely by raising the level of spending.'
2. Tahir (1990a: 102–3) refers to an exchange of letters between Joan and Harrod on the imminent decline in the British population. (Harrod's letters, 12–17 January 1938, may be found in Joan Robinson's papers in King's Modern Archives.) Harrod was concerned about the Brits being outbred (see, e.g., Harrod, 1938), while Joan was concerned to relate population policy to the need to establish and support 'decent living standards everywhere' (Tahir: 103; see, e.g., Robinson, 1960b: 107–13).
3. One of the anonymous referees argued that she was 'then well past the age of youthful naïveté, [that] [s]he had a settled ideological position which led her to put the best possible construction on what she saw ... to believe what she was told by the representative of the regimes.' I think this attributes far too much sense of *Realpolitik* to Joan; she lacked judgement, she had little tactical sense or guile, and she never developed

Austin's acute sense of orders of magnitude. But her utopian idealism, a search, as Paul Samuelson (1989: 136) put it, for that '"true socialism" [which] was her first and ever love, not the pretenders who took its name in vain', was a lifelong constant of her psychological make-up. Samuelson added: 'Who is to say that her value judgements were wrong, or other than noble?' Certainly not this writer.

References

Cairncross, A. (1993) *Austin Robinson. The Life of an Economic Advisor* (London: Macmillan).

Dobb, M. H. (1954) *On Economic Theory and Socialism. Collected Papers* (London: Routledge & Kegan Paul).

Galenson, W. and H. Leibenstein (1955) 'Investment Criteria, Productivity, and Economic Development', *Quarterly Journal of Economics*, vol. 69, 343–70.

Harcourt, G. C. (1997) 'Edward Austin Gossage Robinson 1897–1993', *Proceedings of the British Academy*, vol. 94, 707–31; chapter 8, this volume.

Keynes, J. M. (1919) *The Economic Consequences of the Peace*. Reprinted in *Collected Writings* (*C.W.*), Vol. II (London: Macmillan).

— (1930) *A Treatise on Money*, 2 vols. Reprinted in *C.W.*, Vols V and VI (London: Macmillan).

— (1936) *The General Theory of Employment, Interest and Money*. Reprinted in *C.W.*, Vol. VII (London: Macmillan).

— (1972) *Essays in Biography, C.W.*, Vol. X (London: Macmillan).

Lessing, D. (1994) *Under My Skin* (London: HarperCollins).

Reddaway, W. B. (1996) 'The Bangladesh Economy in a World Perspective', in A. Abdullah, and A. R. Khan (eds), *State, Market and Development: Essays in Honour of Rehman Sobhan* (Dhaka: University Press), 289–304.

Robinson, A. (1931) *The Structure of Competitive Industry*, revd edn, 1953 (Cambridge: Cambridge University Press).

— (1941) *Monopoly* (Cambridge: Cambridge University Press).

— (1947) 'John Maynard Keynes, 1883–1946', *Economic Journal*, vol. 56, 1–68.

— (1974) 'The Economic Development of Malthusia', *Modern Asian Studies*, vol. 8, 521–34.

— (mid-1970s) *Future Tasks for UNDP: Report to the Administrator of the United Nations Development Program*.

Robinson, J. (1933) *The Economics of Imperfect Competition*, 2nd edn, 1969 (London: Macmillan).

— (1943) 'The International Currency Proposals', *Economic Journal*, vol. 53, 161–75.

— (1949) 'Theory of Planning. Review of Maurice Dobb, *Soviet Economic Development since 1917*', *Soviet Studies*, vol. 1, 60–4.

— (1960a) *Exercises in Economic Analysis* (London: Macmillan).

— (1960b) *Collected Economic Papers*, Vol. II, 2nd edn, 1975 (Oxford: Basil Blackwell).

— (1977) 'Michal Kalecki on the Economics of Capitalism', *Bulletin of the Oxford Institute of Economics and Statistics*, vol. 39, 7–17.

— (1978) *Aspects of Development and Underdevelopment* (Cambridge: Cambridge University Press).

Rosenstein-Rodan, P. N. (1943) 'Problems of Industrialisation of Eastern and South-eastern Europe', *Economic Journal*, vol. 53, 202–11.

Samuelson, P. A. (1989) 'Remembering Joan', in G. R. Feiwel (ed.), *Joan Robinson and Modern Economic Theory* (London: Macmillan).

Sen, A. K. (1960) *Choice of Techniques. An Aspect of the Theory of Planned Development* (Oxford: Basil Blackwell).

Solow, R. M. (1956) 'A Contribution to the Theory of Economic Growth', *Quarterly Journal of Economics*, vol. 70, 65–94.

Swan, T. W. (1956) 'Economic Growth and Capital Accumulation', *Economic Record*, vol. 32, 334–62.

Tahir, P. (1990a) 'Some Aspects of Development and Underdevelopment: Critical Perspectives on Joan Robinson', unpublished PhD dissertation, Cambridge.

— (1990b) 'Making Sense of Joan Robinson on China', mimeo, Cambridge.

23
How I Do Economics*

I

Because I am what cricketers call an all-rounder, it is an especially pleasant task the editors have set me. As an undergraduate at Melbourne University in the early 1950s, I decided that I wanted to become a theoretical economist, though I had also thought of becoming an economic historian and I initially wanted to write my fourth year undergraduate dissertation on a topic in the history of economic thought. (I was dissuaded from doing so by a wise teacher who said that HET topics required maturity – in my case a never-never state, for I feel that I have gone straight from my first childhood to my second with nothing in between.) Nevertheless, as one of my two specialisations in my third and fourth (honours) years, I took History of Economic Thought. The other specialisation was Mathematical Economics. In those days the distinction between theoretical and mathematical economists did not exist, though we were told that the maths of our high priest, Paul Samuelson, in

* Originally published in Steven G. Medema and Warren J. Samuels (ed.), *Foundations of Research in Economics? How do Economists do Economics* (Cheltenham, Glos: Edward Elgar, 1996), 93–102. I thank but in no way implicate Roberta Dessi, Aly Fischer, Tim Harcourt, Wendy Harcourt, Prue Kerr, Yougesh Khatri, Steve Medema, Ray Petridis, Warren Samuels, Claudio Sardoni and the members of the Cambridge Workshop on realism and economics for their comments on a draft of this essay.

the *Foundations* ... (1947) was said sometimes to be clumsy and inelegant.

In the event, my undergraduate dissertation was a mixture of theory and applied work, my master's degree pure applied ('Pilot Survey of Personel Savings in Melbourne 1954' (1955)) and my PhD dissertation at King's College, Cambridge, mainly applied. Two and a half of the four years I took to do it were spent pounding out calculations on a Marchand (calculations which now might take a week's (seconds'?) work on a computer), getting the raw data into an appropriate form in order to test the inferences I had drawn from the analysis in the theoretical first chapter. I was interested in the implications, for both the operation of the firm and the economy in a period of inflation, of the use of historical-cost accounting procedures to measure profits for tax and dividend purposes, and to set prices. I contrasted the outcomes of using these procedures with what would follow if replacement cost-accounting procedures were used, instead, for the same purposes.[1]

In the course of doing my PhD I became deeply interested in the writings of Joan Robinson and Nicky Kaldor on accumulation, growth and distribution, and, as a sideline, on capital theory – Joan Robinson published her (in)famous critique of the production function in *R. E. Studs* in 1953–54 and her *magnum opus, The Accumulation of Capital* in 1956, Kaldor, his *R. E. Studs* paper on alternative theories of distribution in 1956 and his *Economics Journal* paper on growth in 1957. (As an undergraduate I had become fascinated by capital theory, principally from reading Hayek's (1941) *Pure Theory of Capital* and some of Boulding's articles and his *Economic Analysis* (1948).) Much of my teaching when I returned to Australia in 1958 to my first lecturing post (at the Economics Department of the University of Adelaide) was on these themes, but I was also soon to give the first year course on Keynesian economics. This eventually became my first book, *Economic Activity* (1967), which was written jointly with the two other people who had given the course, Peter Karmel (who initiated it at Adelaide) and Bob Wallace. I also started to work on themes associated with Wilfred Salter's 1960 classic, *Productivity and Technical Change* and, at Harold Lydall's suggestion, 'The Accountant in a Golden Age' (1965a).

Back in Cambridge in the 1960s I continued working on these themes. I developed a two-sector model of distribution and employment in the short period (1965b). I read Piero Sraffa's 1960 masterpiece, *Production of Commodities...*, with Vince Massaro, writing with Vince an approved review article of it (1964) – Sraffa scrutinised and, ultimately, approved every sentence. I criticised the conceptual foundations of the CES production function in an *Economic Journal* review (1964) of Minhas's book (1963) and my only article ever in the Green Horror (Dennis Robertson's description of *R. E. Studs*) (1966). I also started to apply theory to policy (I had done this in the 1950s and 1960s on taxation policy), extending Salter's work on the choice of technique to take in investment-decision rules and investment-incentive schemes in the West and what was then the 'socialist' East (1968, 1969a).

When I returned to Adelaide in early 1967, as well as becoming an anti-Vietnam War protester, I also started to work on capital theory issues, as a result of Mark Perlman's request in August 1968 that I write the survey on capital theory for the second issue of the *Journal of Economic Literature* (June (1969b)). This survey and its offshoots (which include my 1972 book) absorbed much of my intellectual energies for the next 10 years or so. It was also the first of nine substantial survey articles I was subsequently to write (1969b, 1973, 1975, 1976, 1977, 1979, 1982, 1988 (with Omar Hamouda), 1995 (with Luke Spajic)). By the early 1970s, however, I deliberately turned to policy, mainly because of the emergence of inflationary pressures in Australia (and, of course, elsewhere), following the first oil price rise shock, the breakdown of the Bretton Woods system and other major changes of the late 1960s, early 1970s. These policy writings were centred around designing a permanent incomes policy for Australia, using its traditional centralised wage-setting institutions within a package deal of fiscal, monetary, exchange rate and tariff policies. At the end of the 1970s I was the economist on the Australian Labor Party's national committee of enquiry into why they had done so badly in the elections of 1975 and 1977. I wrote the first draft of the outline of economic policy for the Australian Labor Party governments of the 1980s and 1990s.

Finally, the request by the late Angus Wilson to send him some material on Joan Robinson for the oration to go with the award to her of an honorary degree at the University of East Anglia in the early 1970s and the terrible shock of the sudden death in February 1977 of my greatest friend in Adelaide, Eric Russell, led me to write intellectual biographies, see, for example, Harcourt (1993). This pursuit has taken up much of my time since then, though I have also had the odd 'go' at theory and, more recently, policy as well, as a result of invitations to give certain public lectures and a natural inclination always to respond to economic and political issues.

II

So how do I think we ought to do economics? With Eric Russell, Nicky Kaldor, Joan Robinson and Michal Kalecki and, of course, Keynes as mentors, I am a 'horses for courses' person – how you do it depends upon what the purpose is. If doctrinal debate is the issue – the robustness of a fundamental intuition or insight in a particular approach, say price as an index of scarcity in neoclassical economics, surplus labour and value as the origin of profits in the capitalist mode of production in Marxian economics – it is right and proper to operate at a high level of abstraction, to use simple, *very* unrealistic models which are appropriately closed, for capturing the essence of the problem but which exclude all other 'matters of the real world' as irrelevant for the purpose in hand.

My favourite example is the debate which Ian Steedman (1976, 1977) initiated on whether the existence of joint production destroyed the general validity of what Michio Morishima (1973) dubbed the Fundamental Marxist Theorem (FMT) – the necessary and sufficient condition for positive profits in the sphere of distribution and exchange is positive surplus labour (and value) in the sphere of production. For *that* purpose it was perfectly legitimate to use a Golden Rule, Golden Age (steady growth) model, so ignoring real life puzzles such as the realisation problem. The argument then turned on the correct specification of what were initially ideas expressed in literary form. Steedman inappropriately used equalities in order to estimate necessary and surplus labour (in his examples the latter turned out to be negative) whereas inequalities (linear programming) were the appropriate formal tools in this context to capture the basic idea that the monopoly of capitalists *as a class* of the means of production and of access to finance enabled them to make the wage-earners *as a class* work longer than was necessary to make their wage goods alone with the existing techniques of production and accumulated capital goods. Joint production techniques could be handled as an unessential complication (though an inescapable feature of the real world) which should not destroy this essential insight. If it *appeared* that they did, it was the specification and not the insight which must give way, as indeed happened, see Morishima (1976).

Or, to take another issue with which I have some familiarity: is the demand curve for 'capital' as a whole well-behaved – reswitching, capital-reversing and all that. Again, stationary-state comparisons of long-period competitive equilibrium positions are the simplest and most appropriate method of analysis to test for the robustness in heterogeneous capital good models of the results of simple one all-purpose commodity models in which the marginal productivity theory of distribution and the related neoclassical parables may be shown rigorously to 'go through', see, for example, Harcourt (1976).

III

To descend from these dizzy theoretical heights to a much more practical plane – the testing of inferences of theory against real world data. One approach is to follow the frankness and honesty of Bob Solow in his most famous empirical work on the aggregate production function and technical progress. In his reply to Anwar Shaikh's critique (1974) of his procedure and findings, he wrote:

> It merely shows how one goes about interpreting given time series if one starts by assuming that they were generated from a production function and that the competitive marginal-product relations apply. (Solow, 1974: 121)

What could be fairer or more honest than that? The limitations are set out, the meaning of the findings is coherent, the usefulness of them then turns on whether or not it is believed that the underlying simple theoretical model captures the essence of the processes at work which have thrown up the statistical observations of the times series used in the first place. Solow and his surrogates (especially) presumably believe(d) that they do (did). Their critics do not – and some of them have provided either alternative approaches or different theoretical structures to explain what the data show.

Let me take as another example my empirical work on the effects of using historical-cost accounting procedures in periods of inflation. The inferences to be looked for in the data were rather broad: that if inflation continued, and if the taxation authorities and management insisted on basing taxes and dividends respectively on accounting profits rather than on 'economic' profits – those adjusted for stock appreciation and capital consumption at replacement cost – and if management insisted on setting prices by 'marking up' historical costs while not widening their margins, we ought to see over time a decline in 'economic' rates of return coupled with a deterioration on the liabilities side of balance sheets, that is to say, a rise in the ratio of short-term and long-term debts to total liabilities. The latter would result from financing, not expansions, but firms as 'going concerns', trying to continue to do tomorrow what they had done today. Whereas, if replacement cost procedures were used, such deteriorations should not be observed; or, at least, not for these reasons. Plain competition, or bad management, or changes of fashion could also lead to similar happenings. But, anyway, if the former tendencies were the most powerful at work in the specific concrete situations examined, we knew what we had to look for and, hopefully, find. (As it happened, in my case inflation proved disobliging and, relatively, went away for twenty years.)

It will be noticed that in this example I did not use any sophisticated econometric techniques – the essential aim was to understand the sources and construction of the data set, what processes it was hypothesised lay behind it and threw up the observations, adjust it from its raw form to get it in the appropriate form to allow estimates of the relevant theoretical variables to be made, and then analyse what the results showed. Such a procedure belongs to a well-established Australian tradition (not exclusively, of course, in Cambridge, for example, it is known as the Reddaway method). It involves thorough understanding of the sources and limitations of the data, especially of how 'far off' the actual observations are from their theoretical counterparts, the use of simple tables, ratios, graphs, to get a 'feel' for what the orders of magnitude are, never going further than the data themselves warrant while being ready to take advice from the experts on what traps to look for and what techniques may be used either to avoid them or to tease out answers which otherwise would remain hidden.

IV

I have written about doctrinal debates in high theory and the rough and tumble of applied work, the latter often prefatory to policy. I want now to consider intermediate cases concerning theory and specific issues. There are, at least, two basic approaches. One is axiomatic, for example, as Frank Hahn often says, let us see how far the assumption that the world is inhabited by 'greedy people' will take us. The other starts by observing behaviour, institutions, 'stylized facts' and then constructs simple models incorporating the essence of the observations in order to try to explain the original observations *et al.* Debreu, Arrow, Hahn are outstanding proponents of the first approach, Kaldor, Kalecki, Joan Robinson and Steindl – also Keynes, Marx and Adam Smith – of the second. An interesting, indeed vital, question is whether there are large differences between the answers to the same questions according to which approach is taken.

Let me illustrate this by the work I did in the 1960s on the choice of technique. I compared the investment-labour ratio which would be predicted by the axiomatic approach, using some versions of the set of DCF procedures, with those which would be predicted by starting from 'real world' investment-decision rules – the pay-off period criterion, the accounting rate of profit rule (and, in some instances, the various recoupment period procedures of socialist managers in the 1960s). Using a simple model based on Salter's work, I was able to show that for the orders of magnitudes likely to be met in the real world, the pay-off period criterion always resulted in a more investment-intensive, less labour-intensive technique being chosen than did any of the other investment-decision rules. I also showed that under the conditions assumed the ratio associated with the net present value rule (NPV) was intermediate between those associated with the pay-off period criterion and the internal rate of return rule (IR) respectively (except in long-period competitive equilibrium when the NPV rule and IR rule not surprisingly resulted in the same technique being chosen).[2] I then allied this set of findings with an analysis of the impact of a variety of investment-incentive schemes (then much in vogue) which were combined with the various investment-decision rules, in order to see how robust the main results were and also whether what was predicted to happen was in accord with what the policy-makers had in mind when they introduced the schemes. (I am told I had a file under my name in HM Treasury at the time – which certainly makes a change from the file which the Australian secret service subsequently was to have on me when I was a leader of the anti-Vietnam War movement in South Australia in the late 1960s and 1970s.)

V

Finally, let me say a little about my other two major research preoccupations – surveys and intellectual biographies. A useful survey should put a structure on an area in the literature. It should draw out the main thrust of the arguments, identify the major articles or books, and show how the rest cluster around them. It should suggest the areas and issues of disagreement, try to reconcile what is reconcilable, point out what is not and why, and suggest, where, if anywhere, we should go from here. Doing all this should give perspective and senses of relevance and balance. If in the process it also enlightens and even amuses, why, those are surely acceptable pluses.

What of intellectual biography? I still believe in heroes and heroines and I like to know what makes them tick. I became an economist because I hated injustice, unemployment and poverty. Most of my heroes and heroines had become economists for the same reasons and they devoted their lives to trying to do something about understanding how these ills arose and how to get rid of them. Some – not all – understood the *Realpolitik* of policy advice, as I have tried to myself, because I have been a political animal all of my adult life. Intellectual biography allows us to begin to see the links between the historical settings of the persons concerned, their class, their racial, educational, philosophical and religious backgrounds, and the issues of the day on which they have worked. By analysing the intertwinings of all these aspects, we get a better understanding of the writings and contributions of these economists, of their limitations as well as their achievements, of the particular forms which their analyses take, and, possibly and hopefully, we are also inspired to follow on from where they left off. If not, it is at least to be hoped that we have had a good read on the way.

VI

I have written elsewhere, Harcourt (1995), about why I think mathematics is a good servant but a bad master. My own most ambitious paper was the two-sector model of distribution and employment in the short period (1965b). I had wanted to extend the analysis into a process in historical time, seeing how the model economy moved from period to period but I did not have the necessary mathematics to allow me to do this. (I did show good taste in the two young sorcerer's apprentices I asked to help me do so – the young Jim Mirrlees and the even younger Joe Stiglitz – but both said 'no', Jim immediately, Joe after a week, the opportunity cost of the paper-a-week he wrote then, and now, no doubt being too high.) It is partly because of this paper that I admire Kalecki's contributions so much, for he had the technical expertise and the genius to do superbly what I wanted to do but could not. Dick Goodwin's writings spring to mind also at this juncture. So the most use I ever made of mathematics was in my papers on the choice of technique. Even then I eventually got the argument down to a simple diagram which exploited the properties of the two most useful (and used) constructions of our trade – the 45° line and the graph of a concave-to-the-origin quadratic (Harcourt, 1972: 64).

Similarly, I regard econometrics as a set of valuable tools and techniques which enable us to squeeze information from data in forms which people generally understand, for example, that a regression coefficient is a particular sort of average, sometimes, but not always, to be preferred as the slope of a line to what could be obtained by fitting a line freehand to a scatter diagram. But *always* the guiding principle must be the economics of the problem and its importance and relevance, not what economic problem can we find to which to fit any fancy technique that we have come across. It is most important to get the conceptual aspects of a problem clear, together, sometimes, with conjectures as to outcomes, *before* starting any formal analysis. This I have always tried to do.

Notes

1. I was the first to use the consolidated data on profit and loss accounts, balance sheets and funds statements of all the quoted public companies in the UK which the National Institute for Economic and Social Research in London and the Department of Applied Economics in Cambridge were then starting to process. They were the basic data for the subsequent distinguished studies by, for example, Tew and Henderson (1959), Singh and Whittington (1968) and Meeks (1977).
2. Initially I thought that the orderings were a completely general result but I subsequently found out that I had a wrong sign in one of my differentiations! Showing *why* the result was not general led to some interesting *economic* analysis in itself.

References

Boulding, K. E. (1948) *Economic Analysis*, revd edn (New York: Harper).

Harcourt, G. C. (1964) 'Review of B. S. Minhas (1963), *An International Comparison of Factor Costs and Factor Use*, Amsterdam: North Holland', *Economic Journal*, vol. 74, 443–5.

Harcourt, G. C. (1965a) 'The Accountant in a Golden Age', *Oxford Economic Papers* (NS), vol. 17, 66–80.

Harcourt, G. C. (1965b) 'A Two-Sector Model of the Distribution of Income and the Level of Employment in the Short Run', *Economic Record*, vol. 40, 103–17.

Harcourt, G. C. (1966) 'Biases in Empirical Estimates of the Elasticities of Substitution of C.E.S. Production Functions', *Review of Economic Studies*, vol. 33, 227–33.

Harcourt, G. C. (1968) 'Investment-Decision Criteria, Investment Incentives and the Choice of Technique', *Economic Journal*, vol. 78, 77–95.

Harcourt, G. C. (1969a) 'Investment-Decision Criteria, Capital-Intensity and the Choice of Techniques', chapter 14 of J. T. Dunlop and N. P. Federenko (eds), *Planning and Markets* (New York: McGraw-Hill), 190–216.

Harcourt, G. C. (1969b) 'Some Cambridge Controversies in the Theory of Capital', *Journal of Economic Literature*, vol. 7, 369–405.

Harcourt, G. C. (1972) *Some Cambridge Controversies in the Theory of Capital* (Cambridge: Cambridge University Press).

Harcourt, G. C. (1973) 'The Rate of Profits in Equilibrium Growth Models: A Review Article', *Journal of Political Economy*, vol. 81, 1261–77.

Harcourt, G. C. (1975) *Theoretical Controversy and Social Significance: An Evaluation of the Cambridge Controversies* (Edward Shann Memorial Lecture) (Perth: University of Western Australia Press).

Harcourt, G. C. (1976) 'The Cambridge Controversies: Old Ways and New Horizons – or Dead End?', *Oxford Economic Papers*, vol. 28, 25–65.

Harcourt, G. C. (ed.) (1977) *The Microeconomic Foundations of Macroeconomics* (London: Macmillan).

Harcourt, G. C. (1979) 'Non-Neoclassical Capital Theory', *World Development*, vol. 7, 923–32.

Harcourt, G. C. (1982) 'Post Keynesianism: Quite Wrong and/or Nothing New?', *Thames Papers in Political Economy*, Summer, 1–19.

Harcourt, G. C. (1993) *Post-Keynesian Essays in Biography: Portraits of Twentieth Century Political Economists* (London: Macmillan).

Harcourt, G. C. (1995) *Capitalism, Socialism and Post-Keynesianism. Selected Essays of G. C. Harcourt* (Cheltenham: Edward Elgar).

Harcourt, G. C. and V. G. Massaro (1964) 'Mr. Sraffa's *Production of Commodities*', *Economic Record*, vol. 40, 442–54.

Harcourt, G. C., P. H. Karmel and R. H. Wallace (1967) *Economic Activity* (Cambridge: Cambridge University Press).

Harcourt, G. C. and O. F. Hamouda (1988) 'Post Keynesianism: From Criticism to Coherence?', *Bulletin of Economic Research*, vol. 40, 1–33.

Harcourt, G. C. and L. D. Spajic (1995) 'Post-Keynesianism', *Enciclopedia Italiana*, forthcoming, published in English in Shri Bhagwan Dahiya (ed.), *The Current State of Economic Science*, vol. 2 (Rohtak, India: Spellbound), 909–34.

Hayek, F. A. (1941) *The Pure Theory of Capital* (London: Routledge).

Kaldor, N. (1955–56) 'Alternative Theories of Distribution', *Review of Economic Studies*, vol. XXIII, 83–100.

Kaldor, N. (1957) 'A Model of Economic Growth', *Economic Journal*, vol. 67, 591–624.

Meeks, G. (1977) *Disappointing Marriage: A Study of the Gains from Merger* (Cambridge: Cambridge University Press).

Morishima, M. (1973) *Marx's Economics. A Dual Theory of Value and Growth* (Cambridge: Cambridge University Press).

Morishima, M. (1976) 'Positive Profits with Negative Surplus Value: A Comment', *Economic Journal*, vol. 86, 599–603.

Robinson, J. (1953–54) 'The Production Function and the Theory of Capital', *Review of Economic Studies*, vol. XXI, 81–106.

Robinson, J. (1956) *The Accumulation of Capital* (London: Macmillan).

Salter, W. E. G. (1960) *Productivity and Technical Change* (Cambridge: Cambridge University Press), 2nd edn 1966.

Samuelson, P. A. (1947) *Foundations of Economic Analysis* (Cambridge: Harvard University Press).

Shaikh, A. (1974) 'Laws of Production and Laws of Algebra: The Humbug Production Function', *Review of Economic and Statistics*, vol. LVI, 115–20.

Singh, A. and G. Whittington in collaboration with H. T. Burley (1968) *Growth, Profitability and Valuation* (Cambridge: Cambridge University Press).

Solow, R. M. (1974) 'Laws of Production and Laws of Algebra: The Humbug Production Function: A Comment', *Review of Economics and Statistics*, vol. LVI, 121.

Steedman, I. (1976) 'Positive Profits with Negative Surplus Value', *Economic Journal*, vol. 86, 604–8.

Steedman, I. (1977) *Marx After Sraffa* (London: New Left Books).

Tew, B. and R. F. Henderson (eds.) (1959) *Studies in Company Finance* (Cambridge: Cambridge University Press).

24
The Cambridge Contribution to Economics*

I am a Fellow of Jesus so I must start with the person Keynes called 'the first of the Cambridge economists', Thomas Robert Malthus, as you would say, but according to Keynes, as the name is an adaptation of Malt house, the correct pronunciation is Malthouse. You may see his portrait in the dining hall of Jesus College. Keynes called him 'the first of the Cambridge economists' because he was the first chap to think like Keynes (Keynes never did consider modesty a virtue). I have a great affection for Malthus, partly because he had a stock (or perhaps a flow) of one-liners which I enjoy. In the first edition of his famous essay on population you will find some really funny remarks about the nature of the passion between the sexes which he thought was as near to a constant as would be likely to be found amongst human beings. When he was arguing with his dad, who took a Godwin stance on the possibility of perfection of humanity, Malthus, as befits a member of the Church of England, was more gloomy. He said there are two great constants: one, the passion between the sexes; the other, the fact that, as population grew, since there was a limit to the quantity of land and also to its quality, food and other necessaries would not grow as fast and so we would always be near to the constraints of

---

* Originally published in Sarah J. Ormrod (ed.), *Cambridge Contributions* (Cambridge: Cambridge University Press, 1998), 65–87. This chapter is based on the transcript of the lecture I gave in the Lady Mitchell Hall to the Summer School in July 1996. I have tried to make the text grammatical but otherwise I have left it much as it was delivered.

starvation and misery. In fact, if we temporarily overcame the constraints, the best we ultimately could hope for was a larger population which would be just as miserable as the smaller one. So you can see why economics used to be called the 'dismal science' – we predicted maximum human misery if Malthus was correct.

I must impose two constraints on myself: the first is that there is an inbuilt tendency for sermon-givers in Jesus College Chapel to talk for 13 minutes (not always abided by), for dissenters to talk for 25 minutes and for University lecturers to talk for 50 minutes; that is the first constraint. The second is that I am not going to talk about any economists who are still teaching in Cambridge, not only because I might be indulging in slander, but also because it would be invidious to try to pick out the stars and non-stars amongst my colleagues. I will say this, that they continue the Cambridge tradition in at least one aspect – we still have as many brawls as ever we had in our Faculty since we began. We have always had a propensity to produce bantam cocks who fight with great gusto on a dunghill for their positions. Of course, we do have some tremendous stars, but I am not going to tell you who they are – you have to be retired before you get a mention today. With these provisos, let me get going.

I now jump from Malthus at the beginning of the nineteenth century to the person who is responsible for the foundation of the Economics Tripos, and also for the traditional approach to economics in Cambridge, as we know them today. I mean, of course, Alfred Marshall (1842–1924), whose Library stands opposite the Austin Robinson building.

The tradition that Marshall started was the idea that economics should explain how the world worked and then do something about it, if it did not work well. This should be done by both theorising and doing applied work and then formulating feasible policies. Marshall, who was a strange and convoluted character, rather wavered on aspects of this. But the tradition was taken up, often without any inhibitions, thank goodness, by many of his pupils and followers.[1]

Marshall was not, in many ways, an admirable person, but he was a great economist. He read mathematics at St John's College towards the middle of the last century. He was then a progressive and idealistic person, greatly influenced by Henry

Sidgwick (whose lasting monument is Newnham College), as well by Sidgwick's books and contributions to philosophy. Marshall belonged to the 'Grote Club'; he went from mathematics to flirt with psychology and then into economics. He was in favour of women being allowed into Cambridge and of doing things for the poor and underprivileged. As to the latter, he did continue to think about them and contribute ideas on poverty and its causes until his death, but once he married (in 1876) an absolutely marvellous person, Mary Paley (Marshall), who had been his student, he switched sides on the women question, opposing women's entry to the University, and greatly upsetting his former colleague and supporter, Sidgwick. He told his wife that women could not do economic theory but that she could act, in effect, as his research assistant. He did allow her to be a lecturer, first at Bristol where they went after they married, then at Oxford and then finally here at Cambridge. She served him loyally, in I think a Quixotic way, and indeed she wrote a book with him, which he later suppressed even though it is one of his best books. So I do not like Marshall and I agree with my mentor Joan Robinson, who said, 'the more I learn about economics the more I admire Marshall's intellect and the less I like his character' (1973: 259).

Marshall set about taking economics out of the Moral Sciences Tripos, where it had a niche but did not, on the whole, attract good students, and making it a separate Tripos which, in the event, started in the early years of this century. It is on that foundation that we have built ever since, and though, of course, the structure has changed as the subject has changed, we owe much to Marshall for the way in which economics is taught and practised in Cambridge today. His own major contribution was his huge *Principles of Economics*, first published in 1890 and which for the first five editions was called Vol. I. Marshall intended to write three (or even four) volumes but ill health (which he rather enjoyed) and certain character deficiencies meant he never was able to write down in a systematic form the other volumes. In old age he published two more volumes which were not a patch on the famous first volume. He died in his early eighties without being able to complete his project. He did establish what is known as 'The Cambridge Oral Tradition', that is, Cambridge chaps would say to the lesser breeds without the Law: 'Oh well, of course, we always talk about that at Cambridge – it is in the Oral Tradition, it may not be written down, but that is what we mean' – a good ploy to fall back on, especially when on dangerous ground. People obtained their notion of what Cambridge economic principles were about, partly from the *Principles*, partly from articles and memoranda to Royal Commissions and so on; and partly from people's views and recollections of his lectures and supervisions (he was an excellent supervisor).

What was the structure of Marshallian economics? Putting it simply and not doing full justice to its richness, in the first volume he wrote about the nitty-gritty of economic life – what determines the prices and quantities of commodities, what determines the employment, wages and salaries of different classes of labour, what determines the rate of interest and the rate of profit in various industries: what we now call the theory of relative prices and quantities. His first great analytical contribution in this endeavour was to introduce systematically into economics the use of supply and demand functions and curves. You have often heard it said that economists are just parrots who say 'supply and demand, supply and demand'; if anyone is responsible for us being parrots, it is Marshall. But he was no parrot; rather, he used the supply and demand apparatus to handle in a systematic and rigorous manner the analysis of the determination of prices and quantities in mainly competitive markets. His second contribution was to recognise in a deep way that the most difficult and yet relevant concept which affects economic life is time. You know the saying, 'Time is a device to stop everything happening at once', which is said to be due to the philosopher, Bergson. A group of us in the 1960s were discussing who actually said this. An Indian economist, Dharma Kumar, a Cambridge graduate on leave at the time, said, 'I don't know who said it, but I think that space is a device to stop everything happening in Cambridge' – one of the best spontaneous one-liners I have ever heard. A lot of people would have killed to have said it and indeed many people, though they have not killed, have certainly plagiarised Dharma ever since. In order to handle this intractable concept of time Marshall used three analytical concepts: the market period, the short period, and the long period. The market period is an immediate one; in the central market in Cambridge there will be a length of analytical time during which prices will be set such that the *given* quantities will be bought. The short period is an analytical device which refers to a period that is long enough for the number of people employed in a firm or industry to be changed, in order to change their rates of production, but not long enough for firms to either leave or enter an industry or bring in new capital goods to increase their capacity. The long period is a period of time long enough to allow both the supplies of skilled labour and of capital goods in industries to be changed, and for new firms to enter and old firms to exit. Marshall made clear that these are not one-for-one descriptions of real life, but analytical devices which use the concept of *ceteris paribus* (other things being equal); he called it the *ceteris paribus* pound, in order to allow us to get a grip on what otherwise is an intricate interconnecting process which is impossible to make sense of in a systematic way. In Vol. I he used these devices in order to go systematically through the determination in the market period, the short period, and the long period, of prices and quantities of commodities and prices and employment of the services of the factors of production; and so to develop theories of rent, wages, profits, and interest – all in the supply and demand framework. Strangely enough though, because he was a most realistic person, money did not get a mention except as a ticket – as something with which to measure things. Everything was done in real and relative terms and money might just as well never have existed as far as analysis was concerned. This is a bit unfair for we now know, as a result of the recent publication of the first major biography of Marshall, by Peter Groenewegen (1995), that Marshall was more guarded than this. He always qualified and modified, and whenever you thought you had something new, it would be said, 'there's nothing new about that, it's all in Marshall'. But it was the message which people took away from Vol. I. In Vol. II, if he had ever got round to writing it down systematically, he meant to talk much more about money and monetary institutions and, combined with this, he was to talk about what determined not the prices of individual commodities or of the individual services of factors of production, but the general price level – the concept of the price level of all goods and services in aggregate in the economy. In doing that he would have been one of the first to develop in a systematic way the theory of the general price level which we call the quantity theory of money, which has made a great comeback in recent years via the monetarists and in particular, their high priest Milton Friedman of Chicago, a Marshall admirer.

Marshall developed the quantity theory of money in order to try and describe what determined the general price level; he argued that, at least in the long period, what was happening in the real sector of the economy concerning employment, production, and relative prices, and what was happening in the monetary sector of the economy, the banks, the financial sector generally and the formation of the general price level, were independent of one another. Money was basically a veil. We all know what may be done with a veil; as we are getting to mature years, we could pull it down and provide an aura of mystery; if we are younger we could lift it up. But the vital point is, that what ever is underneath is not affected by the veil itself. That is how, generally speaking, money was treated in the Marshallian tradition – at least in the long period. It is true that in the short period, when looking at the workings of the economy as a whole, it was admitted that money could have real effects on the economy but this was not worked out systematically or satisfactorily because they were constrained by the dichotomy between the real and the monetary.

Marshall, of course, contributed many, many things besides those I have alluded to,[2] but the important thing that I want to emphasise here in the context of the Cambridge contribution to economics is that he systematically developed the idea of the real sector and the monetary sector and the quantity theory of money as an explanation of the general price level in the long term. This meant that the role of the monetary institutions, including central banks, was to make sure that they so controlled the monetary side of the economy that the underlying real things operating in a competitive environment would not be handicapped in their determination of the allocation of resources, with supplies and demands responding to each other. The basic idea was that if we had a lot of competition, on the whole the level of activity and the composition of goods and services that were produced would be responding to what people wanted, as expressed through their demands and reflected in the price mechanism.

It would be wrong to say that Marshall and his followers were uncritical defenders of *laissez-faire*, that if you leave it alone, the system will work well. They were not. They recognised that the system had deficiencies, that there was poverty, unsatisfactory working conditions, and lapses from full employment, and that there *was* a role for government intervention. Yet, on the whole, they were great supporters of creating competitive institutions and then letting the price mechanism do its thing. This was the underlying philosophy to which they admitted definite exceptions, the extent of which varied according to their particular philosophies, personalities, and so on. Nevertheless, they argued that there were strong forces, if there was competition, which would not only ensure that the goods and services produced were the goods and services that people wanted, but also that there was a tendency for people who wanted to work and capitalists who wanted to employ their capital in particular ways, to be able to do so. And, logically, that is what they had to believe, because if there were not a tendency to full employment, it would not be possible to argue that, even for the long period, the quantity theory was an explanation of the general price level because (for those of you who are mathematicians) there would be three unknowns with only one equation. Whereas if it were argued that there was a tendency for prices, that is, real wages, in the labour market – just as in any other market – to settle at the point where what was voluntarily supplied as labour services was voluntarily demanded by employers in aggregate, we could find what the long-period level of activity would be. We could then feed the answer into the quantity theory equation, make an argument about how the velocity of circulation of the typical pound was determined by custom and history, and assume that the monetary authorities controlled the quantity of money, so that the only thing not known would be the general price level. With one equation, and one unknown, we could solve the general price level. That was the thrust of Marshall's teaching, and of the Cambridge teaching of monetary theory generally, up until the end of the 1920s.

I now pass on from Marshall. He retired in the early years of this century, to be succeeded by his protégé, A. C. Pigou (1877–1959), who was in his early thirties. (Those were the days of child professors.) Pigou carried on Marshall's work, though not always in ways Marshall liked because Pigou was much more of a bolshie than Marshall turned out to be. He drew on Marshall's work about how the price mechanism did not always do its thing correctly, and wrote a book which went into several editions, *The Economics of*

Welfare (1920). Pigou's views still influence us today. He pointed out that, often, the social costs and the social benefits of production do not match their private counterparts. Because businesspeople are guided by their private gain (why should they be guided by anything else, they are not there as altruists, they are in business to make profits – that is what capitalism is about), we may often get an allocation of resources, a level and a composition of production, which do not take properly into account their social costs and benefits, which in our jargon are called 'externalities'. The best-known example is that of a factory which belches out smoke, yet its owners do not have to pay the costs of people living nearby who have to do extra washing – yet they ought to. These ideas are now applied to how we may handle the problem of destroying our environment by taking into account the social as well as the private costs of production. Piero Sraffa, who was the Marshall Librarian for many years, had Marshall's copy of an earlier version of Pigou's book, in which Pigou made these suggestions for government intervention; it was full of Marshallian annotations saying things like: 'Oh, he shouldn't have said that, he shouldn't have said that at all.' He wondered what he had let loose on the world, this bolshie chap, Pigou, who was going much farther than he himself was prepared to go. *So far* that in the ridiculous hunt for spies after the Second World War (you know, the Cambridge spies and all that), Pigou was mistaken for a Russian spy – absolute piffle. So, Pigou developed arguments about the sort of government interference which related to social costs and social benefits. He had a most illustrious and important career. Now he is a rather forgotten figure, but he should not be forgotten at all.

But, of course, Marshall's most distinguished pupil was John Maynard Keynes. He dominated Cambridge economics from the 1920s to his death in 1946 – and beyond. Keynes is one of my great heroes. For though he sometimes seemed to have had feet of clay, my judgement is that in a fundamental sense, he was a *good* man. I interpret his life as trying to solve the conundrum posed by the Cambridge philosopher G. E. Moore (who was a defining influence on the young Keynes and other bright young things around Cambridge at the turn of the century): is it possible both to *do* good and *be* good? I think Keynes's life provides a resounding *yes* to that question. His Bloomsbury friends were less sure. They, or some of them anyway, rather drew apart from the world and lived individual lives – we know the sort of lives they lived, they had endless affairs to make copy for their next novels and so on – a circle who lived in squares and loved in triangles, as Lord Annan recently reminded us. Keynes was a naughty man in lots of ways but he was driven, as were/are all the outstanding Cambridge economists, by an intense seriousness: a desire to understand the world and then make it a better place. Keynes was a civil servant as well as a don, and a very courageous man once he grew up. He started off as Marshall's pupil, but in the end he was to overthrow, in fundamental ways, the Marshallian legacy; not out of lack of piety for his teacher but because he followed arguments wherever they led, no matter how unpalatable their conclusions were. He was also very much a man of affairs.

It is interesting that virtually all these people come from either the middle or upper-middle classes of British society except for poor old Marshall, who was barely lower-middle class. When he died his wife connived with Keynes, consciously or unconsciously, to hide what his origins were. For example, he had given his father a more posh role in banking circles than he actually had and he hid the fact that his mother was the daughter of a butcher and the granddaughter of an agricultural labourer (see Coase, 1984: 520); which was silly because Marshall's view of economic progress allowed people in our sorts of society to realise their potential. Indeed he was an excellent example of someone who came from rather lowly origins yet realised his own potential as a professor at Cambridge, but he had that sort of inverted snobbery which made him suppress his origins, whereas his wife was much higher up the social pecking order and so she did not worry about such things; the same was true of Keynes, Austin and Joan Robinson. It gave them a confidence, even an arrogance and imperiousness, which allowed them to think that they could actually do things, that they could fulfil what Harrod (1951) said of Keynes, 'the pre-suppositions of Harvey Road'. (Harvey Road was where the Keynes family lived.) The idea was that there was this group of disinterested people who worked in the civil service, the universities, and the public schools, training intelligent people to go out and find out how the world worked and make it work better; in particular, to stop the malfunctioning of society falling on those who are least able to defend themselves. A noble ideal, I think.

Keynes started as a mathematician but he was only twelfth wrangler, a respectable result but not what was expected of him. He therefore read for the civil service exams, sitting at Marshall's feet. Marshall quickly realised that he was a brilliant student. He said, in effect, we old men will have to kill ourselves, the world's only safe for the young now. Keynes went into the civil service, getting his worst marks, by the way, in economics. 'Presumably, the examiners knew less about the subject than I [Keynes] did'. He was elected to a Fellowship at King's College in 1909, and came to back to teach at Cambridge before the First World War. In the war he went into the Treasury; he was at the Treaty of Versailles as a junior assistant to Lloyd George. Keynes was so horrified at what the French (and the Australians, through Billy Hughes) and Lloyd George were doing to Woodrow Wilson and through Wilson, to the Germans, that in the end he resigned and wrote the book which first made him famous, *The Economic Consequences of the Peace* (1919). In it he examined how the prewar European economy worked and how the vicious reparations that were to be imposed on the Germans would not only wreck Germany's economy but would also disturb the delicate balance of how things were done in Europe, and bring about a catastrophe as well as being inhumane and ungenerous to a defeated enemy. It brought him fame but it also put him in the wilderness as far as official circles were concerned for the interwar years (though not as much as was first thought).

In writing the book he was still applying Marshallian principles; it was during the 1920s and especially in the 1930s that he started to rethink drastically about how the world worked. Of course, he was not alone; in the 1920s his closest ally was Dennis Robertson (1890–1963). They had a most productive intellectual partnership and friendship which, alas, did not survive the making of *The General Theory*. This was both a personal tragedy and a professional one for the development of economic theory.

As Keynes was rethinking Marshall's monetary theory, others at Cambridge were starting to rethink Marshall's theory of the determination of prices at the firm and industry level. The latter development was especially associated with five people. The first was an Italian émigré chased out of Italy by Mussolini, Piero Sraffa, who was one of the most important intellectual influences of the twentieth century. He was the intimate friend of Keynes, Wittgenstein and

Gramsci. He published a most important article in the *Economic Journal* in 1926 (Keynes was co-editor with Edgeworth); it was principally an attack on Marshall's method of doing economics. But Sraffa suggested as well that rather than having competition as the general model of how markets worked and industries and firms behaved, monopoly – the other end of the spectrum – would be more appropriate. Sraffa said that if you asked businessmen, 'Why don't you sell more? Is it because your costs are rising?', they would laugh you out of court, adding, 'We can't sell more because we'd have to cut our prices too much, so it wouldn't be profitable to do so.' Sraffa suggested that we ought to look at the formation of prices and quantities in modern industries as resulting from mini-monopolies surrounded by other mini-monopolies, so that they had to take account of their customers' reactions and other firms' reactions when they set their prices. This was a huge blow to the case for *laissez-faire* because one of the arguments for competition is that it rids the system of the unfit. Marshall (and Pigou, following him), predicted that if there was a fall in demand for products, unfit firms would disappear, only the fittest would survive. (Marshall was not alone in this but we are talking about the Cambridge tradition.) Sraffa showed that this was not true, that most firms would survive but they would be working at under-capacity and therefore competition was not the effective *clean it out* sort of process that it was thought to be.

Sraffa's article precipitated what became known as the imperfect competition revolution. It was developed by Gerald Shove, Richard Kahn (1929, 1989) (Keynes's favourite pupil, in King's), and then by Austin and, especially, Joan Robinson, who published *The Economics of Imperfect Competition* in 1933, in which these ideas were synthesised and systematically expounded. At the same time as the revolution in price theory was occurring here it was independently occurring at the other Cambridge. (For example, Edward Chamberlin of Harvard published *The Theory of Monopolistic Competition* in 1933.)

Keynes himself became more and more dissatisfied with Marshall's way of looking at the workings of the economy as a whole. In particular, he discarded the argument that we could talk about prices and quantities and employment *independently* of what was happening in the financial sector and in the monetary sector generally. He had a go at solving this in what was meant to be his *magnum opus, A Treatise on Money*, which was published in two volumes in 1930. In many ways it was a continuation of the Marshallian tradition. But he was changing his emphasis from the long period, the central core of Marshall's economics, to the short period, though he continued to regard the latter as stations on the way to the long-period cross. In fact, as early as 1923, cheeking Marshall, he had written: *'In the long run* we are all dead. Economists set themselves too easy, too useless a task if in tempestuous seasons they can only tell us that when the storm is long past the ocean is flat again' (1971: 65, italics in original). He tried increasingly to design monetary policy which contained measures which would stop or at least ameliorate the effects of the huge inflations and deflations that had occurred after the end of the First World War. This runs through his work in the 1920s, but it was never satisfactorily done.

So in 1930–31 he started again. In this task he was aided by a remarkable group of young economists ranging from about 26 to 33 in age who were here in Cambridge and who came together in what was called the Cambridge 'Circus'. The principal members were Austin and Joan Robinson, Piero Sraffa, Richard Kahn, and James Meade (who died just before Christmas 1995, the last 'Circus' person to die). Meade had come from Oxford to study economics before he took up a Fellowship at Hertford College. Meade spent a year here and they discussed Keynes's *Treatise on Money* and they helped him (but he, of course, was the major author) to develop what became his authentic *magnum opus, The General Theory of Employment, Interest and Money* (1936).

What did he do in it? As you remember, the 1920s in Britain and then the 1930s all round the world were characterised by terrible mass unemployment, which in those days was thought to be a sin. (These days it is thought to be necessary in order to provide a quiescent and cowed workforce to allow international capital to prosper. Marx understood this much more, I think, than Marshall.) In those days people were shocked by mass unemployment; they were trying to work out why it had occurred because economic theory, by and large, said that, at least in the long term, it could not occur if the impediments to competition working were removed. What Keynes finally decided when he worked through the traditional analysis again was that it was wrong. He went back to his hero Malthus, who had had an argument with another great economist, David Ricardo, about whether it was possible to have a general glut, that is, could there be a failure of *overall* demand? (Everybody accepted that there could be gluts or scarcities in individual markets because individual demands and supplies had not matched temporarily.) But could there be a failure of demand *overall*, so that people and machines lay idle? Ricardo's answer, based on the argument of the French economist, Jean-Baptiste Say, was, 'No, commodities buy commodities, supply creates its own demand.' There cannot be a lack of aggregate demand in the long term. With competition everything will match up, including the labour market where the real wage rate will settle at a level where those who want to work are able to find jobs. Basically that was the argument that Keynes attributed to Ricardo (though now we would say that, while it was implicit in Marshall, Ricardo only argued that machines, that is, capital, could not be idle in the long term). Malthus countered that there could be a deficiency of overall demand, but he never could explain satisfactorily to Ricardo why this was so. Keynes argued (he was not a good historian of thought) that Ricardo conquered Malthus and that from then on we had all believed in Say's Law. We had a theory which deduced that there could not be a general glut, at least as a long-period proposition, in a world where there was up to 29 to 35 per cent unemployment. The theory was nonsense, the practice just did not match. Keynes set out to provide a theory that did. In doing that he argued, following Malthus, that as well as there being aggregate supply we had to have a theory of aggregate demand, a theory which determined the total demand for the production of the economy and therefore the total employment of people in it. He argued that one of the important components of aggregate demand was investment expenditure or capital accumulation – new factories, machines, and so on. A crucially important determinant of investment was the uncertain future – we do not know what is going to happen in the future but in order to invest we have to make guesses about what is going to happen, what we think our future profits will be, and then invest.

Keynes showed that basically there were not persistent forces at work in the economy which, at least on average, would produce enough investment expenditure at any moment of time to absorb the amount which people in the economy would be willing to save voluntarily if they were receiving the incomes they would get if the economy was at full employment: that is to say, if everyone who wanted to work could find a job at ruling wage rates.

What Keynes claimed to have demonstrated was that for prolonged periods of time the economy could settle at much lower levels than full employment, where what people voluntarily saved equalled what people were willing to invest but which left many people and machines idle. The unemployed were willing to work but there was no way of signalling to the people who were trying to make profits, that it would be profitable to employ them. And, indeed, it would not be unless there were to be a rise in aggregate demand as a result. It followed, therefore, that there was a case for government intervention.

One reason why economists had not seen this clearly before was the dichotomy between the real and the money – with money being just a veil. Whereas Keynes said, 'well, let's think about it again. Money is not a veil. Money is there right from the start.' Why? Because one of its properties is that it is a store of value, as well as a medium of exchange. If people are uncertain about the future they can hold money rather than spend it. Therefore, there is a second reason for holding money which plays an important part in determining what the pattern of rates of interest on financial assets is. He worked out a theory of what these patterns of rates of interest were, and he argued that business people have a fundamental choice – either they can hold financial assets on which they get interest payments, or they can do real things like invest. He argued that often rates of interest settled at levels where the amount of investment that people would make before the expected returns to investment had fallen to the level of the rate of interest (the alternative thing to do) was such that aggregate investment was not large enough to absorb full employment saving. Therefore, if we had a theory of the economy where money played a role right from the start and we did not have a dichotomy but an integrated theory we could show that there were tendencies to unemployment – to a failure of aggregate demand.

That was his great contribution[3] and the Cambridge contribution to economics in this century has built on this foundation ever since: first, in developing policies to run a wartime economy, including keeping inflation in check; secondly, in the postwar period in developing longer-term theories of growth and distribution over time. Here, some of Keynes's younger colleagues from the 'Circus', together with Nicholas Kaldor (who came to Cambridge from the London School of Economics after the war), Richard Goodwin and Luigi Pasinetti, came into their own in developing the peculiarly Cambridge contribution to theories of growth and distribution, the issues which had been the preoccupations of the great classical economists, Adam Smith, Ricardo and Malthus, leading on to Marx. That was one aspect of what came out of Keynes's and his colleagues' contributions.

Another aspect was the development of ideas of which Marshall would have approved, though he did not do much himself; this was the often down to earth, pioneering applied work associated with the Cambridge Department of Applied Economics. The first Director was a marvellous man called Dick Stone (Sir Richard Stone), who died a few years ago and who, with James Meade, is the only overwhelmingly Cambridge economist to get the Nobel Prize. (Now we may add Jim Mirrlees, if I may break my vow not to mention any colleagues, and also overlook his 25 years or so at Oxford.)[4] Starting in 1945, Stone headed up an extraordinary group of researchers and research in the Department of Applied Economics (DAE). One of the things for which he was known (and for which he received the Nobel Prize) was his development of National Accounting, which is a way of looking at the production, expenditure, and income that is produced annually in a Keynesian sense. The structure that Stone developed reflects the theoretical developments of Keynes in his theory of aggregate demand and aggregate supply. (Meade and Stone pioneered the structure of such accounts early in the Second World War. Austin Robinson recruited them for this task and he regarded their achievements as his greatest contribution to the war effort.)

Dick Stone not only presided over developing worldwide national accounting standards, he also was a pioneer of demand theory and practice. Here Marshall's contributions were influential in a conceptual sense while Stone was one of the pioneers of the actual *estimation*, through econometric and statistical methods, of demand curves for various commodities. Stone presided over a remarkable ten years in which what are now some of the most famous names in our subject produced highly original econometric and applied work. I should especially mention the seminal work on economic history, using a Keynesian framework, associated with Max Cole, Phyllis Deane, Charles Feinstein, Robin Matthews and Brian Mitchell, which commenced under Stone's benign leadership and encouragement. In a sense this filled an essential gap associated with Marshall's inability to complete his original project.

The tradition which Stone started has been continued, with different emphases, by the various Directors. Brian Reddaway took over from Stone in 1955 (Stone became the P. D. Leake Professor of Accounting and led with J. A. C. Brown the growth project in the DAE). Reddaway undertook himself (and encouraged many others to do likewise) applied projects characterised by the 'Reddaway Method' – thorough knowledge of data and its limitations, careful statistical analysis of it and of what it can be used to show, and what it cannot. When Brian became the Professor of Political Economy in 1970, Wynne Godley, as Director (1970–87), carried on both the Keynes and the Marshall stories, because he was very interested, first of all, in the role of forecasting in economic policy and, secondly, at a theoretical level, in showing how in the short term and in the long term the real and the monetary aspects of the economy may be combined together in a consistent set of stock and flow accounts. He was then succeeded in 1988 by David Newbery, about whom I may only say that I used to beat him at squash (I think!). So, alongside the theoretical developments I discussed earlier, we also have a tradition of applied work.

As I noted above, in the postwar period some of those from the 'Circus' were joined by the man who most resembled Keynes in the postwar period – Nicky Kaldor, who was a larger-than-life figure: a completely honest and ultimately lovable man who always said what he thought, who loved and lived life to the full. Kaldor, Joan Robinson, Richard Kahn, Piero Sraffa, Richard Goodwin and Luigi Pasinetti between them developed theories of growth and distribution peculiarly associated with Cambridge, and also, in my view, a damning critique of the reversion to pre-Keynesian theory associated with the monetarists, and of the theory of value and distribution which was associated with Marshall amongst others. They felt that there were serious flaws in the latter's conceptual foundations. They criticised it in a number of important books and articles while at the same time developing alternative approaches which not only drew on Keynes's insights, but also reached back (not in a retrogressive but in an historical sense) to the classical political economists. They adopted their central concept of the surplus, its creation, extraction, distribution, and use, to give us a new way of thinking about the economy. Included in both these endeavours we may mention, first, Sraffa's edition of the works and correspondence of Ricardo, on which he worked from the early 1930s and which, in collaboration with Maurice Dobb;[5] came to fruition in 11 volumes in the 1950s (1951–73). (The index was published in the 1970s.) Sraffa's Introduction to Vol. I and his 1960 classic, *Production of Commodities by Means of Commodities*, laid the foundations both for the critique of the supply-and-demand theories of mainstream economics and the revival of the classical Marxist method and approach through the concept of the surplus, which was incorporated into the peculiarly Cambridge approach to value, distribution and growth theory. Secondly, we may name Joan Robinson's *magnum opus, The Accumulation of Capital* (1956), her many influential works and articles that cluster around it, and a whole host of Kaldor's articles starting in the 1950s. His ideas reached their final form in his Raffaele Mattioli Lectures. They were given in May 1984, just two years before he died, but have only recently been published as *Causes of Growth and Stagnation in the World Economy* (1996). In this endeavour they were joined by the Polish Marxist economist, Michal Kalecki, who independently discovered the main propositions of Keynes's *General Theory*. As he came from a Marxist background, he found it natural and easy to link his findings to classical political economy as fulfilled in Marx's analysis of capitalism. (While I think Marx on 'how to run an ideal society' can be even more Utopian than the most Utopian Christian Socialist, as an analyst of capitalism he, Kalecki and Keynes had no peers – Marx understood capitalism better than probably anyone else.) Kalecki, who belonged to that tradition, very much influenced Joan Robinson's writings.

Richard Goodwin (who died in August 1996) was a most original and eclectic economist. He absorbed all the elements set out above, together with those that came from his mentors, Joseph Schumpeter and Wassily Leontief at Harvard, to produce a theory of cyclical growth, the indissolubility of trend and cycle. It emphasised both aggregative trade-cycle theory and the production interdependent systems associated with Sraffa and Leontief (see Goodwin and Punzo, 1987). Luigi Pasinetti (Goodwin's pupil at Cambridge) has over a 30-year or more period developed a unified system of distribution and growth which absorbs both classical and Keynesian ideas. He is perhaps the last great system builder of our profession (see Pasinetti 1981, 1993). Finally, on the subject of growth theory, the profession will ever be indebted to Frank Hahn and Robin Matthews for their masterly survey article of the state of the art in growth theory. It was published in the *Economic Journal* in 1964, and it set the standard for survey articles from then on.

I must also add that Marshall's original concern with poverty and injustice and their cures lived on in many of Meade's writings, in the writings of David Champernowne (who died in August 2000) on inequality and the distribution of income and in the writings of Tony Atkinson (who was inspired by Meade and about whom I may talk as he has gone to Oxford) on the distribution of income and wealth and the causes and cures of poverty.

Well, that is what I think the Cambridge contribution and tradition are about. I am a fortunate person because I have been a student in this tradition, I have taught it, most of the people about whom I have written (with the exception of Keynes, and of course Pigou, Marshall and Marx – I am not *that* old) were my teachers, and then my colleagues and my friends. So, it has been my good fortune also to work in this tradition. I have brought to this peculiarly Australian contributions as well, because of the mentors I had in Australia, most of whom came out of the Cambridge tradition. Therefore, you see before you a fulfilled person who has tried to do something to preserve the Cambridge tradition and who is going to play cricket for the Jesus College Long Vacation High Table side this afternoon. On a glorious summer day, what more could anybody ask for?

Notes

1. In writing on the Cambridge approach to applied economics, Michael Kitson and I (1993: 437) put it as follows: 'it emphasises the importance of relevance in economics, incorporating the lessons of history, the international context and prevailing social and political conditions. Theory and measurement are mutually interdependent as robust empirical analysis is dependent on relevant theory, which in turn depends on reliable observations. Cambridge advances in theoretical and applied economics

have ... gone hand-in-hand ... techniques have never been allowed to obscure the analysis – the medium is not the message.'

2. Not least his method of partial equilibrium analysis – looking at particular parts of the economy, locking the rest in the *ceteris paribus* pound, in order to be able to say something concrete. He understood about general equilibrium analysis but thought it could not get much past the profound insight that everything depends upon everything else.

3. It must be added that Richard Kahn was especially influential in the making of *The General Theory*: first, as a remorseless critic of the quantity theory as a causal explanation of the general price level; secondly, through his own remarkable work in the late 1920s on the economics of the short period (Kahn 1929, 1989) in which he made the short period a subject worthy of analysis in its own right, thus reinforcing Keynes's own inclinations; and, thirdly (with James Meade), through his 1931 article on the multiplier which provided the central, indeed, crucial concept for Keynes's new system.

4. Also, since this lecture was first published, Amartya Sen.

5. For many decades Maurice Dobb was the foremost Marxist economist and scholar in the United Kingdom (he died in 1976). He wrote several classics which remain sources of inspiration and instruction. My favourites are *Political Economy and Capitalism* (1937), *Welfare Economics and the Economics of Socialism* (1969) and *Theories of Value and Distribution since Adam Smith* (1973).

References

Chamberlin, E. H. (1993) *The Theory of Monopolistic Competition. A Reorientation of the Theory of Value* (Cambridge, Mass.: Harvard University Press).

Coase, R. H. (1984) 'Alfred Marshall's Mother and Father', *History of Political Economy*, vol. 16, 519–27.

Dobb, M. H. (1937) *Political Economy and Capitalism. Some Essays in Economic Tradition* (London: Routledge).

— (1969) *Welfare Economics and the Economics of Socialism. Towards a Commonsense Critique* (Cambridge: Cambridge University Press).

— (1973) *Theories of Value and Distribution since Adam Smith. Ideology and Economic Theory* (Cambridge: Cambridge University Press).

Goodwin, R. M. and L. F. Punzo (1987) *The Dynamics of a Capitalist Economy* (Oxford: Polity Press).

Groenewegen, P. (1995) *A Soaring Eagle: Alfred Marshall, 1842–1924* (Aldershot: Edward Elgar).

Hahn, F. H. and R. C. O. Matthews (1964) 'The Theory of Economic Growth: A Survey', *Economic Journal*, vol. 74, 779–902.

Harcourt, G. C. and M. Kitson (1993) 'Fifty Years of Measurement: A Cambridge View', *Review of Income and Wealth*, series 39, no. 4, December, 435–47, chapter 17 this volume.

Harrod, R. F. (1951) *The Life of John Maynard Keynes* (London: Macmillan).

Kahn, R. F. [1929] (1989) *The Economics of the Short Period* (London: Macmillan).

— (1931) 'The Relation of Home Investment to Unemployment', *Economic Journal*, vol. 41, 173–98.

Kaldor, N. (1996) *Causes of Growth and Stagnation in the World Economy* (Cambridge: Cambridge University Press).

Keynes, J. M. [1919] (1971) *The Economic Consequences of the Peace* (London: Macmillan, *Collected Writings*, Vol. II).

— [1923] (1971) *A Tract on Monetary Reform* (London: Macmillan, *Collected Writings*, Vol. IV).

— [1930] (1971) *A Treatise on Money*, 2 vols. (London: Macmillan, *Collected Writings*, Vols. V, VI).

— [1936] (1973) *The General Theory of Employment, Interest and Money* (London: Macmillan, *Collected Writings*, Vol. VII).

Marshall, A. (1890) *Principles of Economics* (1967, variorum edn) (London: Macmillan).

Pasinetti, L. L. (1981) *Structural Change and Economic Growth: A Theoretical Essay on the Dynamics of the Wealth of Nations* (Cambridge: Cambridge University Press).

— (1993) *Structural Economic Dynamics: A Theory of the Economic Consequences of Human Learning* (Cambridge: Cambridge University Press).

Pigou, A. C. (1920) *The Economics of Welfare* (London: Macmillan).

Robinson, J. (1933) *The Economics of Imperfect Competition* (London: Macmillan).

— (1956) *The Accumulation of Capital* (London: Macmillan).

— (1973) *Collected Economic Papers*, Vol. IV (Oxford: Basil Blackwell).

Sraffa, P. (1926) 'The Laws of Returns under Competitive Conditions', *Economic Journal*, vol. 36, 535–50.

— (1960) *Production of Commodities by Means of Commodities: Prelude to A Critique of Economic Theory* (Cambridge: Cambridge University Press).

Sraffa, P. with the collaboration of M. H. Dobb (eds) (1951–73) *Works and Correspondence of David Ricardo*, II vols. (Cambridge: Cambridge University Press).

Index

accounting
    double-entry book-keeping   16
    historical-cost   7, 328
accumulation   317–18
    Keynes's theory   266–8
    Post-Keynesianism   272–5
    see also capital; investment
Adelman, I.   215
Africa   135–6, 310–11, 313
Akerlof, G. A.   45
altruism   290–1
Amadeo, E., Keynes's Principle of
    Effective Demand   33
Andrew, R.   148
animal spirits   199, 225, 274
Annan, Lord   342
Araujo, J. A. T. R.   98
Arestis, P.   1, 177, 264
Arndt, H. W.   19
Arrow, K. J.   105, 194, 211–12, 217,
    329
Arrow–Debreu model   59, 188,
    189, 192, 193, 242, 243
Arthur, B.   277
Asimakopulos, A. (Tom)   7, 36,
    198, 223–4, 267, 275
Atkinson, A. B.   351
Atrostic, B. K.   222–3, 225
Australia
    Accord   19
    Adelaide Plan   16
    Adelaide University   9–13
    Arbitration Commission   11,
        18
    policy proposals   16–19
    wages policy   11–12
Australian Council of Trade Unions
    (ACTU)   12
Australian Labor Party (ALP)   5,
    18–19, 325
Ayres, C.   211

Ball, R. J.   14
Balls, E.   203
Balogh, T.   19, 186
banana diagram   267, 274
banana plantation parable   39, 65
Bangladesh   146
banks
    central   203
    commercial   201–3
    Horizontalists versus Verticalists
        280
    stickers and snatchers   201–2,
        203
Baran, P.   122, 124
Baranzini, M.   24
Barens, I.   54
Barker, T.   220
Barro, R. J.   289
Barton, A. D.   12
Bastard Keynesianism   16, 19, 281,
    303
Baumol, W. J.   301
Baxter, M.   73
Bennathan, E.   151–2
Bennett, J. W.   12
Bensusan-Butt, D.   141
Bentley, P.   16
Berle, J. A.   117, 119
Berndt, E. R., Fifty Years of Economic
    Measurement   219–34
Berrill, K.   140–1
Bhaduri, A.   103–4, 304
Bharadwaj, K.   181, 189, 191,
    275–6
Bhaskar, R.   84
Bibow, J.   61
biography   330–1
Blandy, R. J. (Dick)   175
Blecker, R. A.   73, 79
Blinder, A. S.   46
Bliss, C. J.   15, 188–9, 194

Bloomsbury Group 170
Blyth, C. A. 184
Böhm-Bawerk. E. von 163, 193
 *Karl Marx and the Close of his
 System* 163
Bortis, H. 282–3, 297
Boskin, M. J. 74, 118, 220, 222, 226
Boulding, K. E., *Economic Analysis*
 324
Bretton Woods 49, 254, 255, 281
Brown, A. C. B. 131
Brown, A. J. 48, 59, 185
Brown, G. 202–3
Brown, J. A. C. 220, 349
Bryce, R. 116
Buckley, W. 120
Burbidge, J. B. 223–4
bureaucracy 290–1

Cairncross, A. 131, 133, 135–6,
 138–40, 144, 307, 309–10,
 312–13
Cairns, J. F. 13
Callaghan, J. 240
Cambridge 6–9, 13–15, 20–3, 68,
 96, 116, 132, 170–1, 273, 289,
 293, 306, 312, 334–51
 Department of Applied Economics
 219–21, 291, 348–9
Campbell, B. 126
capital
 additions to 58–9
 circuits of 162
 international 79–83
 marginal efficiency 66
 meaning 191
 measurement 191, 229–30
 see also accumulation; investment
capital theory controversies 15,
 188–95, 211, 289
capitalism 166–7
 competitive 160–1
 cyclical 296–7
Carabelli, A. 35
Caspari, V. 54
centres of gravitation 296
Chakravarty, S. 106

Chamberlin, E. H. 3, 177
 *The Theory of Monopolistic
 Competition* 344
Chari, V. V. 10
Chick, V. 44, 72–3, 83
China 102–3, 215, 308, 315, 318,
 319
Churchill, W. S. 232–3
Clark, A. 233
Clark, J. B. 193, 222
Clarke, P., *The Keynesian Revolution
 in the Making* 33
Clausewitz, C. Von, *Principles of War*
 3
Clower, R. W. 52–3, 211
Coakley, J. 73
Coase, R. H. 93, 192, 342
Coates, J. 35, 50, 64
Cochrane, D. 3
Cohen, A. J. 190, 192–3, 268
Cohen, R. 107
Cole, M. 349
competition 339–40
 imperfect 34–5, 213–15, 344
complementarity 247
consumption function 41, 66
Corden, W. M. 7
Cornwall, J. L. 54, 225, 282–3
Cottrell, A. 73, 281
country size 141–2
Cournot, A. 243
credit 200
Cripps, F. 292
Cripps, Sir S. 139
Crotty, J. 197
Crucini, M. J. 73
cumulative causation 22, 282

Dalziel, P. C. 9, 72–84
Darity, W. 68
data
 manipulation 228–32
 political use of 233
 reliability 228–32
 see also measurement
David, M. H. 225
David, P. 277

Davidson, P.   47–9, 57–64, 72,
   210–11, 265, 268, 276, 289,
   295–7
   Money and the Real World   58
Deane, P. M.   141, 221, 349
Debreu, G.   310, 329
debt forgiveness   125
demand
   aggregate   346–7
   curves   59
   effective   47, 52, 59, 266, 295
   theory   348
Denison, E.   224, 231
deregulation   281–2
developing countries   140, 144–6
   see also Africa; China; India
development theory   142–3,
   306–20
Dillard, D.   216
discounted cash flow (DCF)   14
distribution
   and employment   13
   Post Keynesianism   268–71
distribution theory   245–6
Dixon, H.   118
Dobb, M. H.   5, 98, 102, 133,
   159, 177, 274–5, 293, 301, 316,
   350
   Political Economy and Capitalism
   294
doctrinal debate   326–7
Domar, E. D.   246, 274
Dore, M. H. I.   116, 124–5
Dow, J. C. R.   7
Dow, S. C.   1, 48, 204, 278, 280
Downing, R. I.   5
Duesenberry, J. S.   3
Dunlop, J. T.   35, 118

Earl, P.   73
Eatwell, J. L.   265, 276
econometrics   331
Economic Journal   134, 148, 171,
   311, 344
economy
   real and financial   199–200
   spacial factors   251–3

Edgworth, F. Y.   344
education   143–4
Eichner, A. S.   14, 211, 264, 271,
   295
Eisner, R.   55
elasticities   41–2
empirical work   181, 327–9
employment
   and distribution   13
   full   78
   and inflation   257–8
   and pricing policies   9–10
   theory   213–15
Engels, F.   158, 160
environmental policy   227–8
expectations   37, 66
externalities   341

Falk, O. T.   63
Farmiloe, T.   1
Faucett, J.   224
Fay, C. R.   132
Feinstein, C. H.   221, 349
Feiwel, G. R.   211–18
   *Joan Robinson and Modern
      Economic Theory*   209
   *The Economics of Imperfect
      Competition*   209
Feldstein, M.   73, 79, 82
feudalism   160
Filippini, C.   238
financial constraint   61, 100–1
fiscal deficit   232
Fisher, F.   102, 193, 215
Fitzgibbon, A.   35
Frankel, S. F.   136
Frearson, K. S.   7
Friedman, M.   22, 44, 290, 339
Fundamental Marxist Theorem
   (FMT)   163–4

Galbraith, J.   216
Galbraith, J. K.   210–11
Galenson, W.   102, 316
Gallaway, L.   102
Garegnani, P.   188–91, 193, 265,
   276, 304

general equilibrium theory
188–95
Germany   138
Gifford, C.   93
Gilbert, J.   175–6
Godley, W.   220–1, 292, 349
Goldberg, L.   4
Goodwin, R. M.   20, 45, 73, 105,
107, 202–3, 210, 212, 232,
273–4, 277–8, 295, 331, 348–51
Gram, H.   91, 210, 293
Gramsci, A.   344
Grant, J. McB.   7
Griffin, K.   140
Griliches, Z.   222, 224, 226–7,
230–1
Groenewegen, P. D.   338
Grossman, G. M.   45
growth
causes and consequences   242–3
cyclical   203
Harrod/Domar problem   246,
274
natural rate   165, 273
warranted rate   165

Hahn, F. H.   15, 45, 59, 69,
98, 102, 105,149–50, 194,
212, 218, 239, 242, 292, 329,
351
Critical Essay   298
Hailey, Lord, *African Survey*   136
Hall, N.   136
Hall, R.   150
Hamermesh, D. S.   222, 228, 233
Hammond, P.   215
Hamouda, O. F.   115, 127, 264,
325
Harcourt, G. C.   4–5, 9, 11–16,
19–21, 23–4, 55, 69, 72, 74–5,
84, 98, 177, 188, 190, 239, 258,
264, 272, 282, 289, 297, 304,
326–7, 331
Economic Activity   324
'The Accountant in a Golden Age'
324
Harcourt, J. M.   191

Harrod, R. F.   9, 66, 73, 99–100,
165, 170–1, 201, 225, 246, 252,
272–4, 282, 301, 308, 342
Hart, M. K.   120
Hatch, J. H.   1
Hawke, R. J. (Bob)   19
Hawtrey, R.   46, 65, 172
Hayek, F. A. von   193–4, 275, 294
Pure Theory of Capital   324
Hegel, G. W. F.   159
Heilbroner, R.   158
Heim, C.   197
Helpman, E.   45
Henderson, H. D.
Can Lloyd George Do It?   35, 65
Supply and Demand   2
Henderson, R. F.   6–7
Hicks, J. R.   20, 45, 72, 120, 177,
193, 198, 201–2, 239, 281, 295
The Social Framework   2
Value and Capital   3, 276, 294,
177
Hilferding, R.   164
Hopkin, B.   7, 150–1
Horioka, C.   73, 79, 82
Horne, D.   21, 40
Housner, G.   115
Howitt, P.   50, 69
Howson, S.   98, 152
Hufbauer, G. C.   253
Hughes, A.   148
Hughes, B.   16, 41, 343
Hulten, C. R.   222, 224, 229–30
Hurwicz, L.   214

imperfect competition   34–5,
213–15, 339–40
income
and investment   78
process   74–5
incomes policy   186
indexation   18
India   133, 308, 313
industrial organisation   135
inflation   257–8, 279
Innis, H.   115
input measurement   224

interest rates   41
International Economic Association
   (IEA)   140–2
investment   200–1
   and income   78
   process   74–9
   and profits   97–8
   and saving   72–84, 269–70
   see also accumulation; capital
IS–LM   43, 45, 66, 297
Isaac, J. E.   11

Jeffrey, B.   148
Jevons, W. S.   5
Johnson, H. G.   12, 98, 141, 190
Jorgenson, D W.   222, 224, 231

Kahn, R. F.   20, 33, 39–40, 42, 44,
   60, 66, 68, 72, 74–5, 93–4, 99,
   106, 114, 116–18, 217, 266,
   309, 344–5, 349
   The Economics of the Short Period
   34–5
Kaldor, N.   6, 9, 12–13, 15, 19–20,
   45, 73–4, 77, 99, 102, 106, 177,
   201, 211, 221, 269, 273, 276,
   279, 283, 292, 295, 309, 324,
   326, 329, 348–9
   'A Classificatory Note on the
   Determinateness of Static
   Equilibrium'   240
   *Causes of Growth and Stagnation in
   the World Economy*   238–58,
   350
   'Speculation and Economic
   Stability'   239
   two-sector model   247–51
Kalecki, M.   3, 6, 9–10, 12, 19–21,
   23, 35–6, 42–3, 45, 51–2, 61,
   75, 94, 96–8, 118–19, 177–8,
   180, 202–3, 217, 224, 232, 245,
   257, 265, 267, 269–71, 273–4,
   276, 278, 281, 295–7, 301,
   303–4, 308–9, 326, 329, 331,
   350
Karmel, P. H.   2, 175, 324
Katona, G.   6

Keating, P.   19
Kehoe, T.   216
Kendrick, J.   224
Kent, E.   115
Kenyon, P.   14, 272
Kerr, P. M.   19–20, 91, 157–67,
   300–4
Kerry Smith, V.   222
Keynes, F. I.   169
Keynes, G.   169
Keynes, J. M.   10, 20, 23, 78–9, 83,
   93–4, 101, 176–7, 179–80,
   184–5, 192, 198, 200–1, 211,
   217, 224, 241, 254, 274–8, 281,
   292, 294, 298, 303, 309–10,
   326, 329, 348, 350
   A Tract on Monetary Reform   2, 58,
   60, 170
   A Treatise on Money (2 vols)   2,
   33, 35, 38–9, 41–2, 60, 65,
   95–6, 114–16, 123, 135,
   170, 216, 265, 269, 295, 311,
   345
   A Treatise on Probability   36
   biography   169–72
   Can Lloyd George Do It?   35, 65
   classical roots   264–5
   Essays in Biography   171
   Essays in Persuasion   171
   his contribution to economics
   341–7
   How to Pay for the War   137
   philosophy   49–50
   *The Economic Consequences of the
   Peace*   64–5, 132, 170, 307,
   343
   The General Theory   3, 8, 33,
   35–7, 39, 41–55, 57–69, 72,
   95–7, 99–100, 114, 116–19,
   170, 184–5, 198, 216, 245,
   264, 266–7, 280, 295–8, 301,
   315, 343, 345, 350
Keynes, J. N.   169
   *Studies and Exercises in Formal
   Logic*   169
   *The Scope and Method of Political
   Economy*   169

Keynes, L.   64
Keynes, M.   169
Keynesian, chapter   17, 41
Keynesianism   291–2
Kidron, M.   140
Kinda-Hass, B.   118, 267
King, J.   51
Kirman, A.   189, 192
Kitson, M.   74, 219–34
Klein, L. R.   105, 216
Knight, F. H.   193
Kornai, J. L.   194
   Anti-Equilibrium   194
Kregel, J. A.   47, 54, 69, 100, 192,
   211, 264, 277–8, 295
Kriesler, P.   51
Krugman, P.   4
Kumar, D.   337
Kurz, H. D.   190

labour, reserve army of   19, 161,
   164, 166
Labour Party   98
labour theory of value   294
land reform   319
Lane, R. W.   42, 120
Lange, O.   45
Lau, L.   224–5
Lavoie, M.   264
Lawson, T.   84
Lee, F. S.   272
Leeson, R.   183–4
Leibenstein, H.   102, 316
Leijonhufvud, A.   243
   *Keynesian Economics and the
   Economics of Keynes*   52
Lekachman, R.   67
Leontief, W.   270, 350–1
Lessing, D., *Under My Skin*   311
Leubuscher, C.   136
Levhari, D.   15, 101
Levine, D.   216
Lewis, A.   253
Lewis, M. K.   16
Lipsey, R. E.   226
liquidity preference   60–1, 66, 98
List, A.   244

Littleboy, B.   52
Lloyd George, D.   170, 343
Lodewijks, J.   10
long boom   253–5
Lucas, R.   10, 45, 289
Luxemburg, R.   165, 302
   Accumulation of Capital   100
Lydall, H. F.   6, 324

McCombie, J. S. L.   252
Majumdar, M.   216
Malinvaud, E.   294–5
Malthus, T. R.   5, 146, 314–15,
   334–5, 346, 348
Mankiw, N. G.   10, 45, 118
Marcuzzo, M. C.   69
Marglin, S. A.   279
Marris, R. L.   6, 8, 11, 47, 69,
   118
Marshall, A.   5, 36, 41, 52–3, 58,
   64, 92–3, 95, 99–100, 138,
   169–70, 176, 190–1, 214, 221,
   251–2, 265, 273, 277, 290, 292,
   294, 298, 300, 302–3, 309, 312,
   342–5, 351
   contribution to economics
   335–40
   Economics of Industry   132
   Principles of Economics   2, 34,
   37–8, 123, 132, 241, 243, 276,
   336
Marx, K.   10, 19–20, 51, 60,
   96–101, 157–67, 177, 180, 186,
   217, 243–5, 252, 264–5, 268–9,
   272, 274, 276, 278, 293–4, 296,
   301–2, 304, 308–9, 329, 345,
   348, 350
   analytical method   159–60
   biography   157–8
   major works   5, 158–9
   schemes of reproduction   164–5,
   244–5, 295, 315, 318
   technical change   165–6
   value   160–4
Mas-Colell, A.   211
Massaro, V. G.   75, 325

mathematics 180–1, 212, 331
Mathews, R. L. 7
Matthews, R. C. O. 149, 216–17,
  221, 289, 349, 351
Maurice, Major-Gen. Sir F. 92
Meade, J. E. 9, 11, 15, 39–40,
  138, 147, 266, 281, 290, 345,
  348
  Mr Meade's relation 72–82
Means, G. 42, 117, 119
measurement
  scope of 226–8
  see also data
Meek, R. L. 157, 163, 275
Meiszkowski, P. 223
migration 96
Milgate, M. 91, 265, 276, 293
Mill, J. S. 5, 123
Minhas, B. S. 325
Minsky, H. 9, 19, 197–204, 277,
  295–7
  Small and Big Business 180
Mirrlees, J. A. 213, 331, 348
Mitchell, B. 221, 349
Mitra, T. 216
Moggridge, D. E. 57, 63,
  65–9
Monadjemi, M. S. 282
Monetarism 16, 19, 42–3
  Mark I 290, 292
  Mark II 289–90, 292, 295
monetarist policies 255–6
money 98–9
  demand for 60–1
  endogenous 48, 280–1
  importance of 347
  quantity theory of 44,
    338–9
  roles of 41
  store of value 59–60
Moore, B. J. 280
Moore, G. E. 170, 341
Morishima, M. 163–4, 326–7
Morison, D. 93
multiplier 39, 65, 73
Myint, H. 141
Myrdal, G. 45, 239, 252, 279

Naqvi, K. A. 102
national income accounts 138,
  227, 348
Nell, E. J. 210
Newbery, D. M. G. 220–1, 349
Nield, R. R. 292
Nordhaus, W. D. 295
Nunn, C. 140
Nunns, J. R. 222–3, 225
Nurkse, R. 141
Nyarko, Y. 216

O'Donnell, R. M. 35–6, 50, 62–3
Ohlin, B. 35
oil shock 254, 255
Okun, A. 17, 241, 291, 295
OPEC 255
open economy 48–9

Paley, M. 336
Palma, G. 1
Panić, M. 203
Papi, U. 140
Parkin, M. 10
Pasinetti, L. L. 15, 20, 55, 99,
  105–6, 118, 163, 268, 278,
  348–9, 351
Patel, I. G. 144, 152, 218, 312
Patinkin, D. 57, 62, 64, 72–3,
  77
Penner, R. G. 232
Perlman, M. 15, 325
Pesaran, M. H. 24
Petrides, R. 1
Phillips, A. W. H. 183–4
Phillips Curve 43, 184–6
philosophy 35–7, 49–50, 63–4,
  170
Pieper, P. E. 222
Pigou, A. C. 93, 135, 214, 252,
  290, 309–10
  The Economics of Welfare 340–1
  Theory of Unemployment 68
Pincus, J. J. 122
planning 102–3, 315–16
Plumptre, W. 114–15
policy 179, 256–7, 281–3, 325

population   314, 317
Porter, R. B.   232
Post-Keynesianism   16, 45, 52,
    263–83
    accumulation   272–5
    Marshallian–Keynesian roots
        265–6
    method   275–9
    policy   281–3
    value, distribution and
        price-setting   268–71
Prais, S. J.   7
prey–predator model   274
price
    hedonic index   229, 230–1
    level   48, 338
    mechanism   102–3, 316–17
    policies   9–10
    of raw materials   240–1
    and value   162–4
    volatillity   240–1
price-setting   8, 295, 344
    mark-up   271–2
    Post-Keynesianism   268–71
production
    function   223
    joint   326–7
    short-period   39
productivity slowdown   231–2
profits
    and investment   97–8
    rate of   163
psychology   64–5
Punzo, L. F.   274, 351

quantity theory of money   44,
    338–9

Raj, K. N.   308
Ramsey, F. P.   170
Rankin, N.   118
Rappaport, I.-M.   115
raw material prices   240–1
W. B. Reddaway,   48, 67, 147,
    220–1, 229, 315, 349
Reid, G.   149

resource allocation   242
Riach, P. A.   21, 46, 297
Ricardo, D.   5, 161, 190–1, 244,
    293, 296, 302, 304, 346, 348,
    350
Richardson, G.   192
Rizvi, A.   189, 192
Roberts, J.   214
Robertson, D. H.   34, 44, 72, 93,
    116, 133–4, 202–3, 300, 325,
    343
Robinson, E. A. G.   20, 63, 92–3,
    131–54, 172, 345
    *Appropriate Technologies for
        Third World Development*
        144
    on development   306–20
    Monopoly   134
    *The British Crown and the Indian
        States*   133
    'The Economic Development of
        Malthusia'   314
    The Economics of Education   143
    *The Structure of Competitive
        Industry*   134
Robinson, J.   3–4, 6, 12–13, 15, 20,
    35–6, 42, 51, 68, 72, 74, 77,
    114, 117–18, 133, 165, 191,
    193, 209–18, 263, 267, 270,
    273–8, 290, 293, 296, 324–6,
    329, 336, 342, 345, 349
    *Aspects of Development and
        Underdevelopment*   317
    biography   91–108
    and the classics   300–4
    on development   306–20
    Economics is a Serious Subject
        93
    Essay on Marxian Economics   98
    *Essays in the Theory of Economic
        Growth*   98, 101
    Exercises in Economic Analysis
        103, 315
    'Spring Cleaning'   304
    The Accumulation of Capital   7,
        100–1, 105, 301, 324, 350,
        216

Robinson, J. (*cont.*)
  The Economics of Imperfect Competition   93–5, 105, 214, 300, 310, 344, 214
  'The Philosophy of Prices' 316
  'The Second Crisis in Economic theory'   211
  'The Unimportance of Reswitching'   102
Roemer, J.   216
Rogers, C.   154, 265, 276, 297
Romer, D.   118
Romer, P. M.   45, 216
Roosevelt, President   123
Rosenstein-Rodan, P. N.   308
Rostow, W. W.   143, 211
Rothschild, K. W.   177
  'Price Theory and Oligopoly'   3
Rowthorn, R. E.   279
Royal Economic Society (RES) 134
Rubenstein, A.   214
Russell, B.   170
Russell, C. S.   222, 226–7, 229
Russell, E. A.   7, 11–12, 16, 19–20, 183–4, 325–6
Rymes, T. K.   54

Salant, W.   291
Salter, W. E. G.   11–12, 14, 19, 257, 272, 303, 325, 329
  Productivity and Technical Change 324
Samuelson, P. A.   3, 42–3, 104, 118, 123, 151, 185, 210–12, 216–17, 222, 291, 323
  Foundations   3
Sardoni, C.   11, 13–14, 51, 57–69, 164, 244, 272
Sargent Florence, P.   134–5
Sargent, T. J.   289
saving
  and investment   72–84, 269–70
  process   74–9
  propensity to   73, 75
Sawyer, M. C.   1, 177

Say, J. B.   346
Say's Law   38, 40, 68, 116–17, 211, 346
schemes of reproduction   164–5, 244–5, 295, 315, 318
Schor, J.   104, 210
Schultze, C. L.   232–3
Schumpeter, J. A.   5, 177, 274, 350
Scitovsky, T.   118, 121, 197
'Second Edition' of *The General Theory, A*   21, 46–55
Sen, A. K.   102, 316
service sector   226–7
Shackle, G. L. S.   52, 175–6, 278
Shaikh, A.   223, 327
Shapiro, N.   47, 180
Shoup, C.   224
Shove, G. F.   34, 37, 93, 98, 116, 133, 300, 309, 344
Shukla, V.   102
Sidebotham, E.   131
Sidgwick, H.   336
Singer, H.   152
Singer, S.   114
Skidelsky, R.   54, 57, 62–5, 72, 171
Smith, A.   5, 124, 224, 242–3, 264, 276, 293, 296, 304, 309, 329, 348
  The Wealth of Nations   141
Smith, V. K.   226–7, 229
Solow, R. M.   13, 15, 43, 45, 100, 105, 151, 165, 185, 197, 210–13, 217, 223–4, 240, 273, 291, 316, 327
  Critical Essay   298
  Monopolistic Competition and Macroeconomic Theory   10–11
Sonnenschein, H.   189, 192
Soviet Union   14
Spajic, L. D.   325
specialisation   179–80
speculators, and tax rates   23
Sraffa, P.   2, 13, 15, 20, 68, 93, 99, 106, 116–17, 162–3, 190–1, 193–5, 265, 274–5, 278, 296, 309, 341, 343, 345, 349, 351

Production of Commodities by Means of Commodities 163, 270–1, 293, 301–2, 304, 325, 350
stagflation 17, 43, 184–6, 255
Steedman, I. 163–4, 326
Steindl, J. 177–81, 273, 329
Maturity and Stagnation in American Capitalism 180
Stewart, I. A. 232
Stigler, G. J. 190
Stiglitz, J. E. 45, 197, 217–18, 331
Stone, J. R. N. 138, 226, 232, 348–9
Mathematics in the Social Sciences 220
Strachey, J. 97, 301
Streeten, P. 210
'stylized' facts 240, 279
Sunding, D. 215
supply
aggregate function 118, 123–4
curves 58
elasticities 41
supply-side models 225–6
surplus 159, 161, 293–4, 315, 350
surveys 330
Swan, T. W. 7, 100, 217, 273, 292, 303, 316
Sweezy, P. 5, 177
Szenberg, M. 148

Tahir, P. 96, 308, 317
Tappan-Hollond, M. 92, 120
Targetti, F. 118, 238, 267
Tarshis, J. 114
Tarshis, L. 35, 42–3, 194, 197, 210, 216
'An Economic Program for American Democracy' 120
biography 114–28
Introduction to International Trade and Finance 124
The Elements of Economics 120, 122
Taussig, F. W., *Principles* 132
Tawney, R. H., *Acquisitive Society* 132

tax
burden 223–4
incidence 225
and speculators 23
Tobin 258, 282
Taylor, J. B. 10
technical change 327
endogenous 165–6
technique, choice of 14, 316, 329–30
Temple, W. 308
Thatcher, M. 64, 232, 255
Thirlwall, A. P. 21, 238–9, 252–3
time 331
long-period 3, 37, 48, 96, 193, 273, 275, 279, 296–7, 303–4, 337–8, 345
short-period 34–5, 39, 41–2, 44, 276, 303–4, 337–8, 345
Tinbergen, J. 215, 292
Tobin, J. 18, 52–4, 289, 291, 297
Tobin tax 258, 282
Torr, C. 119
Triffin, R. 177
Monopolistic Competition and General Equilibrium Theory 3
Triplett, J. E., *Fifty Years of Economic Measurement* 219–34
Tugan-Baranovsky, M. I. 97
Turner, M. S., *Joan Robinson and the Americans* 104, 209–13, 218

uncertainty 50, 59, 64, 66
unemployment
in developing countries 308–9, 313–15
disguised 308–9
involuntary 53–4
United States 254–5
productivity slowdown 231–2
user cost 119–20

Vaizey, J. 140, 143
value
labour theory of 160–2, 163, 294

value (*cont.*)
  Post-Keynesianism   268–71
  and price   162–4
  Volterra   274

wage unit   59–60
Walker, D.   192
Wallace, R. H.   2, 125, 289, 324
Walras, L.   52–3, 63–4, 188, 191–2
Walsh, V.   91, 210, 215
  Classical and Neoclassical Theories of General Equilibrium   293
Watson, A.   184
Weintraub, S.   18, 43, 58–60, 118, 211, 265, 291, 295, 297
Weller, A. (Sammy)   2
Westphalen, J. von   158

Wheen, F.   158
Whitaker, J. K.   214
Wicksell, K.   188, 191, 302
Wilensky, R.   197
Wiles, P.   147
Willis, R.   19
Wilson, H.   240
Wilson, R.   214
Wilson, W.   343
Wittgenstein, L.   50, 170, 343
wolf-pack analogy   279
Wood, A.   14, 271–2
Worswick, G. D. N.   150

Yellen, J. L.   197
Young, A. A.   45, 239, 243, 251, 279